SOFT FOODS FOR EASIER EATING COOKBOOK

EASY-TO-FOLLOW RECIPES FOR PEOPLE WHO HAVE CHEWING AND SWALLOWING PROBLEMS

SANDRA WOODRUFF, RD
LEAH GILBERT-HENDERSON, PhD

SQUAREONE
PUBLISHERS

The information and advice contained in this book are based upon the research and professional experiences of the authors, and are not intended as a substitute for consulting with a licensed health care professional. The publisher and authors are not responsible for any adverse effects or consequences arising from the use of any of the information, suggestions, or recipes presented in the book. All matters pertaining to your physical health, including your diet, should be supervised by a health care professional who can provide medical care that is tailored to meet individual needs.

COVER DESIGNER: Jeannie Tudor
COVER PHOTO: SuperStock
INTERIOR ART: Vicky Chelf
EDITOR: Joanne Abrams
TYPESETTER: Gary A. Rosenberg

Square One Publishers
115 Herricks Road
Garden City Park, NY 11040
(516) 5335-2010 • (877) 900-BOOK
www.squareonepublishers.com

Library of Congress Cataloging-in-Publication Data

Woodruff, Sandra L.
    Soft foods for easier eating cookbook : easy-to-follow recipes for people who
have chewing and swallowing problems / Sandra Woodruff, Leah Gilbert-Henderson.
        p. cm.
    Includes index.
    ISBN 978-0-7570-0290-8 (pbk.)
    1. Deglutition disorders—Diet therapy—Recipes. 2. Cookery (Soft foods) I.
Gilbert-Henderson, Leah. II. Title.
    RC815.2.W66 2010
    641.5'63—dc22   2009017041

Printed in Canada

10   9   8   7   6   5   4   3   2   1

CONTENTS

PART TWO

The Recipes

Appendices

ACKNOWLEDGMENTS

I would like to thank Michael Rudd, SLP, for his contributions to the book and for all I have learned from him about dysphagia over the years we worked together. I am grateful to Laninda Sande, SLP, for reviewing portions of the book, and for lending me her support and encouragement as a friend. Thanks also go to Dr. Stefan Kiedrowski, ENT specialist, for reviewing the manuscript and advising us on medical matters. Roscoe Thompson, Betty Moore, and Heribert June were kind enough to teach me how to make puréed foods from everyday foods; I am deeply grateful to them. I also extend my appreciation to all of my interns who contributed information (I always learn so much from my students)—especially Heather Page, who contributed to the menu plans. I am grateful to my sister, Penny Kamm, who made it a project to dig up all the useful old family recipes she could find; and to Julia Woodward, Judy Gregory, and Eloise Joyner, who shared their own family recipes. I thank my husband, Tim, for his patience and support, and my children, Peter and Stefanie, who are my greatest inspiration. And, of course, I thank my pets, who eagerly anticipated the failed experiments.

—LG

Our heartfelt thanks go to Rudy Shur, founder and publisher of Square One, for envisioning this book long ago. Rudy's unique insights and ideas have added so much to this project. We are equally grateful to our editor, Joanne Abrams, whose amazing attention to detail, incredible patience, and helpful input greatly enhanced this book. Special thanks go to Dr. Mary Jo Weale for bringing Leah and me together at a time when we were both thinking about writing this book; thus, our decision to collaborate. Thanks also go to the friends, family, and acquaintances who shared their stories and experiences with eating difficulties and mechanically altered diets—both good and bad—adding important insights to the book. Last but not least, thanks go to my husband, Tom, for his ongoing support, and to my favorite taste testers past and present—Wiley, CD, Belle, Moose, and Misty—who have cheerfully sampled all of my creations.

—SW

PREFACE

This book is the result of several minds coming together after many years of thought and inspiration. For me, it was inspired by one of the most delicious foods I ever put in my mouth. I was at a reception following one of Florida State University's Distinguished Lecture Series events, when I saw the most amazing giant fish mold. I just had to try it. I scooped some of the creamy salmon mousse onto my plate, added a little sauce, and was instantly delighted.

Several years later, I began working with patients who had chewing and swallowing problems (dysphagia), and I often thought about that salmon mousse. I wanted to find other ways to create delicious dining experiences for people who had to eat smooth foods due to medical necessity.

As it happened, Sandy Woodruff was also thinking along these lines. A gifted cook as well as a registered dietitian and a nutritionist, Sandy had published numerous cookbooks and was an accomplished teacher of health matters. Over the years, Sandy had talked with Rudy Shur, publisher of Square One, about his ideas for such a project. And so, our common goal became to help people find simple ways of creating smooth and soft-textured meals that are both healthful and delicious. We also wanted to guide people in modifying their diet to accommodate various medical conditions.

I decided that if I wanted to make this book really practical, I had to live on a dysphagia diet myself. I remained on a puréed diet almost exclusively for several months. This gave me firsthand knowledge of the difficulty and monotony that can come with the diet. In the beginning, my breakfast was a smoothie—which I still enjoy every day—and my lunch was the puréed dishes prepared at work for our dysphagia patients. For dinner, I would purée whatever my husband and I were having. Some things puréed well and tasted good, but for the most part, these meals left a lot to be desired.

My biggest problem in the beginning was finding something to grab out of the refrigerator when I came home famished. I could eat just so much yogurt, regardless of the variety of choices. I began to experiment with blended gazpacho, a cold tomato and vegetable soup. Each time I made it, I varied the recipe a little so I never got tired of it.

Another favorite was a puréed peanut butter, honey, and banana sandwich. This took a little experimenting to get good results. Peanut butter alone is too sticky for dysphagia patients, but I found that it blended to a smooth, spreadable consistency when mixed with mashed bananas. The problem, then, was to find something on which to spread the honey. Dry breads are not advisable for people with swallowing difficulties because they pose a choking hazard, and I didn't like gelled breads. I finally came up with a technique that allowed me to soften the bread without making it too mushy. I prepared a slightly thinned honey, which I kept in a squirt bottle, and I squirted a small amount of the honey mixture on a plate. I then spread the peanut butter-banana purée on a crustless slice of bread and placed the bread, topping side up, on the thinned honey. The honey slowly soaked into the bread from the bottom, softening the bread and giving it a purée-like texture. This was really good, and could be easily eaten with a fork or spoon.

Through the practical experience of living on a puréed diet, along with much research and input from people who face eating challenges on a daily basis, Sandy and I began the search for recipes and foods that were naturally soft and smooth and that everyone in the family would find appetizing and delicious. We approached relatives, friends, and coworkers who were willing to share their secrets. In the end, we came up with over 150 delicious and versatile recipe ideas, along with a wealth of information and practical tips for soft and smooth diets.

As you will see, your dietary concerns need not interfere with your enjoyment of life. On the contrary, a wide array of tasty home-style meals—meals that can be prepared quickly in your own kitchen—will not only meet your dietary needs, but also satisfy your desire for wonderful food.

LG

INTRODUCTION

If you or a loved one has recently been told that you must follow an easy-to-chew, soft, or smooth diet, we know that you are going through a difficult time. Whether the problem is long-term or only temporary, it will require change and the ability to learn and accept a new way of eating. This book was written to help you through this challenging period and to convince you that chewing or swallowing difficulties do *not* mean the end of good-tasting food, nor do they mean hours of slaving in the kitchen. Easy-to-eat dishes can also be easy to prepare and easy to enjoy. This book will show you how it's done.

You will be amazed by the variety of tastes and visual delights that can be created while keeping it smooth. Hospitals frequently make puréed diets by simply putting whatever they are cooking for their main course into a food processor. They may add a little liquid and thickener, but otherwise, they are simply blending a food that we don't normally eat in puréed form. Because the results are not very appetizing, people often refuse these foods even when chewing or swallowing problems make a special diet necessary. But if you avoid foods that are easily eaten and digested, you may be unable to maintain a healthy weight and give your body the best chance of healing.

There is an alternative. You can compensate for the variety you lose in texture by emphasizing a range of tastes and colors. Throughout the world, countless dishes featured in gourmet restaurants are not only soft or smooth in texture, but also rich in both taste and visual appeal. This book will show you simple ways to create delicious and appetizing foods so you can more fully enjoy eating.

Part One of this book highlights basic strategies for living with *dysphagia,* or difficulty in swallowing, as well as other problems that require a mechanically altered diet. You will learn about the conditions that can benefit from a soft or smooth diet, and you will find tips for dealing with added difficulties such as nausea, diminished appetite, and altered taste. You will then learn how to stock your pantry and equip your kitchen so that you can make soft and smooth foods with ease—and, when necessary, at a moment's notice. Part One also includes special sections on puréeing and thickening—techniques that you may need to master not only as you follow the recipes in this book, but also as you convert family favorites into easy-to-eat dishes. Finally, you'll find guidelines for keeping your diet healthy as you meet your special needs.

Part Two puts principles into practice with over 150 delicious soft and smooth recipes that cater to a wide range of tastes and dietary needs. From smashing smoothies and sumptuous soups to hearty entrées and sensational sides, you will discover how to prepare healthful and appealing meals. In addition to offering simple step-by-step instructions, each recipe provides comprehensive nutritional information, including diabetic exchanges. It also specifies whether the dish is suitable for easy-to-chew, soft, or smooth/puréed diets. In many cases, tips have been included to help you boost or decrease calories, cut fat, or otherwise modify the recipe so that it is right for you in every way.

We realize that putting together meals can be a challenge to someone who's new to easy-to-chew, soft, and smooth diets. That's why, in addition to the recipes, we include several days of menus that will help you create satisfying and nutritionally balanced meals by joining home-cooked dishes with ready-to-eat foods. Also included are tables of special products—nutritional supplements, handy ingredients such as thickeners, and prepared meals, for instance—that can help you more easily meet your dietary needs. A list of helpful organizations and websites is offered as well, enabling you to find further information about health, diet, and more.

An easy-to-chew-and-swallow diet does not have to mean a decline in the quality of life. Rather, it can signal the beginning of new cooking adventures. We wish you health, happiness, and many satisfying meals to come.

HOW TO USE THIS BOOK

The fact that you picked up this book probably means that you or someone close to you has recently been advised to follow a soft or puréed diet. It is vital that you work with a health care provider who identifies the best diet for you and helps you as you make positive changes in your life. But we know that no doctor, nurse, speech therapist, dietitian, or other professional—no matter how knowledgeable and dedicated—can be with you twenty-four hours a day, ready to answer your questions and guide you as you prepare your meals. That's why *Soft Foods for Easier Eating Cookbook* was written: It will fill the gap between your health care professionals and your need for practical day-to-day help. Whether you require advice on using kitchen equipment to chop or purée foods, you need products designed to thicken liquids to the proper consistency, you would like to transform favorite family dishes to a soft or puréed texture, you're looking for new recipes to meet your new goals, or you need assistance with other aspects of your diet, this book will be there for you.

Throughout this book, we speak directly to the person who requires a special diet, but we know that the individual who prepares these special meals is just as likely to be a family member or other caretaker.

Whether you are preparing these meals for yourself or for someone else, this book can be your practical companion.

Most likely, you have already realized that *Soft Foods* is far more than just a cookbook; it is a comprehensive guide to living well with a mechanically altered diet. It is designed for a wide range of health problems, and therefore addresses a variety of different dietary needs. The next few pages were created to help you better understand what this unique book offers and learn about those sections that are most appropriate for you.

UNDERSTANDING THE DIETS ADDRESSED IN THIS BOOK

If you have already had a chance to flip through the pages of Part Two, "The Recipes," you know that the recipes presented in *Soft Foods for Easier Eating* are designed for three types of diets: easy-to-chew, soft, and smooth/puréed. Generally, when a physician determines that an individual's diet must be mechanically altered—broken down so that it is easier to chew and/or easier to swallow—a diet may be prescribed using one of a variety of terminologies. If you are unsure which of the *Soft Foods* diets is appropriate for your needs, your health care professional will guide you to foods with the proper consistency.

Whichever diet you are now following, be aware that your needs may change over time. You may start off on a soft diet, but as your condition improves—as your body recovers from radiation therapy or surgery, or as you learn more effective swallowing strategies, for instance—you may be able to eat the less mechanically altered easy-to-chew foods. On the other hand, you may have a progressive disorder that makes it necessary to eventually adopt a diet of puréed foods. It is important to stay attuned to your changing needs so that, with the help of your health care providers, you can adjust your diet accordingly.

Our focus in this book is on the three diets discussed above, but we realize that you may have to follow an all-liquids diet. If so, you'll want to turn to the "Liquid Diets" discussion on page 16. There, you'll learn about clear liquid, full liquid, and blenderized diets. Also turn to page 109, where you'll find a selection of recipes for smoothies, shakes, and other beverages; and to page 141, where you'll find soups, many of which are perfect for a liquid diet.

Your doctor may prescribe thickened liquids in order to make swallowing safe. We have addressed that, too, in Chapter 6, "Thickening Liquids." Be aware, though, that you should work closely with a speech therapist to learn the exact consistency that is right for you.

Our discussion of mechanically altered diets would not be complete without a look at tube feedings. When swallowing problems become severe, tube feedings may be necessary for a brief or extended period of time. If your doctor has put you on this form of nutrition, you'll want to turn to the inset "Boosting the Nutrition of Tube Feedings" on page 26. There you will discover how, in some circumstances, you can replace some or all of your commercial tube-feeding formula with wholesome homemade blenderized foods.

You now have a greater understanding of the diets that are addressed in this book. In the remainder of this discussion, you will learn how this book is arranged and where you can find the specific information you need.

USING PART ONE

Part One includes seven chapters designed to provide basic information on following an easy-to-chew, soft, or smooth/puréed diet. Depending on your individual needs, you will want to read one or more of these chapters before you turn to the recipes in Part Two. As your requirements change and as questions arise, you can easily turn back to these chapters for additional guidance.

Chapter 1 begins by looking at common conditions that can make it necessary to follow a mechanically altered diet. It also provides proven tips and tricks for dealing with chewing problems, swallowing problems, and other difficulties that arise from these common conditions. These suggestions can help you more successfully follow your diet. Also included are examples of recommended recipes for each situation, as well as a handy table that guides you to good food choices for each of the three diets addressed. If you want to gain a better understanding of the basic foods you can eat—the most appropriate breads, fruits, vegetables, meats, etc.—Chapter 1 is the place to start.

In addition to the health condition that led your doctor to prescribe a mechanically altered diet, you may have other issues that make it difficult for you to obtain good nutrition. Because of the medications you take, treatments such as radiation or chemotherapy, or other factors, you may be suffering from nausea, altered taste, loss of appetite, heartburn, and a range of other problems. If so, you'll want to read

Chapter 2, which discusses common complications, provides practical tips for coping, and suggests recipes that can help you meet your dietary needs.

If you're like many people, you may now have a very basic question: What foods should I have on hand to follow my new diet? That's why Chapter 3 was written. It will guide you in buying healthful foods that make it far easier to follow a mechanically altered diet. Suggestions are included for people who must limit fat, calories, or sodium. Just as important, a wealth of tips is provided for stocking your pantry with foods that will allow you to make a meal or snack even when time is in short supply.

Your primary task in producing many foods for an easy-to-swallow diet is to mechanically soften foods by chopping, grinding, or puréeing them. Depending on whether your diet must be easy-to-chew, soft, or smooth/puréed, one or several kitchen tools can help you do the job. Chapter 4 introduces you to these tools and assists you in choosing those that can best meet your specific needs. Most likely, you already have some of this equipment on hand—a blender, potato masher, or food processor, for instance. If so, this chapter will guide you in using it more effectively when creating a soft or smooth diet. It will also direct you to other appliances that may help you more quickly and effectively achieve the consistency you desire. Finally, Chapter 4 will fill you in on simple kitchen tools that can make puréed foods look more appetizing.

If you have been told to follow a puréed diet, Chapter 5 provides the basic information you need to transform foods, including treasured family dishes, to the right consistency. This chapter is full of tricks of the trade that can make a range of dishes, from sandwiches and soups to meats and desserts, not only easy to swallow, but also far more appealing. Suggestions are included for achieving appetizing colors and shapes and for avoiding common pitfalls.

As already mentioned, certain swallowing disorders make it necessary to thicken liquids before drinking them. If you have been instructed to thicken your liquids, Chapter 6 will be your guide. It first discusses the different levels of thickness so that you can better understand and identify the desired consistency. It then discusses the pros and cons of different commercial thickeners and instructs you in using them, as well as common household thickeners, with success.

Regardless of the diet you are following, you want your foods to provide you with the nutrition you need to regain or maintain your health. Chapter 7 explains the basic building blocks of nutrition and helps you make good food choices. It also guides you in modifying your diet for common health problems such as diabetes, heart disease, and excess weight.

USING PART TWO

Once you have gathered the information you need from Part One, you'll be ready to look at the over 150 recipes provided in Part Two. As you'll see, each section of Part Two focuses on a different type of dish: beverages; breakfasts; soups; sauces; breads, spreads, and sandwiches; entrées; side dishes; and desserts.

Before you prepare your first *Soft Foods* dish, we suggest that you read "Understanding the Recipes," which begins on page 105. This will help you choose dishes that are right for your diet, understand the Nutritional Facts that accompany each recipe, and follow the step-by-step instructions with success. This section will also point you towards several features that can aid you in varying each recipe according to your nutritional needs and your personal preferences.

As you follow the recipes, always keep in mind your dietary restrictions. If your doctor has told you to drink thickened liquids only, for instance, some of the recipes in the beverages, soups, and sauces chapters may be just fine as prepared, while others may have to be modified. Chapter 6, "Thickening Liquids," will help you determine if the consistency of the finished dish is right for you, and instruct you in thickening it if necessary. Don't hesitate to turn back to this chapter as needed. Similarly, if you are on a smooth/puréed diet, you may want to revisit Chapter 5 for tips on puréeing foods.

If you are experiencing complications such as nausea, altered taste, and decreased appetite, it would be wise to choose your recipes carefully and modify them when warranted. Keep in mind that Chapter 2, "Special Considerations," offers a wealth of tips for coping with these problems. If food has lost its taste, perhaps a splash of hot sauce, a sprinkling of herbs, or another favorite seasoning will increase its appeal. If the odor of foods is aggravating your nausea, it may be wise to eat your meals chilled, because cold foods have less of an odor. Smart decisions like these can help you get the nutrition you need. Remember that only you know which tastes and smells are appetizing to you and which are "turnoffs." A certain amount of trial and error may be necessary as you search for the foods and dishes that work best for you. Moreover, as your condition changes—when an old treatment has ended or a new one has begun, for instance—you may find that you have to make modifications which are better suited to your needs.

USING THE APPENDICES

The more information you have, the more success you will experience in creating foods for your diet. The appendices in this book were designed to provide further information and help you locate any products you may need for your *Soft Foods* dishes.

"Products, Maufacturers, and Distributors," which begins on page 283, will guide you to a wealth of useful products, including thickeners, nutritional supplements, prepared puréed foods, tube-feeding formulas, and more. The "Products" section will allow you to quickly find what you need. Following this, the "Manufacturers and Distributors" list will direct you to the appropriate supplier. A number of organizations and websites can provide additional information about various health conditions, food safety, and other topics of interest. If you need help in understanding a health disorder or its management, the "Organizations and Websites" list is a good place to start.

Many people are daunted by the task of putting together soft and easy-to-swallow meals and menus. "Menu Planning," found on page 298, combines homemade dishes with ready-to-eat foods to create meals that have a healthy balance of proteins, carbohydrates, fats, and other nutrients. If you need to plan a day's worth of meals, or if you simply want ideas for simple, easy-to-swallow dishes and snacks, this appendix will supply the guidance you need.

In creating this book, we have gathered together information and tips gleaned through years of both working with people on mechanically altered diets, and creating dishes and menus for special needs. Nevertheless, as you make diet-related decisions, it is vital that you work with your own health care providers to make sure that the food you choose— and its consistency—is right for you. With the help of knowledgeable health professionals and the *Soft Foods for Easier Eating Cookbook,* you can make a positive difference in your diet, your well-being, and your quality of life.

Part One

Living Well on an Easy-to-Chew, Soft, or Smooth Diet

1. WHO NEEDS AN EASY-TO-CHEW, SOFT, OR SMOOTH DIET?

Eating should be an enjoyable experience, but difficulties with chewing or swallowing can make pleasurable dining seem impossible. Whether your problems develop slowly or suddenly, whether they are temporary or long-term, it's common to have a changed attitude toward food, as well as confusion regarding what you can and cannot eat.

This chapter was designed to start you on the path toward a healthier, more enjoyable diet. A simple table will tell you about some basic conditions that create a need for easy-to-chew, soft, and smooth/puréed diets—the three diets addressed throughout this book. The rest of the chapter provides tips for choosing both individual foods and specific recipes that meet your needs. We think you'll be delighted to learn that regardless of your condition, there is a range of dishes that you can eat and enjoy.

WHY YOU MAY NEED AN EASY-TO-CHEW, SOFT, OR SMOOTH DIET

A number of conditions can make it necessary to switch to a mechanically altered diet—a diet that is easy-to-chew, soft, or smooth-puréed. Some people have a sudden onset of chewing or swallowing prob-

lems following dental work, head and neck surgery, a stroke, or an accident. Some develop these problems gradually as the result of a progressive disease or a treatment such as radiation or chemotherapy. In still other cases, digestive disorders or breathing difficulties can make a regular diet inadvisable or impossible.

Table 1.1 provides an overview of the most common conditions and complications that can make it difficult to eat. The first column lists the condition. The second column informs you of the specific problems that can arise as a result of that disorder, and directs you to the pages in this book that provide additional information about those difficulties.

CHEWING PROBLEMS

The ability to chew makes it possible to enjoy and derive nutrition from a wide range of foods. When chewing problems occur, it can be difficult to eat certain foods, and it may be impossible to chew any foods at all. Even so, it is important to continue eating a variety of nutritious, balanced meals, either by modifying the texture of the foods you normally eat, or by finding high-quality substitutes for them.

TABLE 1.1 CONDITIONS THAT CAN CAUSE EATING DIFFICULTIES

Condition	Associated Problems
Alzheimer's disease.	• Swallowing difficulty (page 12) • Memory loss and increasing dependence on others for feeding
Amyotrophic lateral sclerosis, or ALS (Lou Gehrig's disease); multiple sclerosis.	• Swallowing difficulty (page 12) • Nausea (page 25)
Cancer of the head and/or neck, and surgery.	• Mouth pain (page 14) • Swallowing difficulty (page 12)
Cerebral palsy.	• Swallowing difficulty (page 12)
Chemotherapy and radiation therapy of the head and neck.	• Mouth sores/mouth pain (page 14) • Nausea (page 25) • Dry mouth (page 29) • Loss of sense of taste (page 23) • Loss of teeth/chewing difficulty (page 9) • Swallowing difficulty (page 12)
Connective tissue disorders such as lupus, scleroderma, and rheumatoid arthritis.	• Dry mouth (page 29) • Swallowing difficulty (page 12)
COPD (chronic obstructive pulmonary disease), such as emphysema.	• Breathing difficulty while chewing (page 15)
Facial or jaw fractures.	• Mouth pain (page 14) • Inability to chew (page 9)
Gastrointestinal strictures.	• Risk of obstruction (page 14)
HIV.	• Mouth sores/mouth pain (page 14) • Swallowing difficulty (page 12) • Nausea (page 25)
Loose dentures.	• Mouth sores/mouth pain (page 14) • Chewing difficulty (page 9)
Medication side effects as the result of antibiotics, pain medications, antihistamines, or other drugs.	• Dry mouth (page 29) • Altered taste (page 23) • Nausea (page 25)
Missing teeth or dental surgery.	• Chewing difficulty (page 9) • Mouth pain (page 14)
Mouth infections due to periodontal disease, thrush, herpes, mumps, or other disorders.	• Chewing difficulty (page 9) • Mouth sores/mouth pain (page 14)
Myasthenia gravis.	• Swallowing difficulty (page 12) • Dry mouth (page 29)
Parkinson's disease.	• Swallowing difficulty (page 12) • Tremors and possible need for assistance or special utensils

If you have missing teeth, you may find meats, nuts, and firm cheeses particularly hard to chew. You may also find it difficult to eat many fruits, vegetables, and whole grains. Loose dentures, too, can make it challenging or impossible to chew adequately, and in some cases, can wear painful sores in the lining of your gums. Dentures may become loose due to changes caused by weight loss, periodontal disease, osteoporosis, or other problems. Some people find ill-fitting dentures so bothersome that they take them off when they eat.

If you have missing teeth, loose dentures, or other problems that can be corrected, be sure to see your dentist. Your dentist should be able to refit your dentures, create bridges and other devices that replace missing teeth, and treat any underlying conditions that led to the difficulty. This will allow you to eat the foods you love, including foods that provide important nutrition. If you continue to have problems that affect your ability to chew, soft or smooth foods are the best option, as they will enable you to get the nutrients you need. Also see the suggestions on page 14 for dealing with mouth pain.

If you are having chewing difficulties, the following tips can help you maintain a healthy diet:

❏ Avoid any dry, coarse, or hard foods that need a good deal of chewing and may worsen mouth pain.

❏ Try softer versions of your favorite foods. (See Chapter 5 to learn how you can convert your favorite dishes to a puréed texture.)

❏ If you are losing weight, eat more frequent meals that are high in calories. (Check the Nutritional Facts at the end of each recipe for the calorie count per portion, and see the inset on boosting calories in each of the recipe chapters in Part Two.)

❏ Practice good dental hygiene. Brush with a *soft* toothbrush twice daily, floss, and use a fluoride mouthwash.

If you have had your jaws wired closed as the result of surgery or an accident, you may temporarily need a liquid diet that you can drink through a straw. The discussion of liquid diets, which begins on page 16, presents more information about liquid eating plans, and Part Two of this book offers many delicious drinkable dishes that can help you stay well nourished and battle taste fatigue. Nevertheless, it can be difficult to eat a balanced diet when you are limited to liquids. To make sure that your diet is supplying you with adequate nutrition, it may be important to also use a liquid multivitamin or nutritional supplement while you're following a liquids-only diet. (See the inset "Liquid Vitamin and Mineral Supplements" on page 98.)

RECOMMENDED RECIPES FOR CHEWING PROBLEMS

Soft and Smooth Dishes

❏ Poached Eggs Florentine (page 127)
❏ Fluffy Buttermilk Pancakes (page 130)
❏ Chicken Timbales (page 205)
❏ Barbecue Pulled Pork (page 216)
❏ Potato Croquettes (page 244)
❏ Refried Beans (page 253)
❏ White Chocolate-Strawberry Parfaits (page 269)

Liquid Dishes

❏ Peachy Peanut Butter Shake (page 113)
❏ Carrot-Apple Slush (page 111)
❏ Chilled Beet Soup with Sour Cream and Dill (page 158)
❏ Potato and Leek Soup (page 150)
❏ Aunt Julia's Boiled Custard (page 122)

SWALLOWING PROBLEMS

Most of us swallow about 600 times a day without even thinking about it. This seemingly simple action is really quite complex, involving many muscles of the mouth, throat, and *esophagus*—the tube-like structure that moves food from the throat to the stomach. Swallowing difficulty, also known as *dysphagia,* can occur when illness, injury, diseases of the nervous system, or muscle weakness interferes with the normal function of these muscles. This problem not only can make it difficult to eat, but can cause choking or, by failing to close your airway when you swallow food or drink, can permit food to enter your lungs through a process called aspiration. Aspiration becomes especially likely when liquids are consumed.

A speech therapist, also called a speech pathologist, can often help people with dysphagia to swallow more safely. In addition, the following guidelines can help prevent choking or aspiration:

❑ Chew your food well before swallowing.

When It's Hard to Swallow

If you show signs of a swallowing problem, or dysphagia, your physician should refer you for a Modified Barium Swallow (MBS) study. Performed by a radiologist and a speech therapist, an MBS is used to evaluate the nature of the problem and confirm a diagnosis of dysphagia. If it is determined that you need a *compensatory strategy*—a strategy for swallowing more safely—you will probably be sent to a speech therapist, who is specially trained to provide this instruction.

How You Swallow

There are three phases of the swallow, with each phase performing a unique function.

1. The oral phase. During this phase, the food is chewed and shaped into a *bolus*—a round mass— as it's mixed with saliva. The bolus is then propelled to the back of the tongue, where the tongue pushes the bolus into the pharynx, a passageway connected to the trachea (airway to the lungs) and the esophagus (passageway to the stomach).

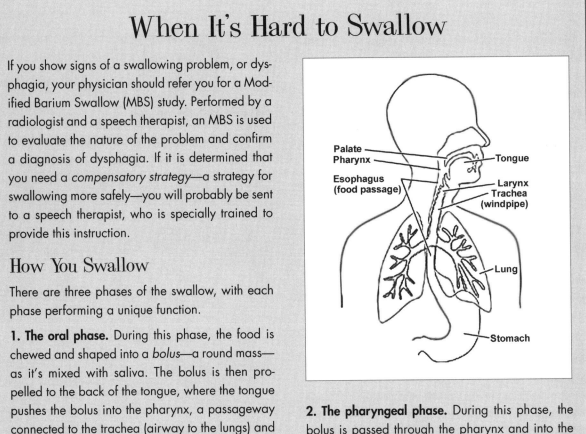

2. The pharyngeal phase. During this phase, the bolus is passed through the pharynx and into the esophagus.

❑ Eat only moist, cohesive foods—foods with a pudding-like or egg salad-like consistency that hold together as you swallow them.

❑ Do not eat dry foods like bread or cookies without dipping or soaking the food in liquids or slurries first. (See Chapter 5, page 76, to learn about slurries.)

❑ Alternate small bites of food with small sips of liquid.

❑ Try to avoid distractions while you eat.

❑ Relax and avoid thinking about things that upset you while you eat. Try playing your favorite calming music during meals.

❑ Avoid talking during a meal, or at least swallow before speaking.

❑ If your doctor or speech therapist recommends that you drink only thickened liquids, follow his or her instructions carefully. (See Chapter 6 to learn about thickened liquids.)

3. The esophageal phase. This phase begins as the bolus moves toward the lower esophagus and then into the stomach.

How You Can Make Your Swallow Safer

A common compensatory strategy for safer swallowing is to change the texture or thickness of the food. For instance, by puréeing a solid food such as chicken or thickening a thin liquid such as fruit juice to a nectar- or honey-like consistency, you can often make foods easier to swallow. (See Chapter 6 for information about thickening a variety of liquids.)

Another useful strategy is to control the amount of food and liquid placed in the mouth. (This is known as *presentation*.) While the mouth can handle a lot, the throat cannot. For that reason, small amounts of food are generally recommended. It is often advisable to alternate small bites of chewed food with small sips of liquid. This aids in the transfer of the food through the pharyngeal and esophageal phases of the swallow.

A final compensatory strategy involves choosing a head position that will make swallowing safer and decrease the risk of choking or aspiration. Three main head positions can be used—the chin tuck, head turned to the left shoulder, and head turned to the right shoulder. Each of these positions needs to be used *before* you initiate the swallow. For instance, if the chin tuck method is recommended, as a sip of liquid is taken in, hold the liquid in your mouth as you lower or tilt your head toward your chest. Once the chin has been tilted, swallow. After the swallow, look up and take another bite or sip. In other words, the chin should not stay down during the entire meal, but only during the swallow itself. Similarly, if you need to turn your head as you swallow, you should turn to the left or right only after the food is in your mouth and you are ready to swallow.

As you can see, a number of steps can be taken to facilitate the swallowing process. Most important is to employ only those strategies that have been recommended by your speech therapist. Use of a strategy that is inappropriate for you can actually cause problems rather than solving them.

RECOMMENDED RECIPES FOR SWALLOWING PROBLEMS

❑ Green Eggs and Ham (page 126)

❑ Stovetop Spoon Bread (page 184)

❑ Chicken Timbales (page 205)

❑ Cheese Soufflés (page 224)

❑ Cauliflower Purée (page 236)

❑ Creamy Fruit Mousse (page 265)

MOUTH AND THROAT PAIN

Mouth and throat pain can make eating very unpleasant. Painful mouth sores can be caused by poorly fitting dentures, HIV/AIDS, and the herpes simplex virus, as well as a number of other conditions. Mouth and throat discomfort can also result from radiation therapy for cancer, infection, thrush, and chemical irritation.

Although your doctor may be able to prescribe medications to treat your condition and/or temporarily numb the pain, a soft or smooth diet can further reduce the discomfort associated with eating. Some of the cool soups, smoothies, and puddings offered in Part Two may be especially helpful. In addition, the following guidelines can help you maintain a healthy diet without aggravating your condition.

❑ Eat soft or smooth foods that will not irritate your mouth and throat.

❑ Eat foods at a moderate temperature—neither too hot nor too cold. When preparing smoothies and milk shakes, use little or no ice.

❑ Avoid spicy foods, especially those that are too salty or contain black or hot peppers.

❑ Avoid acidic foods such as tomato sauces, citrus fruits and juices, and vinegar. If necessary, avoid coffee, tea, and soda as well.

❑ Avoid alcohol.

❑ Avoid foods that are crunchy or have hard, sharp edges such as chips, crackers, and pretzels.

❑ Use a straw when drinking beverages. This will enable you to direct the liquid away from the sore areas of your mouth.

❑ Take pain medications one hour before eating if needed.

❑ Ask your doctor about special mouthwashes that can treat or relieve your pain.

RECOMMENDED RECIPES FOR MOUTH OR THROAT PAIN

❑ Poached Eggs Florentine (page 127)

❑ Creamy Risotto (page 226)

❑ Quick Chicken and Dumplings (page 204)

❑ Polenta Parmesan (page 249)

❑ Fabulous Flan (page 277)

STRICTURES

A *stricture* is an abnormal narrowing of a body passage or tube—in this case, a narrowing of the digestive system. Strictures leave only a small opening through which food can pass, as if a rubber band were wrapped around the affected organ. Some of the most common areas for this to occur are the lower esophagus, usually as a result of scarring from acid reflux; and the lower "valve" of the stomach, where food passes into the intestines. A narrowing can also occur throughout the small and large intestines.

Your doctor may order a liquid, puréed, or soft diet for you in order to prevent food from getting "stuck" and causing an obstruction—an event that could necessitate surgery. If the stricture occurs in the esophagus, you may be referred to a gastroenterologist who can "stretch" the stricture so that food can pass through easily.

The following guidelines can help you maintain a healthy diet and avoid causing an obstruction.

❑ Restrict your diet to the consistency ordered by your physician.

❑ Ask your physician about the signs and symptoms which might indicate that your food has caused an obstruction. If you experience the symptoms, stop eating solid foods and call your doctor immediately.

❑ Eat slowly and take small sips of liquid between bites.

❑ If you have an esophageal stricture, eat in an upright position and remain upright for at least thirty minutes after eating.

RECOMMENDED RECIPES FOR A STRICTURE OF THE DIGESTIVE TRACT

❑ Peaches and Cream (page 117)

❑ Tasty Tomato Soup, puréed (page 156)

❑ Easy Cheese Grits (page 135)

❑ Aunt Julia's Boiled Custard (page 122)

❑ Layered Puréed Spinach Lasagna (page 230)

❑ Savory Carrot Purée (page 235)

❑ Frozen Fruit Whip (page 259)

RESPIRATORY PROBLEMS

Chronic obstructive pulmonary disease (COPD)—an overall term for a group of disorders that include emphysema and chronic bronchitis—can cause shortness of breath during chewing, making it impossible to enjoy a standard diet. In such a case, softer food that is easier to chew, or even a diet of puréed foods, can make it possible to get the nutrition you need without burning extra calories as a result of labored breathing. If your foods are liquid or puréed, they will provide the added benefit of incorporating more fluids into your diet.

The following dietary guidelines can help you cope with chronic obstructive pulmonary disease:

❑ Avoid foods that require a lot of chewing, especially if they cause you to get short of breath. Instead, stick to soft, smooth, and easy-to-chew foods.

❑ Drink plenty of water and other fluids, especially if you use oxygen.

❑ Sip on juices, whole milk, milk shakes, or smoothies throughout the day. This will help keep you hydrated while maintaining your energy.

❑ Instead of having three large meals a day, plan frequent small meals, and eat slowly. This will reduce bloating, which can make breathing uncomfortable.

❑ To ease pressure on your lungs, sit up straight while you eat.

❑ If you are short of breath, avoid high-carbohydrate and high-protein diets, as carbs and proteins demand a good deal of oxygen to metabolize. At the same time, increase the amount of healthy fats in your diet, especially olive oil and foods containing omega-3 polyunsaturated fats. (See Chapter 7, page 94.)

❑ If you are losing too much weight, choose calorie-dense foods or drink a high-calorie nutritional supplement. (Check the Nutritional Facts at the end of each recipe for the calorie count per portion, and see the inset on calorie boosting in each of the recipe chapters in Part Two.)

RECOMMENDED RECIPES FOR RESPIRATORY PROBLEMS

❏ Blueberry Nog (page 121)

❏ Biscuits with Sausage Gravy (page 134)

❏ Peaches and Cream (page 117)

❏ Johnny Marzetti (page 211)

❏ Cheesy Bread Pudding (page 191)

❏ Peanutty Pumpkin Soup (page 149)

❏ Garden Gazpacho (with a dash of olive oil) (page 159)

THE BEST FOODS FOR YOUR DIET

Descriptions of easy-to-chew, soft, and smooth/puréed diets vary as widely as the range of conditions requiring them. Table 1.2 was designed to get you started by listing the different food groups—such as breads, cereals, grains, and pastas—and recommending the best choices for your needs. Column 1 includes good choices for people who are experiencing mild difficulty in chewing and/or swallowing, and therefore follow an easy-to-chew diet—the least limiting of the three mechanically altered diets addressed in this book. Since this diet involves fewer restrictions than the other two, people who follow it can also eat all the foods listed in Columns 2 and 3. Column 2 presents foods for people who have moderate difficulty in chewing and/or swallowing, and therefore follow a soft diet. In addition to all the foods listed in Column 2, people on a soft diet can enjoy the choices listed in

Column 3. The third column lists food choices for people who are experiencing more severe chewing and/or swallowing difficulties, and have to follow a smooth/puréed diet. For the most part, people on this diet have to limit themselves to the types of foods described in Column 3.

Since everyone's needs are unique, some people may find that they can choose items from a more challenging food category. With the help of speech therapists, dietitians, and other health professionals, many people are able to change their diet over time, moving from smooth foods to soft foods, or from soft foods to easy-to-chew options. In general, the greater difficulty you're having with the foods you're currently eating, the smoother your diet will need to be. If you require thickened liquids as well, turn to Chapter 6.

LIQUID DIETS

For the most part, this book addresses the needs of people who are following an easy-to-chew, soft, or smooth/puréed diet. However, sometimes—after certain types of surgery, for instance—you may need to be on a liquid diet for a period of time. When that happens, you will follow one of three liquid eating plans: A clear liquid diet, a full liquid diet, or a blenderized diet.

A *clear liquid diet* may be ordered following gastrointestinal surgery, as preparation for a gastrointestinal test, or to rest the body when you are experiencing vomiting or diarrhea. Clear liquids are those that you can see through and contain little or no pulp. Some examples are apple juice, cranberry juice, grape juice, Jell-O gelatin (no fruit added), tea, clear carbonated and noncarbonated beverages, broth, and fruit ices or popsicles made with clear juices. This diet is not nutritionally adequate, but can be improved through the addition of a clear liquid nutritional supplement.

TABLE 1.2 MAKING GOOD FOOD CHOICES

EASY-TO-CHEW DIET (Mild Difficulty)	SOFT DIET (Moderate Difficulty)	SMOOTH OR PURÉED DIET (Severe Difficulty)
BREADS, CEREALS, GRAINS, AND PASTAS		
• Soft breads (without seeds, nuts, grain pieces, dried fruits, or hard crusts) moistened with margarine, butter, syrup, or sauce. • Pancakes, crepes, and waffles moistened with butter, margarine, syrup, or sauce. • Well-cooked rice (cook until soft by adding extra water and cooking longer than usual) with gravy or sauce. • *Plus* all foods listed in Columns 2 and 3.	• Soft, moist breads (without seeds, nuts, grain pieces, dried fruits, or hard crusts) moistened with syrup or sauce. (Breads may include biscuits, muffins, and French toast.) • Moist cornbread. • Moist stuffing or dressing. • Pancakes and crepes moistened with syrup or sauce. • Soft-cooked smooth hot cereals with some texture, such as oatmeal. • Dry cereals softened in milk. • Soft-cooked pasta, noodles, or dumplings in sauce. • Gnocchi (potato dumplings) in sauce. • *Plus* all foods listed in Column 3.	• Breads and cereals (without seeds, nuts, grain pieces, dried fruit, or crusts) that have been saturated with a liquid, syrup, or sauce so they have a smooth consistency. • Soft-cooked smooth hot cereals such as oat bran, Cream of Wheat, farina, and Cream of Rice. • Grits, soft cornmeal mush, spoon bread, and soft polenta. • Puréed pasta in puréed sauce.
FRUITS		
• Soft, easy-to-chew raw fruits such as kiwis, peaches, and melons. (Remove all hard seeds and tough skins.) • Soft berries such as blueberries, blackberries, raspberries, and strawberries. • Halved grapes as tolerated. • Fruit compotes and chutneys. • *Plus* all foods listed in Columns 2 and 3.	• Soft-cooked or canned fruits. • Chunky applesauce. • Soft, ripe bananas. • Fruit juices, nectars, or smoothies. (May be lumpier than purées.) • Dried fruits that have been cooked until soft. • Fruit jams and preserves. • *Plus* all foods listed in Column 3.	• Fruits that have been blended until smooth (no seeds or nuts). If necessary, strain the fruits after blending. • Applesauce without chunks. • Mashed ripe bananas. • Fruit juices or nectars (avoid too much pulp) and well-blended smoothies. • Fruit jellies.

EASY-TO-CHEW DIET (Mild Difficulty)	SOFT DIET (Moderate Difficulty)	SMOOTH OR PURÉED DIET (Severe Difficulty)
NONSTARCHY VEGETABLES		
• Shredded lettuce, chopped tomatoes, and thinly sliced, peeled cucumbers. (Avoid difficult-to-chew raw vegetables such as carrots and celery.) • *Plus* all foods listed in Columns 2 and 3.	• Soft-cooked nonstarchy vegetables. (Avoid all raw vegetables except those that can be mashed or juiced.) • Vegetable soufflés, puddings, and soups. • *Plus* all foods listed in Column 3.	• All cooked nonstarchy vegetables that have been blended, mashed and strained, or puréed so that they have a pudding-like consistency, with no lumps, chunks, or seeds. (Avoid vegetables that are stringy, tough, or rubbery after cooking, such as celery.) • Vegetable juices and smooth sauces.
STARCHY VEGETABLES		
• Soft French fries and baked potato wedges. • Soft-cooked beans and peas. • Creamed corn. • *Plus* all foods listed in Columns 2 and 3.	• Soft-cooked root vegetables such as potatoes, moistened with butter, sour cream, or sauce. • Cooked pumpkin and winter squash. • Creamed corn without whole corn kernels. • Soft-cooked, mashed beans and peas. • *Plus* all foods listed in Column 3.	• Mashed or puréed root vegetables such as white potatoes, sweet potatoes, beets, and carrots. • Mashed or puréed pumpkin and winter squash. • Beans, peas, or creamed corn that has been puréed and strained.
MILK, YOGURT, AND CHEESE		
• All easy-to-chew cheeses such as Brie, and thinly sliced hard cheeses. (Hard cheeses can also be grated and used in dishes.) • Yogurt with soft fruit chunks (no nuts or coconut). • *Plus* all foods listed in Columns 2 and 3.	• Cottage cheese, feta cheese, ricotta cheese, and other soft cheeses. • Fruit-flavored yogurt with no fruit pieces, or only small bits of fruit. • Tapioca, rice, and bread pudding. • *Plus* all foods listed in Column 3.	• Milk, buttermilk, evaporated milk, soymilk, almond milk, and rice milk. • Yogurt without nuts or chunks of fruit. • Kifer or blended yogurt smoothies. • Smooth-textured puddings and custards. (Avoid those with lumps, such as tapioca, rice, and bread puddings.) • Cheese sauce.

MEATS AND MEAT SUBSTITUTES

• Tender meats and poultry with sauce.

• All fish except fried, moistened with sauce.

• Hard-boiled eggs.

• Casseroles with tender chunks of meat.

• Well-cooked, moist dried beans and peas.

• *Plus* all foods listed in Columns 2 and 3.

• Ground meats served with gravy or sauce.

• Casseroles with ground or shredded meats. (Avoid stringy or tough vegetables such as celery and corn. Also avoid rice unless it is soft-cooked and part of a cohesive mixture.)

• Meatloaf and meatballs.

• Tender, flaky fish (baked or steamed) with sauce.

• Seafood spreads, soft smoked salmon, or lox.

• Soft seafood croquettes or mousse.

• Egg salad, tuna salad, or chicken salad. (Include onion or pickles only if finely chopped. Substitute celery salt for chopped celery.)

• Tofu in soft, moist dishes.

• Scrambled or soft-cooked eggs or egg substitutes.

• Quiches or soufflés made without hard or chunky ingredients such as crisp bacon.

• Refried beans or bean spreads and pâtés.

• *Plus* all foods listed in Column 3.

• Puréed meats and puréed scrambled eggs.

• Egg custards or smooth, crustless quiches.

• Liverwurst and smooth pâtés.

• Smooth meat, poultry, or seafood mousses, timbales, and custards.

• Puréed dried beans and bean spreads such as hummus.

• Smooth soufflés (remove crusted tops).

• Soft tofu used in smooth dishes.

• Smooth nut butters blended with banana or other ingredients to make a soft, nonsticky spread.

SOUPS

• All soups with soft, easy-to-chew ingredients, such as well-cooked carrots and potatoes. (Avoid large chunks of meat and tough meats.)

• *Plus* all foods listed in Columns 2 and 3.

• All soups with ground meat or small, soft chunks of meat and vegetables. Avoid corn and peas (except split peas).

• *Plus* all foods listed in Column 3.

• Soups that are naturally smooth, like tomato soup, or that have been blended and strained.

EASY-TO-CHEW DIET (Mild Difficulty)	SOFT DIET (Moderate Difficulty)	SMOOTH OR PURÉED DIET (Severe Difficulty)
DESSERTS		
• Any cakes, cookies, and candies that are not dry, hard, or chewy and do not contain seeds, nuts, dried fruits, coconut, or pineapple. • Fruit compotes. • *Plus* all foods listed in Columns 2 and 3.	• Soft pies, such as pumpkin, without dry top crust. • Cobblers without hard seeds or nuts. • Soft, moist cakes with sauce or moist topping. • Soft cookies (no nuts or chunks) that are moistened by dunking in milk, coffee, or hot chocolate. • Flavored gelatin or fruited gelatins made with soft canned fruits (no pineapple) and cream cheese (for extra calories). • Parfaits and trifles with no pineapple. • *Plus* all foods listed in Column 3.	• Smooth puddings and custards. • Dessert soups, soufflés, and mousses without chunks. • Frozen desserts (avoid if you need thickened liquids). • Flavored gelatin without chunks (avoid if you need thickened liquids). • Cakes thoroughly moistened with sauce, custard, or milk. • Fondues made with thoroughly moistened, crustless bread or cake cubes. • Soft, smooth candy. • Parfaits and trifles made with puréed fruit and soft cakes or cookies (without nuts or chips) that are thoroughly moistened.

A *full liquid diet* is sometimes used as a "step up" from clear liquids. It contains more protein than a clear liquid diet, but is not generally considered to be nutritionally complete. If this diet includes a good deal of dairy products, it may not be tolerated by people with lactose intolerance. Soymilk, rice milk, or drinkable yogurt with live cultures (if tolerated) can be substituted for milk. Foods that can be added to those found on a clear liquid diet include milk, drinkable yogurt, ice cream, creamed soups (strained), vegetable juices, fruit juices with pulp, smoothies, milk shakes, and all other beverages. Mashed potatoes, Cream of Wheat, Cream of Rice, and grits can be used if they are incorporated into soups or into a beverage that includes enough milk to give it a soupy consistency. Like a

clear liquid diet, this food plan can be improved nutritionally through the addition of liquid supplements. Fiber supplements mixed with liquids would also be beneficial.

A *blenderized diet* is recommended in those relatively rare instances when you need to be on a liquid diet for an extended period of time—for instance, if your jaws are wired shut. If properly planned, this diet can provide adequate nutrition. For a blenderized diet, you can blend entire meals or individual foods as long as you end up with a liquid that is free of particles and can be consumed through a straw. (The difference between a smooth/puréed and blenderized diet is that in the latter, all foods must be drinkable.) This can usually be accomplished with about equal

Daily Blenderized Menu (about 1,800 calories)

Breakfast

Blenderize together until liquefied:

❑ $\frac{1}{2}$ cup pasteurized liquid egg (whole eggs or egg substitute)

❑ $\frac{1}{2}$ cup Cream of Wheat (cooked)

❑ 1 cup drinkable yogurt

❑ 1 cup apple juice

❑ 1 tablespoon walnut oil

Snack

❑ 8 ounces mixed 100% fruit and vegetable juice, such as V8 Fusion

Lunch

Blenderize together until smooth (strain if needed):

❑ 1 cup beef and vegetable soup

❑ 1 slice bread

❑ 1 cup milk (may use soy or rice milk with calcium)

❑ 1 tablespoon canola oil

Snack

❑ 1 cup pomegranate or grape juice

Dinner

Blenderize together until smooth (strain if needed):

❑ $\frac{1}{2}$ cup cubed cooked chicken

❑ 11.5-ounce can vegetable juice, such as V8

❑ $\frac{1}{2}$ cup cooked broccoli or cauliflower florets

❑ $\frac{1}{2}$ cup cooked rice

❑ 1 cup milk (may use soy or rice milk with calcium)

❑ 1 tablespoon olive oil

---

parts solids and liquids. Very dry foods, such as breads, may need more liquid, but very moist foods, such as fruits and vegetables, may need less. You can incorporate meats and vegetables into blended soups; enhance smoothies with phytonutrient-rich additives; and boost the nutritional value of milk shakes with protein powders. You may need to omit seeds, nuts, skins, coconut, pineapple, and any other foods that are difficult to blend unless you strain the mixture through a fine mesh sieve.

When following a blenderized diet, be aware that some foods blend together well and taste good, but other combinations are awful. A rule of thumb is to consider whether you would combine the foods in a casserole, soup, or stew. If you would, there is a good chance that you have a palatable combination. Also consider colors when choosing foods. If all the primary colors are blended together, you may end up with an unappealing brown drink. For that reason, it's helpful to stick with foods within the same color family. (For more on this, see page 74.)

A blenderized diet doesn't have to be boring or inadequate. The box above shows a sample of a daily menu that could be blenderized. Just remember that when following this or any liquid diet, it is essential that you adhere to the instructions of your health care provider. Only a professional who is familiar with your full medical history can approve a diet that will meet your needs without causing further problems. Be aware, too, that sometimes individuals cannot swallow even a liquid diet. In those cases, tube feedings may be necessary. (For more information on this, see the inset "Boosting the Nutrition of Tube Feedings" on page 26.)

FURTHER CONSIDERATIONS

This chapter has discussed some common problems that make it necessary to follow an easy-to-chew, soft, or smooth/puréed diet. It has also provided tips for coping with these common problems, as well as basic guidelines for choosing appropriate foods. But everyone is unique, and for many people, complications such as altered taste, nausea, dry mouth, and/or heartburn can make some of the foods you learned about better choices than others. In the next chapter, you'll read about common complications and learn how to further tune your diet to meet your specific needs.

2. SPECIAL CONSIDERATIONS

Chapter 1 provided a foundation for choosing foods for your easy-to-chew, soft, or smooth/puréed diet. But while a particular food may be appropriate for your chewing and swallowing problems, any complications you're experiencing can prevent you from enjoying it. Altered taste, nausea, and loss of appetite are common problems that can affect people who need mechanically altered foods. Other possible difficulties include dry mouth, heartburn, constipation, diarrhea, and excessive phlegm production.

This chapter provides a wealth of suggestions to help you manage any complications you may be experiencing. For each problem, you'll find a brief explanation followed by lists of coping tips and appropriate recipes. Whether you are having trouble with altered tastes or you are suffering from digestive difficulties, you'll learn that you can find food that's not only nutritious, but also easy to swallow.

ALTERED TASTE (DYSGEUSIA)

Altered taste, known medically as *dysgeusia,* involves a diminished sense of taste or a persistent abnormal taste that can make eating unpleasant. Some people feel that things just taste "wrong" or "bad." Some experience a metallic or chemical taste, especially after eating high-protein foods such as meat. Some find that foods taste very different from the way they used to. And some find that all foods taste alike—or that they have no flavor at all.

While dysgeusia is not in and of itself a life-threatening condition, it can have serious consequences. Diminished or distorted taste can lead to food aversions, loss of appetite, and severe weight loss.

Dysgeusia can result from a number of disorders and conditions, including Bell's palsy, cancer, depression, diabetes, dry mouth, gingivitis, infection, nasal polyps, multiple sclerosis, and some vitamin and mineral deficiencies. It can also be caused by certain medications, particularly antibiotics and chemotherapy drugs, and by radiation therapy. It can even be the result of smoking. In addition, normal aging usually dulls the sense of taste.

In some cases, altered or diminished taste can be resolved by dealing with the underlying problem. For instance, the offending drug can be stopped, the infection can be cleared up, and dry mouth can be treated with increased hydration or artificial saliva. (See page 29 for more information on dry mouth.) However, dysgeusia caused by permanent damage to the neurological system responsible for taste may never improve.

If you are suffering from a reduced or distorted sense of taste, speak to your doctor to discuss a possible course of action. Be aware, though, that there are no specific treatments for this condition. If your dysgeusia cannot be resolved, the following guidelines can help you better enjoy your food:

Odor of Food Is Unpleasant

❑ Eat cold and frozen foods, which have less aroma.

❑ Prevent or lessen cooking smells by cooking on an outdoor grill, buying prepared food, or using an exhaust fan during cooking.

❑ Place beverages and soups in a hot or cold cup fitted with a lid. Then use a straw or the hole at the edge of the cup to sip the food.

Sense of Taste Has Diminished

❑ Add more spices or tart foods to your meal. Also try strongly flavored sauces such as horseradish sauce, barbecue sauce, salsa, and curry sauce.

❑ Use flavorful oils such as extra virgin olive oil and sesame oil.

❑ Add a bit of sweetener to foods, especially if you are experiencing undesirable weight loss. (Check with your doctor if you are diabetic.) Try brown sugar, molasses, or honey, which are more flavorful—and less processed—than white sugar. The sense of taste for sweets often remains after other tastes are lost.

❑ Sip on flavored beverages, such as tea or lemonade, between bites of food.

Food Tastes Different

❑ Add a pinch of salt if foods taste too sweet.

❑ Add sugar if foods taste too salty. (Or use less salt.)

❑ Try mild-tasting dishes if foods taste too strong or bitter.

❑ Choose foods that taste or smell good even if they are unfamiliar to you.

❑ Season your food with new herbs and spices, or use familiar seasonings in different ways. For instance, add cinnamon to savory sauces and turmeric to soups.

Mouth Has Persistent Bad Taste

❑ Brush your teeth before and after meals.

❑ Rinse your mouth with water that has a pinch of baking soda added.

❑ Between meals, suck on sugar-free mint, lemon, or orange hard candies, or chew on sugar-free gum.

Meat or Other Food Tastes Bitter or Metallic

❑ Serve meat cold or at room temperature.

❑ Include meat in mixed dishes such as stews and casseroles.

❑ Choose meat alternatives such as eggs, custards, cheese, yogurt, milk, tofu, or nut butters.

❑ Marinate meat in acidic mixtures such as sweet and sour marinades or those containing lime or lemon juice, vinegar, wine, or pineapple juice.

❑ Use glass cookware and eat with plastic (non-metallic) utensils.

RECOMMENDED RECIPES TO COPE WITH ALTERED TASTE

Loss of Taste

❑ Apricot Frappé (page 110)

❑ Cinnamon-Apple Oatmeal (page 140)

Meat Tastes Bitter or Metallic

NAUSEA AND VOMITING

For those who are undergoing treatment for cancer or who suffer from gastrointestinal disorders, infection, migraine, or inner ear problems, nausea and vomiting can make it difficult to get adequate nutrition. Although powerful drugs are now available to help relieve nausea and vomiting due to cancer treatments, these symptoms cannot always be eliminated. Moreover, the use of strong drugs can cause undesirable side effects.

If you suffer from nausea or vomiting on a frequent basis, make sure to tell your doctor so that he is aware of the problem. If he is unable to substantially lessen or eliminate these symptoms, the following tips should help you cope so that you can get the nourishment you need.

❏ Avoid odors that bother you, including cooking smells, smoke, and heavy perfumes.

❏ Drink a lot of clear, ice-cold beverages such as unsweetened fruit juice, tea, and gingerale. This will replace fluids lost through vomiting. (Drink clear liquids only if still vomiting.)

❏ Sip drinks slowly instead of drinking a lot at once.

❏ If you were unable to eat solid food for a time but have just returned to solids, start with bland foods such as saltine crackers and plain white bread, and eat small amounts throughout the day.

❏ If you are eating meals, choose cold or room-temperature foods so that you won't be bothered by strong odors. Again, eat small amounts throughout the day rather than having a few large meals.

❏ Avoid excessively sweet foods as well as foods that are fried or fatty.

❏ Take ginger in the form of gingerale, ginger tea, ginger candy, or pickled ginger. Studies have shown that ginger can help alleviate nausea. (If you are not taking blood anticoagulants, you can also try 1,000 milligrams of powdered dried ginger root per day.)

❏ Between meals, sip peppermint tea or suck on peppermint candy. Peppermint has been shown to relieve nausea. (Avoid peppermint if heartburn or acid reflux is a problem.)

❏ When feeling nauseated, breathe deeply and slowly. This can help lessen the nausea.

❏ After eating, try to rest and relax. Do not, however, lie flat for at least two hours after you finish a meal, especially if reflux is a problem.

❏ If vomiting has lasted for more than a few days (twenty-four hours for small children and the elderly), contact your doctor. You may need intravenous fluids to prevent dehydration.

RECOMMENDED RECIPES TO COPE WITH NAUSEA

Boosting the Nutrition of Tube Feedings

This chapter explains how a variety of strategies can be used to insure a nutritious diet even when problems such as nausea or loss of appetite make eating difficult or unpleasant. Sometimes, though, tube feedings may be necessary for a brief or extended period of time. If you have been put on tube feedings, your doctor has already ordered a feeding formula appropriate for your condition. Although this ready-made product is sterile, is very convenient, and may be necessary in some cases, you may wish to supplement or replace this formula with natural, unrefined food in the form of a homemade blenderized formula.

Making your own blenderized formula is time-consuming and requires planning, but can offer several advantages. Most important, it allows you to control the ingredients. A variety of wholesome foods such as vegetables, fruits, whole grains, dairy products, lean meats, and healthful oils can be included in the formula. In contrast, many commercial formulas contain large amounts of refined carbohydrates such as corn syrup, sugar, and maltodextrin. Homemade formulas can also include the foods that your family is eating so that you can feel that you are participating in family meals. And you can easily omit any foods to which you are allergic or sensitive.

If you'd like to stick with a commercial formula but want something more wholesome, speak to your doctor about switching to a product that's made from whole foods. (See the "Products" tables, beginning on page 284.) Another option is to use the commercial formula ordered by your doctor, but to fortify your diet by adding some fruit and vegetable juice through the tube. This will enhance your nutrition with important *phytonutrients*—health-protecting plant compounds.

Presented below is a sample blenderized menu that could be used for tube feeding. By following this menu of formulas, rather than making a single formula, you will help insure that your diet is nutritionally complete and balanced. Nevertheless, it is vital to talk to your doctor before switching to a blenderized food. Homemade formulas are not appropriate for certain conditions and feeding methods, such as continuous drip feedings. Blenderized foods can be used only for bolus feedings (feedings given at one time, as a "meal"), preferably through a button-type port.

Sample Blenderized Menu (about 2,000 Calories)

Breakfast
Blenderize together until liquefied; then strain if needed:
- ½ cup pasteurized liquid egg (whole eggs or egg substitute)
- ½ cup cooked whole grain cereal
- 1 cup drinkable yogurt
- 1 cup low-acid orange juice
- ½ cup berries
- 1 tablespoon walnut oil

Snack
- 8 ounces vegetable juice, such as V8

Lunch
Blenderize together until liquefied; then strain if needed:

❏ 1 cup beef stew (homemade or store-bought)

❏ 12 ounces vegetable juice, such as V8

❏ 1 slice whole grain bread

❏ 1 cup milk (may use soy or rice milk with calcium)

❏ 1 tablespoon flaxseed oil

Snack

❏ 1 cup pomegranate or grape juice

Dinner

Blenderize together until liquefied; then strain if needed:

❏ $\frac{1}{2}$ cup diced cooked skinless chicken

❏ 12 ounces vegetable or carrot juice

❏ $\frac{1}{2}$ cup cooked broccoli or cauliflower florets

❏ $\frac{1}{2}$ cup cooked brown rice or whole grain pasta

❏ 1 cup milk (may use soy or rice milk with calcium)

❏ 1 tablespoon olive or canola oil

Once you've received your doctor's approval for your homemade formula, you'll want to become familiar with some general precautions. The following guidelines will help insure that your blenderized food is free of contaminants and provides great nutrition without causing problems.

❏ Flush the tube with water before and after any food or medication has been provided, following your doctor's orders. Clogs can form if food or medication is not flushed completely out of the equipment. By keeping the tube clean, you will also avoid bacterial growth.

❏ If you are just starting tube feedings, begin slowly. You may not be able to tolerate the amount of food your body actually needs until you adjust to this form of nutrition. Follow your doctor's recommendations regarding the increase of feedings.

❏ Always use safe food handling practices when making your tube-feeding formula. (See the inset "Food Safety" on page 46 for more information.)

❏ Never mix medications with the blenderized food, as this may cause clumping and can even alter the effectiveness of your medication.

❏ Allow cold or hot foods to reach room or body temperature before putting them in the tube.

❏ Use a blender that is powerful enough to liquefy whole foods without burning out. (See the discussion of blenders in Chapter 4, page 55, for more information.) If your blenderized formula is not completely smooth, strain it through a fine-mesh sieve before putting it through the feeding tube.

❏ When making your blenderized formula, use adequate amounts of liquid so that the food will not clog the tube. The formula should have a nectar-like consistency. Add more water as necessary to achieve this texture. Also be aware that the formula must provide enough fluids to keep you hydrated. (Work with your doctor or dietitian on this.)

❏ To avoid digestive discomfort, add the blenderized foods through the tube *slowly*. One way to do this is to provide the food in 50-cc (cubic centimeter) increments with a syringe, taking time between each "dose" so that the meal is spread out over at least thirty minutes. This will take a little patience. Notify your doctor right away if you experience abdominal pain, nausea, vomiting, diarrhea, or other intestinal symptoms.

❏ Add a liquid multivitamin through your tube daily. Ask your doctor to prescribe one that is appropriate for your condition.

❏ Cinnamon Applesauce (page 261)

❏ Fabulous Fruit Gelatin (page 264)

❏ Soft Scrambled Eggs (page 128)

❏ Cornmeal Mush (page 135)

❏ Yogurt-Fruit Soup (page 161)

LOSS OF APPETITE

Loss of appetite, also called *anorexia,* can be the result of any number of conditions, therapies, and situations. Cancer, high fever, HIV, viral hepatitis, heart problems, liver disorders, duodenal ulcer, and zinc deficiency are just a few of the conditions that can cause a poor appetite. Various psychological problems, from anxiety and general stress to depression, can also have a marked negative effect on appetite. Finally, a range of treatments, including radiation therapy, chemotherapy, and some medications, can greatly diminish the desire to eat.

Clearly, loss of appetite can be dangerous because your body needs adequate nourishment, including hydration, especially if you are trying to overcome a health condition. Speak to your doctor if your desire to eat has lessened. If the problem is being caused by a medication, it may be possible to reduce your dosage or find a substitute drug. If the problem is an undiagnosed or untreated condition, appropriate therapy may return your appetite to normal. Your physician may also be able to prescribe medications that can stimulate your desire to eat. (To learn more about this, see the inset "Appetite Stimulants" on page 29.)

If your doctor is unable to find a resolution to your problem, the following tips can help you cope with anorexia and avoid a substantial loss of weight. If loss of appetite is caused by altered taste or nausea, see the discussions on pages 23 and 25.

❏ Don't hurry your meals. Take your time.

❏ Eat whenever you are hungry and make the most of those times. Don't worry if this is not your usual mealtime. If you can, eat high-protein, high-calorie foods. (See the inset on calorie boosting in each recipe chapter for tips on increasing calories.)

❏ Keep your home stocked with food that is easy and quick to prepare so that when hunger strikes, you don't have to spend time and energy preparing a meal.

❏ Try eating frequent smaller meals throughout the day. A plate that is loaded with food can be off-putting when your appetite is already small.

❏ To avoid dehydration, be sure to drink plenty of fluids, especially calorie- and nutrient-rich beverages such as juices, shakes, and smoothies.

❏ Avoid strong-smelling foods if they depress your appetite. If all food smells are a problem, eat your meals cold, as this makes odors less noticeable.

RECOMMENDED RECIPES TO COPE WITH LOSS OF APPETITE AND WEIGHT LOSS

❏ Peanut Butter-Banana Smoothie (use whole milk) (page 115)

❏ Pumpkin Nog (use regular eggnog) (page 121)

❏ Cheesy Bread Pudding (page 191)

❏ Creamy Cheese Omelet (page 129)

❏ Biscuits with Sausage Gravy (page 134)

❏ Three-Cheese Manicotti (page 228)

❏ Angel Hair Alfredo (page 223)

❏ Cheesy Twice-Baked Potatoes (page 245)

Appetite Stimulants

If you have a poor appetite and are experiencing undesired weight loss, you should discuss this with your doctor, as unplanned weight loss can be damaging to your health. Fortunately, in many cases, there are steps that you and your doctor can take to help restore your appetite. One possible option is to use medications that can stimulate your desire to eat. Below, you'll learn about a few of the drugs that can be helpful.

❏ *Megace,* or *megestrol acetate,* stimulates appetite and can support weight gain. Unfortunately, the weight gained may be fat and water, rather than muscle. Megace should not be used when you are at risk for blood clots.

❏ *Marinol,* or *dronabinol,* is made form THC, the active ingredient in marijuana. This appetite stimulant is particularly useful for patients whose anorex-

ia is accompanied by pain, nausea, or both. One drawback is that it may increase disorientation in some people, which can be a problem in the case of dementia. On the other hand, this drug can calm people who have a problem with agitation.

❏ *Remeron,* or *mirtazapine,* is an antidepressant that can stimulate appetite, particularly when the problem is linked to depression. A drawback can be increased fatigue in some people. Be aware that other antidepressants can also act as appetite stimulants.

As you can see, the action of drugs can be complex and create both desirable and undesirable effects. For that reason, when discussing appetite loss, you should make your doctor aware of any medications you are already taking.

DRY MOUTH

Dry mouth, also known as *xerostomia,* is a side effect of many prescription and over-the-counter drugs, including medications used to treat anxiety, allergies, asthma, colds, depression, diarrhea, epilepsy, hypertension (high blood pressure), nausea, obesity, pain, Parkinson's disease, and urinary incontinence. It can also be caused by dehydration; disorders such as Alzheimer's disease, diabetes, Parkinson's disease, Sjogren's disease, and stroke; treatments such as chemotherapy; and surgical removal of the salivary glands or destruction of the glands through radiation to the head and neck.

Although dry mouth is not a disease, it can increase the risk of mouth sores, gingivitis, and tooth

decay. It can also be extremely uncomfortable and cause a persistent sore throat, constant thirst, a burning sensation in the mouth, and difficulty in speaking, tasting, chewing, and swallowing. Keep in mind that saliva begins the digestive process by lubricating food and adding enzymes. When the mouth is dry because of insufficient saliva, swallowing becomes not only more difficult but also more risky, as the food remains more intact.

If your dry mouth is being caused by use of a medication, your physician may be able to offer an alternative drug without that side effect or to decrease the dosage of your current prescription. Your doctor may also be able to prescribe a medication that can help relieve dry mouth. In addition, the following steps can improve salivary flow, make your mouth feel more comfortable, and make it easier for you to chew and swallow your food.

❏ Follow a puréed diet. Easy to swallow even with a dry mouth, this will also provide you with the fluids you need to keep hydrated.

❏ Sip on fluids throughout the day to keep your mouth moist and provide hydration.

❏ Eat a lot of foods with high fluid content, such as smoothies, milk shakes, applesauce, puddings, flavored gelatin desserts, yogurt, and soups.

❏ If fluids don't relieve your discomfort, ask your health care professional about an artificial saliva such as Optimoist spray, Salivart Oral Moisturizer spray, or SalivaSure Lozenges. Other options include an all-natural glycerin-based mouth spray, such as Thayers Dry Mouth Spray, and Biotene's gum and toothpaste, which are specifically designed for people who need dry mouth relief.

❏ Chew sugar-free gum, or keep sugar-free candy in your mouth to help stimulate saliva production.

❏ To moisten your mouth during conversations, carry a spray bottle or regular bottle that contains water or one of the solutions listed below. You can also use these solutions to rinse your mouth, which will remove food particles and give your mouth a fresher taste.

- 1 cup water plus ¼ teaspoons salt
- 1 cup water plus ¼ teaspoon baking soda
- 1 cup water plus ¼ teaspoon glycerin
- Soda water

❏ Avoid sticky and sugary foods, such as jams and dried fruits, which can promote tooth decay.

❏ Dunk or soak dry foods in liquids such as tea, hot cocoa, soups, or broths.

❏ Use a room vaporizer to add moisture to the air in your home.

❏ As much as possible, breathe through your nose, not your mouth.

❏ Protect your teeth by brushing with a fluoride toothpaste, using a fluoride rinse, and visiting your dentist on a regular basis.

RECOMMENDED RECIPES TO COPE WITH DRY MOUTH

❏ Frosty Fruit Shake (page 119)
❏ Frosty Frappuccino (page 112)
❏ Celery Bisque (page 146)
❏ Golden French Onion Soup (page 148)
❏ Sweet Cherry Soup (page 160)
❏ Frozen Fruit Whip (page 259)
❏ Peanut Butter Mousse (page 263)

HEARTBURN

When you swallow, a circular band of muscle around the bottom of your esophagus relaxes to allow food and liquid to flow into your stomach. This band of muscle, called the *lower esophageal sphincter,* closes after the "bolus" of food passes into the stomach. But if this valve relaxes abnormally or becomes weak, stomach acid can flow back into the esophagus, causing heartburn—a painful feeling in the chest, under the breastbone, sometimes accompanied by a sour or acid taste in the back of the throat and mouth. Most people have an occasional bout of heartburn, usually after a large meal. Some, however, suffer from heartburn more often, or even on a daily basis.

Frequent heartburn is referred to as *GERD,* or *gastroesophageal reflux disease*. (The term *reflux* refers to the backing up of stomach contents into the esophagus.) Typically, GERD also involves other symptoms, such as chest pain, coughing, difficulty swallowing, and sore throat. If left untreated, GERD can damage your esophagus and lead to esophageal ulcers, a stricture (abnormal narrowing) in the lower esophagus, or even breathing problems.

A number of conditions and medications can lead to GERD. Obesity and pregnancy, both of which put extra pressure on the stomach; hiatal hernia, in which the lower esophagus is pulled up through the diaphragm; diabetes, which can slow the emptying of the stomach; gastric outlet obstruction; connective tissue disorders that cause muscular tissue to thicken; and Zollinger-Ellison syndrome can all cause or worsen heartburn. Many medications—both prescription and over-the-counter—can also result in heartburn, including antianxiety medications, antibiotics, heart medications, potassium, steroids, antihistamines, iron supplements, nonsteroidal anti-inflammatory drugs (NSAIDS), and high doses of vitamin C. In addition, a number of foods, from caffeine-containing beverages to chocolate, fried and fatty foods, tomatoes, citrus fruits, peppermint tea, and alcohol, can aggravate GERD.

If you have frequent heartburn, talk to your doctor about possible therapy. A number of prescription and nonprescription drugs are now available for the prevention and treatment of this condition. Here are some simple diet and lifestyle changes that can further help you manage this problem:

❏ Avoid alcohol, caffeine, regular or decaf coffee, chocolate, peppermint, and fatty foods, all of which can result in or worsen heartburn. Be aware that even if you are trying to gain weight, you may have to avoid greasy foods, fried foods, "fast foods," and even "healthy fats" such as olive oil.

❏ If your heartburn has already resulted in damage to your lower esophagus, avoid foods that can irritate it or cause pain, such as hot and spicy foods, partic-ularly hot peppers. Acidic foods, such as citrus fruits, tomato sauce, and dishes containing vinegar, may also cause pain. You may need a vitamin C supplement when avoiding these foods. (Be sure to take the supplement with meals, and avoid high doses of vitamin C if you find them irritating.)

❏ To reduce the fat in your diet, use low-fat substitutes whenever possible. For instance, make smoothies and puddings with nonfat or low-fat milk; use low-fat sour cream and cheese; and replace fatty meats with leaner products, such as white meat chicken, lean fish, and low-fat cold cuts.

❏ Eat smaller, more frequent meals to avoid overfilling your stomach.

❏ Avoid eating close to bedtime or just before strenuous activity. A full stomach puts extra pressure on the esophageal sphincter, which increases the chance of reflux. If possible, wait three hours after eating before going to bed or exercising.

❏ Sit upright when you eat, and remain upright for thirty minutes after eating. This will help prevent the contents of your stomach from flowing backwards into your esophagus.

❏ Don't drink a lot of fluids with meals, as this can overfill your stomach. Instead, drink plenty of fluids *between* meals.

❏ If you are taking both acid-reducing medication and calcium supplements, choose calcium citrate, which is absorbed better than calcium carbonate (oyster shell calcium)—particularly if the stomach is less acidic.

❏ Elevate the head of your bed so that gravity can help you avoid reflux. Place wooden blocks, cement blocks, or commercial bed props under the legs to raise the head of the bed between six and nine inches. If this can't be done, insert a foam pillow wedge under your mattress to elevate your body from the waist up. Do *not* elevate your head only.

RECOMMENDED RECIPES TO COPE WITH HEARTBURN

❏ Triple Berry Slush (page 118)

❏ Golden French Onion Soup (page 148)

❏ Pancake Roll-Ups (page 132)

❏ Steamed Pumpkin Bread (page 190)

❏ Dilled Chicken Aspic (page 208)

❏ Winter Squash Timbales (page 241)

❏ Saucy Blackberry Crepes (page 270)

CONSTIPATION

Constipation is a condition in which stool becomes hard and dry, and is passed infrequently and with difficulty. It is a very common disorder in the United States, particularly among older adults.

Constipation can be caused by a number of different factors, with one of the most common being a poor diet. Both fiber and fluids are key to healthy bowel function, and these two elements are lacking in many diets.

Dietary fiber can be found in two forms. *Soluble fiber,* also called *viscous fiber,* is found in oats, some fruits and vegetables, and legumes (dried beans). This fiber forms a gel in the digestive tract, keeping the contents soft as long as adequate water is available. *Insoluble fiber,* found in whole grains, bran products, and some fruits and vegetables, adds bulk to stools and helps speed their movement through the bowels.

Even if you eat enough fiber, fluids are necessary to prevent or resolve constipation. Adequate fluids are needed to keep the contents of your bowels soft so that they can be easily moved out of your body. In the absence of sufficient liquids, fiber can actually make stools too hard to move. If severe, this can result in a blockage that requires medical attention.

A number of medications can also cause constipation. Potentially problematic drugs include antacids, anticonvulsants, antidepressants, antispasmodics, codeine-containing painkillers, and iron supplements. Some chemotherapy drugs can also result in constipation, and both cancer and cancer treatment can lead to this disorder by contributing to poor food and fluid intake, decreased activity, and general weakness.

One of the most common causes of constipation is irritable bowel syndrome, or IBS. Other conditions that can lead to this problem include neurological disorders such as Parkinson's and stroke, metabolic disorders such as diabetes, and systemic disorders such as lupus.

If constipation is a chronic problem for you, your doctor may suggest the use of laxatives or stool softeners. However, even if you have a condition that requires a soft or puréed diet, there is much you can do to restore good bowel function.

❏ Eat high-fiber foods like fruits and vegetables, puréeing them if necessary.

❏ Eat cooked whole grains and bran cereals. If a smoother texture is needed, use a food processor to grind the dry cereal to a grits- or cornmeal-like texture before cooking. If you need a perfectly smooth texture, purée the cereal after cooking.

❏ Add bran to puddings, breads, stuffing, and hot cereals. It can even be added to cookies and cakes, which you can eat if softened with milk or sauce. If a smoother texture is needed, grind the bran finely before adding it to the food.

❏ Eat more lentils; split peas; or navy, pinto, or kidney beans. If you are following a smooth diet, purée the legumes with a little liquid. (The liquid in canned beans is usually sufficient.) Add the puréed mixture to soups or casseroles, or enjoy as a side dish. Refried beans are another good source of fiber.

❑ Drink prune juice if you like it, or try orange juice with pulp, tomato juice, or V8 vegetable juice.

❑ Keep well hydrated by drinking eight to ten cups of water a day. Other good choices are herbal teas, clear soups, and the juices mentioned above.

❑ Avoid alcohol and caffeine-containing beverages such as coffee, tea, and colas. These liquids are diuretics and can actually contribute to dehydration.

❑ Increase physical activity as your condition permits. Exercise helps regulate bowel activity.

RECOMMENDED HIGH-FIBER RECIPES TO COPE WITH CONSTIPATION

❑ Triple Berry Slush (page 118)

❑ Hot Barley Cereal (page 138)

❑ Steamed Fig Bread (page 188)

❑ Savory Lentil Soup (page 151)

❑ Layered Puréed Black Bean Enchiladas (page 229)

❑ Lima Beans with Sage and Onions (page 237)

❑ Saucy Blackberry Crepes (page 270)

DIARRHEA

Normally, the food you eat stays in liquid form during most of the digestive process. Then, when the food residue passes through the colon, most of the fluids are absorbed, leaving a relatively firm stool. But if the food and fluids you consume pass too quickly through the colon, the fluids aren't sufficiently absorbed, and the result is diarrhea—frequent loose or watery stools accompanied by pain, cramping, and gas.

Diarrhea can be caused by infections, contaminated foods, and certain medications. Gastrointestinal problems such as Crohn's disease or colitis, irritable bowel syndrome, and lactose intolerance can also cause diarrhea. Some people get diarrhea as the result of fat malabsorption—a condition referred to as *steatorrhea*.

If diarrhea is severe or lasts more than a few days, you could become dangerously dehydrated, so it is important to seek medical attention. If diarrhea is a frequent problem for you, there are steps you can take to help restore normal bowel function:

❑ Initially stick to a clear liquid diet, including water, clear sodas, juices with no added sugar, broths, and flavored gelatin. Avoid very sweet drinks and sports drinks because sugar can actually worsen diarrhea. (See Chapter 1, page 16 for more information on clear liquids.)

❑ Eat small, frequent meals throughout the day instead of a few larger meals.

❑ Do not eat foods at extreme temperatures—very hot or very cold. Extreme temperatures can speed the digestive process and worsen diarrhea.

❑ Avoid candies, gums, and other foods containing sorbitol, a sugar substitute that can act as a laxative.

❑ As your diarrhea improves and you are ready to begin eating semisolid foods again, gradually add low-fiber (low-residue) foods such as soda crackers, white toast, eggs, white rice, Cream of Wheat cereal, and chicken soup until your stools return to normal. Keep in mind that foods like crackers and toast should be well moistened, and rice should be cooked until very soft or eaten in the form of Cream of Rice cereal. If you continue to feel better, tender meats, puréed if necessary, can be added as well. You could also try the BRATT diet—bananas, rice, applesauce, tea, and toast.

❑ Be aware that soluble fiber—the kind found in oats, legumes, and fruit—not only helps prevent constipation but can also relieve diarrhea. Try adding small amounts of foods high in soluble fiber to your diet. (Oatmeal, bananas, and applesauce are good choices.) Another option is to add fiber supplements such as psyllium or guar gum to your beverages.

❏ Avoid dairy products and fatty foods for a while. Even if you normally tolerate these foods, they can worsen bouts of diarrhea.

❏ If your diarrhea is caused by lactose intolerance, try lactose-free milk such as Lactaid, buttermilk, soymilk, rice milk, or almond milk. Also try yogurt with live cultures, as this is often digestible even for lactose-intolerant individuals.

❏ If you can easily digest them, include in your diet yogurt, kefir, and yogurt drinks that contain "active cultures." These foods offer beneficial bacteria that can help prevent or relieve diarrhea, especially when you are using antibiotics, which can kill the good bacteria in your intestines. Probiotics—supplements containing good bacteria—can be found in both health food stores and pharmacies.

❏ Avoid caffeine, alcohol, and highly seasoned foods, all of which can aggravate a case of diarrhea.

RECOMMENDED RECIPES TO COPE WITH DIARRHEA

❏ Spinach, Celery, and Apple Cocktail (page 111)

❏ Buttermilk Drop Biscuits (page 187)

❏ Soft Scrambled Eggs (page 128)

❏ Ham and Potato Puffs (use low-fat cheese) (page 218)

❏ Cauliflower Purée (use soy or lactose-free milk) (page 236)

❏ Cinnamon Applesauce (page 261)

PHLEGM

Excessive production of *phlegm,* a thick mucus, is a common side effect of radiation treatments to the throat, and can also be a complication of disorders such as COPD (chronic obstructive pulmonary disease); CHF (congestive heart failure); and ALS, or Lou Gehrig's disease. By sticking to the walls of the throat and causing a constant drip, phlegm can trigger a chronic cough, choking, nausea, and a persistent bad taste. All of these symptoms can make it difficult to get adequate nutrition.

If phlegm production is causing you discomfort, speak to your doctor, who may be able to prescribe a medication that can alleviate the problem. Also try the following tips, which can help dissolve the phlegm and minimize the effect that it has on your diet and other aspects of your life.

❏ Drink lots of fluids—especially water—to thin the phlegm so that it becomes less sticky. Many people find noncaffeinated hot liquids such as herbal teas and soups especially helpful.

❏ Try eating pear sauce, which has been reported to help relieve the phlegm. (See the recipe found on page 262.)

❏ Try avoiding dairy products such as milk, cheese, ice cream, sour cream, and yogurt, which may make the phlegm thicker.

❏ As much as possible, remain in an upright position, as this will allow the phlegm to drain freely and minimize choking and congestion. When in bed, raise the head of the bed, if possible, to lift the upper portion of your body. If this is not an option, use cushions to remain upright even when sleeping. A "husband" pillow—which has a back and arms, much like the top of an armchair—can provide comfortable support in bed.

RECOMMENDED RECIPES TO COPE WITH EXCESSIVE PHLEGM

❑ Pear Sauce (page 262)

❑ Melon Magic Smoothie (page 110)

❑ Triple Berry Slush (page 118)

❑ Carrot-Apple Slush (page 111)

❑ Savory Lentil Soup (omit the Parmesan) (page 151)

❑ Winter Squash Soup (page 157)

CONCLUSION

This chapter has explained how you can adjust your diet—and, in some cases, your environment—so that you are able to obtain the nutrition you need even when faced with problems such as loss of appetite, altered taste, and digestive difficulties. As you modify your menu, remember to consult with your physician, dietitian, or speech therapist as needed to make sure that you are properly integrating the treatments for your different medical problems. A coordinated approach is essential so that the treatment for one problem improves your well-being without aggravating other health conditions.

3. STOCKING YOUR PANTRY

The earlier chapters of this book explained some of the more common conditions that can make an easy-to-chew, soft, or smooth/puréed diet necessary. They also showed you how to adjust your diet to maximize comfort and nutrition in the presence of problems such as nausea and altered taste. This chapter will bring you one step closer to a more satisfying, easy-to-chew-and-swallow diet by guiding you as you stock your pantry, refrigerator, and freezer. We think you'll find that once you have the ingredients you need on hand—including convenience products that require little or no cooking—you'll be able to eat well without long hours of preparation. A wise choice of pantry items will also enable you to more easily meet any special needs you have for higher-calorie, lower-calorie, higher-fiber, lower-sodium, or reduced-fat foods.

DAIRY PRODUCTS

The dairy case of your supermarket is packed with products that are naturals for a soft and smooth diet. Many of these items—yogurt and cream cheese, for instance—are already creamy, while products such as milk can help you turn casseroles and other foods into easy-to-swallow dishes. Moreover, most dairy products provide calcium, protein, minerals such as potassium, and vitamins such as A and D. These nutrients can help you heal faster and maintain your health.

It is worth noting that dairy products come in different varieties to suit a range of dietary needs. Milk, for instance, is available in full-fat, reduced-fat, fat-free, and lactose-free versions. You can even find milk made from rice, almonds, or soy. So whatever your culinary preferences or dietary requirements, you're sure to find some healthful and delicious products in the dairy case.

Cheese

An excellent source of calcium and protein, cheese can take a dish from ordinary to extraordinary. Be aware, though, that some cheeses are more suitable than others for a soft and smooth diet. Firm products like Cheddar and Swiss must be shredded and incorporated into soft spreads, soups, or sauces if you are following a puréed diet. Cheeses that are more easily made part of an easy-to-swallow diet include blue cheese, feta, ricotta, cottage cheese, cream cheese, and soft-curd farmer's cheese.

If you are following a heart-healthy lifestyle, you'll want to take advantage of the many available lower-fat cheeses, as well as nondairy alternatives made from soymilk and nut milks. Lower-fat cheeses, of course, offer less fat, less cholesterol, and less calories than their full-fat counterparts. Vegan cheeses made from nonanimal milks are usually lower in saturated fat than dairy cheeses, but may provide less protein and calcium, as well. (Always check the label.) Be aware, though, that hard dairy cheeses which are entirely fat-free can be difficult to chew, and may become tough and rubbery when cooked. A better choice would be a reduced-fat cheese, although you will have to experiment to find products that melt well in smooth sauces. Vegan cheese may also not melt well, so you'll want to look for brands that specifically advertise good melting properties.

Cream cheese is particularly helpful for people on an easy-to-swallow diet. However, it is much lower in protein and calcium than cheeses such as Cheddar and Swiss. If you have chewing or swallowing difficulties, you may not be able to spread cream cheese on crackers or a bagel, but you can thin it a little with water, milk, or juice and spread the resulting slurry on a slice of crustless bread to moisten and flavor it. (See Chapter 5 for details on making and using slurries.) You can also blend this versatile cheese into sauces, smoothies, and other dishes for a richer, smoother consistency.

Regular calorie-packed cream cheese is great if you're trying to gain weight or avoid weight loss, but the saturated fat that is the source of all those calories should be avoided by anyone who's trying to shed pounds or lower cholesterol. If you are following a heart-healthy diet, look for reduced-fat cream cheese.

Kefir and Drinkable Yogurt

Cultured milk products such as kefir and drinkable yogurt are convenient smoothie-type beverages with a nectar-like consistency. Like regular yogurt, they are good sources of protein, calcium, and potassium. Kefir and drinkable yogurt are available in several varieties—flavored, with added fruit, low-fat, low-

sugar, and organic. Look for these products in supermarkets and health food stores.

Milk and Milk Alternatives

A variety of milk products and milk alternatives are perfect for soft and smooth diets, making them essential ingredients in many of the recipes in this book. Milk, is in fact, a great snack in and of itself, as it is rich in protein, calcium, and potassium, and is often supplemented with vitamins A and D, as well. People who cannot tolerate milk sugar (lactose) can choose lactose-free milk products such as Lactaid, or use nondairy milks made of soy, rice, or almonds.

Almond Milk. Made from ground almonds blended with water and vegetable thickeners, almond milk has a sweet nutty flavor that is delicious in smoothies, desserts, and baked goods, and also nice on cereal. This product is sold in natural food stores and supermarkets, and may be found in shelf-stable containers and the dairy case. To make almond milk at home, soak one cup of almonds in three cups of water overnight, or from eight to twelve hours, placing the mixture in the refrigerator. Then transfer the nuts and their soaking liquid to a blender and process for a minute or two, or until the almonds are completely pulverized and the liquid is milky. Add a couple of tablespoons of honey and/or a few drops of vanilla extract if desired. Strain the mixture, discarding the solids, and store in the refrigerator for three to five days.

Nutritionally, almond milk is cholesterol-free, lactose-free, and low in saturated fat. However, it is lower in protein than cow's milk, and may also be lower in calcium and vitamin D. Check the label, though, as some brands are fortified with calcium, vitamin D, and other nutrients.

Buttermilk. Buttermilk is a naturally thick beverage that may be included when "nectar-thick" liquids are prescribed. Ask your speech therapist if this is an appropriate choice for you, and be sure to find a brand that is adequately thick. In some cases, you may have to add a commercial thickener to reach the desired consistency. (See Chapter 6 for information on thickening liquids.)

Evaporated Milk. Evaporated milk is an excellent substitute for cream in sauces, gravies, quiches, puddings, and many other dishes. Since it is concentrated, it has twice the protein and nutritional value of regular milk. To limit fat and calories, choose nonfat or low-fat evaporated milk.

Milk. A glass of milk is a great way to add important nutrients to your diet as you meet your fluid needs. Milk also makes a good creamy base for smoothies, sauces, and puddings. If you are following a heart-healthy diet and want to reduce calories and saturated fat, use reduced-fat (2-percent) milk, low-fat (1-percent) milk, or nonfat (skim) milk. If necessary, add a commercial thickener to make the milk easy to drink. (See Chapter 6 for details.)

Nonfat Dry Milk Powder. When preparing smoothies, quiches, cream soups, sauces, custards, and puddings, try adding a tablespoon or two of nonfat dry milk powder for each cup of milk being used. You will boost calcium, protein, potassium, and vitamin D while enriching flavor and texture.

Rice Milk. Rice milk is typically made from brown rice, brown rice syrup, water, and vegetable thickeners. With a light, slightly sweet taste, this product is good in smoothies, desserts, and baked goods, as well as on cereal. Like almond milk, rice milk is sold in both shelf-stable and refrigerated containers in natural food stores and supermarkets.

In general, rice milk is cholesterol-free, lactose-free, and low in saturated fat. However, it is substantially higher in carbohydrates and lower in protein than cow's milk. Check the label to learn about calcium, vitamin D, and other nutrients, as many brands are fortified with amounts similar to those found in cow's milk.

Soymilk. Soymilk is an excellent beverage that can be substituted for cow's milk in most recipes. When added to breads and baked goods, this product will make little if any difference in flavor. The taste difference will be more noticeable in smoothies, sauces, and cream soups. Do not use soymilk to prepare instant puddings, as the pudding will not set firmly.

Nutritionally speaking, soymilk is an excellent source of high-quality protein. It is low in saturated fat and is cholesterol- and lactose-free. Many brands are fortified to provide amounts of calcium and vitamin D similar to those present in cow's milk, but check the label to be sure.

Ready-Made Pudding

Most supermarket dairy cases offer snack-sized puddings that make good light meals for anyone on a puréed diet. Vanilla, chocolate, and other flavors of creamy-style puddings have an excellent consistency for most people on a soft and smooth diet. But rice, bread, and tapioca varieties, which have mixed textures, may be a problem for some people. Ask your speech therapist if you can tolerate these as is, or if they have to be be puréed. In addition to whole-milk sugar-sweetened puddings, you'll find low-fat and low-sugar versions in most supermarkets, and soymilk-based versions in most health food stores.

Sour Cream

Sour cream is a must-have ingredient for spreads, dressings, sauces, and many other dishes. To trim fat and calories, choose nonfat or light versions. Flavor and texture can vary greatly among brands, so shop around to find one to your liking. Also look for flavored sour cream dips, which can be thinned with a little milk and used to moisten soft breads.

Yogurt

Like milk, yogurt is an excellent source of protein, calcium, and potassium. Yogurt is a great snack on its own, and is also delicious in smoothies, sauces, desserts, and other dishes. Unflavored, it is a good substitute for sour cream.

Because yogurt is so versatile and popular, you will find a wide range of products in your local stores. Low-fat and no-added-sugar versions are widely available. For a change of pace, try plain Greek yogurt, which is particularly creamy, or a pourable Mexican yogurt. Yogurt has the added advantage of being low in lactose, so in many cases it can be enjoyed by people with lactose intolerance—especially if the label states that "live active cultures" have been included. These cultures are a plus for everyone, in fact, as they help promote the growth of beneficial bacteria in the gut.

For many people on soft and smooth diets, any type of yogurt is fine whether eaten straight from the container or included in a recipe. If you are on a puréed diet, though, you will need to avoid yogurts that contain chunky fruits, or you will have to purée the product before eating it.

EGGS AND EGG SUBSTITUTES

From omelets and quiches to casseroles and custards, eggs are an essential ingredient in many soft and smooth recipes. They also make an excellent meat substitute, with each egg supplying about 6 grams of protein. However, one large egg uses up about two-thirds of the recommended 300-milligram daily cholesterol budget. This may not seem like much until you consider that a three-egg omelet contains two days' worth of cholesterol!

Fortunately, it's a simple matter to make dishes with more whites (which are cholesterol-free) and fewer yolks. It's also a good practice to purchase eggs that are higher in heart-healthy omega-3 fats. Made by feeding hens a diet enriched with flaxseed or other omega-3-rich foods, these products are a smart choice when you're using whole eggs or egg yolks in a recipe. Although whole eggs are high in cholesterol, most experts agree that a healthy diet can include up to seven eggs per week. Your physician or dietitian can tell you if this guideline is appropriate for your dietary needs.

Another good option is egg substitutes. Products like Egg Beaters are made from fat- and cholesterol-free egg whites, and colored with plant-based substances so that they look like beaten whole eggs. Sold in small cartons, egg substitutes are easy to use and can replace whole eggs in quiches, custards, omelets, and many other dishes. Most brands are pasteurized so that they are safe to use in eggnog and other dishes that call for uncooked eggs. (Check the labels to be sure.) In fact, because raw eggs carry the risk of salmonella poisoning, pasteurized egg substitutes are a good choice for anyone who is very young, elderly, or immune-compromised. Alternatively, pasteurized whole eggs are available in some markets. You will find egg substitutes in both the refrigerated foods section and the freezer case of your grocery store. As a rule, a quarter cup of the substitute equals one large egg.

GRAINS AND GRAIN PRODUCTS

How can you instantly boost the nutrients in your diet? Replace refined grain products like white rice and white bread with whole grains and whole grain products. While refined grains have been stripped of disease-fighting nutrients, whole grains are loaded with fiber, B-vitamins, minerals, antioxidants, and phytonutrients. For this reason, they can actually reduce your risk of heart disease, diabetes, and many other health problems. Here are some ways to get healthful grains into your soft and smooth diet.

Bread. When told that they must follow a soft or smooth diet, many people fear that they will have to give up bread. The fact is, though, that by choosing your bread carefully and softening it as described in Chapter 5, you can make bread part of your daily menu.

For the greatest health benefits, choose breads made with 100-percent whole grain flours. Whole wheat or another whole grain should be the first ingredient listed on the package. Make sure that the bread is smooth in texture and does not contain pieces of nuts, seeds, fruits, or grains. Then soften your bread with the desired spread or slurry before eating.

Pasta. A wide range of whole grain pasta is now available. If you are not on a puréed diet, you may be able to tolerate soft-cooked (not al dente) whole wheat pasta tossed with plenty of sauce. Angel hair pasta is the thinnest cut and can be made the most tender, but you may also be able to enjoy tender-cooked macaroni, orzo, and other pasta shapes. If you are on a puréed diet, your pasta will have to be cooked until soft, blended in a food processor along with a little cooking liquid, and then served with the puréed sauce of your choice. If you can tolerate a little texture, you can use a blender or food processor to grind dry pasta to a grits-like texture, and then cook it as you would hot cereal. (See Chapter 5 for more details on puréeing pasta.) You can also buy instant puréed pasta, which comes as a powder that you cook with water. (See page 286 of the "Products" table.)

Whole Grains and Whole Grain Cereals. People on soft and smooth diets cannot eat grains in their whole kernel form. However, dry uncooked whole grains such as barley, brown rice, and wheat can be ground in a blender until they reach a texture similar to grits or cornmeal, and then cooked into a hot cereal. For many people, these cereals are a pleasing way to get great nutrition. If you are on a low-fiber or low-residue diet, though, you will want to limit your whole grain consumption.

Commercial whole grain cereals can also be part of a soft or smooth diet. Oats, oat bran, and Wheatena (a toasted-wheat cereal) are all excellent choices. If you're following a low-residue (low-fiber) diet, select farina (a finely milled wheat), regular Cream of Wheat, or Cream of Rice cereal instead. Cold cereals can also be included in your diet. Just choose one that does not contain dried fruits, seeds, or nuts, and that will become soft in milk. If you require a *very* smooth diet, you may have to swirl the cereal and milk in a blender to achieve the proper consistency.

Whole Wheat Flour. Many people on an easy-to-chew-and-swallow diet can enjoy foods like pancakes, crepes, and moist cakes and breads as long as they are softened adequately with a sauce or syrup. A simple way to boost the fiber and nutritional content of these foods is to substitute whole wheat flour for part or all of the white flour being used. We recommend *whole wheat pastry flour*—also called *whole grain pastry flour*—for the recipes in this book. Whole wheat pastry flour is lower in gluten than regular whole wheat flour, and therefore results in a softer, more tender texture. It also has a lighter, sweeter flavor than regular whole wheat flour. Look for whole wheat pastry flour in natural food stores and many grocery stores, where it is often found in the health food aisle. Like all wheat products, whole wheat pastry flour is not appropriate for anyone on a gluten-free diet.

FATS AND OILS

If you need to gain weight, fats and oils can help you add extra calories to your diet. Just one tablespoon of oil provides 120 calories, and an equal amount of full-fat margarine, butter, or mayonnaise offers about 100 calories. Fats and oils can also make foods smoother and easier to swallow, which is a big bonus when you're following a soft or smooth diet.

Of course, if excess weight is a problem, you should use fats only in moderation. And whether you want to shed pounds or put them on, you should always opt for the most healthful fats and oils that will work in your recipe.

Butter. Negative publicity about the harmful effects of trans fats in margarine has caused many people to switch to butter in cooking and baking, and as a spread. This is not ideal, however, since butter is high in saturated fat, which can raise blood cholesterol levels. The latest consensus among nutrition experts is that butter is preferable to hard, trans-fat-laden margarines, but that soft trans-free margarines are an even better choice. Spreads made by blending butter with canola oil are another option for people who want the flavor of butter, with less saturated fat. Some of these spreads also contain added plant sterols or stanols—natural substances that help to lower the levels of LDL (bad) cholesterol.

If you love the taste of butter, unaltered by the addition of oil, consider using either light butter, which is bulked up with water, or whipped butter, which is bulked up with air. Either product has only about half the calories of regular butter.

Canola Oil. Low in saturated fat and rich in healthful monounsaturated fat and omega-3 fatty acids, canola oil is a good choice for both cooking and baking. Canola oil also has a very mild, bland taste, making it an excellent all-purpose oil when you want no interfering flavors.

Flaxseed Oil. Flax oil is the richest plant source of omega-3 fatty acids available. For a nutritional boost, add a few teaspoons of this product to smoothies and other cold dishes. Just remember that flaxseed oil should always be used cold, never heated.

Margarine. Historically, margarine has been a major source of harmful trans fats—a substance that has been linked to heart disease and diabetes. This is quickly changing, though, as manufacturers respond to the public's health concerns with a selection of "trans-free" brands. Look for soft trans-free margarines that list liquid canola or soybean oil as the first ingredient. These products will boost your intake of beneficial essential fats as they trim trans fats from your diet. A margarine made with olive oil is another good option. You can also try liquid margarine. Generally low in trans fats, this product has the added advantage of being pourable over a wide range of temperatures, enabling you to drizzle it over breads as a means of softening them and infusing them with a buttery taste.

If you are watching your weight, be aware that you can trim calories by switching to a reduced-fat margarine, which has about half the calories of its full-fat counterpart. Because light margarine is part water, it is especially useful for softening breads. Just spread it over a warm slice of your favorite bread, and as it melts, it will soften and moisten the product, making it easy to swallow.

Nonstick Cooking Spray. Most nonstick cooking sprays are primarily liquid vegetable oil—usually canola, olive, or soybean oil—mixed with a small amount of lecithin, a component of soybeans that helps prevent sticking. Like all oils, cooking sprays have 120 calories per tablespoon. The advantage to using them is that the amount expelled during a one-second spray is so small that it adds an insignificant quantity of fat and calories to your dish.

Olive Oil. Olive oil is rich in monounsaturated fat and contains phytonutrients that may help reduce blood cholesterol and protect against cancer. Unlike most vegetable oils, which are very bland in taste, olive oil adds its own delicious flavor to foods. Extra virgin olive oil is the least processed and most flavorful form of this product, so if you love the taste of olive oil, this is the type you'll want to buy. If you don't care for olive oil's distinctive flavor, look for a product that's labeled "light." Just be aware that this variety is light in flavor, not calories, and that some of the oil's beneficial phytonutrients have been removed to tone down its taste.

Sesame Oil. This aromatic oil adds Far Eastern flair to stir-fried dishes, tofu, and sauces. Like olive oil, sesame oil is rich in heart-healthy monounsaturated oils, Vitamin E, and beneficial phytochemicals. Just remember that this product is a flavoring and cannot be used as a cooking oil.

Soybean Oil. Most cooking oils that are simply labeled "vegetable oil" are derived from soybeans. Soybean oil is also used as an ingredient in many brands of margarine, mayonnaise, and salad dressing. This oil is a good source of the essential omega-6 fat *linoleic acid*. It also supplies a fair amount of the omega-3 fat *linolenic acid,* although not as much as you'll find in canola oil. Like canola oil, soybean oil has a bland taste that works well when you want the flavor of the food to shine through.

Walnut Oil. Walnut oil—and other nut oils, as well—makes a delicious addition to smoothies, desserts, fruit and vegetable purées, and other dishes that would benefit from a nutty flavor and a boost in calories. Walnut oil is also a good source of healthy omega-3 fats.

SWEETENERS AND SYRUPS

While sugar is not the most nutritious food in the pantry, when used in moderation, it adds wonderful sweetness to smoothies, baked goods, and other treats. If you are trying to gain weight or just keep it on, sugar is also a good source of calories, as are syrupy sweeteners like maple syrup and honey. Syrups have the added advantage of being able to soften and moisten breads, pancakes, and other foods

so that they become not only more flavorful, but also easy to chew and swallow—a big plus for people on easy-to-chew, soft, or smooth diets.

Granulated Sugar. Many kinds of sugar are available. The most common type, of course, is white granulated sugar (sucrose), which is refined from sugar cane. To make white sugar, the sugar cane juices are extracted and boiled into dark, molasses-rich syrup. The syrup is then spun down to remove most of the molasses, and the resulting light brown crystals are rinsed, leaving refined white sugar crystals. Since all of the nutrients from the sugar cane juice are retained in the molasses, white sugar has no nutritional value other than calories.

A variety of less-refined forms of granulated sugar—often sold as evaporated cane juice, turbinado sugar, Demerara sugar, and natural cane sugar—are available in grocery stores and natural food stores. These amber- to brownish-colored sugars have a delicious light molasses flavor and contain some of the nutrients naturally present in molasses, including B-vitamins, calcium, copper, iron, magnesium, manganese, potassium, selenium, chromium, and phytonutrients. In general, the darker the sugar, the more nutrients should be present. Keep in mind that coarse sugars like Demerara and turbinado will not dissolve as easily as finely granulated sugars.

Honey. This syrupy sweetener adds moistness and distinctive flavor to many kinds of foods. Honey has been found to contain an array of nutrients, including small amounts of B-vitamins, calcium, copper, iron, magnesium, manganese, phosphorus, potassium, and zinc. This sweetener also contains a variety of antioxidants; the amount and type depend largely on the nectar source of the honey. In general, darker honeys, such as buckwheat, are higher in antioxidants than light-colored honeys.

Honey is a great addition to the easy-to-chew-and-swallow diet. Drizzle it over pancakes, French toast, or cereal, or thin it with a little water and use the mixture to soften bread when making puréed peanut butter-and-banana sandwiches.

Maple Syrup. The boiled-down sap of sugar maple trees, maple syrup adds delicious flavor to all baked goods, and even provides some potassium and other nutrients. Use it as you would honey to top breakfast foods and moisten breads.

Using Sugar Substitutes

If you are trying to trim calories and/or carbohydrates from your meals, sugar substitutes are a handy ingredient that can provide the sweetness of sugar without its well-known disadvantages. In fact, many of the smoothie and dessert recipes in this book include the option of using sugar substitutes in place of sugar.

As anyone who does grocery shopping knows, there are a number of sugar substitutes now available. Are some artificial sweeteners better suited for certain purposes than others? How much sugar substitute do you need to match a given amount of sugar? Knowing the answers to these questions is key to your success as you trim the sugar from your favorite recipes.

When replacing sugar with sugar substitutes, keep in mind that sugar plays some key roles in the chemistry of cooking. For instance, sugar adds volume and tenderness, helps retain moisture, and promotes browning. These properties are especially important in baked goods like cakes, muffins, quick breads, and cookies, which can develop a rubbery texture and pale color if too much sugar is omitted from the recipe.

How much sugar can you trim from recipes and still expect a good result? In general, you can replace up to half of the sugar in baked goods with a sugar substitute. On the other hand, dishes like smoothies, puddings, pie fillings, and dessert sauces may turn out quite well even if you replace all of the sugar. Be aware that some sugar substitutes can lose their sweetness if exposed to heat, and may not work in cooking and baking. Refer to Table 3.1 to learn which ones can be used in cooked dishes.

What about calories? Two teaspoons of sugar contain 32 calories and 8 grams of carbohydrate. If you use a lot of sugar, the calories and carbs can add up quickly. Most sugar substitutes claim to have "zero calories per serving." Keep in mind that many of these products contain bulking agents (such as dextrose or maltodextrin), which can add 2 to 4 calories per packet. However, foods that contain less than 5 calories per serving can legally list the calories as zero.

As for amounts to use, a single-serve packet of sugar substitute is typically equivalent to two teaspoons of sugar. However, some sugar substitutes are also available in a granular form (packaged in large bags or containers) that measures cup-for-cup like sugar. The following table provides general guidelines for swapping sugar substitutes for sugar. This information is also listed on product labels, so always double-check to make sure you are using the correct amount of the brand you have selected.

Sugar Substitutes. While most people love the sweet taste of sugar, certain conditions—from diabetes to the simple need to lose weight—make low-calorie, low-carbohydrate sugar substitutes a useful ingredient. If you have to limit your carbs and calories, you may already be acquainted with at least one brand of sugar substitute. If not, you'll find a range of artificial sweeteners on the shelves of your local supermarket. (For specific information on using these sweeteners to replace sugar in recipes, see the inset "Using Sugar Substitutes," which begins on page 44.)

MEAT, POULTRY, AND SEAFOOD

When buying beef and pork, choose lean cuts to reduce the saturated fat in your diet, and cut any visible fat off the meats when you get them home. When buying poultry, you can minimize saturated fat by removing the skin and any visible fat before cooking. You can also speed preparation by choosing skinless, boneless cuts of poultry. This will not only make the finished dish more healthful, but will also make the job of chopping, grinding, or puréeing the food easier once it has been cooked.

TABLE 3.1   SUGAR SUBSTITUTE EQUIVALENCY CHART

Sugar Substitute	Approximate Amount Needed to Replace 1 Tablespoon of Sugar	Approximate Amount Needed to Replace 1 Cup of Sugar	Comments
Equal (Aspartame)	• 1$\frac{1}{2}$ packets • 1 tablespoon granulated	• 24 packets • 1 cup granulated	Can be used in cold dishes. Prolonged heating can cause a decrease in sweetness under certain circumstances (related to combined effects of temperature, pH, and time). When cooking or baking, the manufacturer recommends using recipes specifically designed for Equal.
Splenda (Sucralose)	• 1$\frac{1}{2}$ packets • 1 tablespoon granulated	• 24 packets • 1 cup granulated	Can be used in cold dishes, cooked dishes, and baking without losing sweetness.
Sweet 'N Low (Saccharin)	• 1$\frac{1}{2}$ packets • $\frac{1}{2}$ teaspoon granulated • $\frac{1}{3}$ teaspoon liquid	• 24 packets • 8 teaspoons granulated • 2 tablespoons liquid	Can be used in cold dishes, cooked dishes, and baking without losing sweetness.
Sweet One (Acesulfame-K)	• 1$\frac{1}{2}$ packets	• 24 packets	Can be used in cold dishes, cooked dishes, and baking without losing sweetness.
Truvia (Stevia)	• 1$\frac{1}{2}$ packets • 1$\frac{1}{8}$ teaspoons granulated	• 24 packets • $\frac{1}{3}$ cup plus 1 tablespoon	Can be used in cold dishes, cooked dishes, and baking without losing sweetness.

Some supermarket and deli meat sections have ready-made pulled pork, chopped barbecued beef, or cooked and seasoned ground taco meat. These prepared dishes are often already suitable for a soft diet. Also look for prepared entrées like roast beef or turkey with gravy, as they can be chopped, ground, or puréed for a quick main dish. Just be sure to check the label for fat and sodium content, as many ready-to-eat foods are high in both.

Because many fish are delicate in texture, they are perfect for soft diets, especially when served with sauce. Look for thin fish fillets, which cook quickly, or for products that have been premarinated or seasoned. Then cook the fish just until flaky. Another fast

Food Safety

Bacteria are naturally present in foods, and some are even beneficial—especially those found in yogurt and other fermented foods. But some bacteria, such as salmonella, can make you very ill, leading to symptoms like nausea, vomiting, diarrhea, and fever. Although food-borne illness poses a risk to everyone, the risk rises with the need for a soft or smooth/puréed diet, as this necessitates an increased handling of foods. If you are elderly, have nutritional deficiencies from a poor diet, or have been diagnosed with a medical condition that compromises your immune system, you may also have an increased chance of contracting a food-borne illness. It has been estimated that 76 million cases of food-borne sickness occur each year in the United States.

It is, of course, always important to use safe food-handling techniques, but it becomes even more essential when you have to alter the texture of your foods. By adhering to the following USDA food safety guidelines, you can help insure that your easy-to-swallow food is as safe as it is tasty.

❑ Always refrigerate perishable foods within two hours—sooner, if possible. When the temperature is above 90°F, get the foods into the refrigerator within an hour. Wrap foods securely for storage to keep them fresh and to prevent their juices from getting onto other foods.

❑ Cook or freeze fresh poultry, ground meat, and fish within two days. Cook or freeze whole (unground) cuts of beef, veal, lamb, and pork within three to five days. When freezing, keep the food in its original package and wrap again with plastic wrap or foil that has been designed for the freezer.

❑ Thaw foods in the refrigerator, which allows slow, safe thawing; in cold water, which allows faster thawing; or, for the speediest results, in a microwave oven. Cook foods immediately after they have thawed. (If you decide not to cook the thawed food, keep in mind that only foods thawed in the refrigerator can be safely refrozen.)

❑ Always wash your hands with warm, soapy water for at least 20 seconds before and after handling food.

❑ Wash all raw meats, vegetables, and fruits thoroughly before cutting, cooking, or eating them.

❑ Avoid cross-contamination by keeping raw meat, poultry, and fish—as well as their juices—away from clean and cooked foods. After cutting boards, knives, and other handling equipment

seafood option for an easy-to-chew diet is pre-steamed crabmeat, available in some supermarkets and fish stores. Dip it in seafood sauce or your condiment of choice to add flavor and moisture. Keep in mind, too, that soft ready-made seafood spreads are a good choice for sandwich fillings. (See Chapter 5 for information on making puréed sandwiches.)

TOFU

Made from soybeans, tofu is high in protein and therefore is a great soft vegetarian meat alternative. You can find it in shelf-stable unrefrigerated containers and in the refrigerated section of your local supermarket or health food store.

---

make contact with raw foods, wash them thoroughly with hot, soapy water. Also clean counters between uses. Sanitize cutting boards with a solution of 1 tablespoon of unscented liquid chlorine bleach mixed with 1 gallon of water.

❑ Marinate meat and poultry in a covered dish in the refrigerator.

❑ Cook meats until a food thermometer registers the minimum internal temperature recommended for that specific food. (See Table 3.2.) Note that reheated leftovers, purées included, also must reach a minimum temperature.

❑ Keep cold food cold (40°F or colder) and hot food hot (140°F or hotter). In other words, do not allow foods to remain in the "danger zone" between 40°F and 140°F any longer than necessary. (Make sure your refrigerator cools to 40°F or less.)

❑ Transfer leftovers to shallow containers and immediately place in the refrigerator or freezer for rapid cooling. Use most refrigerated leftovers within three to four days.

❑ Discard any perishable foods that have been left out for more than two hours if the temperature is under 90°F, and more than one hour if the temperature is over 90°F. Also discard foods that have visible mold growth unless, like blue cheese, the foods are intended to be moldy.

TABLE 3.2 RECOMMENDED MINIMUM INTERNAL COOKING TEMPERATURES

Food	Minimum Internal Temperature
Beef, Pork, and Game Animals, ground	160°F
Beef, Lamb, and Veal, solid piece, rare	145°F
Beef, Lamb, Pork, and Veal, solid piece, medium	160°F
Beef, Lamb, Pork, and Veal, solid piece, well done	170°F
Egg Dishes (quiches, casseroles, etc.)	160°F
Eggs	145°F (until yolk and white are firm)
Fish	145°F
Ham (precooked, to reheat)	140°F
Ham (raw)	160°F
Leftovers (to reheat)	165°F
Poultry and Stuffed Meats	165°F
Soups, Stews, and Casseroles	165°F

For more information on safe food handling, check the government hotlines provided on page 297 of "Organizations and Websites."

There are two main types of tofu: regular and silken. Each of these types comes in soft, firm, and extra-firm textures. The firmer the tofu, the less water it contains. All silken-style tofu is good for soft and smooth diets, as it has a creamy texture that blends well into smoothies, puddings, dips, and spreads. Silken tofu is also delicious when mashed into egg salad or cooked with scrambled eggs.

NUTS

Rich in heart-healthy fats, protein, and a wide range of phytonutrients, vitamins, and minerals, nuts rank high on the list of healthful foods. In fact, people who eat an ounce of nuts (3 to 4 tablespoons) several times a week are 30- to 50-percent less likely to suffer from heart disease than people who avoid nuts.

If you are on a soft or smooth diet, you cannot, of course, eat whole or chopped nuts. However, you can use nut butters; nut flours, which can be purchased from specialty stores; and nuts that you have finely ground at home using a food processor or, for small batches, a coffee grinder. Incorporate the nut butters and flours into sauces, smoothies, and mousses, and enjoy the goodness of nuts in an easy-to-swallow form. Also try adding whole or chopped nuts to a smoothie and blending until the solids are finely ground.

FROZEN FOODS

Frozen foods have long been the friend of the cook who's low on time, and this is doubly true for anyone who's following a soft or smooth diet. In the frozen food aisle, you will find foods that are already suitable for your diet, as well as foods that may need only a quick whirl in a blender or food processor to make them soft or smooth. Look for the following items in your supermarket.

Berries. Full of flavor and nutrients, frozen berries are wonderfully convenient—especially when berries are not in season. Berries are rich in beneficial phytonutrients, which are preserved well when frozen. Add frozen berries to your smoothies, or just blend them into delicious fruit purées. Another option is to freeze your homemade fruit purées into luscious sorbets.

Ice Cream. Ice cream, sherbet, and sorbet are convenient snack and dessert items. Choose the flavors you like best, being sure to avoid any products that include bits of fruits, nuts, or other chunky additions. Keep in mind that super-premium ice creams contain as much as 600 calories per cup. This makes them useful for weight gain, but high in saturated fat. If you need to shed pounds and lower your cholesterol, opt for light and lower-calorie brands, or choose sherbets and sorbets instead. Also be aware that because frozen desserts melt to a thin consistency in the mouth, they are not appropriate for a thickened liquids diet. (For more on thickened liquids, see Chapter 6.)

Ready-to-Eat Entrées. Frozen entrées provide an easy alternative to cooking from scratch. Some good choices include stuffed peppers, cheese lasagna, vegetable lasagna, macaroni and cheese, cheese ravioli, and bean enchiladas. These are all soft foods that can, if necessary, be blended to a smooth consistency. If you are watching calories, fat, or sodium, look for lighter and lower-sodium versions of your favorites.

Vegetables. Vegetables retain a high nutritional value when frozen, and are easy to prepare in your microwave oven or saucepan. Many of these products also come in convenient bags that allow you to use only what you need, and return the rest to the freezer. Frozen creamed spinach is a delicious soft side that can be made completely smooth through use of your blender or food processor. Also look for frozen vegetables in cheese sauce, as the sauce will allow you to make a delicious purée with ease. If you need to trim calories or fat, though, you'll also find a number of vegetables that have been prepared in lighter sauces.

CONDIMENTS, SAUCES, AND GRAVIES

Although sauces, gravies, and condiments play a role in most people's diets, they are especially important in an easy-to-swallow diet. These ingredients not only add great flavor but also provide much-needed liquid, softening foods and, when necessary, allowing them to be puréed to the proper consistency. Experiment with the following condiments as you create your soft and smooth dishes.

Barbecue Sauce. Barbecue sauce is similar to ketchup but tends to be spicier and more flavorful, with a smoky taste. Naturally smooth, it provides an easy way to flavor chopped or ground meats. Like ketchup, all tomato-based barbecue sauces contain the cancer-fighting phytonutrient lycopene. If sugar is a concern, look for low-sugar brands.

Canned or Jarred Gravies and Sauces. When you're in a rush, nothing is easier to use than a canned or jarred gravy or sauce. Ready-made gravies can flavor and soften a range of foods, from meat to vegetables, while tomato and pasta sauces can turn pasta, chicken, beef, or pork into a hearty entrée or side dish.

Ketchup. Made of tomatoes, vinegar, and spices, ketchup is naturally smooth and can quickly add flavor and moisture to a dish. Ketchup has the added benefit of being rich in lycopene, a phytonutrient shown to help protect against some cancers. Regular ketchup is high in sugar and sodium, so if this is a concern, look for low-sugar and low-salt brands.

Mayonnaise. Made chiefly of vegetable oil, egg yolks, and a little lemon juice, mayonnaise delivers about 100 calories and 11 grams of fat per tablespoon. Lower-fat mayonnaise is available for people who need to watch their calories. Most brands of nonfat mayonnaise contain just 10 calories per tablespoon, while light mayo provides about 50 calories per tablespoon.

Mustard, Prepared Horseradish, and Hot Sauce. These spicy condiments will allow you to perk up foods quickly and easily, without adding a lot of fat and calories to your dish. Mustard, horseradish, and hot sauce are great for people who have a diminished sense of taste, and hot sauce has the added benefit of being low in sodium. If you have mouth sores or pain, though, you'll want to avoid these products.

Packaged Sauce Mixes. Available in powder form, these mixes allow you to quickly whip up Hollandaise sauce, pesto, cheese and Alfredo sauces, and a range of gravies—products that will add moisture and flavor to your foods. These mixes are also highly adaptable. Prepare them with low-fat milk, olive oil, or trans-free margarines to create delicious, healthier versions of the original.

Ready-Made Pesto. Made chiefly of olive oil and basil, pesto is available in both shelf-stable jars and refrigerated plastic containers. Use this savory condiment to flavor and moisten pasta, puréed vegetables, puréed meats, and sandwich spreads.

Salsas and Chutneys. Prepared with a variety of ingredients, from tomatoes and onions to peaches and mangos, these condiments can be easily blended to a smooth consistency and used as toppings for soft foods or as a moist flavoring for meats. If spice is a concern, though, check the label for ingredients such as chilies and vinegar. While some salsas and chutneys are fairly mild in flavor, others can be quite hot and spicy.

Vinegar. Vinegar is available in a variety of types and flavors, from hearty red wine vinegar to delicate rice vinegar and sweet balsamic vinegar. A splash of this condiment can enhance the taste of meats, vegetables, and many other dishes while reducing the need for salt. If you have mouth sores or pain, though, you'll want to steer clear of vinegar and other highly acidic products.

CANNED AND JARRED FOODS

In the previous pages, we discussed how jarred condiments, sauces, and gravies can add vibrant flavor and much-needed moisture to your smooth or soft dishes. But these aren't the only convenience foods that can help you out in the kitchen. The following canned and jarred foods can be blended for quick side dishes or entrées, or used as sauces or flavorings in a number of dishes.

Applesauce. Available in a variety of flavors, applesauce can be found in large jars as well as single-serving containers. Applesauce contains a small amount of fiber, but is a good source of quercetin, a powerful antioxidant. This product makes a great quick snack on its own, and is also good sprinkled with a little cinnamon or eaten with cottage cheese or plain yogurt. If you are on a smooth/puréed diet, either avoid the chunky styles or blend the sauce into a smooth consistency before eating.

Canned and Jarred Fruits. Canned and jarred peaches, pears, apricots, mangos, and other fruits are convenient ways to add some fiber and important nutrients to your soft or smooth diet. Depending on your dietary needs, you may be able to eat them as is. If not, purée the fruits for a delicious soft dessert, a sauce for ice cream, or an addition to your favorite smoothie.

Canned and Jarred Vegetables. Although canned and jarred veggies generally have a higher sodium content than their fresh and frozen counterparts, they have a long shelf life and are convenient to use. Soft vegetables like carrots can simply be blended, seasoned, and heated for an easy puréed side dish. When using stringy or coarse vegetables like creamed corn and peas, though, you may have to strain the food after blending to make the result sufficiently smooth.

Canned Beans. A good source of protein and cholesterol-lowering fiber, canned beans can be puréed to a creamy consistency. For a quick dish, sauté some garlic in olive oil and stir in puréed white beans. Black beans, garbanzos, pintos, and other varieties also make good purées, especially when flavored with a little sauce or salsa.

Canned Soups. Tomato soup is a convenient naturally smooth soup that can be heated and served as is—without further processing—for a puréed diet. Other canned soups, such as bean, lentil, and cream of chicken, can be puréed to a smoother consistency for a quick meal or snack. If sodium and fat are a concern, look for lighter versions of your favorite flavor. Many soups are now available in full-fat, low-fat, and low-sodium varieties, and some brands cater specifically to people who follow a heart-healthy lifestyle.

Canned Tomatoes. Available whole and diced, canned tomatoes are a convenient ingredient for many recipes. To make a quick sauce, purée a can of diced Italian- or Mexican-style tomatoes with a few tablespoons of olive oil. Heat and serve over meat, eggs, pasta, and other entrées.

Fruit Nectars. Nectars are fruit juice beverages that include some puréed fruit, giving them a thicker consistency. If you need nectar-thick liquids, these nutrition-packed drinks are the perfect substitute for juices, and are also great ingredients in smoothies and other dishes. Apricot and pear nectars are available in most supermarkets.

Refried Beans. Already smooth, and packed with protein, antioxidants, and soluble fiber, refried beans have only to be reheated to make a great side dish. For extra flavor and a softer, smoother texture, add a little salsa and process to the desired consistency. Black-bean dip is also a good source of protein and soluble fiber, and can add flavor and texture when blended with other foods, such as well-cooked rice.

Roasted Red Bell Peppers. Full of great flavor, nutrients, and color, jarred roasted peppers can be puréed along with some olive oil or mayonnaise and savory herbs. The resulting sauce is delicious on eggs, meats, soufflés, and other dishes.

Vegetable Juice Cocktail. Products like V8 vegetable juice and carrot juice make it easy to get your veggies when your ability to eat solid foods has been compromised. These juices are often thick enough for people who need nectar-consistency liquids, but if you're in doubt, check with your health professional. Vegetable juices made with a juicer usually need to be thickened. And as you will learn in Part Two of this book, an excellent sandwich bread slurry can be made by mixing a tablespoon or two of vegetable juice with an equal amount of olive oil. (See the recipe on page 198.)

DELI FOODS

Whether you prefer your local delicatessen or the deli counter of your favorite supermarket or health food store, a deli is a great place to pick up convenience foods for your soft or smooth diet. Many delis offer a range of sandwich fillings, soups, prepared entrées, and other freshly made dishes. Below, we mention just a few of the useful items you may find at your deli.

Fresh-Ground Peanut Butter and Other Nut Butters. Often featured in the deli section of supermarkets and in health foods stores, nut butters provide a boost of calories and protein. If you have swallowing problems, nut butters are too sticky to be eaten plain, but they make excellent additions to smoothies, sauces, and other dishes. Your favorite nut butter can also be blended with banana or anoth-

er soft fruit to make a smooth, easy-to-swallow sandwich spread.

Guacamole. Avocado-based guacamole is delicious served as an accompaniment to bean enchiladas, refried beans, and other dishes. Many guacamoles can be eaten right out of the container, while others include chunks of avocado, tomato, or onion, and therefore may have to be blended for a puréed diet. If you prefer your guacamole with chips, soften the chips with a salsa-flavored slurry.

Hummus. Made from chickpeas and sesame tahini, and available in various flavors, hummus is a delicious spread over softened bread, or may be eaten plain. Unlike some empty-calorie spreads, hummus is also a good source of fiber, protein, and other nutrients.

Liverwurst and Pâtés. A smooth, ready-to-eat sandwich filling, liverwurst is appropriate for both soft and puréed diets. Keep in mind, though, that this product is high in saturated fat and cholesterol, and therefore is not a good choice for anyone who is overweight or has high cholesterol levels. Some deli sections also carry pâtés, most of which are smooth. (Avoid those that include nuts or other hard chunks of food.) Like liverwurst, pâtés are high in saturated fat and cholesterol, but may be good when excess weight loss is a concern.

Prepared Entrées. Ready-made dishes such as macaroni and cheese can often be found in the deli section. These dishes tend to be higher in fat than their homemade counterparts, so if weight loss is desired, you may want to skip these prepared foods except on an occasional basis. When you do choose prepared entrées, it's a simple matter to process them to a smooth consistency, adding a little thinned mayonnaise, olive oil, or cheese sauce as necessary.

Sandwich Spreads. Pimento cheese, egg salad, chicken salad, ham salad, and tuna salad can make a quick sandwich filling for soft and easy-to-chew diets. If you are following a puréed diet, though, you will need to process these spreads to a creamy consistency and serve them on moistened bread. (See Chapter 5 for details.)

Tabouli. A Mediterranean-style bulgur wheat salad, tabouli easily forms a bolus (ball) in the mouth for easy swallowing. This salad does require some chewing so it is not suitable for puréed diets, but it can work well in soft and easy-to-chew diets. When blending gazpacho, enhance the flavor by adding a few tablespoons of tabouli to the soup.

THICKENERS

If you are on a puréed diet or need thickened liquids, you should have on hand thickeners that can be used to correct the consistency of foods and beverages. Arrowroot, cornstarch, flour, and instant mashed potato flakes are four commonly available household thickeners. Keep in mind, though, that they work only in hot dishes. On the other hand, specially made commercial thickeners can work in both hot and cold dishes. Some are designed for thickening beverages only, while some can thicken other types of food. (For information on using both household and special commercial thickeners, see Chapter 6.)

Arrowroot. This starchy white powder is extracted from the arrowroot plant. Like cornstarch, arrowroot adds a clear sheen to sauces, making it well suited to the preparation of fruit sauces and glazes. To prevent clumping, mix arrowroot with an equal amount of cold liquid before adding it to hot liquids, and cook the dish briefly to thicken. Arrowroot has about twice the thickening power of flour.

Cornstarch. This powdery white flour is ground from the starchy portion of corn kernels. Cornstarch is often used in Asian cooking, fruit sauces, and fruit pies and fillings, where it lends a clear sheen as it thickens. To prevent clumping, mix cornstarch with an equal amount of cold liquid before adding to hot liquids, and cook until thickened. Cornstarch has about twice the thickening power of wheat flour.

Flour. Wheat flour is frequently used to thicken gravies, stews, gumbos, and cream soups. Unlike cornstarch and arrowroot, flour lends an opaque quality as it thickens. To prevent lumps from forming, flour can either be made into a roux—a cooked mixture of flour and fat—or dissolved into a cold liquid before it is added to the dish. The dish must then be simmered for several minutes to allow thickening to occur. For extra fiber and nutrition, use whole wheat pastry flour instead of white flour to thicken your foods. Just keep in mind that whole wheat flour is light brown in color, so it works best in brownish sauces such as chicken and beef gravy. When preparing white sauces, stick to white (refined) flour.

Instant Mashed Potato Flakes. Made of potatoes that have been cooked, mashed, and dried, potato flakes can be sprinkled into hot soups and sauces to add thickness. This product can also be mixed with some hot water and puréed with foods like cooked vegetables and meats to enhance thickness and create a more cohesive texture.

Commercial Thickeners. A variety of starch- and gel-based thickeners have been specially developed for people who need thickened foods and beverages. Some thickeners are made for beverages, while others are designed for foods. These products are available in drugstores and through manufacturers and distributors. (See page 287 of the "Products" tables.)

READY-MADE PUREED FOODS AND MIXES

A number of companies offer ready-made puréed foods that you can have delivered to your home. (See page 286 of the "Products" tables.) Ready-to-eat and heat-and-serve products include fruits, meats, vegetables, breakfast items, and entrées. Some of these products are offered in individual servings, while others combine several dishes to create whole meals. Some are shaped like the original food—chicken, pork chops, peas, or pears, for instance—and some even come in molds that can be reused when you prepare your own purées. Manufacturers also offer a variety of mixes, such as instant puréed pasta, rice, and bread. You may find these mixes handy staples to keep in your pantry.

Whether you are stocking your pantry, filling your refrigerator, or looking for a quick prepared dish, try to be as creative as possible while keeping your dietary needs in mind. A new chutney, salsa, or barbecue sauce may add just the flavor you need to make your puréed meat dish appealing. A local restaurant may be able to give you a take-home container of your favorite soup or pasta. Your fish store may be willing to provide fresh-cooked filets that are already perfect for a soft diet. By thinking along new lines and keeping your eyes open, you'll find many great ingredients and ready-made foods that can help you enjoy your soft or smooth diet.

4. Choosing and Using Kitchen Equipment

Everyone knows that the right tools can get a job done more quickly and easily. This is certainly true of preparing soft foods. The appropriate equipment can help you better chop, grind, or purée food, and then present it in a more appealing manner.

You may be happy to learn that all of the recipes in this book were made with moderately priced equipment that many people already have in their kitchens. This chapter highlights both basic equipment like blenders and strainers, and optional tools such as pastry bags and food molds. You will find these products sold in a variety of places, including the kitchenware section of department and discount stores, restaurant supply stores, cooking and gourmet shops, and supermarkets, as well as on Internet shopping sites. Choose only those tools that suit your particular needs and fit your budget, and you'll be able to create soft and smooth foods that satisfy.

TOOLS FOR CHOPPING, GRINDING, AND PUREEING FOODS

Your primary task in producing foods for an easy-to-swallow diet is to mechanically soften foods by chopping, grinding, or puréeing them. Depending on whether your diet must be easy-to-chew, soft, or smooth/puréed, one or several of the following kitchen tools can help you do the job.

STANDING BLENDERS

A standing blender—a traditional blender composed of a base, a container with spinning blades, and a lid—is ideal for puréeing soups, smoothies, and other foods that have a high liquid content. It is also useful for grinding whole grains such as uncooked barley and rice into a cornmeal- or grits-like texture suitable for hot cereal. Blenders come in many shapes and sizes, and you may want to have several types on hand to suit different purposes. The following tips will help you choose the blender that's right for your needs.

Choosing a Standing Blender

When selecting a standing blender, keep the following points in mind:

❑ Most moderately priced blenders can effectively purée soups and beverages made with vegetables and fruits, and are adequate for many people on soft or smooth diets. But if you must have foods that are ultra-smooth or liquefied, and if your dish contains meat and grains, you will get better results with a more powerful high-speed model. Most low- to moderately priced blenders have 450- to 500-watt motors. Higher priced "professional" and "high-performance" models such as a Vita-Mix or Blendtec blender may have two to three times as much power. These blenders are capable of liquefying dishes such as soups into very fine particles, which is important if you are following a liquid diet or preparing a homemade blenderized formula for tube feedings. Be aware, though, that if you want to purée very thick mixtures such as beef stews and casseroles, you will need a food processor instead. (See page 58.)

❑ Most standard blenders have a five- to eight-cup capacity, which is good for puréeing large batches of food that can then be divided among smaller containers and frozen for later use. These blenders will not, however, do a good job with a small amount of food. If you think you'll be blending both small and large volumes, look for a standard-size blender with a mini-jar attachment. If you have an Oster blender, you can purchase eight-ounce Oster mini-blender jars for use with your appliance.

❑ A mini-blender can typically handle one to two cups of food. If you intend to process only single servings, this may be your best option, since it is difficult to efficiently blend small amounts of food in a larger blender.

❑ If you don't already own a food processor, consider purchasing a blender that has a mini-food processor attachment. This will make the appliance much more versatile.

❑ Look for blenders that have a lid with a feeder hole in the top. This will allow you to easily add foods or liquids during the blending process. The feeder hole can also be cracked open to allow steam to escape when processing hot foods.

❑ Many people prefer blenders that have a see-through glass or plastic jar, as opposed to stainless steel, which requires you to stop blending and remove the lid to check the consistency of your mixture. Glass containers are heavier than plastic and thus tend to be more stable during use. Glass containers are also less likely to scratch and absorb stains and odors.

Using a Standing Blender

When using a standing blender, keep the following tips in mind:

❑ For best results, fill the blender a third to a half full. This will leave enough space in the jar for the contents to move and blend efficiently.

❑ When blending both wet and dry ingredients, place the liquids in the blender first. Then add the dry ingredients, such as ground flaxseed or wheat germ. If dry ingredients are placed in the blender first, they may remain stuck between the blades even after the liquids have been added.

❑ When making a beverage that contains ice, add

the liquids first and the ice last. This will prevent the ice from hampering the motion of the blades.

❏ When puréeing hot liquids in a blender, the pressure from the steam can blow the cover off. To guard against accidents, never fill a blender more than half full with a hot liquid. If the machine has a feeder cap, crack it open slightly to allow the steam to escape. Start blending the mixture at the lowest speed, and gradually increase to higher speeds as needed. As an extra precaution, cover the blender lid with a towel to protect yourself in the event that the top pops off.

❏ Vegetables that are coarse or stringy—celery, onions, corn, or peas—may be difficult to blend to a completely smooth texture. If you find that your puréed vegetables contain fibrous pieces, push them through a wire strainer to create a smooth texture. (See page 65 for information on using a strainer.)

❏ When placing several foods in the blender at once, consider the color of the resulting mixture. Foods of contrasting colors—the green and red vegetables found in a stew, for instance—may turn into a brownish-looking mush when blended together. On the other hand, foods that contain similar colors—an asparagus and leek soup or a smoothie made with mixed berries—will maintain an appealing color when processed.

IMMERSION BLENDERS

An immersion blender, also called a stick or hand-held blender, is essentially a long handle or wand that has electrically powered blades attached to the bottom. Unlike a standing blender, which makes it necessary to transfer food from a pot or bowl to the appliance's container, an immersion blender can be inserted directly in the food—in a pot of soup or a tall glass, for instance. You then press the power button, which activates the blades until the food reaches the proper consistency.

The immersion blender is obviously a handy device. Besides making it unnecessary to transfer your food in batches from one container to another, it is much more easily cleaned than a standing blender. In most cases, you simply unplug the device and hold the blades under hot running water. There is no container to detach and scrub. And for some jobs, an immersion blender is perfect. For instance, it makes easy work of blending smoothies and bean soups, puréeing canned tomatoes, and processing other soft foods. However, even a relatively powerful immersion blender will typically not produce the very smooth purée created by a conventional blender, and will not be able to handle dishes like beef stew, which require a food processor.

Choosing an Immersion Blender

When selecting an immersion blender, keep the following points in mind:

❏ Some immersion blenders have only a few accessories—such as a small beaker for making drinks—while others include a number of different gizmos, such as whisks, food choppers, and ice crushers. Consider how you'll be using the blender before making your purchase, and don't pay extra money for accessories that you don't need and that will simply take up space in your kitchen.

❏ Like standing blenders, immersion blenders come

with different size motors. Inexpensive models typically have motors with less than 200 watts of power, while heavy-duty or "professional" models have motors of 300 watts or more. If you plan to make frequent use of your blender, and you intend to blend soups containing beans or chunks of veggies, it makes sense to opt for a more powerful model. Just keep in mind that a standing blender is preferred when smoother results are desired.

❑ Immersion blenders with variable speeds will give you more control over the consistency of your purées. Some models have one speed only. For better results, choose a blender that has at least two speeds: High and Low.

❑ In most cases, you can easily clean your immersion blender by holding the end of the stick and the blades under hot running water. Some models come with detachable wands that are dishwasher-safe. If you like the idea of being able to pop the wand into your dishwasher, look for this option.

Using an Immersion Blender

When using an immersion blender, keep the following tips in mind.

❑ If you have a choice of pots or other containers in which to prepare your food, choose one that's narrow and deep rather than wide and shallow. This will make it easier to keep your blender submerged, and will help the puréeing process move more quickly.

❑ Fully immerse the blade end of the blender in your food before hitting the power button. There is a reason it's called an immersion blender; it has to be kept submerged in the food while it's working. If you lift this tool while it's in operation, it may splatter food all over your kitchen.

❑ Always release the power button before lifting the blender out of the food.

FOOD PROCESSORS

One of the most useful tools for creating easy-to-chew, soft, and smooth/puréed foods is the food processor. This is, in fact, the appliance of choice when dealing with thick mixtures like stews and casseroles. Because a food processor has a shallow bowl, the food can be more easily stirred and redistributed in a processor than would be possible in the deep, narrow container of a blender. In most cases, the food processor can quickly grind meat and vegetables to a soft or easy-to-chew texture. With the addition of adequate liquid, this appliance will also allow you to purée foods to a smooth texture.

Choosing a Food Processor

When selecting a food processor, keep the following points in mind:

❑ Most full-size food processors hold six to eleven cups of food. This is a good size if you want to process large batches of food and freeze leftovers, but will not work efficiently if you are going to process small amounts of food. If you think you'll be processing both small and large volumes, look for a standard-size food processor with a versatile mini-bowl attachment.

❑ Mini-food processor capacities range from one to three cups. If you intend to process only single servings, this may be the best option for you.

❑ By far, the most useful and important accessory that comes with a food processor is the standard chopping blade, which can finely chop foods or—if you process for a long enough period of time with adequate liquids—can transform foods into a purée. If you have no need for shredding discs and dough hooks, opt for a simple model that omits these accessories.

❑ Most full-size food processors have handy feed tubes or chutes that allow you to add ingredients while the machine is running. If possible, buy a machine with a wider chute, which will save on prep time by enabling you to feed larger pieces of food into the processor.

❑ Like blenders, food processors come with different size motors. Moderately priced models have 400- to 500-watt motors, while heavy-duty models may boast 700 or more watts of power. If you plan to buy a new food processor, opt for a more powerful model. If you already have a lower-power machine, be aware that a thick mixture can cause the motor to strain. For smooth and efficient functioning, add more liquid as necessary.

Using a Food Processor

When using a food processor, keep the following tips in mind:

❑ For best results, fill the food processor a third to a half full. This will leave enough space for the food to move around and be processed efficiently.

❑ If you want to chop or grind food, do not add liquid. If you want a smoother texture, add a small amount of liquid. Approximately two to three tablespoons of liquid will be needed for every two ounces of meat. (Two ounces is just shy of half a cup.) When processing fruits and vegetables, start with one tablespoon of liquid for each half cup of cooked vegetables or grains, and add more as needed during processing. Fruits and "watery" vegetables such as zucchini may not need any added water at all. If necessary, once the contents is smooth, add thickeners so that the food will hold together as it's swallowed. (See Chapter 5 for more information on puréeing.)

❑ Use flavored liquids such as broth or gravy to enhance the taste of meat or poultry. When processing fish, try mayonnaise, tartar sauce, or cocktail sauce. When puréeing ham, add V8 vegetable juice or honey mustard. Mix a bit of broth, cheese sauce, yogurt, olive oil, or trans-free margarine into vegetables or grains.

❑ Foods that are coarse or stringy—celery, onions, corn, and peas—may be difficult to process to a completely smooth texture. If you find that your puréed vegetables contain fibrous pieces, push them through a wire strainer to make them completely smooth. (See page 65 for information on using a strainer.)

❑ When placing several foods in the processor at once, consider the color of the resulting purée. Foods of contrasting colors, such as those found in casseroles and stews, may turn into a brownish-looking mush when processed together. Foods of similar colors—a sorbet of mangos and strawberries, or a casserole of zucchini, onions, and celery—will be more appealing after being processed.

POTATO MASHERS

Most people are already familiar with potato mashers, which are simple hand-held kitchen tools that are good not just for mashing potatoes, but also for mashing other soft-cooked vegetables, beans, and fruits. Mashers are inexpensive and readily available in a wide variety of stores, including supermarkets. Just keep in mind that although this handy device can make foods softer and easier to chew, it cannot produce a truly smooth purée. For that, you'll need a food processor.

Choosing a Potato Masher

When selecting a potato masher, keep the following points in mind:

❑ Some models have a zigzag wire head that tends to leave lumps in the food. Other models have a broad stainless steel head that more evenly mashes food through a grid. We recommend the latter style for a smoother texture.

❑ Look for a durable, comfortable handle. Some brands have a soft rubber horizontal handle that absorbs pressure and cushions your grip as you press downward. If you'll be doing a lot of mashing, you'll appreciate this feature.

Using a Potato Masher

When using a potato masher, follow the instructions below for the best results:

❑ Remember to cook your potatoes, vegetables, or fruits until completely soft. Foods that are still firm will be much more difficult to mash, and might never approach the smoothness of a food that was soft-cooked.

❑ Place the cooked food in a bowl and mash to the desired consistency. If you need extra moisture, mash in a bit of liquid such as milk, broth, juice, olive oil, or trans-free margarine.

POTATO RICERS

Resembling a large garlic press, a potato ricer processes food by forcing it through small holes that are about the size of a grain of rice. Ricers have long been used to make light and fluffy mashed potatoes and baby food. What types of food can your ricer handle? Starchy vegetables without skins or seeds, such as rutabaga, winter squash, and sweet potatoes, are especially well-suited to processing in a ricer. You can also make applesauce by ricing soft-cooked apples, or transform canned pears into pear sauce. Finally, to add interest to puréed pasta meals, you can take soft-cooked pasta that's been blended with liquid until smooth, and force it through the ricer holes to give the illusion of noodles.

Be aware that while the ricer works very well with some foods, it does have its limits. If you attempt to rice "watery" foods that have large proportions of skin, stems, or other fibrous parts—zucchini or spinach, for instance—you may find that the ricer expels mostly liquid while the fibrous vegetable remain in the hopper, clogging the holes. That's why it's important to choose the right foods and prepare them properly before ricing. Also keep in mind that a ricer will not get foods as perfectly smooth as a food processor.

Choosing a Potato Ricer

When selecting a potato ricer, keep the following points in mind:

❏ Look for sturdy stainless steel construction and handles that have a comfortable grip.

❏ Some ricers come equipped with interchangeable discs, each of which has different size holes to control the coarseness of the food. If possible, opt for a ricer with these different discs so that you can use smaller holes for mashing vegetables and fruits, and larger holes when you're trying to imitate pasta noodles.

❏ Some ricers have holes only at the bottom of the hopper—the portion of the ricer that holds the food before processing. Others have holes in both the bottom and the sides. Be aware that the first type is easier to control. If you get the second type, you will have to position the ricer carefully over a large bowl to prevent the food from creating a mess as it squirts out the sides.

Using a Potato Ricer

When using a potato ricer, follow the instructions below for the best results:

❏ Remember to cook your vegetables or fruits until completely soft. Foods that are still firm will be much more difficult to force through the ricer, and will include coarse bits even after ricing.

❏ When processing vegetables or fruits, drain off the cooking liquid and place the remaining food in the ricer. Then squeeze the handles and allow the mashed food to be extruded through the holes and into your container or onto a serving plate. If the resulting texture isn't smooth enough, push the food through a fine-mesh sieve.

❏ To make puréed pasta dishes more appealing, first overcook the pasta until very soft, and use a food processor to make it completely smooth. Add some water, milk, or olive oil to develop a texture similar to thick mashed potatoes. If desired, add a little grated Parmesan cheese, Alfredo sauce, or pesto to enhance the flavor. Then press the resulting product through your ricer and directly onto a serving plate to resemble pasta noodles. (For more information on puréeing pasta, see page 80 of Chapter 5.)

❏ If the ricer starts to get clogged with fibrous bits of food during use, periodically scrape out the interior with the side of a spoon.

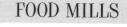

FOOD MILLS

Food mills have been used for generations to grind, mash, purée, and strain foods. A food mill is essentially a bottomless bowl fitted with a perforated disc. A hand crank turns a blade and forces the food through the disc, where it can be collected in a container.

A food mill can be especially useful when you need to both purée a food and remove its skins and seeds. For instance, when milling foods like stewed tomatoes, only the tomato flesh will pass through the disc.

Food mills can be used to purée a variety of cooked vegetables and soft fruits. For instance, they are perfect for making mashed potatoes or processing cooked apples or pears into a sauce. Just be aware that this kitchen tool will give you a bit more texture than you would get if you used a food processor, since the food is extruded through holes rather than being pulverized by whirling blades.

Choosing a Food Mill

When selecting a food mill, keep the following points in mind:

❏ Many food mills come with interchangeable discs that allow for varying consistencies. Consider your needs before buying a mill, and make sure that the discs will give you the texture you require.

❏ Review all the features of each mill and decide if they are important to you. For instance, some mills come with bowl attachments that collect the processed food, some have non-slip legs, and some have handles that hold the mill securely over a bowl or pot.

❏ Determine the volume of food you'll be milling, and select the capacity that's right for you. A smaller size mill—one with a two-cup capacity, sometimes sold as a "mini food mill" or "baby food mill"— makes sense if you will typically be processing single servings. If you intend to process larger quantities of food, you'll want a mill with a larger capacity.

❏ For durability, choose a mill made of a sturdy material such as stainless steel. A plastic food mill may not stand up to frequent use.

❏ Look for a model that can be easily disassembled and is dishwasher-safe. This will save you time and energy.

Using a Food Mill

It's simple to use a food mill. The following instructions will insure success.

❏ Fit the mill with the desired size disc, using a finely perforated disc for the smoothest texture. Place the food in the mill, position the mill over a bowl or pot, and turn the crank.

❏ During the milling process, periodically turn the crank in the opposite direction. This will help dislodge any food that has accumulated under the blade.

MEAT GRINDERS

In generations past, the meat grinder was a staple in many homes, where it processed beef, pork, poultry, and fish for use in sausages, burgers, soups, and other dishes. Although products vary, in general, the food is placed in a chute or hopper and—either through hand-cranking or electric power—is forced through a series of blades and pushed out through a screen. The advantage for the soft-foods cook is that this sturdy machine can take meats and vegetables and chop them finely or even grind them to a pâté-like consistency.

Choosing a Meat Grinder

When selecting a grinder, keep the following points in mind:

❏ Some grinders are powered by a hand crank and clamp onto the side of a table for stability, while others are electrically powered and sit on a tabletop. Choose the style that meets your needs.

❏ Unless you intend to grind a lot of food and freeze some of it for future use, choose a small grinder with a hopper that measures about two and a half by three and a half inches. This will be adequate if you plan to prepare single servings or only a couple of servings at a time.

❏ Look for durable construction utilizing materials such as stainless steel or cast iron.

Using a Meat Grinder

When using a grinder, follow the instructions below for the best results.

❏ Since different grinders work in different ways— and some are manually operated while others are electrically powered—be sure to read the user's manual that accompanies your appliance. Then follow the directions carefully for best results.

❏ Most grinders come with interchangeable cutting blades. Choose the finest blade to create a pâté-like consistency, and a coarser blade for a hamburger-type consistency.

❏ For easier use and better results, chill the meat, poultry, or fish in the freezer for thirty minutes. Then cut it into cubes before grinding.

❏ Assemble the grinder and fill the hopper with the cubed food. Feed the meat into the grinder tube with a long pusher or other utensil, positioning a bowl under the grinder to catch the processed food.

❏ Always clean the equipment meticulously after use. Remember that because ground meat has more exposed surface area, it allows bacteria to grow quickly.

JUICERS

A juicer is a great way to add the goodness of fresh vegetables and fruits to your diet when you can't tolerate fiber and texture. A mind-boggling array of juicers are available these days, ranging from simple manual citrus juicers, which cost just a few dollars, to elaborate electric "juice extractors," which are sold for hundreds of dollars each. The trick is to decide what your needs are and to find a juicer that will meet them.

Choosing a Juicer

When selecting a juicer, keep the following points in mind:

❏ Citrus juicers are made for the sole purpose of extracting juice from oranges and other citrus fruits. Both manual and electric-powered versions are available, but the process is the same: The fruit is halved and pressed onto the peak of a cone. This extracts the juice, leaving the rind, membranes, and pulp behind. Relatively inexpensive, this is a good choice if you're interested in juicing citrus fruits only.

❏ Juice extractors can remove juice from a wide variety of vegetables and fruits. Some juice extractors use a combination of grinding and centrifugal force to isolate the juice. Others masticate or crush the produce to a pulp and then squeeze out the juice. The pulp, which is often expelled into a separate container, can be added to other dishes, tossed onto a compost pile, or discarded.

❏ Read the descriptions of various juicers to learn the foods for which they are best suited. Some machines will not extract juices from leafy greens or wheatgrass, and some are not able to handle hard produce like carrots and beets. The recipe book that comes with the machine generally provides a good idea of the foods that can be processed efficiently by the appliance. Be sure to choose one that does the job you have in mind.

❏ Make sure that the juicer has sturdy construction and dishwasher-safe parts. Also check for ease of assembly and cleaning.

Using a Juicer

When using a juicer, keep these guidelines in mind:

❏ Since different juicers work in different ways, be sure to read the user's manual that accompanies your appliance. Then follow the directions carefully for best results.

❏ If you cannot tolerate any pulp that remains after juicing, pour the juice through a fine wire mesh strainer and toss out any solids. Generally, this added step is necessary only for a clear liquids diet.

❏ Most juicers come with a variety of tasty recipes to get you started. By following a few of the recipes and adjusting them for your tastes, you will be able to enjoy great juice from the very beginning.

STRAINERS

A fine mesh wire strainer, also known as a sieve, is a hand-held filtration device traditionally used to remove lumps from soups and sauces and to eliminate unwanted seeds, skins, strings, and hulls from vegetables. If your foods need to have an ultra-smooth texture, and your blender or food processor isn't doing the job, a sieve is a must. All you have to do is place the already-processed food in the strainer and push it through the mesh. The lumps and other unwanted particles stay in the strainer, while the mashed or puréed food ends up in your serving bowl or plate.

Choosing a Strainer

When selecting a strainer, keep the following points in mind:

❏ Look for a strainer in your supermarket or discount store, where you'll probably find one for just a few dollars. Professional restaurant-quality models can easily cost ten times as much, but a higher price does not necessarily mean that the tool will do a better job. On the other hand, you don't want to buy a very cheap and flimsy strainer, as it may quickly dent or tear.

❏ Most wire strainers are made of stainless steel. They have a rounded or conical bottom and can range in diameter from three to eight inches. Either shape will produce the desired results, but you may want to have several sizes on hand to perform different jobs.

❏ If you can compare several different strainers, look not only at the tool's sturdiness but also at the size of the mesh. The finer the mesh, the smoother your food will be.

❏ Look for a strainer that has a hook or handle that allows you to clamp or rest the tool on the sides of pots or bowls. This will help prevent the strainer from slipping into the container as you push your food through the wire mesh.

❏ If you intend to strain coarser foods, such as corn and peas, consider buying a strainer that comes with a pestle. This device can help you efficiently press the food through the mesh.

Using a Strainer

When using a strainer, follow the instructions below for the best results:

❏ Place the food in your strainer, filling it about a quarter to a third full, and place the strainer over a bowl or plate. Use a wooden spoon or pestle to push the food through the wire mesh into the serving dish. Continue—working in batches, if necessary—until the food is strained. Then discard any pieces that remain in the strainer.

If you are not sure of the appliances that will be most useful to you, turn to Table 4.1. This table guides you to the most appropriate food-processing equipment for each type of diet, and also suggests optional tools that may be helpful as you create your easy-to-chew, soft, or smooth/puréed foods.

TOOLS FOR MOLDING AND PRESENTING SOFT FOODS

A common complaint of people on a soft or smooth diet is that the food looks unappealing. Certainly, there's nothing appetizing about a mound of puréed beef stew or chicken, unshaped and unadorned. But soft food doesn't have to look that way. With just a few simple tools and a modest effort, you can make any food look as good as it tastes.

SCOOPS

Probably the simplest, easiest way to make puréed foods look more familiar is to use ice cream and cookie dough scoops to dispense them onto the serving plate. By giving foods a clean and attractive

TABLE 4.1 CHOOSING FOOD-PROCESSING TOOLS

Dietary Requirements	Best Tools for the Job	Other Helpful Tools
Easy-to-Chew Foods	• For meats, use a meat grinder or food processor only if the meat is not tender enough for easy chewing and swallowing. A home grinder will allow you to produce a very fine texture and enjoy a wide variety of ground products. • For soups that are not adequately soft, use a standing or immersion blender. • For soft-cooked vegetables and fruits, simply mash the food with a fork.	• Use a slow cooker to give foods an exceptionally moist and tender texture.
Soft Foods	• For meats, use a meat grinder or food processor. • For soups, use a standing or immersion blender as needed. • For soft-cooked vegetables and fruits, use a blender, food processor, food mill, or ricer.	• Use squeeze bottles to quickly add your favorite sauce for extra moisture and flavor.
Smooth/ Puréed Foods	• For meats, use a food processor. • For soups, use a standing blender. • For soft-cooked vegetables and fruits, use a blender or food processor. • For beverages, use a juicer or a blender. Once the mixture is smooth, thicken it as needed.	• If you need an ultra-smooth texture, use a strainer to remove any lumps or fibrous bits of food. • Use scoops to give puréed foods a more pleasing shape. • Use pastry bags to dispense puréed foods in interesting shapes and designs. • Use molds, custard cups, and ramekins to improve the appearance of puréed dishes. • Use squeeze bottles to decorate and moisten puréed foods with a smooth sauce.

shape, these simple utensils—which you may already have on hand—make puréed dishes more appealing, especially when you drizzle a tasty gravy or sauce over them.

Choosing Scoops

When selecting scoops, keep the following points in mind:

❑ Ice cream scoops can be made of plastic or stainless steel. For greater durability and ease of use, buy a stainless steel scoop and opt for one with a trigger-release mechanism that ejects the food with the press of a lever. These scoops, which generally hold about a half a cup, are great for portioning out entrées and side dishes.

❑ Cookie scoops come in various sizes, ranging from about an inch in diameter to two or more inches in diameter. Small scoops are perfect for portioning foods like butter, margarine, and cream cheese, and larger scoops work well for shaping meatballs. Again, you'll want a trigger-release mechanism that allows you to easily and cleanly dispense the scoop of food onto the plate.

Using Scoops

When using scoops to shape your soft foods, follow the instructions below for the best results:

❑ Use the ice cream scoop to portion out puréed meat, poultry, chicken, fish, or vegetables. Arrange the scoops in a pleasing way on the serving plate, and to make the food even more attractive and tasty, top it with a smooth gravy or sauce.

❑ Use the cookie scoop to add little balls of butter or margarine to the plate. This will not only look attractive but also give the diner another means of enhancing the flavor of the foods being served.

PASTRY BAGS

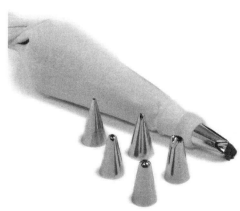

A pastry bag is a soft cone-shaped bag with two open ends, one large and one small. A decorative tip is inserted in the small end and the food is inserted through the larger, more open end. This enables you to pipe the food out in decorative designs.

Bakers and chefs have long used pastry bags to pipe semisolid foods such as cake icing and mashed potatoes into decorative shapes. But these bags are equally handy for piping an array of homemade puréed foods. By keeping one or more pastry bags and several different tips at your disposal, you will be able to give soft foods all-important eye appeal.

Choosing Pastry Bags

When selecting pastry bags, keep the following points in mind:

❑ Pastry bags come in a range of sizes, from about eight inches long to more than twenty inches long. When preparing individual portions, an eight- to ten-inch bag is about right.

❑ Some pastry bags are washable and reusable, while others are made of disposable plastic. Choose the material that's most convenient for you.

Using Pastry Bags

When using pastry bags to dispense your puréed foods, follow the instructions below for the best results:

❏ Make sure that the consistency of the food lends itself to piping. Thick mashed potatoes and puréed starchy vegetables like lima beans and winter squash usually pipe well. But when using other foods like puréed meats and nonstarchy vegetables, you may have to process them with some added liquid, potato flakes, or crustless bread so that they hold their shape when piped.

❏ Place a decorative tip at the end of the bag—try a star tip for easy, attractive designs—and fill the pastry bag up to half full with the prepared food. Close the bag by twisting it halfway down, and force the contents toward the tip.

❏ Position the bag so that the tip faces the plate or other serving dish. Squeeze the bag, gently forcing the contents through the tip and creating designs on the plate. Remember that artful piping can take a lot of practice, but even simple designs can add a touch of elegance to a meal.

❏ If you don't have a professional pastry bag on hand, but you do own a set of tips, make your own disposable bag from a quart-size zip-type plastic bag. Snip a hole in one corner and insert the decorating tip through the hole. Fill the bag and squeeze the food through the tip and onto your serving dish.

MOLDS

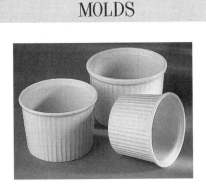

Many people find that puréed foods are more appetizing when they are cooked or gelled in molds. Whether these molds are simple in form or actually imitate the shape of the original food, they can make a big difference in eye appeal.

Choosing Food Molds

When selecting molds for soft and puréed foods, keep the following points in mind:

❏ Look for ovenproof ramekins and custard cups in a range of sizes, from six to twelve ounces. Various sizes and shapes are useful for making entrées, side dishes, and desserts.

❏ Get creative by using mini-bundt pans for aspics and mousses, mini-loaf pans for meatloaf, and individual pie slice pans for custards and quiches.

❏ Be aware that some ready-to-eat puréed foods come in reusable molds that resemble the food's original form—chicken, pork chops, peas, or pineapple, for instance. After enjoying the tasty entrée, side dish, or dessert, you can save the mold for your own use. (See page 286 of the "Products" section.)

Using Food Molds

When using molds to shape your soft foods, follow the instructions below for the best results.

❏ When making molded custards and timbales, coat the custard cups, ramekins, or decorative molds with nonstick cooking spray before filling to facilitate the release of the food.

❏ After baking, allow the custard or timbale to sit for five to ten minutes or longer to allow the food to firm up a bit. Then run a sharp knife around the edges of the cups to loosen the edges, and invert onto a serving plate.

❏ If you want to convert one of your favorite dishes

into a puréed, molded food, use a commercial thickener specifically made for puréed foods that will be shaped or molded. (See page 287 of the "Products" section.)

SQUEEZE BOTTLES

Ask any professional chef and he'll tell you that a decorative drizzle of sauce under or over a food is one of the simplest ways to create a stunning presentation as well as a burst of flavor. For people on a soft or smooth diet, a drizzle of sauce also adds important moisture, making everything easier to swallow.

It's a good idea to have several filled bottles on hand so that you'll always be ready with an appropriate condiment. In "The Secret's in the Sauce," which begins on page 163, you'll find a variety of sauce recipes that work well with a soft or smooth/puréed diet. And, of course, old standbys like ketchup, mustard, and barbecue sauce are favorites with many people.

Choosing Squeeze Bottles

When selecting squeeze bottles, keep the following points in mind:

❑ Use only food-grade plastic bottles such as those intended for ketchup and mustard. You will find these in restaurant supply stores and some grocery stores. Sizes range from two to twelve ounces or even larger. Choose the bottle size based on the type of sauce you intend to store. For instance, if you make a sweet and vinegary sauce, which can keep fresh for several weeks, you can prepare a larger amount, which will necessitate a larger bottle. If you make a sauce that will stay fresh for only a few days, you'll probably prepare a smaller amount and need a smaller bottle.

❑ To save money, wash and reuse the squeeze bottles in which you purchased ketchup, mustard, and other condiments.

Using Squeeze Bottles

When using squeeze bottles to dispense gravies, sauces, and condiments, follow the instructions below for the best results.

❑ Fill the bottle at least half full with the sauce of your choice. If less liquid is used, it may be difficult to dispense.

❑ To make the presentation as decorative as possible, squirt some of the sauce over the plate before adding the food. Then squirt more sauce over the food to moisten it and make it attractive and flavorful.

❑ If the sauce can be used for several days or weeks, label the bottle, including the date prepared, and place it in the refrigerator. Cap it to maintain freshness, and shake the bottle well before using.

SLOW COOKERS

The tools discussed earlier in this chapter are intended to help you mechanically soften foods or present them in a more appetizing manner; they do not cook foods. But as the name implies, the slow cooker, or crockpot, is different. It does take foods from raw to cooked. Why has it been included in this chapter? Because, especially if you need easy-to-chew foods, this appliance can be an important ally in your kitchen.

The slow cooker is actually an electric "casserole" that cooks food through low, steady heat. Because this appliance remains covered during the entire cooking time, steam does not escape, which causes the food to become very tender and exceptionally moist. That's what makes the slow cooker perfect for soft and smooth cooking. When meat is cooked in this device, it becomes so tender that it can be easily shredded with a fork, and the ample juices that are produced are wonderful for moistening puréed meats.

In Part Two, you'll find a number of recipes that utilize the slow cooker to make flavorful soft and smooth foods. The following information will guide you in choosing a crockpot and in making the best use of it when you prepare your own favorite recipes.

Choosing a Slow Cooker

When selecting a slow cooker, keep the following points in mind:

❏ Consider the size you need. Slow cookers typically range in capacity from three to seven quarts, with some smaller versions holding only one and a half to two quarts. Some models even come with interchangeable crocks of different sizes, which greatly increases their versatility. A three-quart crockpot will allow you to make the slow-cooker recipes presented in this book.

❏ Look for a model with a removable liner since it will make the slow cooker easier to clean.

❏ Make sure that the model has both a High and a Low setting. This will enable you to adjust the cooking time as necessary, as some foods can be cooked on either setting. Note that some slow cookers also have a "keep warm" setting.

Using a Slow Cooker

When using slow cookers, follow the instructions below for the best results.

❏ Always thaw frozen meat or poultry before putting it in the slow cooker. Otherwise, the food may not cook in the desired time. Even worse, for several hours, it may remain at a temperature that harbors the growth of bacteria.

❏ Vegetables cook more slowly than meats and poultry in a slow cooker, so place any vegetables at the bottom and around the sides of the crock, as these areas tend to get hotter. Arrange the meat over the vegetables and cover the food with a liquid such as broth, wine, canned tomatoes, or barbecue sauce.

❏ To promote moist and even cooking, fill the slow cooker half full to two-thirds full.

❏ For maximum tenderness, cook meats on Low for eight to ten hours, or on High for four to five hours. Tough cuts of meat, such as brisket and chuck, are best suited to slow cooking at lower settings.

❏ Brown ground meats—used in chili or Sloppy Joes—before placing them in the slow cooker. If the meat is not first browned in a skillet, it will not separate into crumbles. It also will remain unappealingly pale in color.

❏ Do not lift the lid during cooking. By keeping the lid closed, you will help insure that the food cooks in the stated time. Remember that every time you lift the lid, the temperature in the cooker drops rapidly.

❏ If you are not at home during the entire cooking process, and you return to find that the power went off during your absence, discard the food to avoid the risk of bacterial growth.

Having the proper equipment and tools on hand is key to preparing quick, easy, and attractive meals. If you need further information before purchasing a kitchen appliance or tool, we suggest perusing product reviews published by groups such as Consumer Reports. These reviews compare the cost and performance of a wide range of products, and provide frequent updates to evaluate the latest goods to enter the marketplace. You can also check out Internet cooking and shopping sites to compare products and evaluate their features and prices.

5. CONVERTING FAVORITE RECIPES TO A PURÉED TEXTURE

Earlier in the book, you learned that some conditions make it necessary to follow a puréed diet—a diet of foods that have a smooth consistency, similar to that of mashed potatoes or pudding. Part Two of *Soft Foods* offers a variety of recipes for dishes that are perfect for a puréed meal plan, but if you know a few tricks of the trade, you can also convert many of your favorite foods to a puréed texture. This chapter will show you how. In the first part of the chapter, we offer general tips for puréeing foods. We then show you how to convert specific types of food into puréed dishes while boosting taste and maintaining all-important eye appeal.

GENERAL CONSIDERATIONS

Many of your favorite foods can simply be swirled in a blender or food processor with a little liquid to convert them to a purée. On the other hand, this practice can have some surprisingly bad results! The most obvious problem is that puréeing robs food of the texture and appearance to which you are accustomed. Puréeing a mixture of foods—like those found in casseroles, soups, and many other dishes—can also result in a very unappetizing color. Some people find this so disturbing, in fact, that they lose their appetite

at the sight of the dish. They may begin to lose weight involuntarily, which can be a blessing for some, but a serious health hazard for others.

Fortunately, some simple tips can help you maintain appetizing colors and even appealing shapes when blending foods, allowing you to enjoy familiar dishes. The following guidelines will help you take family and personal favorites and transform them into dishes that have not only an easy-to-chew-and-swallow texture, but also an appealing color, shape, and flavor.

Achieving Appropriate Texture

If you are following a puréed diet, you may think that the foods you have eaten in the past are now off-limits. The truth is that the texture of nearly any dish can easily be changed with a food processor or blender, and many foods can be successfully puréed—although not made *completely* smooth—with a potato masher, ricer, or food mill.

Although a blender is usually the best tool for puréeing soups, smoothies, and other foods that have a high liquid content, when puréeing thicker foods such as meats and stews, you will have to use a food processor. (To read more about these and other kitchen tools, see Chapter 4.) Unless a dish already contains a good deal of liquid, you will probably have to thin it with added liquid to achieve a smooth texture. To create a tastier and more nutritious purée, use a flavored ingredient with nutritional value, such as milk, yogurt, fruit juice, vegetable juice, gravy, or cheese sauce. Add just enough liquid so that the food can be processed until smooth. At that point, you may have to thicken it to improve consistency and appearance. This can be accomplished by mixing in a bit of instant potato flakes, crustless bread, or a commercial thickening agent. (For listings of commercial thickeners, see page 287 of the "Products" section.) Puréed foods should have the consistency of pudding or mashed potatoes.

It can be difficult to achieve a smooth texture when puréeing coarse or stringy foods. When preparing dishes that include stringy vegetables, such as celery and onions, and foods with coarse hulls, such as corn and peas, you may have to strain the foods to attain a smooth consistency. Seeds, nuts (except softened nut butters and nut flours), and coarse grains should be avoided entirely.

When puréeing sticky foods, such as peanut butter and other nut butters, blend them with softer, smoother foods to create a velvety, easy-to-swallow texture. The addition of bananas results in a smooth and tasty sandwich spread that is not at all sticky. Nut butters can also be included in puréed mixtures like mousses, puddings, and even smoothies, where they add flavor and nutrients.

When preparing rice, be sure to overcook it, adding extra water or broth as needed for a softer result. Then blend the cooked rice with a bit of liquid such as sauce or soup so that it can be puréed to a smooth consistency. Alternatively, you can substitute store-bought Cream of Rice cereal for the rice, or replace it with Hot Brown Rice Cereal. (See the "For a Change" suggestions under the Hot Barley Cereal recipe on page 138.) If cornbread is on the menu,

soak the bread in a little milk or buttermilk. This will make the bread soft, smooth, and cohesive without the use of a food processor or blender. For a similar taste, replace the cornbread with soft polenta, yellow corn grits, or Stovetop Spoon Bread (page 184).

Avoiding Unappetizing Colors

When puréeing foods with mixed textures, like soups and casseroles, keep in mind that you are blending all of the colors in the foods you combine. What was once a collage of color may turn into a brown soupy mush if you don't plan ahead. Try to think like an artist. Artists know that when you mix opposite colors such as red and green, blue and orange, or yellow and purple, you get brown. While tomato juice with flecks of green herbs such as parsley looks great when lightly blended, it may look brownish when blended until smooth. Fresh herbs, while enhancing taste, can turn a dish into a strange greenish color if used in excess. Here are some tips for avoiding color disasters when puréeing:

❏ When blending tomato-based dishes, try using dried herbs instead of fresh, as you will then be able to add a smaller amount. (Typically, you need only about a third as much dried herb as fresh.) If you can tolerate some texture, another option is to stir in some finely chopped fresh herbs *after* the dish has been blended. When making tomato-based dishes, use ingredients such as red bell peppers, onions, and garlic. These foods will add flavor without altering color. (Fragments of onion and garlic may have to be strained out of the processed mixture.)

❏ When making smoothies, avoid combining fruits with opposite colors such as blueberries and peaches—unless you use so much of one fruit that it overpowers the color of the other.

❏ When preparing vegetable soups, avoid blending veggies of opposite colors. For instance, do not add green beans or peas to a tomato-based soup, as this will result in a brown color when processed. The best bets are single-vegetable soups such as pumpkin, broccoli, tomato, or beet soup.

Creating Appetizing Shapes

A plate containing three piles or blobs of puréed food is not likely to stimulate anyone's appetite. Instead, try to create appealing shapes when serving puréed dishes. You can, for instance, cook the dish in ramekins or custard cups, pipe the food through pastry bags or cookie presses, form neat balls of purée with an ice cream scooper, or layer or swirl foods that have been puréed separately. When puréeing pasta, you can even use a potato ricer to give the food a pasta-like shape.

If you really want to make your puréed dishes look more familiar, you can buy ready-to-heat puréed foods in molds that resemble their original form, such as chicken or pork chops. (See page 286 of the "Products" section.) After you've eaten the purée, some of these molds can be refilled with your own foods. Just be sure to use a commercial thickener that is specifically designed for shaping food (see page 287), and to follow the manufacturer's directions for mixing, baking, and unmolding.

Enhancing Flavor

Flavor enhancement is the true secret of transforming "purée" into "gourmet." Make the most of seasonings and sauces. You can enhance the flavor of a dish while cooking the food prior to puréeing, or you can add savory sauces, spices, and herbs during the puréeing process. You can also pour a tasty sauce over the puréed food, or dispense it from a handy squeeze bottle to add an artistic drizzle of flavor. Either method will serve the dual purpose of flavoring the dish and making it look more appetizing. Use your own favorite condiment or turn to Part Two to find a wealth of recipes for simple and satisfying sauces. (See page 163.)

GETTING DOWN TO SPECIFICS

Each individual ingredient and dish presents a unique challenge when foods have to be puréed to a smooth consistency. Here are some ideas for making the most of your favorite dishes.

Puréeing Soups

One of the easiest dishes to convert to a puréed texture is soup. Vegetable soups and other soups with mixed textures need to be swirled in a blender for a very smooth texture, or puréed with an immersion (hand-held) blender for a coarser texture. Remember to keep color in mind, since dishes containing multi-colored ingredients may end up an unappetizing brown when puréed. (For more on this, see page 74.) Foods made with just one kind of vegetable, such as tomatoes, look very appealing when puréed, as do soups made with vegetables of similar colors, such as asparagus and leeks. Part Two of *Soft Foods* presents some delicious soup recipes, but you can make your own favorite soups smooth and easy to swallow by following the directions below. Keep in mind that these directions work equally well with prepared soups purchased at your favorite supermarket, deli, or restaurant.

If making homemade soup, begin by preparing the soup according to your recipe. If the dish contains rice, pasta, or firm foods such as string beans, cook it until these ingredients are very soft, adding extra liquid as necessary. This will help insure that the soup has a smooth texture when blended. Then follow these directions:

1. Blend the soup until it is smooth by inserting a hand-held blender into the pot, or by placing the soup in a

standing blender. If using a blender to purée a hot soup, cover the appliance with a kitchen towel so that you will be protected from splatters if the steam forces the top off. Never fill a blender more than half full with a hot liquid.

2. If you need a very smooth consistency, and your soup contains ingredients such as corn, onion, peas, and celery—foods that are tough or stringy—pour the blended soup through a wire strainer to filter out any stringy pieces. This will allow you to obtain the texture you need.

3. If necessary, thicken the soup to the consistency advised by your doctor. Generally, creamed soups and soups that include potatoes, noodles, or other pasta do not need thickening. If your soup does have to be thickened, you can add a commercial thickener, potato flakes, or a mixture of flour, arrowroot, or cornstarch and water. (For complete details on thickening soups, see page 87 of Chapter 6.)

4. If necessary, reheat the soup to the proper temperature or chill it before serving.

Puréeing Breads and Other Baked Goods

Breads and other baked goods such as cakes and muffins pose a special problem for people with swallowing difficulties because they can form a dry, dense bolus (round mass) in the mouth, which can cause choking. Crumbly breads, too, can get caught in airways because they can't be formed into a cohesive, easy-to-swallow mass. For this reason, you will need to moisten and soften breads before eating them. You may already be accustomed to eating bread or biscuits with gravy, crumbling cornbread or crackers into soup, pouring syrup over pancakes, or dunking cookies or muffins into a glass of milk. If so, you know that breads and similar

foods can be delicious and satisfying when softened with liquids.

The secret to making puréed bread is to start with a smooth-textured bread—a bread without grainy pieces, seeds, hulls, nuts, coconut, or dried fruit. You then must remove the crusts and soften the remaining bread with a *slurry*—a moderately thick liquid. Below, you will learn how to make a variety of simple slurries. You will then learn how to use these flavored liquids to transform bread, cake, and even sandwiches into easy-to-swallow foods.

Making a Slurry

Slurries can be made by starting with a variety of common ingredients, and then thinning or thickening them as necessary to achieve the appropriate consistency. You will have to experiment to find the flavors that appeal to you, and then further experiment to learn how to adjust each ingredient to reach the right texture. Ideally, the slurry should be a moderately thick sauce that will thoroughly moisten the bread without making it soggy.

Thick sauces and other liquids can be easily modified for use as slurries. Gravy, cheese sauce, mayonnaise thinned with a little water, honey thinned with a little water or fruit juice, and thinned honey butter are examples of simple thick liquids that can be used to soften bread. Another option is to thin solid chocolate or cheese by melting the ingredient and blending it with equal parts of milk or cream. You can then either dip your bread or cake in the fondue-type sauce, or pour the sauce over the bread or cake. Just make sure that your slurry is thin enough to soak the bread, and thick enough so that it won't turn the bread into mush. Also consider the flavor of the sauce. For instance, although barbecue sauce may be the right consistency for a slurry, you would probably find the taste overwhelming on bread.

Thinner ingredients can also make good slurries, although they generally have to be modified through use of a commercial thickener. Following the package directions, you will sprinkle the commercial thickener over a hot or cold flavored liquid such as juice or milk. Allow the thickener to dissolve; then blend with a wire whisk or spoon until smooth. Depending on the product, you may have to let the mixture stand for about fifteen minutes before pouring it on the baked goods. If the thickener instructions provide specific directions for achieving different consistencies, use the guidelines for making nectar-thick liquids. Keep in mind that your favorite slurries can be transferred to a squeeze bottle and stored in the refrigerator for several days. This will enable you to soften and flavor breads whenever you desire, with minimum fuss.

You can also thicken a thin liquid by combining it with unflavored gelatin. Depending on the desired consistency, simply sprinkle 1 to 2 teaspoons of unflavored gelatin over 2 tablespoons of a cold liquid, and allow it to soften for a couple of minutes. Then add $\frac{1}{4}$ cup of boiling hot liquid, such as broth or juice; stir until the gelatin is dissolved; and mix in a small amount of flavoring if desired. You will need about $\frac{1}{4}$ cup of slurry for 1 slice of bread, but this recipe can be easily doubled and tripled as desired. Place the gelled bread in the refrigerator until it has set. Be aware that the gelatin-thickened slurry should be used only for dishes that are served cold, since the gelatin will liquefy if heated.

Through trial and error, you will find the type of slurry that is most appealing to you. Many people, for instance, prefer the results achieved with naturally thick ingredients, while others like the flexibility provided by thickeners, which allow you to use a wide range of liquids.

Making Slurried Bread or Cake

Once you have prepared your slurry, you will be ready to use it in the preparation of puréed bread or cake. You have already learned that it is important to choose smooth-textured baked goods—bread that has no grainy pieces, seeds, chocolate chips, dried fruit, etc.—and to remove and discard any crusts unless they are very soft. Then just follow the simple directions below:

1. Arrange the crustless bread or cake on a plate. If you are using biscuits or muffins that have a soft crust, cut the baked goods in half horizontally and place them crust-side-down. This will insure that the food becomes thoroughly moistened.

2. Pour 2 tablespoons to $\frac{1}{4}$ cup of your slurry over each slice of bread or cake, and allow the liquid to soak through and completely soften the bread until it has the consistency of a purée. This should take about 10 minutes, depending on the texture of the baked goods. Eat with a spoon or fork.

Making Slurried or Gelled Bread Sandwiches

When people are told that they have to follow a puréed diet, they usually assume that sandwiches will no longer have a place in their life. The fact is, though, that by pairing slurried bread with a puréed filling, you can make a dish that is easy to swallow and has much of the appeal of a regular sandwich. The directions below will guide you in making both layered (closed) and open-faced sandwiches.

MAKING LAYERED SANDWICHES

1. For each sandwich you are preparing, arrange 2 slices of crustless bread in a baking dish or pan—any container that can hold the liquid.

2. Using 2 tablespoons to $\frac{1}{4}$ cup of slurry or gelatin mixture per slice of bread, pour your liquid of choice over both slices.

3. Allow the bread to sit until it is thoroughly soaked—for about 10 minutes, depending on the texture of the bread. If using the gelatin method, place

the pan in the refrigerator for 30 minutes to an hour, or until the liquid has gelled.

4. Place your sandwich filling of choice in a food processor and add a small amount of flavored slurry or other sauce. Process until smooth, adding more liquid as necessary to make the filling spreadable. If the filling is too liquidy, add thickener just until the filling is moist and easy to spread. If desired, add lettuce and tomato to the filling while puréeing. Another option is to purée and thicken each ingredient separately so that the finished filling will have familiar layers. Note, though, that it can be tricky to get a desirable result with puréed, thickened lettuce and tomato.

5. For each sandwich, carefully spread your filling on 1 slice of the slurried or gelled bread, being careful not to disturb the shape of the bread. Alternatively, place the spread in a pastry bag and pipe the filling onto the bread. Next, use a spatula to flip the other slice of slurried bread on top of the filling. Eat the sandwich with a spoon or fork.

MAKING OPEN-FACED SANDWICHES

1. For each sandwich you are preparing, pour enough flavored slurry or gelatin mixture into a plate or shallow bowl to saturate the bread—about 2 tablespoons to $\frac{1}{4}$ cup per slice. Set aside.

2. Place your sandwich filling of choice in a food processor and add a small amount of flavored slurry or other sauce. Process until smooth, adding more liquid as necessary to make the filling easily spreadable. If the filling is too liquidy, add thickener just until the mixture is moist and easy to spread.

3. For each sandwich you are making, spread the filling over 1 slice of crustless bread. Then place the bread, filling-side-up, on top of the slurry.

4. Allow the bread to sit for about 15 minutes, or until it is thoroughly soaked. Add more slurry if the

bread still has dry spots. If using the gelatin method, place the dish in the refrigerator for 30 minutes to an hour, or until the liquid has gelled. Eat the sandwich with a spoon or fork.

Puréeing Meats

Meat—and by this we mean all beef, pork, poultry, and fish—poses a challenge to the person on a puréed diet simply because it is difficult to make puréed meat look appetizing. Fortunately, there are many ways to enhance both flavor and appearance so that this important food can be included in a puréed menu.

You'll want to begin by grilling, sautéing, baking, broiling, steaming, microwaving, or boiling your meat. In other words, cook it in whatever way you normally do, but avoid frying, as the crust that forms will make it nearly impossible to create a smooth purée. Oven-fried meats are fine to use as long as the coating does not get too crusty. A good way to prevent this from happening—not only during oven-frying, but also during baking—is to place a water-filled pan in the oven on the rack below the meat. The steam that forms as the meat cooks will discourage the formation of a crust.

Be aware that certain meat dishes are easier to purée than others. For instance, beef, pork, or poultry that has been ground, made into meatloaf or meatballs, and cooked in your favorite sauce is much simpler to purée than a solid unsauced piece of meat or poultry.

Once the beef, pork, poultry, or fish has been cooked, remove and discard any bones, skin, or shells. If you wish to avoid this step, start with a boneless cut of meat or with deboned or shelled seafood. Then cut or tear the food into small chunks or strips before following the directions below.

1. For each individual serving, place the meat in a small food processor along with a small amount of

flavored liquid—about 2 to 3 tablespoons of liquid for every 2 ounces of meat. (This amount of meat is just shy of a half cup.) Some good choices for the liquid include gravy for use with beef, pork, or poultry; tartar or cocktail sauce with fish; or a slurry made with brown sugar or molasses, allspice, and orange juice for ham. Add more liquid as necessary until you get the desired consistency.

2. If the flavored liquid you used was made with thickening agents such as flour, cornstarch, or arrowroot, you may not need to add thickeners. In most cases, though, commercial thickeners, crustless bread, baby cereal, or potato flakes are needed to make the meat hold together as it is swallowed. If using potato flakes or baby cereal, mix it with hot water before adding it to the meat purée. (You'll get the best control if you add the thickener directly through the chute while the food processor is running.) Unflavored gelatin can be used to thicken meat dishes that are to be served cold as an aspic. (See Dilled Chicken Aspic on page 208 and Salmon Mousse on page 221.)

3. Serve by scooping the purée onto a plate, and pour or squirt your choice of sauce over it as desired. Another option is to place the mixture in ramekins or other molds and bake before serving. (If choosing this option, you will have to use a commercial thickener specially made for shaping cooked foods.)

Puréeing Vegetables

If you're like most people, you're already eating some of your vegetables puréed. Mashed white or sweet potatoes, for instance, are a common puréed food. This dish is perfect for a smooth diet as long as no skin is left on the potatoes and the vegetables are made truly smooth in consistency. For variety, you can even serve the potatoes in cooked skins to give them the look of twice-baked potatoes.

If you're preparing watery vegetables, such as spinach, summer squash, or tomatoes, it's generally best to make a soufflé or a creamed dish such as creamed spinach, or to use the vegetables in a soup. If you're using salad vegetables such as lettuce, cucumber, cabbage, and tomatoes, they will probably be most appealing in juice form (whether homemade or store-bought) or in a cold blended soup such as gazpacho. But successful purées can be made with vegetables that are less watery and/or contain some starch. This last group includes acorn squash; butternut squash; broccoli; carrots; cauliflower; lima beans; and white potatoes, sweet potatoes, and other root vegetables. Canned black beans and pinto beans also purée especially well.

Begin by cooking the vegetables as you normally would. Then remove the peel, if any, and cut the vegetables into small pieces before following the guidelines below.

1. Place the cooked vegetables in a food processor and process until smooth.

2. If the vegetables are dry, like potatoes or cauliflower, add broth, milk, lemon juice, cheese sauce, or butter, which will boost both flavor and moistness. If the vegetables are too loose to hold together, like squash or tomatoes, add a thickener such as crustless bread, potato flakes, or cooked potatoes. If using potato flakes—which soak up more liquid than bread or potatoes—make the puréed vegetables hot enough to dissolve the flakes. Add the flakes a little at a time, or you may end up having to add hot water to compensate. Alternatively, mix the flakes with hot water to form thick mashed potatoes, and blend with the vegetables.

3. Serve simply by mounding the vegetable on a plate, scooping with an ice cream scoop, or piping onto the plate with a pastry bag. Another option is to place the mixture in ramekins or other molds and bake before serving. (If choosing this option, you

will have to use a commercial thickener specially made for shaping cooked foods.)

Puréeing Pasta

Pasta can be easily puréed, but to make a pasta dish appetizing, a little care has to be taken. Usually the result is most appealing when each component of the dish—the spaghetti and the sauce, for instance—is puréed separately. When you top the puréed pasta with the sauce, not only will the dish look more familiar, but it will taste more familiar than it would if the pasta and sauce were blended together. You can even approximate the look of conventional lasagna by creating layers of puréed pasta, sauce, and ricotta cheese. If you can tolerate some texture, soft polenta, an Italian-style cornmeal mush, is a delicious alternative to puréed pasta. (See the recipe for Polenta Parmesan on page 249.) If convenience is a high priority, you might want to try instant puréed pasta, which is available as a powder that you mix with water. (See page 286 of the "Products" section.)

For best results when puréeing pasta, start with orzo or angel hair, as the ample surface area of these products will enable the pasta to soak up a good deal of water during cooking. Cook the pasta until very soft—overcook it, in other words. If cooked al dente (firm), the pasta may never become completely smooth in texture. Then follow the directions below.

1. For each individual serving, place about a cup of cooked pasta in a small food processor along with a little of the hot cooking liquid—1 or 2 tablespoons to start. Blend until the pasta is smooth but not sticky. As necessary, add more cooking liquid or a small amount of milk, olive oil, or butter to achieve the right texture. If desired, add a little Parmesan cheese to enhance the flavor.

2. Serve the purée in a mound on a plate or bowl, as you would serve mashed potatoes, or force the purée through a ricer to resemble spaghetti. Top with puréed sauce and serve hot.

As an alternative to the method described above, you can grind some orzo pasta in a blender or food processor, and then cook it as you would hot cereal. Here are the basic directions:

1. Place the desired amount of uncooked orzo in a blender or food processor and grind for 30 to 60 seconds, or until the pasta has a texture similar to grits or cornmeal. You will need about $\frac{1}{4}$ cup of ground pasta for a side dish, and about $\frac{1}{2}$ cup for an entrée-size portion.

2. Fill a pot with three times as much water as orzo, and bring to a boil. Whisk the orzo into the boiling water. If desired, add 1 to 2 tablespoons of olive oil or butter to every cup of uncooked orzo. Cover and simmer for about 10 minutes or until the water is absorbed. If you desire a softer texture, use four parts of water to one part orzo and cook for about 15 minutes.

3. If you need a perfectly smooth purée, transfer the cooked pasta to a food processor and process until smooth, adding more liquid if needed. Serve by scooping the purée into a bowl and topping it with the puréed sauce of your choice, olive oil, trans-free margarine, or butter.

Puréeing Grains

People on puréed diets cannot eat grains in their whole kernel form. However, whole grains such as barley, brown rice, and wheat berries can be ground to a texture similar to grits or cornmeal, and cooked into a hot cereal or side dish. Here are the basic directions:

1. Place the desired amount of uncooked grain in a blender or food processor and grind for 30 to 60 seconds, or until it has the texture of grits or cornmeal.

You will need about ¼ cup of ground grain per portion.

2. Fill a pot with four times as much water as grain, and bring to a boil. Whisk the grain into the water, cover, and simmer for about 20 minutes, or until the water is absorbed and the grain is soft. For hot cereal, you can substitute milk for half of the water. For a savory side dish, use broth instead of water.

3. If you need a perfectly smooth purée, transfer the cooked grain to a food processor and process until smooth, adding more liquid if needed. If making hot cereal, serve in a bowl and top with trans-free margarine, butter, sweetener, or puréed fruit. For a side dish, serve on a plate or a bowl as you would mashed potatoes, and top with trans-free margarine, butter, or the puréed sauce of your choice.

Puréeing Fruit

It is easy to incorporate fruits into a puréed diet. You are not doomed to eat applesauce every day, although an increasing variety of applesauce flavors is now available in grocery stores. As you will learn in Part Two, you can include fruits in smoothies, soups, breakfast dishes, and desserts. You can also purée your favorite fruit and use it as a deliciously smooth sauce on meat, poultry, pancakes, and waffles. Alternatively, you can take that same purée and use it to replace part of the liquid in your favorite fruit-flavored gelatin mix, or blend it with plain unflavored gelatin. (See the recipe for Fabulous Fruit Gelatin on page 264.)

Some fruits need to be cooked before puréeing, and some don't. If you are using fresh peaches or apricots, and they are very soft and ripe, simply peel the fruit and remove the stem and pit. You do not have to cook the flesh. If you are using semisoft fruits such as berries, you can cook them or use them raw, as you wish. If you are using firm fruits like apples and pears,

you will need to remove the peel and seeds and cook the fruit until it is very soft. Once the food has been prepped, follow the guidelines below to create a purée.

1. Place the fruit in a food processor and process until smooth. Because fruits contain a good deal of water, most purées don't need added liquid, but if necessary, pour in a little juice or water. If, on the other hand, the purée is too loose to hold together, add a little commercial thickener as needed until you reach the desired consistency.

2. If some fibrous bits or seeds remain in the purée, push the fruit through a strainer to sieve out any lumps.

3. If desired, add some sugar or other sweetener and a splash of lemon juice to the purée to bring out the flavor of the fruit.

4. If the purée is thin, use it as a sauce to drizzle over ice cream or moisten foods like pound cake, crepes, pancakes, or meat. Otherwise, spoon the purée into a custard cup, a small wine glass, or a pretty cordial glass, and serve at room temperature or chilled.

Puréeing Desserts

Many desserts—puddings, custards, ice cream, sherbets, mousses, fruit soups, smoothies, and milk shakes—are perfect for the puréed diet without alteration. Just keep in mind that foods like ice cream, sherbet, and flavored gelatin, all of which melt into thin liquids in your mouth, should not be used if you require thickened liquids.

As you already know from reading the section on breads, plain cakes—those without nuts, chips, or pieces of dried fruit—can easily be made soft and smooth by following the technique used to purée bread. (See page 76.) Of course, you'll want to soften the cake with a liquid that is appropriate for desserts. A sweet slurry, thin custard, milk, or cream would work well.

If you love cookies, you'll be happy to learn that it is easy to soften most plain cookies simply by dipping them into milk or hot cocoa. As you might expect, though, cookies that contain nuts, chips, or pieces of dried fruit should be avoided.

Unfortunately, other than cream and custard varieties, pies are generally not smooth enough for the puréed diet. Pie fillings, however, can easily be puréed and served in ramekins or custard cups.

Puréeing a Full Meal

Part Two of this book offers recipes specifically designed to meet the needs of someone on a soft and smooth diet. But sometimes you may want to take part in your family's meal and eat the same foods that they are enjoying. In this case, you can prepare each dish as usual and then purée it individually in a food processor, adding just enough broth, sauce, or other liquid to create a smooth consistency. As this will be time-consuming, you may want to take some shortcuts by combining certain foods. For instance, you might choose to purée potatoes and meats together. Just be sure to keep the foods' colors and flavors in mind as you do so. This will prevent you from ending up with a brown, unidentifiable mush on your plate. You can also layer purées to make the foods more interesting and appealing.

Whether you intend to purée your family's conventional dishes or to create special puréed meals, you must discuss your dietary needs with your doctor, dentist, dietitian, or speech therapist. This step is necessary if you are to make the best food choices for your health.

6. THICKENING LIQUIDS

In Chapter 1, you learned that swallowing is a complex action which involves many muscles of the mouth, throat, and esophagus. When the timing of these muscles is perfect, all of the food and liquid moves from the mouth to the esophagus and, finally, to the stomach. Sometimes, though, illness, injury, disorders of the nervous system, or muscle weakness can interfere with the normal function of these muscles. The result is *dysphagia,* or difficulty in swallowing.

Dysphagia not only makes eating and drinking difficult, but also poses a very real threat to your health. When your swallow malfunctions and fails to close your airway when you eat or drink, small amounts of food or liquid can enter your airway—a process known as *aspiration.* This can put you at risk for aspiration pneumonia.

Thickened liquids can reduce your risk of aspiration. A thicker consistency makes liquids easier to control in the mouth, and allows them to go down your throat a little more slowly so that your airway has time to close.

Part Two of this book presents a wealth of recipes for beverages, soups, and sauces. Although all of these foods were designed for easy swallowing, people who need thickened liquid may have to adjust the consistency of these dishes to meet their special needs. That's what this chapter is all about. You will first learn about different levels of thickness so that you will more completely understand the level you want to achieve. You will then learn about the commercial thickeners designed specifically for people with swallowing difficulties. Finally, you will discover tricks of the trade for modifying the thickness of not only the recipes offered in this book, but all your favorite beverages, soups, and sauces.

THE DIFFERENT LEVELS OF LIQUID THICKNESS

Speech therapists and doctors who treat swallowing difficulties generally categorize liquids into four categories of thickness, as follows:

❏ **Thin liquids,** which have the consistency of water, include water, juice, milk, coffee, tea, carbonated drinks, and broth, as well as melted ice cream, sherbet, sorbet, frozen yogurt, and Jell-O flavored gelatin. Even though ice cream, frozen yogurt, sherbet, sorbet, and flavored gelatin are thick when you take them out of the freezer or refrigerator, once they are warmed in your mouth, they become thin liquids. For this reason, they are not appropriate for someone who needs thickened liquids.

❑ **Nectar-thick liquids** have the slightly thicker consistency of fruit nectar. Most speech therapists include the following liquids in this category: Fruit nectars, tomato juice, V8 vegetable juice, eggnog, most buttermilk, creamed soups, and nutritional supplements such as Ensure shakes. People who can drink only nectar-thick liquids must modify any thinner liquids with a common household or commercial thickener.

The Importance of Staying Hydrated

Because some people dislike the feel and taste of thickened liquids, they avoid drinking them. Unfortunately, this puts them at risk for dehydration, a condition in which there is too little water in the body. It is believed that a large segment of the population is at least *mildly* dehydrated at times, probably from an insufficient intake of water. But when an individual refuses liquids for a long period of time, as can happen when fluids must be thickened, dehydration can become quite severe, and even life-threatening.

Why is dehydration so dangerous? The human body is estimated to be 60 to 70 percent water. Water is needed for all body functions, from the regulation of body temperature to the transportation of oxygen and nutrients to cells and organs. Water also removes waste from the body and protects your joints and organs. When you become mildly dehydrated, you may experience chronic pain in muscles and joints, headache, lower back pain, dry mouth, fatigue or weakness, and constipation. Your urine may have a yellow or amber color and a strong odor due to insufficient water. Thirst, of course, is also a sign of dehydration, but your body may need water long before you feel thirsty. When dehydration worsens, the electrolytes in your blood, such as sodium and potassium, become too concentrated. Because electrolytes must be within normal concentrations for body functions to occur properly, more severe problems develop, including increased heart rate and respiration, high body temperature, decreased sweating and urination, extreme fatigue, muscle cramps, and tingling of the limbs. If dehydration reaches 10-percent fluid loss, the results can be fatal.

Most people require about a half ounce of water per every pound of body weight. If you divide the total number of ounces by 8, you will know how many cups of liquid you have to consume each day. For example, a 160-pound person would have to take in about 80 ounces of liquid, or about 10 cups per day. Realize that this is only a general rule and that you must follow the guidelines set by your health care provider, as the need for fluids can be affected by many factors.

You can meet some of your fluid requirements by eating plenty of semisolid foods that naturally contain a lot of water. Puréed or soft fruits, vegetables, puddings, custards, and soups can all help you keep hydrated. Even meat contains a significant amount of water, especially when it is puréed with fluids. Nevertheless, it is important to drink fluids. If you are on thickened liquids, your health care provider should monitor you closely to make sure that that your body is getting the water it needs to function properly.

❏ **Honey-thick liquids** are so-called because they have the consistency of honey. Since no beverages naturally have this consistency, people who need honey-thick liquids must modify their drinks with a commercial thickener. They can also get some of their fluids from pudding-thick foods, which are generally more appetizing than honey-thick liquids. (In most cases, it is safe to drink liquids that are *thicker* than the prescribed consistency.)

❏ **Pudding-thick liquids,** which are also referred to as *spoon-thick liquids,* are so thick that they must be eaten with a spoon. As the name indicates, most puddings fit into this category. Most puréed foods are included in this group, as well. Although people typically don't think of a pudding as a liquid, it actually contains a great deal of water and, if consumed in sufficient quantities, can provide all of the fluid that you need. Since many people find it difficult to remain hydrated on a thickened-liquid diet, pudding-thick liquids are a valuable food because of their high water content. (See the inset "The Importance of Staying Hydrated" on page 84.)

Your doctor or speech therapist will tell you the level of thickness you need to make swallowing safe, advise you on the specific liquids that are right for you, and explain how you can check for appropriate consistency. Generally, you can determine liquid consistency by pouring the substance slowly from a spoon. If it pours like honey, for instance, it has a honey-thick consistency. Through time and experience, you will develop a knack for accurately judging if a food has the level of thickness that has been prescribed for you.

MAKING THICKENED LIQUIDS

As you learned on page 84, if your doctor or speech therapist has advised you to drink nectar-thick liq-uids, you'll find that a variety of beverages already have that consistency, including fruit nectars, some tomato juice, V8 vegetable juice, some buttermilk, some nutritional supplements, and more. Milk shakes and smoothies can be consumed only if they have been thickened with fruit, regular yogurt, pudding, or thickened ice, rather than ice cream, frozen yogurt, or ice. Because ice and frozen desserts melt, they will dilute the beverage to a thinner consistency. (You will learn more about smoothies and milk shakes on page 87.)

If you wish to drink liquids other than those that are naturally nectar-thick, or if your doctor has said that you need a thicker consistency than nectar, you can buy special pre-thickened liquids, as well as mixes for making thickened beverages such as coffee. (See page 287 of the "Products" tables.) You can also thicken your beverages of choice, as well as soups and other foods, so that they meet your needs. In Chapter 3, you learned about some of the common household thickeners, such as flour and cornstarch, that you can use to thicken hot soups, gravies, and sauces. In the remainder of this chapter, you will learn about the two categories of commercial thickeners available, and you will discover how to use both commercial and household thickeners to adjust the consistency of foods.

Choosing Commercial Thickeners

Commercial thickeners are of two types: Starch-based and gel-based. These products change the consistency of a liquid, usually without changing its flavor. However, you will discover that some perform better than others.

Starch-based thickeners come in powder form and are generally made from cornstarch, although they can also contain wheat, tapioca, potato, rice, and other starches. They are sold in both pre-measured packets and larger cans, and the packets are available to create both nectar- and honey-thick consistencies. (The envelopes designed to yield a thicker liquid contain a greater amount of the product.)

If you are gluten intolerant or have problems with wheat or other grains, you'll want to check the label on your starch-based thickener carefully. Some product labels specifically state that they are gluten-free.

Most starch-based thickeners work equally well in hot and cold liquids. (Check the manufacturer's directions to be sure.) However, these products are not effective in carbonated beverages. Also be aware that with some starch thickeners, you will have to wait about five minutes after mixing for the liquid to thicken. Some starch-thickened liquids will continue to thicken over time, too, so it is generally best to consume the beverage within fifteen to twenty minutes of preparation. Finally, some starch-based products will turn a glass of plain water cloudy, and can change the taste of the water as well.

Gel-based thickeners usually rely on the thickening powers of xanthan gum, a soluble fiber. Like starch-based thickeners, these products come in powder form and are available both in bulk and in pre-measured packets designed for different consistencies.

Because soluble fiber slows digestion, gel-based thickeners may help stabilize blood sugar levels, which can benefit people with diabetes. These thickeners may also help to lower cholesterol, as soluble fiber binds with bile acids in the intestines, reducing the body's production of cholesterol. However, a caveat is in order. Because some fluid will remain in the intestines bound to the product's xanthan gum, it is particularly important to drink adequate fluids when you are using gel-based products. Additionally, if you are not accustomed to eating much soluble fiber, you may experience some gastrointestinal discomfort when you first begin to use gel thickeners.

Gel thickeners are more costly than starch thickeners, but have certain advantages. They thicken all liquids (including carbonated beverages) equally well; work immediately, rather than over a period of several minutes; and do not continue to thicken beverages as they stand. A gel thickener also leaves beverages clear and does not affect taste, making it an ideal thickener for water. You can even use this product to thicken ice so that when the ice is used to cool your drink, it will not thin the beverage as it melts.

You will probably be able to find some brands of commercial thickeners at your local drugstore. You can also order these products directly from their manufacturers and suppliers. (See page 287 of the "Products" tables for a list of thickeners and their sources.)

Thickening Beverages

Household thickeners like flour and cornstarch require a period of cooking to work. For that reason, commercial thickeners are needed when you want to change the consistency of a beverage.

When using a commercial thickener, it is important to follow the directions on the product's package. In addition, for best results, you will want to keep the following information in mind.

Starch-based thickeners can clump if they are not correctly mixed into your beverage. These thickeners usually work best if you slowly add them to the beverage while stirring with a spoon until the product is dissolved. A small whisk or hand-held blender also works well.

Once the starch-based thickener has dissolved in the liquid, wait about five minutes, or the amount of time stated on the package, before you check the product's consistency. If necessary, add a little more of the product to make the liquid thicker, or add a little more liquid to make it thinner. Some experimentation may be needed to get the exact consistency you want, but if you add too much starch-based thickener too soon, you could end up with a glass full of pudding-thick liquid. As explained earlier, some starch-thickened liquids will continue to thicken over time, so it is generally best to consume the beverage within fifteen to twenty minutes after preparing it.

To use a gel-based thickener, add the directed amount to your beverage. A spoon will not blend the gel into a liquid effectively. If you're thickening a cold noncarbonated liquid, either shake the mixture in a covered container for five to ten seconds, or blend the product into the liquid using a whisk or fork. If you're adding the gel product to a hot liquid or a carbonated beverage, you should not use the shaker method. Instead, use a whisk or fork. If you are thickening a beverage made with a powder that's added to water, such as a hot chocolate mix, thicken the water *before* you add the mix. Once the thickener has been combined with the water, you can stir in the mix.

Making Ice Cream-Thickened and Iced Beverages

As mentioned earlier, milk shakes, smoothies, and other beverages blended with ice, ice cream, or frozen yogurt present a special challenge for the individual on a thickened-liquids diet. The drink may appear quite thick when it is prepared, but once it is warmed in your mouth, it will melt to a thinner consistency. That is why ice cream and other frozen treats are listed in the "thin liquids" category on page 83, and—along with ice—must be avoided if you require thickened liquids.

Fortunately, there are ways to enjoy some of your favorite "iced" beverages. If you love milk shakes, you can use a specially formulated ice cream that melts to a pudding-like consistency. (See page 287 of the "Products" tables.) Thicken the beverage as needed; then add the ice cream product. As the ice cream melts, the beverage will remain safe to drink.

If you like drinks that have been blended with ice, you can make thickened ice cubes. Simply thicken water to the desired consistency and freeze it in ice cube trays. (Use gel-based thickeners for best results.) Store the frozen cubes in a marked plastic container or freezer-safe zip-lock bag so that they will always be ready for use. Add the thickened ice to your pre-thickened beverages, along with fruit and yogurt as desired, and blend until smooth. Or simply drop the ice cubes into your thickened beverages as a means of keeping them chilled during the warm summer months. Whether blended or left whole, this ice will not change the consistency of your drink as it melts.

Thickening Soups and Sauces

Like beverages, soups and sauces can be thickened with the commercial products already discussed. Since your homemade dishes, as well as commercial thickeners, are variable in consistency, you will want to follow the manufacturer's directions.

Because soups and sauces often contain foods that have thickening properties, you can also adjust their thickness by altering the recipe. Simply reduce the amount of water, broth, or milk used, or increase the amount of potatoes, potato flakes, vegetables, or fruits that are puréed into the dish. By changing the proportions of liquids and solids, you will end up with a thicker dish.

It is also easy to modify the consistency of soups and sauces by using household thickeners such as flour, cornstarch, and arrowroot. Once the soup or sauce has been prepared and blended to a smooth consistency, you simply dissolve the flour, cornstarch, or arrowroot in a small amount of cold liquid. Stir the mixture until smooth and then add it to the soup or sauce while stirring. As the dish simmers, it will thicken. (For more pointers on using these starches, see the inset "Tips for Using Common Household Thickeners" on page 88.)

How much starch will you need to thicken your soup or sauce? In general, one tablespoon of flour

Tips for Using Common Household Thickeners

Wheat flour, cornstarch, and arrowroot are familiar thickeners that can effectively change the consistency of cooked foods. The following tips will help you achieve good results when you use these products.

Thickening With Flour

Wheat flour lends a smooth, velvety texture and an opaque quality to the liquids it thickens. For this reason, it is a good thickener for gravies, white sauces, cheese sauces, gumbos, and stews. To use successfully:

❑ Choose either white flour or, for extra fiber and nutrition, whole wheat pastry flour to thicken your foods. Keep in mind that the whole wheat flour will add a brown color, so it is best used in brown sauces and gravies, where the flour will enhance the final appearance.

❑ You can prevent lumps using one of two methods. First, you can make a slurry: Mix one part flour with two parts cold liquid, such as water, broth, or milk, and stir until smooth. Alternatively, you can knead together equal parts of flour and oil, softened butter, or margarine, mixing until the mixture is pasty.

❑ Once your starch mixture is ready, whisk it into the simmering soup or sauce. Continue to simmer, stirring constantly, until the liquid has thickened and has no uncooked starch taste.

❑ If the liquid is not thick enough, prepare and add more of the starch mixture. Be aware that if your dish contains acidic ingredients like fruit juice or tomatoes, or a high proportion of sugar, you may need to increase the amount of thickener.

Thickening With Cornstarch or Arrowroot

Cornstarch and arrowroot give the liquids they thicken a translucent quality and a glossy sheen. While this makes cornstarch and arrowroot common ingredients in fruit sauces and pie fillings, these starches will work in *any* sauce or soup. To use successfully:

❑ To prevent lumps, mix one part cornstarch or arrowroot with one part cold liquid, and stir until smooth.

❑ When the starch mixture is ready, stir it into your soup or sauce. Continue to simmer and stir for about a minute, until the mixture becomes clear and thickened. Cooking too long can cause the starch to break down so that the liquid actually becomes thinner.

❑ If the liquid is not thick enough, prepare and add more of the starch mixture. Be aware that if your dish contains acidic ingredients like fruit juice or tomatoes, or a high proportion of sugar, you may need to increase the amount of thickener.

will thicken a cup of liquid, such as milk or broth, to about the consistency of nectar. Two tablespoons will thicken a cup of liquid to about the consistency of honey. To gauge the amount of starch needed for

your recipe, consider the consistency you are starting with and the consistency you desire. For instance, if you are beginning with celery bisque, your soup may already be nectar-thick. To increase it to honey-thickness, you might try adding about one tablespoon of flour per cup of soup. Keep in mind that cornstarch and arrowroot have about twice the thickening power of flour. In other words, for every tablespoon of flour you would use to thicken a liquid, you would need only a half-tablespoon of cornstarch or arrowroot.

If your soup or sauce must have a pudding-thick consistency, be aware that the amount of household thickener required would create an overwhelmingly starchy taste. In this case, a gel-based commercial thickener would give you better results.

This chapter has explained how virtually any beverage, soup, or sauce can be modified to obtain the consistency you need while retaining the flavor you love. But as you may already know, making food easy to swallow isn't enough. You also want your diet to be healthful—especially if you are recovering from surgery or coping with a health disorder. The next chapter will guide you in creating a diet that is not only easy to swallow, but also high in the nutrients your body requires.

7. Keeping Your Diet Healthy While Meeting Your Special Needs

Eating a healthy diet is important whether you are nine or ninety years of age, and that does not change just because you need an easy-to-chew, soft, or smooth/puréed diet. If you are coping with or recovering from a health disorder, it's more vital than ever to make wise dietary choices, as good nutrition can enhance your body's ability to fight disease and can speed the healing process, as well. Eating smart can also go a long way toward helping you avoid future health problems.

This chapter reviews the elements of a healthy diet and explains how you can modify your food intake to meet your special needs. Whether you need to gain weight, shed unwanted pounds, control blood sugar, or slow the progression of cardiovascular disease, you will learn how—in the context of an easy-to-chew, easy-to-swallow diet—you can improve your overall health by making the best food choices possible.

WHAT IS A HEALTHY DIET?

We live in an age of information overload, and in no area is this more apparent than diet. Books, magazines, professional journals, newsletters, television shows, radio broadcasts, and the Internet present an abundance of conflicting information on what constitutes a healthy diet. Should you eat a high-carb diet or one that's low in carbs? Should you eat meat or become a vegetarian? Are dairy products bad? Are soy products good? Is it best to follow a Mediterranean diet or to stay in the Zone? Conflicting information even overwhelms people in the health profession, so we can readily understand how it confuses the average person. But it's not as difficult to eat wisely as you might think. Basically, a healthy diet is one that:

❏ Has balanced proportions and types of fats, carbohydrates, and proteins to suit your particular needs.

❏ Includes a variety of vegetables, fruits, and whole grains to supply a generous amount of vitamins, minerals, fiber, and *phytonutrients*—health-promoting plant compounds.

❏ Provides enough protein to maintain muscle mass and support the natural processes that keep your body healthy.

❏ Helps you to maintain or gradually approach a healthy weight.

One Size Does Not Fit All

In 1992, the United States Government developed the Food Guide Pyramid, which recommended specific daily servings of each food group. Over time, though, it became apparent that because people come in all shapes and sizes, they need personalized eating plans that point them toward the best foods—and the best amounts—for their height, weight, age, gender, and level of activity. One size simply does not fit all.

To better meet individual needs, the United States Department of Agriculture (USDA) created MyPyramid.gov, an interactive website that helps you make healthful food choices. Once on the site, you can click on "My Pyramid Menu Planner," which will allow you to enter your age, gender, height, weight, and other important facts. You will then be presented with a personalized food plan that suggests a daily calorie level and lists the amounts of each food group you should consume each day, including grains, vegetables, fruits, dairy products, and meats or vegetarian alternatives. The recommendations—which emphasize healthy choices such as lean meats and fish, whole grain breads, and low-fat dairy—are based on the Dietary Guidelines for Americans and closely match the DASH (Dietary Approaches to Stop Hypertension) diet, which has been shown to benefit people with diabetes, high blood pressure, and high cholesterol. This diet is a healthy choice for *all* Americans, actually, because it can help prevent the development of many chronic disorders.

If you don't have access to the Internet, some simple guidelines can enable you to design a healthful diet. Most adults need to eat between 13 and 15 calories per pound to maintain a healthy body weight. If you are under- or overweight, use your goal weight to estimate your calorie needs. Of course, individuals can vary greatly in their requirements, depending on activity level, metabolic rate, and the presence of certain health disorders. The DASH diet, created by the National Heart, Lung, and Blood Institute (NHLBI), provides estimates of daily calorie needs based on a group of factors. See Table 7.1 for these approximations.

The Food Guide Pyramid suggests the daily amount needed of each food group to meet the

TABLE 7.1 APPROXIMATE DAILY CALORIE NEEDS

Gender	Age in Years	Calories Needed for Sedentary Lifestyle	Calories Needed for Moderately Active Lifestyle	Calories Needed for Active Lifestyle
Female	19 to 30	2,000	2,000 to 2,200	2,400
	31 to 50	1,800	2,000	2,200
	51 and over	1,600	1,800	2,000 to 2,200
Male	19 to 30	2,400	2,600 to 2,800	3,000
	31 to 50	2,200	2,400 to 2,600	2,800 to 3,000
	51 and over	2,000	2,000 to 2,400	2,400 to 2,800

TABLE 7.2 RECOMMENDED DAILY FOOD PORTIONS BASED ON CALORIE NEEDS

Daily Calorie Needs	Grains	Vegetables	Fruits	Milk	Meat and Beans	Fats and Oils	Discretionary Calories*
1,600	5 ounces	2 cups	1.5 cups	3 cups	5 ounces	5 teaspoons	132
1,800	6 ounces	2.5 cups	1.5 cups	3 cups	5 ounces	5 teaspoons	195
2,000	6 ounces	2.5 cups	2 cups	3 cups	5.5 ounces	6 teaspoons	267
2,200	7 ounces	3 cups	2 cups	3 cups	6 ounces	6 teaspoons	290
2,400	8 ounces	3 cups	2 cups	3 cups	6.5 ounces	7 teaspoons	362
2,600	9 ounces	3.5 cups	2 cups	3 cups	6.5 ounces	8 teaspoons	410
2,800	10 ounces	3.5 cups	2.5 cups	3 cups	7 ounces	8 teaspoons	426
3,000	10 ounces	4 cups	2.5 cups	3 cups	7 ounces	10 teaspoons	512

* Discretionary calories are those that remain in your daily budget if you select especially low-calorie items in each food group. This discretionary allowance is part of—not in addition to—your daily budget, and may be spent on additional foods from the food groups or on "luxuries" such as desserts.

nutritional requirements of people at each calorie level. Table 7.2 presents these amounts for levels ranging from 1,600 to 3,000 calories per day.

Although the information provided in Table 7.2 is helpful, it is sometimes difficult to translate a recommended amount such as *5 ounces of grains* into measured servings of the foods you actually eat each day. The following guidelines should help:

❑ **Grains.** 1 ounce equals: 1 slice of bread; 1 cup of ready-to-eat cereal; or ½ cup of cooked rice, pasta, or cereal. Choose whole grains and whole grain foods whenever possible.

❑ **Vegetables.** 1 cup equals: 1 cup of raw or cooked vegetables, 1 cup of 100-percent vegetable juice, or 2 cups of raw leafy greens.

❑ **Fruits.** 1 cup equals: 1 cup of fruit, 1 cup of 100-percent fruit juice, or ½ cup of dried fruit.

❑ **Milk and Other Dairy Products.** 1 cup equals: 1 cup of milk or yogurt or 1½ ounces of cheese. Most

of your milk group choices should be fat-free or low-fat. If you don't include dairy products in your diet, you may need to add extra protein as well as calcium supplements.

❑ **Meats and Beans.** 1 ounce equals: 1 ounce of lean meat, poultry, or fish; 1 egg; 1 tablespoon of peanut butter; ¼ cup of cooked dried beans; or ½ ounce of nuts or seeds.

❑ **Fats and Oils.** 1 teaspoon equals: Approximately 1 teaspoon of regular mayonnaise or margarine (or 2 to 3 teaspoons of a light product), or 1 tablespoon of regular salad dressing (or 2 tablespoons of a light product). Emphasize unsaturated fats such as olive oil, canola oil, and soybean oil.

The guidelines provided above are considered appropriate for the majority of adults. If you have health disorders, though, you should always consult your physician or dietitian before changing your diet.

In the remainder of this chapter, you will find basic but important information about the building blocks of nutrition listed above—fats, carbohydrates, proteins, and more. You will then find tips for tailoring your diet to cope with several common disorders, including heart disease, diabetes, and unhealthy weight.

Choosing Healthy Fats

Nearly everyone knows about the health dangers posed by a high-fat diet. What you may not know is that fats—the right fats in the right amounts—are necessary for good health. Fats are the main form in which your body stores energy. Fats are also the chief components of cell membranes, the structures that hold your cells together. But not all fats are equal, and your selection and use of these substances can have a profound effect on your health. For instance, depending on the type chosen, fats can fuel or quench inflammation, make the blood more or less likely to clot, and raise or lower blood cholesterol levels. New research is revealing that fats can even affect mood and the ability to learn. Clearly, the kinds of fat you choose to eat are critical to your well-being. The following discussions will help you tell the good from the bad so that you can make smart dietary choices.

Saturated Fats

Saturated fats are found mainly in animal products such as fatty cuts of beef and pork, and high-fat dairy products like whole milk, butter, cream, full-fat cheese, ice cream, and sour cream. Tropical oils, such as coconut and palm oil, also contain saturated fats. Saturated fat is usually easy to spot because it is solid at room temperature—visualize the strip of fat around a steak, the streak of fat in a slice of bacon, or a solid stick of butter.

You probably already know that there is a strong link between diets high in saturated fat and the risk of heart disease. One reason for this is that saturated fats raise levels of low-density lipoproteins (LDLs), the "bad" blood cholesterol that sets the stage for atherosclerosis (clogged arteries). Meals high in saturated fats can also make blood vessels stiffer, and blood more likely to form dangerous clots.

Considering the dangers posed by saturated fat, it is not surprising that intake should be kept as low as possible. This can be accomplished by choosing lean meats, skinless chicken, and low-fat dairy foods, and by avoiding tropical oils.

Trans Fats

Trans fats, also known as trans-fatty acids, are formed when liquid vegetable oils are hydrogenated to make them more solid. Because hydrogenation makes fats more shelf-stable and improves their baking and cooking qualities, trans fats have long been used in commercial products such as hard margarine, baked items, processed snack foods, and fast foods. Unfortunately, researchers have found that trans fats behave much like saturated fats in the body, but are even worse for your health. Like saturated fats, trans fats raise the level of LDLs, the "bad" cholesterol. In addition, they lower the level of high-density lipoproteins (HDLs), which are thought to carry cholesterol away from the cells for disposal. Diets high in trans fats have also been linked to a greater risk of type 2 diabetes.

Trans fats should be avoided as much as possible. This means eliminating partially hydrogenated vegetable oils, vegetable shortenings, and hard margarines, as well as foods made with these substances. Now that the Nutrition Facts food labels list trans fats, this is relatively easy to do. Because trans fats are widely known to be harmful, you will also find that many commercially prepared foods contain "No

Trans Fats" statements on their packaging. In fact, in recent years, a variety of items have been reformulated to replace trans fats with healthier oils.

Regardless of current trends, trans fats can be found in many foods. Beware of the prepared foods that often contain trans fats: Fast foods such as fried chicken, biscuits, fried fish sandwiches, and fried pie desserts; donuts; muffins; crackers; cookies; cake and cake icing; pies; microwave-popped popcorn; canned biscuits; and instant latte-type coffee beverages. Be vigilant, too, when eating in restaurants. Many restaurants still use hydrogenated fats when preparing French fries and other fried foods. It makes sense to ask which fats are being used.

Monounsaturated Fats

Popularized by the heart-healthy Mediterranean diet, monounsaturated fats have become a staple in many people's diets. Olive oil is the best known source of monounsaturated fats, but you can also find monounsaturates in canola oil, avocados, and most nuts. Why are these fats considered so beneficial? They have been long known to lower LDL cholesterol levels without reducing levels of HDL cholesterol.

While monounsaturated fats are a wholesome choice, keep in mind that they are a concentrated source of calories, with 120 calories per tablespoon. If you need to gain weight, liberal use of olive oil and other healthful oils is a good way to boost the calorie content of your diet. But if you need to lose weight, all fats—even healthy ones—should be used in moderation.

Polyunsaturated Fats

Like monounsaturates, polyunsaturated fats are considered heart-healthy because they can help reduce LDL cholesterol. Liquid vegetable oils and fatty fish are the main dietary sources of polyunsaturated fats.

It is important to understand that two types of polyunsaturated fats, known as *omega-6* and *omega-*

3 fatty acids, are actually essential for life. It is easy to consume plenty of omega-6 fats, since they are abundant in nuts, seeds, and a variety of vegetable oils. However, omega-3 fatty acids can be harder to come by, and many people do not consume adequate amounts. How can you get more omega-3 fats in your diet? Fatty fish—salmon, herring, and trout, for instance—are the best source of some especially potent omega-3 fats known as EPA and DHA. The American Heart Association recommends the consumption of fatty fish at least two times per week, as long as you avoid fish that have high levels of mercury. (See the inset "Is Your Seafood Safe?" on page 96.) Among plant foods, flaxseeds, flaxseed oil, and walnuts are concentrated sources of an essential omega-3 fatty acid known as ALA. Canola oil, walnuts, and soy are also good sources of ALA. Finally, omega-3 fatty acids can be added to the diet through fish oil and DHA/EPA supplements.

The Final Skinny on Fats

If you find all this talk of fats overwhelming, don't worry. You don't have to carry a copy of this book around with you to choose foods that provide healthy fats. If you select lean meats, low-fat dairy foods, and low-mercury fish; use olive oil and canola oil as your primary fats; and avoid processed foods containing trans fats, you will be well on your way to achieving a healthy diet. Chapter 3 provides more information on choosing the best products to achieve this goal.

Choosing Healthy Carbohydrates

Carbohydrates are an important part of a healthy diet. They supply energy for the body and are the chief fuel source for the brain, nervous system, and red blood cells.

Many studies have looked at the health effects of carbohydrates, and it's clear that not all carbohydrates are created equal. When choosing foods, perhaps the most important difference to keep in mind is that some carbs are unrefined and some are refined. *Unrefined carbohydrates*—found in vegetables, fruits, whole grains, and legumes—are rich in disease-fighting vitamins, minerals, phytonutrients, and fiber. *Refined carbohydrates*—present in white flour, white sugar, low-fiber cereals, and processed snack foods—have been stripped of most of their nutritional value. Diets high in refined carbohydrates have been linked to obesity, insulin resistance, cardiovascular disease, cancer, and many other health disorders.

There has been much debate over the years about low-carbohydrate versus high-carbohydrate diets for weight loss, diabetes control, and other health problems. The truth is that the body can adapt to a wide range of carbohydrate levels. The Institute of Medicine, a component of the National Academy of Sciences, suggests that a range of 45 to 65 percent of calories from carbohydrates is acceptable for good health. A minimum of 130 grams of carbohy-

drate per day is considered essential to support proper functioning of the brain. If you decide to follow a very-low-carb diet, do so under a physician's supervision and for a limited period of time. Then add back healthy carbohydrates, particularly vegetables and fruits. Keep in mind that unrefined carbohydrates such as vegetables, fruits, whole grains, and legumes can actually help you lose weight because of their high-fiber content, which makes you feel fuller, longer. Whether or not you are dieting, in most cases, you should choose unrefined carbohydrates as much as possible to promote optimal health. Softened whole grain breads and cereals, stuffings and puddings made with whole grain breads, vegetable and bean purées and soups, and fruit smoothies and sauces are just some of the ways in which you can include healthy carbohydrates in your soft or smooth diet.

Before we leave the subject of carbohydrates, it is worthwhile to focus on the indigestible carbohydrate known as fiber. There are two types of fiber:

Is Your Seafood Safe?

Seafood is a good source of protein and omega-3 fatty acids, but all of it contains at least trace amounts of mercury, and some fish have high levels of this poison. Below, you'll learn which commonly available seafood has low, moderate, and high levels of mercury. You will also find recommendations for including healthy amounts of fish in your diet.

❏ **Low-Mercury Seafood.** This group includes anchovies, catfish, clams, bay scallops, canned "light" tuna, crab, freshwater trout, herring, mussels, oysters, pollock, shrimp, and wild Alaska salmon. Eat two or more servings of these fish a week.

(Pregnant women, nursing women, and young children may consume up to twelve ounces a week.)

❏ **Moderate-Mercury Fish.** Seafood with moderate levels of mercury includes albacore, bluefin, and yellowfin tuna; Atlantic cod; Chilean sea bass; flounder; grouper; halibut; mahi-mahi; monkfish; orange roughy; and sole. Eat up to six ounces a week of this seafood. (Pregnant women, nursing women, and young children should not eat *any* moderate-mercury fish.)

❏ **High-Mercury Fish.** Included in this category are Gulf tilefish, king mackerel, shark, and swordfish. Avoid eating all high-mercury fish.

Soluble and insoluble. *Soluble fiber*—found in barley, some fruits and vegetables, legumes, and nuts—forms a gel in your intestines that holds water and binds cholesterol, thus helping to lower cholesterol levels. *Insoluble fiber*—found in leafy greens, fruit skins, whole wheat, seeds, and nuts—forms bulk in your intestines, helping to promote regular bowel movements. Both types of fiber add to a feeling of fullness and help to prevent overeating. And because of the impact fiber has on the body, it has been found to protect against a number of chronic disorders and complications. It should be noted, though, that in some situations, such as when recovering from bowel surgery, it is necessary to restrict the consumption of fiber by following a low-residue diet.

Choosing Healthy Proteins

Protein is the building block of all living things. Many people know that protein is the chief component of muscles, but it is needed for far more than just healthy muscles. Protein is required to build, maintain, and replace all body tissues, and is also used in the manufacture of antibodies, hemoglobin, and certain hormones.

Meat, fish, eggs, and dairy products are typically regarded as the most important sources of protein, but plant foods such as legumes, nuts, whole grains, and vegetables contain protein as well. You may have heard that plant proteins are of lower quality than animal proteins. That is because plant proteins are low in certain essential amino acids, the building blocks of proteins. However, you can easily get all of the amino acids you need by eating a variety of plant foods. For instance, beans supply the amino acids that grains lack, and vice versa. So a meal that includes both foods will provide all of the essential amino acids, just as a serving of meat would.

If you are on a soft or smooth diet, some good sources of protein include dairy foods such as milk, yogurt, and cheese sauces; and soy products such as soymilk, soy yogurt, and tofu. These can be used in a variety of recipes, including smoothies, soups, sauces, casseroles, and fondues. Other good sources of protein are bean purées and pâtés; nut butters; and egg-based dishes such as custards, quiches, and egg breads.

MODIFYING YOUR DIET FOR COMMON HEALTH PROBLEMS

The earlier discussions in this chapter provided information about the most basic components of a healthy diet so that you can more easily zero in on nutritious foods. But what if you have one of the common health problems that are known to be diet-related? Is it possible to choose foods for a soft or smooth diet that will maximize your overall health and also help you cope with a condition such as high cholesterol, hypertension, type 2 diabetes, or excessive weight loss? Fortunately, you can meet both your consistency requirements and your health needs. Below, you'll learn how it's done.

Heart Disease

The American Heart Association lists several lifestyle-related factors that increase the risk of heart disease and heart attack: Obesity, elevated cholesterol, hypertension (high blood pressure), inactivity, smoking, and excessive alcohol consumption. Of these, obesity, elevated cholesterol, and hypertension—all common in Western culture—are directly related to diet. In this portion of the chapter, we will focus on cholesterol and hypertension. Obesity is discussed on page 99.

If you have high cholesterol levels, it's critical to choose foods that are low in saturated and trans fats, and high in fiber, vitamins, minerals, and *antioxi-*

dants—nutrients that can prevent or slow oxidative damage to the body. Lean meats, low-fat dairy products, healthy oils, and foods made with non-hydrogenated healthy oils should be substituted for their less-wholesome counterparts. To help keep blood pressure under control, it is also important to reduce salt intake. Emphasize unprocessed foods over processed versions, which are often loaded with sodium, and add flavor to foods with herbs and spices instead of salt. And, of course, make sure that your diet features healthy carbohydrates such as fresh vegetables, fruits, and whole grains, instead of sugar, white flour, and refined grains. Healthy carbs provide a wide range of nutrients, including potassi-

um, magnesium, and other substances that help control blood pressure.

It's important to highlight another reason why a diet high in vegetables, fruits, and whole grains is associated with a lower risk of heart disease. Heart disease has been linked with inflammation, which is thought to lead to cell damage in the cardiovascular system. Unrefined vegetables, fruits, and grains, as well fatty omega-3-rich fish, have been found to have an anti-inflammatory effect in addition to all the other benefits they provide.

When you're eating a soft or smooth diet, these heart-healthy guidelines may sound difficult to follow, as a lot of naturally soft and smooth foods are

Liquid Vitamin and Mineral Supplements

A wholesome diet is, by far, the best way to get your nutrients. Foods provide an array of vitamins, minerals, and plant-derived phytonutrients in a balance designed by nature—a balance that cannot be replicated by supplements. In fact, many of the beneficial substances in foods have not yet been identified. However, if you are on a mechanically altered diet and/or you have a medical condition that limits your ability to eat a wide selection of foods, you may benefit from a supplement that provides important vitamins and minerals.

Taking vitamin supplements can be difficult if you have trouble swallowing. One option is to crush tablets or open liquid-gel capsules, and mix the product with foods such as pudding or applesauce. An easier option, though, is to use liquid supplements. These products can be taken as is or added to smoothies, shakes, or other foods, and can even be added to tube feedings. If you need

thickened liquids, be sure to mix your liquid supplements with foods or beverages of the appropriate consistency.

Liquid supplements can be found in many pharmacies and health food stores, and can often be special-ordered by your pharmacist. (In health food stores, look for these products in both the vitamin and bodybuilding aisles.) Another good option is to order vitamin and mineral supplements through the Internet. (See page 285 of the "Products" tables.) It is best to ask your physician to prescribe a supplement that suits your particular health needs and takes into consideration both your medications and any treatments you are undergoing. For instance, high doses of antioxidants like vitamins A and C can actually interfere with chemotherapy. The right supplement formula will meet your body's nutrient requirements without compromising medical treatments.

traditionally made with cream, butter, and high-fat cheeses. But in Part Two, you'll learn that these dishes can also be prepared with ingredients that are beneficial to the heart.

Diabetes

If you are diabetic, whether type 1 or type 2, your primary concern should be controlling the amount and type of carbohydrates you consume. Unless you have trouble eating enough food to keep your blood sugars normal—not an uncommon problem when chewing and swallowing difficulties occur—the need to control the carbohydrates you eat will not change.

A detailed discussion of a diabetic diet is not within the scope of this book, but it is important to cover a few basics. We will start by exploding the old notion that controlling diabetes is just about avoiding sugar. Research has shown that it's vital to regulate amounts of *all* carbohydrates, including starches such as breads, grains, and starchy vegetables; fruit; and milk. Understand that your goal is not to eliminate these foods from your diet, but to manage the amounts and kinds of carbohydrates consumed.

Some people are taught to monitor carbohydrates by counting them, while others are taught to use the exchange method. As you follow your easy-to-chew, soft, or smooth diet, you can continue using whichever method you have always used to track carbs. Just keep in mind that if your diet must be puréed, it is best to prepare single servings of the foods and to measure the servings *before* you purée them. Liquids such as milk and juice can still be measured in cups. (Note that all recipes in Part Two list serving sizes, carbohydrates, and diabetic exchanges.)

As you learned earlier in the chapter, all carbohydrates are not equal. Unrefined carbohydrates, such as those found in whole grain breads, provide a wealth of nutrients and fiber. Just as important, the carbohydrates found in whole, unprocessed foods tend to be slowly absorbed, and therefore do not raise blood sugar levels as much as more refined foods. A food's potential to raise blood sugar is referred to as its *glycemic index (GI)*. Basically, the higher the GI of a food, the more the food will trigger a rise in blood sugar after it is consumed. The lower the GI of a food, the lower the rise in blood sugar will be.

If you have diabetes, you will want to build your diet primarily around low-GI foods, which will help you control your blood sugar levels. Be sure to ask your physician or dietician for lists of low- and high-GI foods, or purchase a glycemic index food guide. As you already may have guessed, a good general guideline is to include *whole* foods in your diet as much as possible. Choose fruit purées rather than juices, and use soft whole grain breads that do not contain bits of grain, seeds, nuts, or raisins. If you must use thickeners, count the starches you use to thicken your foods, making sure that they do not push your carbohydrate count above your daily limits. Alternatively, try a gel-based thickener, as this will not increase your carb intake. (See page 287 of the "Products" tables.) If you are following a smooth/puréed diet, and the fibrous portions of your food must be removed—a sure way to cause a spike in blood sugar—try adding back smooth fiber supplements such as Metamucil and Citrucel.

People with diabetes are at higher risk for heart disease, so when making food choices, you will want to follow a heart-healthy diet as well. (See page 97.) Fortunately, these diets are very compatible, as both emphasize lean protein, low-fat dairy products, whole grains, vegetables, and fruits.

Excess Weight

The United States is now experiencing an epidemic of obesity associated with the widespread consumption of refined foods, junk foods, high-fat foods, and calorie-packed treats. You probably already know that over the years, people have recommended low-fat diets, low-carb diets, and many other types of restricted programs as a means of losing weight. We advocate a more balanced diet that emphasizes the healthy foods already discussed in this chapter, and limits portion size so that you consume fewer calories than you are able to burn. In addition, consider the following helpful tips for weight loss:

❏ Eat frequent small meals, eat slowly, and stop eating when you are satisfied.

❏ Fill up on fruits, vegetables, and other foods that are high in fiber. These foods will make you feel full for a longer period of time.

❏ Make sure that most meals and snacks include some protein, such as lean meats, low-fat dairy products, legumes, and nuts. Protein-rich foods are exceptionally filling and will keep you feeling satisfied until your next meal.

❏ Drink plenty of water or calorie-free fluids to insure that you stay well hydrated. People often mistake thirst for hunger, and turn to food when their body is really signaling a need for fluids. Adequate fluid intake will help provide a feeling of fullness and prevent you from eating due to thirst.

❏ Move more. Walk, run, swim, ride a bike, work in the garden, dance, or just play. You might try lessons in karate, tai chi, or yoga, or you might want to join a gym. By building muscle through exercise, you will increase your metabolism and burn more calories through your daily activities.

❏ Find ways to reduce stress. Most people tend to eat more and move less when they are stressed. Moreover, stress changes the body's metabolic makeup in ways that are damaging to your health. Exercise is a good stress reducer, but you may also find solace in music and art, a good book, playing with your kids, or involving yourself in an activity that helps someone else.

Unintentional Weight Loss

Whether you have lost weight due to a health disorder or as the result of a soft and smooth diet, this can be a serious problem. Adequate nutrition is needed not only for energy, but also for the countless metabolic activities that keep your body healthy. Poor nutrition can affect your immune system, which protects your body from infection as well as diseases such as cancer. It can also affect your skin, which may not heal as well after an injury, and can even contribute to pressure sores in those who are bedbound. And it can affect the organs that carry out essential body functions such as digestion. In this case, malnutrition can create a vicious cycle by decreasing your ability to absorb nutrients.

A book could be written about the harmful effects of inadequate nutrition, but we hope we have said enough to inspire you to eat well in spite of your dietary limitations. The *Soft Foods for Easier Eating Cookbook* was designed to tempt your taste buds while providing foods that meet your special needs. This, alone, may help you reach a healthy weight. In addition, the tips below can aid you in getting the calories and nutrients you require on a daily basis.

❏ Make your beverages a good source of calories by choosing to drink whole milk, fruit juice, milk shakes, smoothies, and cappuccinos.

❏ Whenever possible, add extra calories to dishes by stirring in condensed milk (also high in protein), butter, cream cheese, cheese sauces, oils, and peanut and other nut butters. When using oils, try to make heart-healthy choices such as olive, canola, and walnut oil.

❏ As long as you are not diabetic, indulge in rich, sweet desserts. For once in your life, you won't have to feel guilty! As far as possible, improve the nutritional value of these sweet treats by incorporating fruits, nut butters, and nut flours into the recipes.

❏ Perform more resistance exercises—exercises that involve lifting free weights, lifting your own weight, or moving against external resistance such as special elastic bands. These activities help build muscle, improve muscle tone, and keep all of your organ systems working better.

You now know that while it isn't difficult to make your soft and smooth diet healthy, it does take a basic knowledge of nutrition. If you're worried about putting this new information into practice, you can relax. In Part Two, you'll find over 150 easy-to-follow recipes for beverages, breakfast, soups, sandwiches, and more, and all are designed to be just as wholesome as they are easy to chew and swallow.

PART TWO

THE RECIPES

UNDERSTANDING
THE RECIPES

The recipes in this book have been designed to provide a wealth of options so that you can meet your dietary needs while satisfying your personal preferences. In addition to specifying the type of diet (or diets) for which each dish has been created, the recipes often suggest modifications that will allow you to change the consistency of the dish as needed. In some cases, you are offered a choice of ingredients for those times when you want a change of pace, or tips for trimming calories, carbohydrates, and/or fat. At the end of every recipe, comprehensive nutritional data is presented.

Because these recipes, while simple, provide much more information than those found in standard cookbooks—and because some of them involve techniques that may be new to you—it makes sense to learn a little about them before you prepare your first soup, entrée, side dish, or dessert. Below is a guide to understanding and following the recipes found in *Soft Foods* so that every dish is a resounding success.

FINDING THE DIET YOU NEED

Every recipe in *Soft Foods* begins with a box that clearly highlights the diet or diets for which that dish

is appropriate. You will find that most recipes are suitable "For All Diets"—for the easy-to-chew, soft, and smooth/puréed dietary needs addressed in this book. In a few cases, because of the ingredients used or the nature of the dish, the box states that the recipe is appropriate only "For Easy-to-Chew Diets" or "For Easy-to-Chew and Soft Diets." This box—found at the top of each and every recipe—makes it fast and simple to zero in on those dishes that are right for you.

Sometimes, you need only follow the recipe's basic directions to create a dish that is appropriate for all the diets listed. In other cases, the numbered recipe directions guide you in preparing the dish for the least mechanically altered diets—usually easy-to-chew and soft diets—and additional instructions for a smoother version are found below the basic recipe, under the heading "For Smooth/Puréed Diets." These supplementary directions focus on a specific step of the basic recipe that must be modified to make the finished product sufficiently smooth. For instance, you may be instructed to blend the finished dish in a food processor, to omit a certain hard-to-purée ingredient, or to grind an individual food before adding it to the dish. When following these instructions, always keep in mind the desired texture. Only you know the consistency that you need.

Since texture is such an important part of your diet, we recommend that before preparing a dish, you spend an extra moment or two making sure that the chosen recipe will suit you. Check the box at the top of the recipe to see the diets listed. Then see if you can simply follow the numbered instructions, or if you need to add an additional step to create the perfect consistency. These few moments spent choosing and familiarizing yourself with the recipe will save you time later on and help avoid possible disappointments.

RECOMMENDED APPLIANCES

Within the numbered instructions, virtually every recipe recommends a specific kitchen appliance—a food processor or hand-held blender, for instance—that will enable you to achieve the desired texture. We have suggested each appliance on the basis of what we found easiest to use and most efficient in that particular recipe. You should, however, feel free to use what you have on hand. If you don't own a hand-held (stick) blender, for instance, you can get the same results by processing the food in batches in a standing blender. If your dietary needs demand that you process the dish into a smooth purée, and your blender or food processor is unable to achieve that texture, don't panic. First, add more fluid to the dish and continue to blend. If that doesn't produce a sufficiently smooth texture, simply place the mixture in a fine-mesh sieve and push it through the mesh with a wooden spoon or pestle. Any lumps and tough pieces of vegetables and meat will remain in the sieve, leaving you with a perfect purée. (To learn more about choosing and using kitchen appliances, see Chapter 4.)

THE NUTRITIONAL FACTS

The Food Processor (ESHA Research) computer nutrition analysis software, along with product infor-mation from manufacturers, was used to calculate the nutrition information for the recipes in this book. For each recipe, information on calories, carbohydrates, dietary fiber, fat, saturated fat, cholesterol, protein, sodium, calcium, and potassium is provided. Nutri-ents are always listed per one serving—one bever-age, one bowl of soup, one helping of quiche, etc. This gives you the information you require to choose recipes that meet any special needs or limitations you may have regarding fat, cholesterol, sodium, and other important nutrients.

Every recipe also provides diabetic exchanges to assist people who use these lists as a meal-planning tool. For those not familiar with this system, let us say that these lists group foods which are similar in carbohydrate, fat, and protein content, allowing foods of comparable value to be swapped or "ex-changed" for one another so that you can have more dietary choices. (For instance, a quarter of a large bagel can be substituted for half an English muffin.) Most of the recipes in this book are broken down into meat, milk, starch, fruit, vegetable, and fat exchanges, as appropriate. Most desserts are broken down into more general carbohydrate exchanges so that you can swap them for other carbohydrates such as starches, fruits, and milk. Some desserts also list fat exchanges. Certain foods—for instance, smooth-ies and quick breads that contain a significant amount of added sugar—also list general carbohy-drate exchanges. A registered or licensed dietitian or a certified diabetes educator can provide more infor-mation about using exchange lists for meal planning.

Sometimes, recipes give you options regarding ingredients. For instance, you might be able to choose between 95-percent lean ground beef or ground turkey, nonfat or low-fat milk, or margarine or butter. This will help you create dishes that suit your tastes, your nutrition goals, and the ingredients you typically keep in your pantry and fridge. Just keep in mind that the nutritional analysis and diabetic exchanges are based on the first ingredient listed.

SPECIAL FEATURES

We've already explained that many recipes include additional instructions for changing the texture of a dish so that it suits a smoother diet. Headings such as "For Smooth/Puréed Diets" will guide you to these directions. A number of recipes also provide sections that instruct you in modifying the nutritional value or flavor of the dish.

Dietary Variations

The Dietary Variations that accompany some recipes guide you in substituting ingredients so that you can reduce calories and carbohydrates, decrease cholesterol, or otherwise modify the nutritional value of the dish. For instance, by making Triple Berry Slush (page 118) with low-calorie cranberry juice cocktail and sugar substitute, you can eliminate nearly 100 calories, 24 grams of carbohydrates, and $1^1/_2$ carbohydrate diabetic exchanges from each serving. Similarly, by using egg substitute and reduced-fat Cheddar instead of the listed ingredients, you can pare over 100 calories, 11.5 grams of fat, 232 milligrams of cholesterol, and $2^1/_2$ high-fat meat diabetic exchanges from your Cheese Soufflé (page 224). These simple changes can help you reach your dietary goals without making any sacrifice in taste.

For a Change

Most of us get bored eating the same dishes day in and day out. This monotony can become an even greater problem when you have to follow a mechanically altered diet. Although this cookbook was designed to present you with a wide range of choices, we realize that you may find several dishes that

perfectly meet your specific dietary needs and tastes, but that nonetheless can get a little dreary after constant repetition. With this in mind, we have added "For a Change" suggestions to a number of recipes. Each "For a Change" section highlights ingredient substitutions and additions that can give you a twist on an old favorite, or help you tune up a recipe so that it better suits your preferences. For instance, you can make Soft Scrambled Eggs (page 128) more flavorful through the easy addition of herbs, cheese, or finely ground ham. Or you can "change up" Oat Bran with Peaches and Almonds (page 139) by substituting pears for the peaches and walnuts or pecans for the almonds.

CALORIE BOOSTERS

While some people who follow mechanically altered diets have to limit calories and fat, many have problems consuming the calories they need to maintain a healthy weight, and may even need to gain weight. Because of this, virtually every chapter includes a boxed inset on boosting calories. You will find that by making simple changes—by adding more olive oil to a recipe, substituting whole milk or half and half for reduced-fat milk, or topping your dish with a homemade or store-bought sauce—you can boost both the calories and the flavor of your favorite meals. Just make sure that the selected ingredient increases calories *without* compromising other important dietary goals. If high cholesterol is a problem for you, for instance, it might be smarter to add more healthful olive oil to a dish than it would be to top it with a dollop of full-fat sour cream. Similarly, a wholesome fruit sauce might make a better choice than a butter-laden caramel sauce.

While this book provides plenty of options, at the heart of each *Soft Foods* dish are common, healthy ingredients and simple instructions that can be successfully followed by virtually any cook. Whether you are preparing these dishes for yourself or for a member of your family, you will find that the more recipes you follow, the more comfortable you become using the book and creating meals that have the desired texture. Moreover, as you prepare various dishes and use the techniques described in each one, you are sure to learn how to take many of your own favorite recipes and transform them into easy-to-chew, soft, or smooth/puréed dishes. (See Chapters 5 for tips on converting favorite recipes to a puréed texture, and Chapter 6 for tips on thickening beverages, soups, and other liquids.) We wish you many easy-to-eat, satisfying meals to come.

SMASHING SMOOTHIES, SHAKES, AND OTHER BEVERAGES

S moothies, milk shakes, and other blended beverages are among the most delicious and easy-to-prepare of all foods. They are highly versatile, as well. Drinkable "dishes" can be used for any mechanically altered diet, whether easy-to-chew, soft, smooth/puréed, or liquid, and are perfect for breakfast, snacks, or dessert. You can easily take these beverages with you if you are in a hurry, and if you are unable to take in much volume at one time, you can slowly sip them. You can make your drinks high-calorie or low-calorie, high-protein or low-protein. If you're trying to get more nutrition into your diet, incorporate healthful fruits and vegetables and fortify with add-ins like wheat germ, flaxseed meal, oat bran, nuts, nut butter, protein powder, and beneficial oils. If a smoother texture is needed, you can finely grind hard ingredients like nuts in a food processor or coffee grinder, and add the resulting powder to the other ingredients in your blender.

If you require thickened liquids, follow the guidelines presented in Chapter 6 for using commercial thickeners to modify your beverages. Once the blended liquids have reached the right consistency, you can, if you wish, add thickened ice or thickened ice cream (see page 87). Just remember that if you use regular ice or ice cream, although the smoothie or shake may appear to be thick at first, the frozen portion will melt in your mouth as you drink it, causing it to become dangerously thin.

All of the smoothies and shakes offered in the following pages are suitable for easy-to-chew, soft, and smooth/puréed diets when prepared as directed. However, if you need a *very* smooth texture, and your blender does not do the trick, you may have to pour the beverage through a sieve to remove any fibrous bits of food.

Many of the beverages presented in this chapter include milk or yogurt to provide a creamy base, as well as protein and calcium. If you prefer, you can substitute a nondairy alternative such as soymilk or soy yogurt, almond milk, or rice milk, but look for products that are fortified with calcium. In some cases, alternative ingredients are suggested for individuals who want to prepare their drinks with fewer carbohydrates and calories, or with additional calories. That's the beauty of smoothies, shakes, and other beverages. They're infinitely adaptable—and undeniably delicious.

Apricot Frappé

**Nutritional Facts
(Per Serving)**

Calories: 301
Carbohydrates: 67 g
Fiber: 2.7 g
Fat: 0.3 g
Sat. Fat: 0.2 g
Cholesterol: 5 mg
Protein: 11 g
Sodium: 154 mg
Calcium: 383 mg
Potassium: 655 mg

Diabetic Exchanges

1$\frac{1}{2}$ fruit
1 nonfat/low-fat milk
1$\frac{1}{2}$ carbohydrate

1. Place all of the ingredients in a blender in the order listed, and process until smooth.

2. Pour into a 16-ounce glass and serve immediately.

Dietary Variation

To reduce calories and carbohydrates:

Replace the sugar with a sugar substitute and you will eliminate 84 calories, 22 grams carbohydrate, and 1$\frac{1}{2}$ carbohydrate diabetic exchanges. (See page 44 for details on using sugar substitutes.)

YIELD: 1 serving

$\frac{2}{3}$ cup canned apricots in juice or light syrup, drained

$\frac{1}{2}$ cup evaporated nonfat or low-fat milk

$\frac{3}{4}$ cup crushed ice

2 tablespoons sugar or honey

2 tablespoons oat bran or toasted wheat germ (optional)

Melon Magic Smoothie

**Nutritional Facts
(Per Serving)**

Calories: 225
Carbohydrates: 54 g
Fiber: 2 g
Fat: 1 g
Sat. Fat: 0.2 g
Cholesterol: 0 mg
Protein: 3 g
Sodium: 18 mg
Calcium: 48 mg
Potassium: 1,059 mg

Diabetic Exchanges

2$\frac{1}{2}$ fruit
1 carbohydrate

1. Place all of the ingredients in a blender in the order listed, and process until smooth.

2. Pour into a 16-ounce glass and serve immediately.

* Whenever you have leftover melon, purée it and freeze the purée in ice cube trays. Store the cubes in a freezer-safe resealable plastic bag until needed. Then use 3 to 4 of the frozen cubes instead of fresh melon, and either omit the ice or use less.

YIELD: 1 serving

1 cup orange juice

1 cup cantaloupe cubes*

$\frac{1}{2}$ cup crushed ice

1$\frac{1}{2}$ tablespoons frozen limeade concentrate

For All Diets

Carrot-Apple Slush

**Nutritional Facts
(Per Serving)**

Calories: 175
Carbohydrates: 43 g
Fiber: 3.4 g
Fat: 0.4 g
Sat. Fat: 0.1 g
Cholesterol: 0 mg
Protein: 1 g
Sodium: 39 mg
Calcium: 35 mg
Potassium: 575 mg

Diabetic Exchanges

$2\frac{1}{2}$ fruit
1 vegetable

1. Place all of the ingredients except for the ice in the blender, and process until smooth. Add the ice and blend again until smooth.

2. Pour into a 16-ounce glass and serve immediately.

YIELD: 1 serving

$\frac{1}{2}$ cup water
$\frac{1}{4}$ cup frozen apple juice concentrate
$\frac{1}{2}$ cup chopped carrot
$\frac{1}{2}$ cup chopped peeled apple
1 teaspoon freshly grated ginger (optional)
$\frac{3}{4}$ cup crushed ice

For All Diets

Spinach, Celery, and Apple Cocktail

**Nutritional Facts
(Per Serving)**

Calories: 60
Carbohydrates: 15 g
Fiber: 3.4 g
Fat: 0.4 g
Sat. Fat: 0.1 g
Cholesterol: 0 mg
Protein: 1 g
Sodium: 46 mg
Calcium: 42 mg
Potassium: 305 mg

Diabetic Exchanges

1 fruit

1. Place all of the ingredients in a blender in the order listed, and process until smooth.

2. Pour into a 16-ounce glass and serve immediately.

YIELD: 1 serving

$\frac{3}{4}$ cup water
$\frac{3}{4}$ cup chopped Granny Smith apple (include the peel if desired)
$\frac{1}{3}$ cup packed fresh spinach
$\frac{1}{3}$ cup chopped celery
2 tablespoons chopped fresh parsley
1 teaspoon freshly grated ginger (optional)

For All Diets

Frosty Frappuccino

1. Place all of the ingredients in a blender in the order listed, and process on high for about a minute, or until smooth and frothy.

2. Pour into a 16-ounce glass and serve immediately.

Dietary Variations

To reduce calories and carbohydrates:

Use light (reduced-sugar) chocolate syrup, or use sugar substitute instead of the dulce de leche or turbinado sugar. (See page 44 for details on using sugar substitutes.) This will eliminate 52 calories, 12 grams carbohydrate, and 1 carbohydrate diabetic exchange.

To increase calories:

Add 2 tablespoons of sliced almonds or 1 tablespoon of almond butter, and you will boost the calorie count by 100. If necessary, grind the nuts to a fine powder before adding them to your frappuccino.

YIELD: 1 serving

½ cup evaporated low-fat milk

⅓ cup chilled strong black coffee or espresso

¾ cup crushed ice

2 tablespoons chocolate syrup, dulce de leche,* or turbinado sugar

* Dulce de leche is caramelized sweetened condensed milk that has long been popular in South America. It is available near the regular sweetened condensed milk in many grocery stores.

For All Diets

Leah's Super Breakfast Smoothie

**Nutritional Facts
(Per Serving)**

Calories: 277
Carbohydrates: 43 g
Fiber: 5.6 g
Fat: 8.8 g
Sat. Fat: 0.3 g
Cholesterol: 0 mg
Protein: 10 g
Sodium: 138 mg
Calcium: 171 mg
Potassium: 601 mg

Diabetic Exchanges

2 fruit
1 nonfat/low-fat milk
1½ fat

1. Place all of the ingredients in a blender in the order listed, and process until smooth.

2. Pour into a 16-ounce glass and serve immediately.

For a Change

■ Substitute almond or dairy milk for the soymilk.

■ Substitute raspberries, strawberries, or mixed berries for the blueberries.

YIELD: 1 serving

½ cup soymilk

½ cup kefir or yogurt, plain or vanilla

½ cup mixed fruit, orange, or pomegranate juice

½ cup frozen blueberries

1 tablespoon wheat germ

1 tablespoon flaxseed meal*

*You can find flaxseed meal in most health food stores.

For All Diets

Peachy Peanut Butter Shake

**Nutritional Facts
(Per Serving)**

Calories: 329
Carbohydrates: 43 g
Fiber: 3.2 g
Fat: 12.8 g
Sat. Fat: 2.8 g
Cholesterol: 5 mg
Protein: 15 g
Sodium: 240 mg
Calcium: 316 mg
Potassium: 746 mg

Diabetic Exchanges

1 fruit
1 nonfat/low-fat milk
1 carbohydrate
2½ fat

1. Place all of the ingredients in a blender in the order listed, and process until smooth.

2. Pour into a 16-ounce glass and serve immediately.

Dietary Variation

To reduce calories and carbohydrates:

Replace the honey with a sugar substitute equal to 1 tablespoon sugar, and you will eliminate 60 calories, 16 grams carbohydrate, and 1 carbohydrate diabetic exchange. (See page 44 for details on using sugar substitutes.)

YIELD: 1 serving

1 cup nonfat or low-fat milk

½ cup diced fresh, canned, or frozen peaches

½ cup crushed ice

2 tablespoons toasted wheat germ (optional)

1½ tablespoons peanut butter

1 tablespoon honey

For All Diets

Cranberry-Banana-Orange Smoothie

Nutritional Facts (Per Serving)

Calories: 186
Carbohydrates: 46 g
Fiber: 6 g
Fat: 0.8 g
Sat Fat: 0.2 g
Cholesterol: 0 mg
Protein: 2.7 g
Sodium: 3 mg
Calcium: 54 mg
Potassium: 725 mg

Diabetic Exchanges

3 fruit

1. Place all of the ingredients in a blender in the order listed, and process until smooth.

2. Pour into a 16-ounce glass and serve immediately.

YIELD: 1 serving

$\frac{1}{2}$ cup orange juice

$\frac{1}{2}$ cup fresh seedless orange or tangerine sections

$\frac{1}{2}$ cup frozen or fresh cranberries

$\frac{1}{2}$ cup frozen or fresh sliced bananas

$\frac{1}{2}$ cup crushed ice (omit if frozen fruit is used)

1 scoop protein powder (optional)

For All Diets

Banana Cream Pie Smoothie

Nutritional Facts (Per Serving)

Calories: 313
Carbohydrates: 61 g
Fiber: 1.9 g
Fat: 2.5 g
Sat Fat: 1.3 g
Cholesterol: 9 mg
Protein: 14 g
Sodium: 214 mg
Calcium: 493 mg
Potassium: 889 mg

Diabetic Exchanges

$1\frac{1}{2}$ nonfat/low-fat milk
1 fruit
$1\frac{1}{2}$ carbohydrate

1. Place all of the ingredients except for the graham cracker crumbs in a blender in the order listed. Process until smooth.

2. Pour into a 16-ounce glass and sprinkle the cracker crumbs over the top. (If you need a smoother texture, omit the graham cracker crumbs or blend them into the smoothie in Step 1.) Serve immediately.

Dietary Variation

To reduce calories and carbohydrates:

Replace the sugar or honey with a sugar substitute, and use sugar-free yogurt. (See page 44 for details on using sugar substitutes.) This will eliminate 67 calories, 15 grams carbohydrate, and 1 carbohydrate diabetic exchange.

YIELD: 1 serving

$\frac{1}{4}$ cup plus 2 tablespoons evaporated nonfat or low-fat milk

$\frac{1}{2}$ cup low-fat vanilla yogurt

$\frac{1}{2}$ cup fresh or frozen sliced bananas (about $\frac{1}{2}$ large)

$\frac{1}{4}$ cup crushed ice

1 tablespoon sugar or honey

2 teaspoons finely ground graham cracker crumbs

For All Diets

Banana-Berry Smoothie

Nutritional Facts (Per Serving)

Calories: 386
Carbohydrates: 67 g
Fiber: 4.7 g
Fat: 10.1 g
Sat Fat: 1 g
Cholesterol: 5 mg
Protein: 13 g
Sodium: 130 mg
Calcium: 323 mg
Potassium: 844 mg

Diabetic Exchanges

1$\frac{1}{2}$ fruit
1 nonfat/low-fat milk
1$\frac{1}{2}$ carbohydrate
2 fat

1. Place all of the ingredients in a blender in the order listed, and process until smooth.

2. Pour into a 16-ounce glass and serve immediately.

Dietary Variation

To reduce calories and carbohydrates:

Replace the honey or sugar with a sugar substitute, and you will eliminate 88 calories, 24 grams carbohydrate, and 1$\frac{1}{2}$ carbohydrate diabetic exchanges. (See page 44 for details on using sugar substitutes.)

YIELD: 1 serving

1 cup nonfat or low-fat milk
$\frac{1}{2}$ cup frozen or fresh blueberries or strawberries
$\frac{1}{2}$ cup frozen or fresh sliced bananas (about $\frac{1}{2}$ large)
2 tablespoons walnuts
1$\frac{1}{2}$ tablespoons honey or sugar
1 scoop protein powder (optional)
$\frac{1}{2}$ cup crushed ice (omit if frozen fruit is used)

For All Diets

Peanut Butter-Banana Smoothie

Nutritional Facts (Per Serving)

Calories: 430
Carbohydrates: 64 g
Fiber: 3.8 g
Fat: 16.9 g
Sat. Fat: 3.6 g
Cholesterol: 2 mg
Protein: 13 g
Sodium: 215 mg
Calcium: 170 mg
Potassium: 736 mg

Diabetic Exchanges

1 fruit
$\frac{1}{2}$ nonfat/low-fat milk
2$\frac{1}{2}$ carbohydrate
3 fat

1. Place all of the ingredients in a blender in the order listed, and process until smooth.

2. Pour into a 12-ounce glass and serve immediately.

Dietary Variation

To reduce calories and carbohydrates:

Replace the honey with a sugar substitute equal to 2 tablespoons sugar, and you will eliminate 117 calories, 31 grams carbohydrate, and 2 carbohydrate diabetic exchanges. (See page 44 for details on using sugar substitutes.)

YIELD: 1 serving

$\frac{1}{2}$ cup frozen or fresh sliced bananas (about $\frac{1}{2}$ large)
$\frac{1}{2}$ cup nonfat or low-fat milk
$\frac{1}{2}$ cup crushed ice
2 tablespoons smooth peanut butter
2 tablespoons honey
2 tablespoons toasted wheat germ (optional)

Mocha Banana Smoothie

Nutritional Facts (Per Serving)

Calories: 287
Carbohydrates: 62 g
Fiber: 2 g
Fat: 0.6 g
Sat Fat: 0.3 g
Cholesterol: 5 mg
Protein: 11 g
Sodium: 314 mg
Calcium: 378 mg
Potassium: 786 mg

Diabetic Exchanges

1 nonfat/low-fat milk
1 fruit
2 carbohydrate

1. Place all of the ingredients in a blender in the order listed, and process until smooth.

2. Pour into a 12-ounce glass and serve immediately.

Dietary Variation

To reduce calories and carbohydrates:

Replace the sugar with a sugar substitute and you will eliminate 90 calories, 23 grams carbohydrate, and 1½ carbohydrate diabetic exchanges. (See page 44 for details on using sugar substitutes.)

YIELD: 1 serving

½ cup evaporated nonfat or low-fat milk

½ cup coffee, frozen into cubes or chilled

½ cup frozen or fresh sliced bananas (about ½ large)

2 tablespoons sugar

1 tablespoon sugar-free instant chocolate pudding mix

1 pinch ground cinnamon

Berry Fresh Smoothie

Nutritional Facts (Per Serving)

Calories: 293
Carbohydrates: 59 g
Fiber: 2.1 g
Fat: 2.3 g
Sat. Fat: 1.2 g
Cholesterol: 20 mg
Protein: 10 g
Sodium: 120 mg
Calcium: 307 mg
Potassium: 800 mg

Diabetic Exchanges

1½ fruit
1 nonfat/low-fat milk
1½ carbohydrate

1. Place all of the ingredients in a blender in the order listed, and process until smooth.

2. Pour into a 16-ounce glass and serve immediately.

Dietary Variation

To reduce calories and carbohydrates:

Use reduced-sugar yogurt and you will eliminate 77 calories, 19 grams carbohydrate, and 1 carbohydrate diabetic exchange.

YIELD: 1 serving

½ cup orange juice

½ cup fresh or frozen strawberries, blueberries, or mixed berries

8 ounces berry-flavored yogurt

4–5 ice cubes (omit if frozen berries are used)

For All Diets

Peaches and Cream

Nutritional Facts (Per Serving)

Calories: 303
Carbohydrates: 61 g
Fiber: 3 g
Fat: 3.2 g
Sat. Fat: 1.6 g
Cholesterol: 10 mg
Protein: 10 g
Sodium: 147 mg
Calcium: 286 mg
Potassium: 843 mg

Diabetic Exchanges

1½ fruit
1 nonfat/low-fat milk
1½ carbohydrate

1. Place all of the ingredients in a blender in the order listed, and process until smooth.

2. Pour into a 12-ounce glass and serve immediately.

Dietary Variation

To reduce calories and carbohydrates:

Use light, no-added-sugar ice cream and replace the sugar or honey with a sugar substitute. (See page 44 for details on using sugar substitutes.) This will eliminate 106 calories, 14 grams carbohydrate, and 1 carbohydrate diabetic exchange.

YIELD: 1 serving

³/₄ cup diced fresh or canned peaches in juice, drained

³/₄ cup low-fat or light vanilla ice cream

¹/₄ cup evaporated nonfat or low-fat milk

1–2 tablespoons sugar or honey

For All Diets

Strawberry-Almond Smoothie

Nutritional Facts (Per Serving)

Calories: 313
Carbohydrates: 54 g
Fiber: 4.5 g
Fat: 6.5 g
Sat. Fat: 4.5 g
Cholesterol: 4 mg
Protein: 12.6 g
Sodium: 135 mg
Calcium: 384 mg
Potassium: 739 mg

Diabetic Exchanges

1 fruit
1 nonfat/low-fat milk
1½ carbohydrate
1 fat

1. Place all of the ingredients in a blender in the order listed, and process until smooth.

2. Pour into a 12-ounce glass and serve immediately.

Dietary Variation

To reduce calories and carbohydrates:

Use reduced-sugar yogurt and replace the sugar or honey with a sugar substitute. (See page 44 for details on using sugar substitutes.) This will eliminate 79 calories, 20 grams carbohydrate, and 1 carbohydrate diabetic exchange.

YIELD: 1 serving

1 cup coarsely chopped frozen or fresh strawberries

¹/₂ cup crushed ice (omit if frozen berries are used)

¹/₂ cup nonfat or low-fat vanilla yogurt

¹/₄ cup plus 2 tablespoons nonfat or low-fat milk

2 tablespoons sliced almonds or walnuts, or 1 tablespoon almond butter

1 tablespoon sugar or honey

Triple Berry Slush

**Nutritional Facts
(Per Serving)**

Calories: 186
Carbohydrates: 47 g
Fiber: 3.8 g
Fat: 0.7 g
Sat. Fat: 0 g
Cholesterol: 0 mg
Protein: 1 g
Sodium: 5 mg
Calcium: 22 mg
Potassium: 175 mg

Diabetic Exchanges

1½ fruit
1½ carbohydrate

1. Place all of the ingredients in a blender in the order listed, and process until smooth.

2. Pour into a 16-ounce glass and serve immediately.

Dietary Variation

To reduce calories and carbohydrates:

Use low-calorie cranberry juice cocktail and replace the sugar with a sugar substitute. (See page 44 for details on using sugar substitutes.) This will eliminate 92 calories, 24 grams carbohydrate, and 1½ carbohydrate diabetic exchanges.

YIELD: 1 serving

½ cup coarsely chopped frozen or fresh strawberries

½ cup frozen or fresh blueberries

½ cup crushed ice (omit if frozen berries are used)

½ cup cranberry juice cocktail or pomegranate juice

1 tablespoon sugar

Boosting the Calories in Beverages

Trying to gain weight? Beverages are one of the best foods to help you add pounds. Liquids tend to be less filling than solid foods, enabling you to take in more calories. You can also easily modify the recipes in this chapter to add extra calories. For instance, before blending, try tossing in a tablespoon of healthful oil such as canola, walnut, almond, or flaxseed. This will add 120 calories to each serving.

Or include some almond butter, peanut butter, or other nut butter. For every tablespoon you use, you'll be adding about 100 calories. If cholesterol and saturated fat are not a concern, you can also substitute whole evaporated milk, half and half, or cream for the nonfat milk or evaporated low-fat milk listed in the recipe. Simple add-ons like these can easily double or triple the calories per serving.

For All Diets

Frosty Fruit Shake

1. Place all of the ingredients in a blender in the order listed, and process until smooth.

2. Pour into a 16-ounce glass and serve immediately.

Dietary Variations

To reduce calories and carbohydrates:

Use light, no-added-sugar ice cream and replace the sugar or honey with a sugar substitute. (See page 44 for details on using sugar substitutes.) This will eliminate 100 calories, 25 grams carbohydrate, and 1½ carbohydrate diabetic exchanges.

To increase calories:

Toss in 2 tablespoons chopped walnuts, almonds, or pecans, and you will boost the calorie count by 100. Be sure to blend until the nuts are very finely ground. For a smoother texture, grind the nuts to a fine powder before adding them to your shake.

YIELD: 1 serving

¾ cup low-fat or light vanilla ice cream

⅔ cup coarsely chopped frozen or fresh fruit such as strawberries, pitted sweet cherries, blueberries, peaches, or bananas

½ cup crushed ice (omit if frozen berries are used)

½ cup evaporated nonfat or low-fat milk

2 tablespoons sugar or honey

Nutritional Facts (Per Serving)

Calories: 380
Carbohydrates: 71 g
Fiber: 2.1 g
Fat: 5.6 g
Sat. Fat: 3.2 g
Cholesterol: 35 mg
Protein: 14 g
Sodium: 217 mg
Calcium: 476 mg
Potassium: 746 mg

Diabetic Exchanges

1 fruit
1½ milk
2½ carbohydrate

Mocha Smoothie

1. Place all of the ingredients except for the toppings in a blender in the order listed, and process until smooth.

2. Pour into a 12-ounce glass, top with the whipped cream and a dusting of chocolate, and serve immediately.

Dietary Variations

To reduce calories and carbohydrates:

Use light, no-added-sugar ice cream and light (reduced-sugar) chocolate syrup. This will eliminate 82 calories, 16 grams carbohydrate, and 1 carbohydrate diabetic exchange.

To increase calories:

Toss in 2 tablespoons of chopped walnuts, almonds, or pecans, or 1 tablespoon almond butter, and you will boost the calorie count by 100.

YIELD: 1 serving

¼ cup chilled strong black coffee or espresso

¼ cup evaporated nonfat or low-fat milk

¾ cup low-fat or light vanilla ice cream

¼ cup plus 2 tablespoons crushed ice

2 tablespoons chocolate syrup

⅛ teaspoon ground cinnamon

TOPPINGS

3 tablespoons whipped light cream

½ teaspoon ground dark chocolate

Ice Cream Smarts

Ice cream can be a creamy, flavorful addition to shakes and smoothies. But if you have to follow a thickened-liquids diet, be aware that when an ice cream-thickened drink is warmed in your mouth, the frozen treat begins to melt, causing the liquid to become thin. If you want to include ice cream in your thickened drinks, consider using a specially formulated brand that melts to a pudding-like consistency. (See page 287 of the "Products" section.) When prepared with this product, your smoothies and shakes will remain safe to drink throughout your meal. (See Chapter 6 for more information on thickening liquids.)

Nutritional Facts (Per Serving)

Calories: 342
Carbohydrates: 61 g
Fiber: 1.1 g
Fat: 6.5 g
Sat. Fat: 3.5 g
Cholesterol: 17 mg
Protein: 10 g
Sodium: 169 mg
Calcium: 283 mg
Potassium: 628 mg

Diabetic Exchanges

1 nonfat/low-fat milk
3 carbohydrate

For All Diets

Blueberry Nog

Nutritional Facts (Per Serving)

Calories: 280
Carbohydrates: 53 g
Fiber: 2.1 g
Fat: 2.5 g
Sat. Fat: 1.5 g
Cholesterol: 90 mg
Protein: 10 g
Sodium: 161 mg
Calcium: 306 mg
Potassium: 502 mg

Diabetic Exchanges

1/2 fruit
1 low-fat milk
2 carbohydrate

1. Place all of the ingredients in a blender in the order listed, and process until smooth.

2. Pour into a 16-ounce glass and serve immediately.

Dietary Variation

To increase calories:

Use regular eggnog, and you will boost the calorie count by about 150 calories.

YIELD: 1 serving

1 cup low-fat eggnog
1/2 cup fresh or frozen blueberries
1/2 cup crushed ice (optional if using frozen blueberries)

For All Diets

Pumpkin Nog

Nutritional Facts (Per Serving)

Calories: 250
Carbohydrates: 46 g
Fiber: 0.9 g
Fat: 2.1 g
Sat. Fat: 1.5 g
Cholesterol: 90 mg
Protein: 10 g
Sodium: 161 mg
Calcium: 308 mg
Potassium: 523 mg

Diabetic Exchanges

1 low-fat milk
2 carbohydrate

1. Place all of the ingredients in a blender in the order listed, and process until smooth.

2. Pour into a 16-ounce glass and serve immediately.

Dietary Variation

To increase calories:

Use regular eggnog, and you will boost the calorie count by about 150 calories.

YIELD: 1 serving

1 cup low-fat eggnog
1/2 cup crushed ice (optional)
2 tablespoons plain canned pumpkin
Pinch ground nutmeg or pumpkin pie spice (optional)

Aunt Julia's Boiled Custard

1. Place the eggs and sugar in a medium-size bowl, and whisk to mix well. Set aside.

2. Place the milk in a 1-quart double boiler and heat until steamy and just beginning to boil.

3. Whisk 1/2 cup of the hot milk into the egg mixture. Then whisk the egg mixture into the heated milk in the double boiler.

4. Cook over simmering water, stirring frequently, for about 5 minutes, or until the mixture thickens slightly and coats the spoon. It should be about the consistency of heavy cream. Whisk in the vanilla extract and salt, if using, and pour the custard through a strainer.

5. Pour the warm custard into 12-ounce glasses, and sprinkle each serving with some nutmeg if desired. Or transfer to a covered container, refrigerate for several hours, and serve chilled. Note that the custard will thicken a bit as it chills, so if a thinner consistency is desired, you will want to add a little milk. You can also use the warm or chilled custard as a sauce to moisten cakes, or pour it into an ice cream freezer to make homemade ice cream.

Dietary Variations

To reduce calories and carbohydrates:

Replace the sugar with a sugar substitute. (See page 44 for details on using sugar substitutes.) This will eliminate 128 calories, 32 grams carbohydrates, and 2 diabetic carbohydrate exchanges.

To reduce fat and cholesterol:

Use nonfat or low-fat milk, and substitute 1/2 cup of fat-free egg substitute for the eggs. This will eliminate 109 calories, 12.5 grams fat, and 243 milligrams cholesterol. Diabetic exchanges for whole milk will become nonfat/low-fat milk, and medium-fat meat will become lean meat.

YIELD: 2 servings

2 eggs

1/3–1/2 cup sugar

2 cups milk

1/2 teaspoon vanilla extract (optional)

Pinch salt (optional)

Ground nutmeg (optional)

Nutritional Facts (Per Serving)

Calories: 352
Carbohydrates: 46 g
Fiber: 0 g
Fat: 13 g
Sat. Fat: 6.5 g
Cholesterol: 248 mg
Protein: 14 g
Sodium: 188 mg
Calcium: 284 mg
Potassium: 461 mg

Diabetic Exchanges

1 whole milk
2 carbohydrate
1 medium-fat meat

For All Diets

Luscious Latte

Nutritional Facts (Per Serving)

Calories: 112
Carbohydrates: 18 g
Fiber: 0 g
Fat: 0.4 g
Sat. Fat: 0.3 g
Cholesterol: 5 mg
Protein: 9 g
Sodium: 146 mg
Calcium: 336 mg
Potassium: 528 mg

Diabetic Exchanges

1 nonfat/low-fat milk

1. Combine the milk and milk powder in a small pot and place over medium heat. Cook, stirring frequently with a wire whisk, until hot and steamy. Alternatively, place in a 2-cup glass measure and microwave on high power for about 1½ minutes or until hot and steamy. When the milk is hot, whisk briskly until foamy.

2. Pour the coffee into a 12-ounce mug and stir in the sugar or sugar substitute, if desired. Pour the hot milk over the top. Sprinkle with some cinnamon or chocolate, and serve immediately.

For a Change

∎ To make a Mocha Latte, eliminate the sweetener and stir 1 to 2 tablespoons of chocolate syrup into the coffee before adding the milk. Top with some light whipped cream, if desired.

YIELD: 1 serving

¾ cup nonfat or low-fat milk

2 tablespoons nonfat dry milk powder

½ cup hot strong black coffee

1–2 teaspoons turbinado sugar, light brown sugar, or sugar substitute (optional)

Ground cinnamon or grated chocolate (garnish)

For All Diets

Café Caramel

Nutritional Facts (Per Serving)

Calories: 154
Carbohydrates: 27 g
Fiber: 0 g
Fat: 2.2 g
Sat. Fat: 1.6 g
Cholesterol: 12 mg
Protein: 7.3 g
Sodium: 105 mg
Calcium: 252 mg
Potassium: 393 mg

Diabetic Exchanges

1 nonfat/low-fat milk
1 carbohydrate

1. Place the milk and dulce de leche in a small pot and place over medium heat. Cook, stirring frequently with a wire whisk, until hot and steamy. Alternatively, place in a 2-cup glass measure and microwave on high power for about a minute or until hot and steamy. When the milk is hot, whisk briskly until foamy.

2. Pour the coffee into a 12-ounce mug, and pour the hot milk mixture over the top. Serve immediately.

YIELD: 1 serving

½ cup nonfat or low-fat milk

2 tablespoons dulce de leche*

½ cup hot strong black coffee

* Dulce de leche is caramelized sweetened condensed milk that has long been popular in South America. It is available near the regular sweetened condensed milk in many grocery stores.

Cinnamon Hot Chocolate

1. Place ¼ cup of the milk and all of the milk powder, chocolate, and cinnamon in a 1-quart nonstick pot. Cook over medium heat, stirring frequently, for a couple of minutes, or until the chocolate is completely melted.

2. Stir in the remaining milk and the vanilla extract and cook, whisking frequently, for a couple of additional minutes, or until heated through.

3. Pour the hot chocolate into an 8-ounce mug. Top with the whipped topping and a sprinkling of cinnamon. Serve immediately.

For a Change

■ To make Cinnamon-Mocha Hot Chocolate, add ½ teaspoon instant coffee granules to the chocolate mixture in Step 1.

YIELD: 1 serving

¾ cup nonfat or low-fat milk, divided

1 tablespoon nonfat dry milk powder

¾ ounce chopped dark chocolate or semi-sweet chocolate chips (about 1 tablespoon plus 1 teaspoon)

1 pinch ground cinnamon

⅛ teaspoon vanilla extract

TOPPINGS

2 tablespoons nonfat or light whipped topping

Ground cinnamon

Nutritional Facts (Per Serving)

Calories: 151
Carbohydrates: 21 g
Fiber: 0.8 g
Fat: 4.6 g
Sat. Fat: 2.7 g
Cholesterol: 4 mg
Protein: 8.3 g
Sodium: 123 mg
Calcium: 283 mg
Potassium: 429 mg

Diabetic Exchanges

1 nonfat/low-fat milk
½ carbohydrate
1 fat

BOUNTIFUL BREAKFASTS

"**B**reakfast is the most important meal of the day." You've heard it a million times, but have you ever asked why? The answer can be found in the name. When you break the fast that you experienced overnight, you begin to replenish your body's glucose (energy) stores, which slowly dwindle as you sleep. Breakfast should also supply a renewed mix of the high-quality proteins needed to nourish cells and support essential body processes.

This chapter will help you get your day off to a delicious and energizing start. Some of these dishes are smooth enough for a puréed diet just as they are, while several others include easy instructions for converting the food to a puréed consistency. Often, all that's needed to transform a dish from easy-to-chew to smooth is additional topping, which is allowed to soak into the food until it becomes thoroughly moistened and deliciously silky. You will also find that several recipes offer tempting but simple variations for those times when you want a change of pace and a welcome new taste.

If you thought that adopting a soft or smooth diet meant giving up your favorite foods, this chapter will soon change your mind. Whether you like creamy omelets, tender pancakes, cheesy grits, or steaming hot cereal, you're sure to find a satisfying way to break your fast. And because breakfast can also make a great light midday or evening meal, you will discover new ways to keep your body going strong all day long.

For All Diets

Green Eggs and Ham

1. Preheat the oven to 325°F. Coat four 8-ounce ramekins with nonstick cooking spray, and set aside.

2. Place the spinach and water in a 1-quart pot. Cook over medium heat for several minutes, tossing occasionally, until the spinach is wilted and tender. Drain off the water.

3. Place the spinach, milk, ham or bacon, cream cheese, pepper, and nutmeg in a blender. Process on medium speed until finely ground (for soft or easy-to-chew texture) or until completely smooth (for smooth/puréed texture).

4. Pour the mixture into a 2-quart pot and cook over medium heat, stirring frequently, until the mixture begins to boil. Remove the pot from the heat. Stir 1/2 cup of the spinach mixture into the egg substitute. Then slowly stir the eggs into the pot.

5. Divide the egg mixture among the ramekins. Arrange the ramekins in a 9-by-13-inch pan and add hot water to reach halfway up the sides of the dishes. Bake for about 25 minutes or until a sharp knife inserted in the center of a dish comes out clean.

6. Transfer the ramekins to a wire rack and allow to cool at room temperature for 10 minutes before serving.

YIELD: 4 servings

1 cup (packed) chopped fresh spinach

2 tablespoons water

1 cup evaporated nonfat or low-fat milk

1/2 cup chopped lean ham or Canadian bacon

3 tablespoons garlic-and-herb or vegetable-flavored light cream cheese

1/8 teaspoon ground black pepper

Pinch ground nutmeg

1 cup fat-free egg substitute, or 4 large eggs

Making Eggs Work for You

Eggs are an essential ingredient in many soft and smooth recipes. They are also a highly nutritious food, with a single egg supplying about 6 grams of protein and a range of other nutrients. But each of these protein-packed products also contains about two-thirds of the recommended 300-milligram daily cholesterol budget. What's the answer? If you're trying to lower your cholesterol, consider replacing some of the eggs in your recipe with egg whites, which are cholesterol-free. Also consider using an egg substitute such as Egg Beaters. Made from egg whites, these products can replace eggs in quiches, custards, and many other dishes. As an added benefit, most brands are pasteurized so that they are safe to use in eggnog and other dishes that call for uncooked eggs. (Check the labels to be sure.)

Nutritional Facts (Per Serving)

Calories: 136
Carbohydrates: 9 g
Fiber: 0.4 g
Fat: 3.6 g
Sat. Fat: 2 g
Cholesterol: 16 mg
Protein: 16 g
Sodium: 453 mg
Calcium: 232 mg
Potassium: 407 mg

Diabetic Exchanges

1/2 nonfat/low-fat milk
2 lean meat

For Easy-to-Chew and Soft Diets

Poached Eggs Florentine

1. Fill a pot or deep skillet with 3 inches of water, and bring to a boil. Reduce the heat to a gentle simmer. Break one egg into a custard cup. Hold the cup close the water's surface and slip the egg into the water. Repeat with the remaining eggs. Cook until the whites are set and the yolks have thickened, 3 to 5 minutes. Use a slotted spoon to transfer each egg to a serving plate, and set aside to keep warm.

2. Place the cornstarch and 1 tablespoon of the milk in a medium-size bowl and stir to dissolve the cornstarch. Add the remaining milk and the cream cheese, and whisk until smooth. Set aside.

3. Place the spinach in a medium nonstick skillet and add ½ cup water. Bring to a boil, reduce the heat to medium, and cover. Cook, stirring occasionally, for several minutes or until tender. Drain off any excess liquid.

4. Add the cream cheese mixture to the spinach, and cook, stirring frequently, for several minutes, or until the sauce is bubbly. Add a little more milk if needed.

5. Place a quarter of the spinach mixture on each of 4 serving plates and top each mound with a poached egg. Sprinkle some paprika over the top and serve immediately.

YIELD: 4 servings

4 eggs

1 teaspoon cornstarch

3 tablespoons nonfat or low-fat milk, divided

½ cup garlic-and-herb-flavored light cream cheese

10-ounces frozen chopped spinach

Ground paprika

Nutritional Facts (Per Serving)

Calories: 158
Carbohydrates: 8 g
Fiber: 2.1 g
Fat: 9.7 g
Sat. Fat: 4.1 g
Cholesterol: 227 mg
Protein: 12 g
Sodium: 379 mg
Calcium: 157 mg
Potassium: 308 mg

Diabetic Exchanges

1 vegetable
1 medium-fat meat
1 fat

For All Diets

Soft Scrambled Eggs

For Easy-to-Chew and Soft Diets

1. Place the eggs, milk, salt, and pepper in a medium-size bowl, and whisk until the whites and yolks are completely mixed.

2. Coat a medium-size nonstick skillet with nonstick cooking spray, and preheat over medium heat. Add the eggs and cook without stirring for about a minute, or just until the mixture begins to set around the edges. Using a wooden spoon or spatula, gently push the eggs toward the center of the skillet and stir them into soft curds.

3. Reduce the heat to medium-low and cook for another minute or 2, or just until the eggs are set, but still creamy and moist. Serve hot.

For Smooth/Puréed Diets

You may be able to eat this dish as is. If not, blend the fully cooked eggs in a food processor until smooth, adding a little milk, thickened milk, or sauce as needed.

For a Change

■ To make Herbed Egg Scramble, add $3/4$ teaspoon each dried parsley and chives (or $2^{1}/4$ teaspoons each finely chopped fresh parsley and chives) to the beaten egg mixture before cooking.

■ To make Cheesy Egg Scramble, sprinkle $1/4$ to $1/3$ cup grated Cheddar or Swiss cheese over the eggs after they begin to set.

■ To make Ham and Egg Scramble, stir $1/4$ cup finely ground baked ham into the beaten egg mixture prior to cooking.

Dietary Variation

To reduce calories, fat, and cholesterol:

Use 1 cup of fat-free egg substitute instead of the eggs. This will eliminate 89 calories, 10 grams of fat, and 425 milligrams of cholesterol. Diabetic exchanges will change to 2 lean meat.

YIELD: 2 servings

4 large eggs

2 tablespoons evaporated nonfat or low-fat milk, or regular milk

$1/8$ teaspoon salt

$1/8$ teaspoon ground black pepper

**Nutritional Facts
(Per Serving)**

Calories: 161
Carbohydrates: 4 g
Fiber: 0 g
Fat: 10 g
Sat. Fat: 3.1 g
Cholesterol: 425 mg
Protein: 14 g
Sodium: 290 mg
Calcium: 95 mg
Potassium: 174 mg

Diabetic Exchanges

2 medium-fat meat

For All Diets

Creamy Cheese Omelet

For Easy-to-Chew and Soft Diets

1. Coat an 8-inch nonstick skillet with nonstick cooking spray, and preheat over medium heat. Add the eggs and reduce the heat to medium-low. Cook without stirring for a couple of minutes, or until set around the edges.

2. Use a spatula to lift the edges of the omelet, and allow the uncooked egg to flow below the cooked portion. Cook for another minute or 2, or until the eggs are almost set.

3. Spoon the cream cheese over half of the omelet. Fold the other half over the filling and cook for another minute, or just until the cheese is melted and the eggs are set.

4. Slide the omelet onto a plate, sprinkle with the paprika, and serve hot.

For Smooth/Puréed Diets

You may be able to eat this dish as is. If not, blend the fully cooked omelet in a food processor until smooth, adding a little milk or thickened milk as needed.

For a Change

■ In Step 3, add 3 to 4 tablespoons of finely chopped leftover soft-cooked vegetables such as spinach, cauliflower, or broccoli along with the cream cheese.

■ In Step 3, add 2 tablespoons of finely chopped or ground ham along with the cream cheese.

YIELD: 1 serving

½ cup fat-free egg substitute, or 2 eggs, beaten

1½–2 tablespoons light vegetable or garlic-and-herb-flavored cream cheese

Ground paprika

Nutritional Facts (Per Serving)

Calories: 112
Carbohydrate: 4 g
Fiber: 0 g
Fat: 3.8 g
Sat. Fat: 2.6 g
Cholesterol: 11 mg
Protein: 14 g
Sodium: 362 mg
Calcium: 70 mg
Potassium: 211

Diabetic Exchanges

2 lean meat

For All Diets

Fluffy Buttermilk Pancakes

For Easy-to-Chew and Soft Diets

1. Place the flour, sugar, and baking soda in a medium-size bowl and stir to mix well. Set aside.

2. Separate the egg whites from the yolks. Place the yolks in a small bowl, add the buttermilk, and whisk to mix well. Set aside.

3. Place the egg whites in a medium-size bowl and beat with an electric mixer until soft peaks form when the beaters are raised.

4. Add the buttermilk mixture to the flour mixture and stir with a wire whisk to mix. Gently fold in the whipped egg whites.

5. Coat a large nonstick griddle or skillet with nonstick cooking spray, and preheat over medium heat until a drop of water sizzles when it hits the heated surface. For each pancake, pour about $\frac{1}{4}$ cup of batter onto the griddle and use a spoon to spread it into a 4-inch circle. Cook for about $1\frac{1}{2}$ minutes, or until the top is bubbly and the edges are dry. Turn and cook for an additional 30 seconds, or until the second side is golden brown. Repeat with the remaining batter to make 12 pancakes.

6. As the pancakes are done, transfer them to a serving plate and keep warm in a preheated oven. Serve hot, moistened with Warm Berry Syrup (page 172), Cinnamon-Apple Syrup (page 174), or maple syrup. If there are any leftovers, separate them with sheets of wax paper and store in a zip-type freezer bag.

For Smooth/Puréed Diets

To insure that the pancakes are thoroughly moistened before eating, use a fork to poke holes in them before adding the syrup. You may need to slightly dilute the syrup with a bit of fruit juice or water for extra moisture. For a smoother texture, blend the pancakes, the syrup, and some milk in a food processor to yield the desired consistency.

For a Change

■ For a different flavor and a heartier texture, substitute oat bran or buckwheat flour for half of the whole wheat pastry flour.

**YIELD: 4 servings
(3 pancakes each)**

1 cup whole wheat pastry
   flour

1 tablespoon sugar

$\frac{1}{4}$ teaspoon baking soda

2 eggs

$1\frac{1}{4}$ cups nonfat or low-fat
   buttermilk

**Nutritional Facts
(Per 3-Pancake
Serving)**

Calories: 189
Carbohydrates: 30 g
Fiber: 3.9 g
Fat: 3.6 g
Sat. Fat: 1.2 g
Cholesterol: 108 mg
Protein: 9.6 g
Sodium: 189 mg
Calcium: 102 mg
Potassium: 267 mg

Diabetic Exchanges

2 starch

For All Diets

Pumpkin Pancakes

For Easy-to-Chew and Soft Diets

1. Place the flour, oat bran, sugar, and baking powder in a medium-size bowl and stir to mix well. Set aside.

2. Combine the milk, pumpkin or squash, and egg substitute or eggs in a bowl and whisk to mix. Add the milk mixture to the flour mixture and whisk to mix.

3. Coat a large nonstick griddle or skillet with nonstick cooking spray, and preheat over medium heat until a drop of water sizzles when it hits the heated surface. For each pancake, pour about $1/4$ cup of batter onto the griddle and use a spoon to spread it into a 4-inch circle. Cook for about $1\frac{1}{2}$ minutes, or until the top is bubbly and the edges are dry. Turn and cook for an additional minute, or until the second side is golden brown. Repeat with the remaining batter to make 15 pancakes.

4. As the pancakes are done, transfer them to a serving plate and keep warm in a preheated oven. Serve hot, topping each serving with Cinnamon-Apple Syrup (page 174), Cinnamon-Pear Sauce (page 175), or maple syrup. If there are any leftovers, separate them with sheets of wax paper and store in a zip-type freezer bag.

For Smooth/Puréed Diets

To insure that the pancakes are thoroughly moistened before eating, use a fork to poke holes in them before adding the syrup. You may need to slightly dilute the syrup with a bit of fruit juice or water for extra moisture. For a smoother texture, blend the pancakes, the syrup, and some milk in a food processor to yield the desired consistency.

YIELD: 5 servings (3 pancakes each)

$3/4$ cup whole wheat pastry flour

$3/4$ cup oat bran

1–2 tablespoons sugar

1 tablespoon baking powder

1 cup nonfat or low-fat milk

$3/4$ cup plain canned pumpkin or cooked mashed butternut squash

$1/2$ cup fat-free egg substitute, or 2 eggs, beaten

Nutritional Facts (Per 3-Pancake Serving)

Calories: 137
Carbohydrates: 30 g
Fiber: 5.6 g
Fat: 1.5 g
Sat. Fat: 0.2 g
Cholesterol: 0 mg
Protein: 7.8 g
Sodium: 346 mg
Calcium: 192 mg
Potassium: 279 mg

Diabetic Exchanges

2 starch

Pancake Roll-Ups

For Easy-to-Chew and Soft Diets

1. Place the flour, oat bran, sugar, and baking powder in a medium-size bowl and stir to mix well. Add the milk and egg substitute or egg, and whisk until smooth. Set the batter aside for 5 minutes. Then whisk again.

2. Coat a large nonstick griddle or skillet with nonstick cooking spray, and preheat over medium heat until a drop of water sizzles when it hits the heated surface. For each pancake, pour about 1/4 cup of batter onto the griddle and use a spoon to spread it into a 6-inch circle. Cook for about 1 1/2 minutes, or until the top is bubbly and the edges are dry. Turn and cook for an additional 30 seconds, or until the second side is golden brown. Repeat with the remaining batter to make 8 pancakes.

3. As the pancakes are done, spread each one with 1 tablespoon of the syrup. Then spread 2 tablespoons of cottage cheese or ricotta along one side. Roll up the pancake to enclose the filling, and set aside to keep warm.

4. To serve, place 2 roll-ups on each of 4 serving plates and top each serving with 1/4 cup of the syrup. Serve hot.

For Smooth/Puréed Diets

To insure that the pancakes are thoroughly moistened before eating, use a fork to poke holes in them before adding the syrup. You may need to slightly dilute the syrup with a bit of fruit juice or water for extra moisture. Spread the filling over the moistened pancake, but do not roll up. Eat with a fork or spoon. For a smoother texture, blend the pancakes, the syrup, and some juice in a food processor to reach the desired consistency.

Dietary Variation

To reduce calories and carbohydrates:

Use the reduced-sugar version of Warm Berry Syrup and eliminate 48 calories, 12 grams carbohydrate, and 1 carbohydrate diabetic exchange.

**YIELD: 4 servings
(2 roll-ups each)**

1/2 cup whole wheat pastry flour

1/2 cup oat bran

2 teaspoons sugar

1 1/2 teaspoons baking powder

1 cup nonfat or low-fat milk

1/4 cup fat-free egg substitute, or 1 large egg, beaten

1 1/2 cups Warm Berry Syrup (page 172), or Cinnamon-Apple Syrup (page 174), divided

1 cup low-fat cottage or ricotta cheese

**Nutritional Facts
(Per 2-Roll-Up Serving)**

Calories: 256
Carbohydrates: 53 g
Fiber: 5.3 g
Fat: 272 g
Sat. Fat: 0.6 g
Cholesterol: 4 mg
Protein: 15 g
Sodium: 476 mg
Calcium: 228 mg
Potassium: 272 mg

Diabetic Exchanges

1 starch
1 fruit
1 carbohydrate
1 lean meat

For All Diets

Baked French Toast

For Easy-to-Chew and Soft Diets

1. Coat a 9-by-13-inch baking pan with nonstick cooking spray, and arrange the bread slices over the bottom of the pan in a single layer.

2. Combine the milk, egg substitute or eggs, sugar or maple syrup, nutmeg or cinnamon, and vanilla extract in a medium-size bowl, and whisk to mix well. Pour the egg mixture over the bread slices, cover, and refrigerate for several hours or overnight.

3. When ready to bake, remove the dish from the refrigerator and allow to sit at room temperature for 30 minutes. Preheat the oven to 350°F. Drizzle the margarine or butter over the bread slices.

4. Bake uncovered for about 30 minutes or until puffed and lightly browned. Serve hot, moistened with Warm Berry Syrup (page 172), Cinnamon-Apple Syrup (page 174), or maple syrup.

For Smooth/Puréed Diets

To insure that the French toast is thoroughly moistened before eating, use a fork to poke holes in it before adding the syrup. Then allow it to soak until softened throughout. You may need to slightly dilute the syrup with a bit of fruit juice or water for extra moisture. For a smoother texture, blend the French toast, the syrup, and some milk in a food processor to yield the desired consistency.

YIELD: 4 servings

8 slices (each 1-inch thick and about 1 ounce) whole-wheat, oat bran, or French bread, cut from an oblong loaf (choose bread made without added nuts, seeds, or grain pieces)

12-ounce can evaporated nonfat or low-fat milk

1 cup fat-free egg substitute, or 4 large eggs, beaten

1 tablespoon sugar or maple syrup

¼ teaspoon ground nutmeg or cinnamon

1 teaspoon vanilla extract

2 tablespoons melted margarine or butter

**Nutritional Facts
(Per 2-Slice Serving)**

Calories: 290
Carbohydrates: 41 g
Fiber: 4 g
Fat: 6.6 g
Sat. Fat: 1.7 g
Cholesterol: 0 mg
Protein: 17 g
Sodium: 552 mg
Calcium: 285 mg
Potassium: 524 mg

Diabetic Exchanges

2 starch
1 nonfat/low-fat milk
1 lean meat

For Easy-to-Chew and Soft Diets

Biscuits with Sausage Gravy

1. Place ½ cup of the milk and all of the flour in a jar with a tight-fitting lid. Shake until smooth and set aside.

2. Coat a large nonstick skillet with nonstick cooking spray, and preheat over medium heat. Add the sausage and cook, stirring to crumble, until nicely browned. Add the remaining 1½ cups of milk to the skillet along with the salt and pepper. Cook, stirring frequently, until the mixture begins to boil.

3. While stirring constantly, slowly add the reserved flour mixture, cooking until thickened and bubbly. Cook and stir for another minute or 2, adding a little more milk if necessary.

4. To serve, place each biscuit on a serving plate and split open. Top each biscuit with about ¾ cup of the gravy and serve hot.

YIELD: 4 servings

2 cups low-fat milk, divided*

¼ cup unbleached flour

8 ounces bulk turkey breakfast sausage (no casings)

¼ teaspoon salt

⅛ teaspoon ground black pepper

4 Buttermilk Drop Biscuits (page 187)

* For a richer gravy, use 1 cup milk plus 1 cup evaporated milk.

Smoothing It Out With Milk

Looking for a food that's not only nutritious and satisfying, but also a big help in making foods smooth and easy to swallow? Consider milk. Milk is rich in protein, calcium, and potassium, and is often supplemented with vitamins A and D, as well. It's great as a snack on its own, but can also be used to create a wide range of smooth and creamy soups, sauces, gravies, shakes, side dishes, and puddings. Milk is also available in many different forms, so it can help you meet different dietary needs. If you want to reduce calories and saturated fat, use reduced-fat (2-percent) milk, low-fat (1-percent) milk, or nonfat (skim) milk. If you are trying to put on extra pounds, choose whole milk, half and half, cream, or evaporated milk. If you cannot tolerate milk sugar (lactose), look for a lactose-free brand such as Lactaid or try soy, almond, or rice milk. Any of these products can provide the benefits of milk while helping you make foods easier to swallow.

**Nutritional Facts
(Per Serving)**

Calories: 292
Carbohydrates: 31 g
Fiber: 1.9 g
Fat: 11.7 g
Sat. Fat: 0.5 g
Cholesterol: 50 mg
Protein: 17 g
Sodium: 718 mg
Calcium: 273 mg
Potassium: 439 mg

Diabetic Exchanges

1½ starch
½ nonfat/low-fat milk
2 lean meat
1 fat

Easy Cheese Grits

**Nutritional Facts
(Per ⅔-Cup Serving)**
Calories: 169
Carbohydrates: 24 g
Fiber: 1.3 g
Fat: 3.9 g
Sat. Fat: 2.5 g
Cholesterol: 15 mg
Protein: 11 g
Sodium: 190 mg
Calcium: 269 mg
Potassium: 187 mg

Diabetic Exchanges
1 starch
½ nonfat/low-fat milk
1 medium-fat meat

1. Place the milk, water, grits, and pepper in a 2½-quart nonstick pot. Cook over medium-high heat, stirring frequently, just until the mixture begins to boil.

2. Reduce the heat to medium-low, or just until the mixture reaches a simmer. Cover and cook, stirring occasionally, for about 7 minutes, or until the grits are tender.

3. Add the cheese to the pot and stir until melted. Add a little more water or milk if a thinner consistency is desired. Serve hot.

YIELD: 6 servings

2 cups nonfat or low-fat milk
2 cups water
1 cup quick-cooking (5-minute) grits
Pinch ground white pepper
1 cup shredded reduced-fat sharp Cheddar cheese or diced American cheese

Cornmeal Mush

**Nutritional Facts
(Per 1-Cup Serving)**
Calories: 173
Carbohydrates: 29 g
Fiber: 2.2 g
Fat: 3.5 g
Sat. Fat: 0.9 g
Cholesterol: 2 mg
Protein: 6.6 g
Sodium: 210 mg
Calcium: 152 mg
Potassium: 306 mg

Diabetic Exchanges
1½ starch
½ nonfat/low-fat milk
½ fat

1. Place 1 cup of the milk and all of the cornmeal and salt in a 3-quart nonstick pot. Whisk to mix well.

2. Stir the remaining cup of milk and the water into the cornmeal mixture and bring to a boil over high heat, stirring frequently. Reduce the heat to a simmer, cover, and cook, stirring frequently, for about 15 minutes, or until the cornmeal is no longer gritty and the mixture is thick and creamy. The cooking time, which depends on the texture of the cornmeal, may be longer if you are using coarser meal.

3. Remove the pot from the heat and stir the margarine or butter into the cereal. Cover and allow to sit for a couple of minutes. Serve hot with honey, maple syrup, sugar, or sugar substitute, pouring in additional milk if desired.

YIELD: 4 servings

2 cups nonfat or low-fat milk, divided
1 cup yellow cornmeal
¼ teaspoon salt
2 cups water
1–2 tablespoons margarine or butter

Fabulous Dried Fruit

Although tasty and a good source of fiber and other nutrients, dried fruit is not appropriate for a soft or smooth/puréed diet—or at least it wasn't until now. Fabulous Fruit Butter uses cooked dried fruit to make a delicious butter that can be stirred into hot cereal, yogurt, and other soft foods for added flavor. Best of all, this all-fruit spread is perfect for any diet, no matter how smooth.

Fabulous Fruit Butter

Nutritional Facts (Per 2-Tablespoon Serving)

Calories: 51
Carbohydrates: 14 g
Fiber: 1.5 g
Fat: 0 g
Sat. Fat: 0 g
Cholesterol: 0 mg
Protein: 0.5 g
Sodium: 0 mg
Calcium: 10 mg
Potassium: 158 mg

Diabetic Exchanges

1 fruit

YIELD: 8 servings

1 cup pitted chopped dried plums (prunes), apricots, dates, or other dried fruit

3/4 cup water

1. Place the dried fruit and water in a 1-quart pot. Cover and bring to a boil. Reduce the heat to a simmer and cook for 5 to 10 minutes, or until the fruit has softened and absorbed most of the water. Remove the pot from the heat and allow to sit for about an hour, or until the fruit reaches room temperature.

2. Drain the fruit, reserving any unabsorbed liquid, and place in a mini-food processor. Process for several minutes or until smooth, adding some of the reserved liquid if needed to bring the mixture to the desired consistency.

3. Transfer the fruit butter to a covered container and refrigerate until ready to serve. Swirl into oatmeal and other hot cereals, plain yogurt, or vanilla yogurt for a burst of fruit flavor.

Boosting the Calories in Breakfast

If you need to put on extra pounds, you'll want to begin boosting calories as early in the day as possible. Eating a hearty breakfast is a great way to start.

Begin by spreading pancakes and breads with plenty of trans-free margarine, which packs 80 to 100 calories per tablespoon. If high blood sugar is not a problem, pour on lots of honey or maple syrup, too, and you'll be adding 50 to 60 calories per tablespoon. Instead of using nonstick cooking spray when frying eggs and pancakes, use margarine, canola oil, or olive oil to prevent sticking. If cholesterol and saturated fat are not an issue, use whole eggs, full-fat cheese, and extra butter instead of their low-fat counterparts. And if you want to increase calories even more, replace low-fat milk with evaporated whole milk or half and half, which includes about 340 calories per cup, or opt for cream, which offers about 700 calories per cup. The result will be a calorie-enhanced meal that's high on taste and wonderfully easy to swallow.

For All Diets

Low Country Grits

For Easy-to-Chew and Soft Diets

1. Coat a 2½-quart nonstick pot with nonstick cooking spray. Add the sausage and cook over medium heat, stirring to crumble, until no pink remains. Remove the sausage and set aside. If you need a finer texture, place the cooked sausage in a food processor and grind it into smaller bits.

2. Add the milk and water to the pot, and cook over medium-high heat just until the mixture begins to boil. Stir in the grits and white pepper and reduce the heat to medium-low, or just until the mixture reaches a simmer. Cover and cook, stirring occasionally, for about 7 minutes, or until the grits are tender.

3. Add the cheese and reserved sausage to the pot, and stir until the cheese has melted. Add a little more water or milk if a thinner consistency is desired. Serve hot.

For Smooth/Puréed Diets

After the cheese has melted in Step 3, place the grits in a blender and process until smooth.

YIELD: 6 servings

4 ounces bulk reduced-fat turkey or pork breakfast sausage (no casings)

2 cups nonfat or low-fat milk

2 cups water

1 cup quick-cooking (5-minute) grits

¼ teaspoon ground white pepper

1 cup shredded reduced-fat white Cheddar cheese

Nutritional Facts
(Per ¾-Cup Serving)

Calories: 210
Carbohydrates: 27 g
Fiber: 0.3 g
Fat: 5.6 g
Sat. Fat: 2.8 g
Cholesterol: 27 mg
Protein: 14 g
Sodium: 270 mg
Calcium: 241 mg
Potassium: 239 mg

Diabetic Exchanges

1½ starch
½ nonfat/low-fat milk
1 medium-fat meat

Hot Barley Cereal

YIELD: 4 servings

1. Place the barley in a blender and process for 45 to 60 seconds, or until it has the texture of grits or cornmeal.

2. Place the processed barley, milk, water, and salt, if desired, in a $2\frac{1}{2}$-quart nonstick pot. Cover and bring to a boil. Reduce the heat to low and simmer, stirring occasionally, for about 20 minutes, or until the barley is soft. Add a little more water or milk if needed.

3. Serve hot, topping with some additional milk or margarine and a drizzle of honey or maple syrup, if desired. Or swirl in a tablespoon of Fabulous Fruit Butter (page 136.)

1 cup pearl or hulled barley

2 cups nonfat or low-fat milk

2 cups water

$\frac{1}{8}$ teaspoon salt (optional)

For a Change

■ Substitute other whole grains such as brown rice, spelt, or whole wheat berries for the barley.

■ Replace $\frac{1}{4}$ to $\frac{1}{3}$ cup of the barley with wheat bran or wheat germ.

**Nutritional Facts
(Per 1-Cup Serving)**

Calories: 218

Carbohydrates: 45 g

Fiber: 7.8 g

Fat: 0.8 g

Sat. Fat: 0.3 g

Cholesterol: 2 mg

Protein: 9.1 g

Sodium: 68 mg

Calcium: 165 mg

Potassium: 343 mg

Diabetic Exchanges

2 starch

$\frac{1}{2}$ nonfat/low-fat milk

For All Diets

Oat Bran with Peaches and Almonds

1. Place the peaches in a mini-food processor and process until smooth. Set aside.

2. Place the oat bran and ground almonds or almond butter in 1-quart pot. Add the milk and water, stir to mix, and bring to a boil over high heat, stirring occasionally.

3. Reduce the heat to medium and cook for 1 minute, or until the liquid has been absorbed and the oat bran is soft. Cover, remove from the heat, and allow to sit for a couple of minutes.

4. Stir or swirl the peaches into the oats, and top with some trans-free margarine or butter and some sweetener, if desired. Serve hot.

For a Change

■ Substitute pears for the peaches and walnuts or pecans for the almonds.

YIELD: 1 serving

$1/3$ cup canned peaches in juice, drained

$1/2$ cup oat bran

$1 1/2$ tablespoons finely ground almonds, or 1 tablespoon almond butter

$3/4$ cup nonfat or low-fat milk

$1/2$ cup water

**Nutritional Facts
(Per 1$1/2$-Cup Serving)**

Calories: 267
Carbohydrates: 51 g
Fiber: 9.3 g
Fat: 8.2 g
Sat. Fat: 1.2 g
Cholesterol: 3 mg
Protein: 17 g
Sodium: 103 mg
Calcium: 279 mg
Potassium: 743

Diabetic Exchanges

2 starch
$1/2$ nonfat/low-fat milk
$1/2$ fruit
1 fat

For All Diets

Cinnamon-Apple Oatmeal

For Easy-to-Chew and Soft Diets

1. Place the oats, water, milk, and cinnamon in a 1-quart pot, and bring to a boil over high heat. Reduce the heat to medium and cook for 1 minute or until the liquid has been absorbed. Cover, remove from the heat, and allow to sit for a couple of minutes.

2. Stir in the applesauce and the walnuts or flaxseed meal. Top with some margarine and sweetener, if desired, and serve hot.

For Smooth/Puréed Diets

Increase the water or milk by $\frac{1}{4}$ cup and substitute oat bran for the oatmeal.

For a Change

■ Replace the applesauce with a tablespoon or 2 of Fabulous Fruit Butter (page 136.)

YIELD: 1 serving

$\frac{1}{2}$ cup quick-cooking (1-minute) oatmeal

$\frac{1}{2}$ cup water

$\frac{1}{2}$ cup nonfat or low-fat milk

$\frac{1}{4}$ teaspoon ground cinnamon

$\frac{1}{3}$ cup applesauce

$1\frac{1}{2}$ tablespoons finely ground walnuts or flaxseed meal*

---

*You can find flaxseed meal in most health food stores. Another option is to grind whole flaxseeds to a fine powder in a mini-blender and store any leftovers in the refrigerator or freezer.

Nutritional Facts (Per $1\frac{1}{4}$-Cup Serving)

Calories: 304
Carbohydrates: 43 g
Fiber: 5.8 g
Fat: 9.4 g
Sat. Fat: 1 g
Cholesterol: 2 mg
Protein: 14 g
Sodium: 67 mg
Calcium: 181 mg
Potassium: 467

Diabetic Exchanges

2 starch
$\frac{1}{2}$ nonfat/low-fat milk
$\frac{1}{2}$ fruit
$1\frac{1}{2}$ fat

SUMPTUOUSLY SMOOTH SOUPS

Soups are the ultimate comfort food. You probably already have a favorite that you turn to when you're feeling under the weather, as well as soups that are especially welcome when winter winds blow. But even on a pleasant spring day, there is something both soothing and reviving about a hot bowl of soup.

Most soups are naturally healthful, as well. Packed with a bounty of vegetables, from onion and celery to beets and winter squash, these savory brews offer a wealth of vitamins and minerals, as well as a wholesome dose of fiber. And with the addition of ingredients like beans, cheese, beef, and milk, soups can also be a rich source of protein.

Although you may be used to enjoying soups only as a prelude to your entrée, these are among the most versatile of dishes. You can enjoy soup as an appetizer, a snack, or a complete meal. Fruit-based soups make great desserts, too.

Perhaps most important to the individual who's following a soft diet, soups are easy to chew and swallow. Some soups are naturally smooth, as well, and through use of a blender, virtually all can be modified for a puréed diet. If you can tolerate a few lumps, a hand-held (immersion) blender provides the quickest and easiest way to turn a mixed-texture dish into a purée. If a perfectly smooth consistency is needed, you will have to use a standing blender, and perhaps even a strainer to eliminate coarse bits of vegetables. The result, though, is always the same—a sumptuously smooth, wonderfully nutritious dish that can satisfy your hunger any time of the day.

Asparagus Soup with Asiago Cheese

For Easy-to-Chew Diets and Soft Diets

1. Place the margarine or butter in a 3-quart pot and melt over medium heat. Add the onion or leek, cover, and cook for several minutes to soften, adding a few teaspoons of water if the pot becomes too dry. Add the garlic, and cook for 30 seconds more.

2. Add the broth, asparagus, potato, thyme or marjoram, and pepper to the pot. Cover and bring to a boil. Reduce the heat to medium-low and simmer for about 10 minutes, or until the vegetables are soft.

3. Purée the soup with a hand-held blender until smooth. Serve hot, topping each serving with a sprinkling of cheese and, if desired, a drizzle of olive or walnut oil.

For Smooth/Puréed Diets

Working in batches, purée the entire pot of soup in a standing blender until smooth. (See the inset on page 156 for safety considerations.)

Nutritional Facts
(Per 1-Cup Serving)

Calories: 124
Carbohydrates: 13 g
Fiber: 2.5 g
Fat: 6.2 g
Sat. Fat: 2.1 g
Cholesterol: 4 mg
Protein: 4.7 g
Sodium: 504 mg
Calcium: 93 mg
Potassium: 391 mg

Diabetic Exchanges

$1/_2$ starch
1 vegetable
1 fat

YIELD: 5 servings

$2^1/_2$ tablespoons margarine or butter

$3/_4$ cup chopped onion or leek (white and light green parts only)*

2 teaspoons crushed fresh garlic

3 cups chicken or vegetable broth

3 cups 1-inch pieces fresh asparagus (about 1 pound)

1 cup diced peeled baking potato

$3/_4$ teaspoon dried thyme or marjoram

$1/_4$ teaspoon ground black pepper

$1/_4$ cup grated Asiago or Parmesan cheese

Extra virgin olive or walnut oil (optional)

---

* To make sure the leek is free of dirt, cut it in half lengthwise and rinse well before chopping.

Beef and Barley Soup

Nutritional Facts (Per 1-Cup Serving)
Calories: 152
Carbohydrates: 17 g
Fiber: 3.2 g
Fat: 3.5 g
Sat. Fat: 1.1 g
Cholesterol: 30 mg
Protein: 12.8 g
Sodium: 439 mg
Calcium: 22 mg
Potassium: 319 mg

Diabetic Exchanges

1 starch

1½ lean meat

For Easy-to-Chew and Soft Diets

1. Coat a 4-quart pot with nonstick cooking spray and place over medium heat. Add the ground beef and cook, stirring to crumble, for several minutes or until the meat is no longer pink. Drain off and discard any fat.

2. Add all of the remaining ingredients to the pot and bring to a boil. Reduce the heat to a simmer, cover, and cook for 1 hour or until the barley is tender. Serve hot.

For Smooth/Puréed Diets

Working in batches, purée the entire pot of soup in a standing blender until smooth. (See the inset on page 156 for safety considerations).

YIELD: 7 servings

12 ounces 95% lean ground beef

4 cups water

10 ½-ounce can condensed French onion soup, undiluted

1 cup grated carrot

¾ cup V8 vegetable juice

½ cup pearl barley

1 teaspoon dried thyme

½ teaspoon ground black pepper

Boosting the Calories in Soup

Besides being highly versatile, soups present a great opportunity to boost calories when you need to gain weight or prevent weight loss. Here are just a few ideas.

First, consider adding several tablespoons of olive oil or canola oil to your soup recipe. Every tablespoon you pour into the pot will add 120 calories to the soup. Then drizzle each serving of soup with a bit more extra virgin olive oil. This high-quality oil will give your soup an extra burst of flavor.

If cholesterol and saturated fat are not an issue, you can use extra butter, or substitute evaporated whole milk, half and half, or even cream for the low-fat milk in your recipe. With evaporated whole milk and half and half weighing in at about 340 calories per cup, and cream offering as much as 700 to 800 calories per cup, you can easily double or triple the calories in each serving while making your soup extra smooth, creamy, and flavorful.

For All Diets

Capellini Chicken Soup

For Easy-to-Chew and Soft Diets

1. Place the carrots, onion, celery, and chicken in a 4-quart pot. Add the water, bouillon granules, garlic, and white pepper, and bring to a boil. Reduce the heat to a simmer, cover, and cook for about 20 minutes, or until the vegetables are soft and the chicken is tender.

2. Transfer the chicken to a cutting board and set aside. Use a slotted spoon to transfer about half of the vegetables to a blender. Add about 1½ cups of the broth, and carefully blend at low speed until smooth. Pour the mixture back into the pot.

3. Bring the soup to a boil and add the pasta. Reduce the heat to medium-low, cover, and, stirring occasionally, cook for about 8 minutes, or until the pasta is soft.

4. Chop the chicken (grind it in a food processor if a finer texture is desired) and add it to the soup. Cook for another minute to heat through.

5. Serve hot, topping each serving with a sprinkling of parsley.

For Smooth/Puréed Diets

Working in batches, purée the entire pot of soup in a standing blender until smooth. (See the inset on page 156 for safety considerations.)

1¼ cups diced carrots

½ cup chopped onion

⅓ cup chopped celery

2 boneless skinless chicken breast halves (about 4 ounces each)

4 cups water

1 tablespoon chicken bouillon granules

2 teaspoons crushed fresh garlic

Scant ¼ teaspoon ground white pepper

2½ ounces whole wheat capellini (angel hair) pasta, broken into 1-inch pieces (about 1½ cups)

3 tablespoons finely chopped fresh parsley, or 3 teaspoons dried parsley, finely crumbled

Nutritional Facts (Per 1-Cup Serving)

Calories: 106
Carbohydrates: 14 g
Fiber: 2.2 g
Fat: 0.7 g
Sat. Fat: 0.2 g
Cholesterol: 22 mg
Protein: 11 g
Sodium: 487 mg
Calcium: 27 mg
Potassium: 267 mg

Diabetic Exchanges

1 starch
1 lean meat

For All Diets

Cauliflower-Cheese Soup

For Easy-to-Chew and Soft Diets

1. Place the margarine or butter in a 3-quart pot and melt over medium heat. Add the onion or leek, cover, and cook for several minutes, or until the vegetable starts to soften. Add the garlic and cook for 30 additional seconds.

2. Add the cauliflower, water, bouillon granules, marjoram, and pepper to the pot. Cover and bring to a boil over high heat. Reduce the heat to a simmer and cook for about 10 minutes, or until the vegetables are soft.

3. Stir the evaporated milk into the soup. Purée the soup with a hand-held blender until smooth.

4. Add the cheese to the pot and, stirring constantly, cook over medium heat for a minute or 2, or just until the cheese has melted. Serve hot.

For Smooth/Puréed Diets

Working in batches, purée the entire pot of soup in a standing blender until smooth. (See the inset on page 156 for safety considerations.)

YIELD: 5 servings

3 tablespoons reduced-fat margarine or light butter

½ cup chopped onion or leek (white and light green portions only)*

1½ teaspoons crushed fresh garlic

4 cups fresh or frozen cauliflower florets

2½ cups water

1½ teaspoons chicken or vegetable bouillon granules

½ teaspoon dried marjoram

⅛ teaspoon ground white pepper

1 cup evaporated nonfat or low-fat milk

½ cup plus 2 tablespoons shredded sharp Cheddar cheese

---

* To make sure the leek is free of dirt, cut it in half lengthwise and rinse well before chopping.

Nutritional Facts (Per 1-Cup Serving)

Calories: 152
Carbohydrates: 12 g
Fiber: 2.3 g
Fat: 8.2 g
Sat. Fat: 3.8 g
Cholesterol: 7 mg
Protein: 9.1 g
Sodium: 425 mg
Calcium: 271 mg
Potassium: 451 mg

Diabetic Exchanges

1 vegetable
½ nonfat/low-fat milk
½ high-fat meat
½ fat

For All Diets

Celery Bisque

For Easy-to-Chew and Soft Diets

1. Place the margarine or butter in a 3-quart pot and melt over medium heat. Add the onion, cover, and cook for several minutes or until the onion softens. Add a few teaspoons of water if the pot becomes too dry. Add the garlic and cook for 15 additional seconds.

2. Add the celery, broth, potato, marjoram, and pepper to the pot. Cover and bring to a boil over high heat. Reduce the heat to medium-low and simmer for about 10 minutes or until the vegetables are soft. Stir in the evaporated milk.

3. Purée the soup with a hand-held blender until smooth. Serve hot.

For Smooth/Puréed Diets

Working in batches, purée the entire pot of soup in a standing blender until smooth. (See the inset on page 156 for safety considerations.)

YIELD: 5 servings
2½ tablespoons margarine or butter
¾ cup chopped onion
1½ teaspoons crushed fresh garlic
3 cups chopped celery (include some leaves)
2 cups chicken or vegetable broth
1 cup diced peeled baking potato
¾ teaspoon dried marjoram
¼ teaspoon ground black pepper
1 cup evaporated nonfat or low-fat milk

The Handy Hand-Held Blender

Whether called an immersion, stick, or hand-held blender, this device is essentially a long handle or wand that has electrically powered blades attached to the bottom. Unlike a standing blender, which makes it necessary to transfer food from a pot or bowl to the appliance's container, a hand-held blender can be inserted directly in a pot of soup, where it will quickly purée the food. This versatile device is also great for smoothing out sauces, blending salad dressing ingredients, and making beverages. Just be aware that the stick blender is best used with soft dishes (not thick stews), and that when a completely smooth consistency is needed, a standing blender is the better choice.

Nutritional Facts
(Per 1-Cup Serving)

Calories: 137
Carbohydrates: 16 g
Fiber: 2.6 g
Fat: 6.2 g
Sat. Fat: 1.5 g
Cholesterol: 2 mg
Protein: 5.5 g
Sodium: 438 mg
Calcium: 194 mg
Potassium: 553 mg

Diabetic Exchanges

1 vegetable
½ starch
½ nonfat/low-fat milk
1 fat

Crock Pot Chili

For Easy-to-Chew and Soft Diets

1. Coat a large skillet with nonstick cooking spray and add the ground beef. Cook over medium heat, stirring to crumble, for about 5 minutes or until no longer pink. Drain off and discard any fat. Transfer the meat to a 3-quart slow cooker.

2. Place the undrained tomatoes in a blender and blend until smooth. Add to the slow cooker along with the remaining ingredients. Stir to mix, cover, and cook for 8 to 10 hours on low power, or 4 to 5 hours on high power. Serve hot.

To Make on a Stovetop:

1. Coat a 3-quart pot with nonstick cooking spray and add the ground beef. Cook over medium heat, stirring to crumble, for about 5 minutes or until no longer pink. Drain off and discard any fat.

2. Place the undrained tomatoes in a blender and blend until smooth. Add to the pot along with the remaining ingredients. Stir to mix, cover, and simmer for 1 hour. Serve hot.

For Smooth/Puréed Diets

Working in batches, purée the entire pot of soup in a standing blender until smooth. (See the inset on page 156 for safety considerations.)

YIELD: 8 servings

1 pound 95% lean ground beef

14½-ounce can Mexican-style stewed tomatoes, undrained

2 cans (15 ounces each) pinto or kidney beans, drained

1½ cups V8 vegetable juice

1¼ cups chopped yellow onion

½ cup beer (light or regular) or beef broth

¼ cup chili powder

1 teaspoon dried oregano

1 teaspoon ground cumin

1 teaspoon crushed fresh garlic

**Nutritional Facts
(Per 1-Cup Serving)**

Calories: 221
Carbohydrates: 28 g
Fiber: 9 g
Fat: 3.9 g
Sat. Fat: 1.5 g
Cholesterol: 35 mg
Protein: 19 g
Sodium: 525 mg
Calcium: 73 mg
Potassium: 724 mg

Diabetic Exchanges

1 starch
1 vegetable
2½ lean meat

For All Diets

Golden French Onion Soup

For Easy-to-Chew and Soft Diets

YIELD: 4 servings

1. Pour the olive oil into a 2-quart nonstick pot, and add the onion and thyme. Cover and cook over medium heat, stirring occasionally to prevent scorching, for about 15 minutes, or until the onions are lightly browned. Reduce the heat to medium-low and cook, stirring occasionally, for an additional 20 minutes, or until the onions are golden brown. Stir in the sherry and cook uncovered for about a minute, or until the sherry evaporates.

2. While the onions are cooking, place the broth, carrot, celery, garlic, and pepper in a 2-quart pot. Cover and bring to a boil. Reduce the heat to low and simmer for about 10 minutes, or until the vegetables are soft. Use a hand-held blender to purée the mixture until smooth.

3. Stir the broth mixture into the cooked onions. If necessary, use the hand-held blender again to slightly purée the onions. Cook over medium heat for a minute or 2 to heat through, adding a little more broth if needed.

4. To assemble the individual servings, place about ¾ cup of the soup in each of four 8-ounce ovenproof soup bowls or ramekins. Spread each bread slice with some of the margarine or butter. Top each soup with a piece of bread, and sprinkle 1½ teaspoons of Parmesan over the top of each slice.

5. Arrange the dishes of soup on a baking sheet and place 2 inches below a preheated broiler. Broil for a couple of minutes, or until the cheese is lightly browned. Serve hot.

For Smooth/Puréed Diets

In Step 3, add the Parmesan cheese to the soup (instead of using it as a topping) and blend until completely smooth, using a standing blender for a smoother texture. (See the inset on page 156 for safety considerations.) Then proceed with the recipe as directed, topping each serving with the bread only (omit the broiling). Make sure that the bread is completely saturated with the broth before eating.

Nutritional Facts (Per Serving)

Calories: 197
Carbohydrates: 17 g
Fiber: 2.4 g
Fat: 12.8 g
Sat. Fat: 2.9 g
Cholesterol: 3 mg
Protein: 3.7 g
Sodium: 562 mg
Calcium: 76 mg
Potassium: 237 mg

Diabetic Exchanges

2 vegetable
½ starch
2½ fat

---

2 tablespoons extra virgin olive oil

1 Spanish onion (about 12 ounces), thinly sliced and cut into quarter rings (about 3 cups)

¾ teaspoon dried thyme

2 tablespoons dry sherry

2¼ cups beef broth

¼ cup diced carrot

¼ cup diced celery

1 teaspoon crushed garlic

¼ teaspoon ground black pepper

TOPPINGS

4 slices (about 3-x-3-inches and ½ inch thick) French bread, lightly toasted

2–3 teaspoons margarine or butter, softened

2 tablespoons grated Parmesan cheese

For All Diets

Peanutty Pumpkin Soup

For Easy-to-Chew and Soft Diets

1. Place the onion, marjoram, thyme, and ¼ cup of the broth in a 3-quart pot over medium heat. Cover and cook for several minutes or until the onion starts to soften.

2. Add the pumpkin, garlic, pepper, and remaining 2¾ cups of broth to the pot, and bring to a boil over high heat. Reduce the heat to a simmer, cover, and cook for 10 minutes.

3. Stir the peanut butter into the soup. Then purée with a hand-held blender until smooth.

4. Add the milk to the pot, and stir over medium heat for a couple of minutes to heat through. Serve hot.

For Smooth/Puréed Diets

Working in batches, purée the entire pot of soup in a standing blender until smooth. (See the inset on page 156 for safety considerations.)

YIELD: 5 servings

1½ cups chopped yellow onion

1 teaspoon dried marjoram

½ teaspoon dried thyme

3 cups chicken or vegetable broth, divided

15-ounce can plain pumpkin, or 1¾ cups cooked mashed pumpkin

2 teaspoons crushed fresh garlic

¼ teaspoon ground black pepper

½ cup smooth peanut butter

1 cup nonfat or low-fat milk

The Healing Power of Culinary Herbs and Spices

Creative cooks have long known that the liberal use of herbs and spices is one of the best ways to boost flavor in foods, especially when you are trying to cut back on sodium. Just as important, these tasty additions are rich in health-promoting phytonutrients. Common garden herbs such as oregano, rosemary, sage, thyme, and marjoram have been found to contain antioxidants, cancer-fighting compounds, anti-inflammatory agents, and other beneficial substances. Many other plant-based flavorings—ginger, garlic, celery seed, caraway seed, and orange and lemon zest, for instance—also provide these important nutrients.

As you prepare your *Soft Foods* dishes, expand your seasoning savvy by experimenting with herbs and spices. You will not only open up a whole new world of flavors, but also reap the many health benefits that these foods have to offer.

Nutritional Facts
(Per 1⅛-Cup Serving)

Calories: 217
Carbohydrates: 19 g
Fiber: 6.1 g
Fat: 13 g
Sat. Fat: 2.2 g
Cholesterol: 1 mg
Protein: 10 g
Sodium: 496 mg
Calcium: 113 mg
Potassium: 506 mg

Diabetic Exchanges

1 starch
1 vegetable
2½ fat

For All Diets

Potato and Leek Soup

For Easy-to-Chew and Soft Diets

1. Place the margarine or butter and the leak in a 2-quart pot. Cover and cook over medium heat, stirring occasionally, for about 5 minutes or until the leeks are soft.

2. Add the water, potato, garlic, and salt to the pot, and bring to boil over high heat. Reduce the heat to medium, cover, and cook for about 10 minutes or until the potato is tender.

3. Stir the milk and the turmeric or other seasoning into the potato mixture. Purée the soup with a hand-held blender until smooth. Simmer for 5 additional minutes and serve hot, or chill for at least 2 hours and serve cold.

For Smooth/Puréed Diets

Working in batches, purée the entire pot of soup in a standing blender until smooth. (See the inset on page 156 for safety considerations.)

YIELD: 4 servings

1 tablespoon margarine or butter

3/4 cup diced leek (white portion only)*

2 cups water

2 cups diced peeled baking potato

2 teaspoons crushed fresh garlic

1/2 teaspoon salt

1 cup milk, evaporated milk, or soymilk

1/2 teaspoon ground turmeric, herbes de Provence, fines herbes, or other salt-free seasoning

---

* To make sure the leek is free of dirt, cut it in half lengthwise and rinse well before dicing.

**Nutritional Facts
(Per 1-Cup Serving)**

Calories: 125
Carbohydrates: 22 g
Fiber: 1.5 g
Fat: 2.5 g
Sat. Fat: 0.7 g
Cholesterol: 1 mg
Protein: 3.9 g
Sodium: 349 mg
Calcium: 92 mg
Potassium: 435 mg

Diabetic Exchanges

1 starch
1/2 milk

For All Diets

Savory Lentil Soup

For Easy-to-Chew and Soft Diets

1. Place all of the ingredients up to and including the black pepper in a 3-quart pot. Cover and bring to a boil. Then reduce the heat to low and simmer for 45 to 60 minutes, or until the lentils are soft.

2. Remove 1 cup of the soup and purée it in a blender until smooth. Return the purée to the pot and stir in the olive oil. Serve hot, topping each serving with some of the Parmesan cheese and a drizzle of olive oil, if desired.

For Smooth/Puréed Diets

Working in batches, purée the entire pot of soup in a standing blender until smooth. (See the inset on page 156 for safety considerations.)

YIELD: 5 servings

4 cups chicken or vegetable broth

1 cup dried brown lentils

$3/4$ cup finely chopped onion

$3/4$ cup finely chopped or grated carrot

$1/2$ cup finely chopped celery

$1/2$ cup tomato or V8 vegetable juice

2 teaspoons crushed fresh garlic

1 teaspoon dried thyme

1 teaspoon dried marjoram

$1/2$ teaspoon ground black pepper

2–3 tablespoons extra virgin olive oil

$1/3$ cup grated Parmesan cheese (optional)

Olive oil (optional)

**Nutritional Facts
(Per 1-Cup Serving)**

Calories: 196
Carbohydrates: 26 g
Fiber: 9.2 g
Fat: 5.9 g
Sat. Fat: 0.8 g
Cholesterol: 0 mg
Protein: 10.6 g
Sodium: 465 mg
Calcium: 36 mg
Potassium: 504 mg

Diabetic Exchanges

1 starch
1 vegetable
1 lean meat
1 fat

For All Diets

Spicy Black Bean Soup

For Easy-to-Chew and Soft Diets

1. Place the olive oil in a 2½-quart pot over medium heat, and add the celery, onion, bell pepper, and carrot. Cover and cook, shaking the pan frequently, for about 4 minutes or until the vegetables start to soften. Add the garlic and cook for an additional 30 seconds.

2. Add the broth, vegetable juice, black beans, chili powder, cumin, and oregano to the pot. Cover and bring to a boil. Reduce the heat to a simmer and cook for 15 minutes.

3. Purée the soup with a hand-held blender until smooth. Serve hot, topping each serving with a dollop of sour cream.

For Smooth/Puréed Diets

Working in batches, purée the entire pot of soup in a standing blender until smooth. (See the inset on page 156 for safety considerations.)

YIELD: 5 servings

2–3 tablespoons extra virgin olive oil

⅓ cup chopped celery

⅓ cup chopped onion

⅓ cup chopped green bell pepper

⅓ cup chopped carrot

2 teaspoons crushed fresh garlic

1½ cups low-sodium chicken broth

1 cup low-sodium vegetable juice cocktail, such as V8

2 cans (15 ounces each) black beans, drained

1 teaspoon chili powder

1 teaspoon ground cumin

¾ teaspoon dried oregano

½ cup nonfat or light sour cream

**Nutritional Facts
(Per 1-Cup Serving)**

Calories: 181
Carbohydrates: 28g
Fiber: 9 g
Fat: 5.6 g
Sat. Fat: 0.8 g
Cholesterol: 0 mg
Protein: 9.6 g
Sodium: 480 mg
Calcium: 94 mg
Potassium: 632 mg

Diabetic Exchanges

1 starch
1 vegetable
1 lean meat
1 fat

For All Diets

Split Pea Soup with Ham

For Easy-to-Chew and Soft Diets

1. Place the ham, split peas, celery, onion, and carrot in a 4-quart pot. Add the water, parsley, garlic, thyme, and pepper. Cover and bring to a boil.

2. Reduce the heat to a simmer, cover, and cook, stirring occasionally, for 1 hour and 15 minutes, or until the peas are soft. Stir in the bouillon and cook for another 15 minutes.

3. Remove 1½ cups of the soup and purée in a blender until smooth. Return the blended soup to the pot and stir. Serve hot.

For Smooth/Puréed Diets

Working in batches, purée the entire pot of soup in a standing blender until smooth. (See the inset on page 156 for safety considerations.)

YIELD: 6 servings

- 1¼ cups diced lean ham (grind in a food processor if you want a finer texture)
- 1 cup plus 2 tablespoons green split peas
- 1 cup finely chopped celery
- ¾ cup chopped onion
- ½ cup diced carrot
- 5 cups water
- 2 tablespoons finely chopped fresh parsley, or 2 teaspoons dried parsley
- 2½ teaspoons crushed fresh garlic
- 1 teaspoon dried thyme
- ½ teaspoon ground black pepper
- 2 teaspoons chicken bouillon granules

**Nutritional Facts
(Per 1-Cup Serving)**

Calories: 161
Carbohydrates: 23 g
Fiber: 8.6 g
Fat: 1.8 g
Sat. Fat: 0.5 g
Cholesterol: 13 mg
Protein: 14 g
Sodium: 543 mg
Calcium: 31 mg
Potassium: 595 mg

Diabetic Exchanges

1 starch
2 lean meat

For All Diets

Summer Squash Soup

For Easy-to-Chew and Soft Diets

1. Place the margarine or butter in a 3-quart pot and melt over medium heat. Add the onion, cover, and cook for several minutes or until the onion softens. Add a few teaspoons of water if the pot becomes too dry. Add the garlic and cook for 15 additional seconds.

2. Add the squash, broth, potato, and marjoram or savory to the pot. Cover and bring to a boil over high heat. Reduce the heat to medium-low and simmer for about 10 minutes, or until the vegetables are soft. Stir in the evaporated milk and heat through.

3. Purée the soup with a hand-held blender until smooth. Serve hot, topping each serving with a sprinkling of Parmesan cheese.

For Smooth/Puréed Diets

Working in batches, purée the entire pot of soup in a standing blender until smooth. (See the inset on page 156 for safety considerations.)

YIELD: 5 servings

2½ tablespoons margarine or butter

¾ cup chopped onion

2 teaspoons crushed fresh garlic

3 cups diced unpeeled zucchini or summer squash

2 cups chicken or vegetable broth

1 cup diced peeled baking potato

1 teaspoon dried marjoram or savory

1 cup evaporated nonfat or low-fat milk

3 tablespoons grated Parmesan cheese

**Nutritional Facts
(Per 1-Cup Serving)**

Calories: 153
Carbohydrates: 17 g
Fiber: 1.8 g
Fat: 6.6 g
Sat. Fat: 1.9 g
Cholesterol: 5 mg
Protein: 7 g
Sodium: 437 mg
Calcium: 220 mg
Potassium: 532 mg

Diabetic Exchanges

1 vegetable
½ starch
½ nonfat/low-fat milk
1 fat

For All Diets

Sweet Potato Soup with Cilantro Pesto

For Easy-to-Chew and Soft Diets

1. To make the pesto, place all of the pesto ingredients except for the water in a mini-food processor, and process until the herbs and nuts are finely ground. Add the water and process just until mixed in. Add a little more water or olive oil, if needed, to bring the pesto to a consistency that can be drizzled from a spoon or squeeze bottle. Transfer to a small squeeze bottle or other container, and chill until ready to use.

2. To make the soup, place the olive oil, onion, and celery in a 3-quart pot. Cover and cook over medium heat, shaking the pan occasionally, for several minutes or until the vegetables begin to soften. Add a little water if needed to prevent scorching. Add the garlic and cook for 15 additional seconds.

3. Add the sweet potato and broth to the pot, and bring to a boil over high heat. Reduce the heat to a simmer, cover, and cook for 10 minutes or just until the potatoes are soft.

4. Add the jalapeño pepper to the pot, and purée the soup with a hand-held blender until smooth. Serve hot, drizzling each serving with about a tablespoon of the pesto.

For Smooth/Puréed Diets

Working in batches, purée the entire pot of soup in a standing blender until smooth. (See the inset on page 156 for safety considerations.) Process the pesto until smooth and, if necessary, push through a strainer to remove any coarse bits before drizzling the condiment over the soup.

**Nutritional Facts
(Per 1-Cup Serving)**

Calories: 204
Carbohydrates: 28 g
Fiber: 3.8 g
Fat: 9.2 g
Sat. Fat: 1.6 g
Cholesterol: 2 mg
Protein: 3.7 g
Sodium: 488 mg
Calcium: 64 mg
Potassium: 305 mg

Diabetic Exchanges

$1\frac{1}{2}$ starch
1 vegetable
2 fat

YIELD: 5 servings

1 tablespoon extra virgin olive oil

$\frac{3}{4}$ cup chopped yellow onion

$\frac{1}{2}$ cup chopped celery (include some leaves)

$1\frac{1}{2}$ teaspoons crushed fresh garlic

$4\frac{1}{2}$ cups diced peeled sweet potato (about $1\frac{1}{2}$ pounds)

3 cups chicken broth

1–2 teaspoons chopped pickled jalapeño pepper

PESTO

$\frac{1}{4}$ cup (moderately packed) fresh spinach

$\frac{1}{4}$ cup (moderately packed) fresh cilantro

2 tablespoons pine nuts or pumpkin seeds

2 tablespoons grated Parmesan cheese

2 tablespoons extra virgin olive oil

1 teaspoon crushed fresh garlic

1 tablespoon water

Tasty Tomato Soup

For Easy-to-Chew and Soft Diets

1. Place the broth, tomatoes, onion, celery, carrot, basil, and pepper in a 2½-quart pot. Cover and bring to a boil over high heat. Reduce the heat to a simmer and cook for about 12 minutes, or until the vegetables are soft.

2. Stir the evaporated milk and olive oil into the tomato mixture, and purée the soup with a hand-held blender until smooth. Serve hot, topping each serving with a dollop of sour cream or a drizzle of olive oil, if desired.

For Smooth/Puréed Diets

Working in batches, purée the entire pot of soup in a standing blender until smooth. (See the inset below for safety considerations.)

Puréeing Under Pressure

Standing blenders can allow you to purée soups to a smooth and silky consistency. Just be aware that whenever you process hot liquids in a blender, the pressure from the steam can blow the cover off, causing the hot liquid to splatter both you and your kitchen. To guard against accidents, never fill a blender more than half full with a hot liquid. If the machine has a feeder cap, crack it open slightly to allow the steam to escape. Start blending the mixture at the lowest speed, and gradually increase to higher speeds as needed to achieve the desired consistency. As an extra precaution, cover the blender lid with a towel to protect yourself in the event that the top pops off.

YIELD: 5 servings

2 cups chicken or vegetable broth

14½-ounce can no-added-salt diced tomatoes, undrained

¾ cup chopped onion

¾ cup chopped celery

¾ cup chopped carrot

1 teaspoon dried basil

¼ teaspoon ground black pepper

½ cup evaporated nonfat or low-fat milk

2 tablespoons extra virgin olive oil

¼ cup plus 1 tablespoon light sour cream, or additional olive oil (optional)

**Nutritional Facts
(Per 1-Cup Serving)**

Calories: 105
Carbohydrates: 12 g
Fiber: 2.1 g
Fat: 5.6 g
Sat. Fat: 0.8 g
Cholesterol: 1 mg
Protein: 3.3 g
Sodium: 317 mg
Calcium: 116 mg
Potassium: 422 mg

Diabetic Exchanges

2 vegetable
1 fat

For All Diets

Winter Squash Soup

For Easy-to-Chew and Soft Diets

1. Place the margarine or butter in a 2½-quart pot and melt over medium heat. Add the onion, marjoram, and thyme to the pot. Cover and cook for several minutes, or until the onion starts to soften. Add a few teaspoons of water if the pot becomes too dry.

2. Stir the broth, squash, garlic, and pepper into the onion mixture, and bring to a boil over high heat. Reduce the heat to a simmer, cover, and cook for 10 minutes. If using raw squash, continue to cook until the squash is tender.

3. Purée the soup with a hand-held blender until smooth. Serve hot, topping each serving with a tablespoon of Parmesan cheese and a sprinkling of parsley.

For Smooth/Puréed Diets

Working in batches, purée the entire pot of soup in a standing blender until smooth. (See the inset on page 156 for safety considerations.)

YIELD: 4 servings

2 tablespoons margarine or butter

1½ cups chopped yellow onion

¾ teaspoon dried marjoram

½ teaspoon dried thyme

3 cups reduced-sodium chicken or vegetable broth

3 cups cubed, peeled butternut squash or pumpkin, 15-ounce can plain pumpkin, or 1¾ cups frozen (thawed) cooked mashed winter squash*

2 teaspoons crushed fresh garlic

¼ teaspoon ground black pepper

¼ cup grated Parmesan cheese

1 teaspoon dried parsley, finely crumbled

---

* If you decide to use the frozen winter squash, note that this product usually comes in 12-ounce packages. You will need about 1⅓ packages to yield the 1¾ cups of mashed squash required for this recipe.

**Nutritional Facts
(Per 1⅛-Cup Serving)**

Calories: 144
Carbohydrates: 17 g
Fiber: 4.1 g
Fat: 7.2 g
Sat. Fat: 2.3 g
Cholesterol: 5 mg
Protein: 4.3 g
Sodium: 485 mg
Calcium: 146 mg
Potassium: 430 mg

Diabetic Exchanges

1 starch
1½ fat

For All Diets

Chilled Beet Soup with Sour Cream and Dill

For Easy-to-Chew and Soft Diets

1. Place the broth, beets, onion, carrot, and garlic in a 3-quart pot, and bring to a boil over high heat. Reduce the heat to a simmer, cover, and cook for about 35 minutes, or until the vegetables are soft.

2. Purée the soup with a hand-held blender until smooth, adding a little more broth if needed. If desired, add the canola or walnut oil and blend again. Cover and chill for several hours or overnight.

3. To serve, place one cup of soup in each bowl and top with a rounded tablespoon of sour cream and a sprinkling of dill.

For Smooth/Puréed Diets

Working in batches, purée the entire pot of soup in a standing blender until smooth. (See the inset on page 156 for safety considerations.)

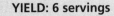

YIELD: 6 servings

3³/₄ cups reduced-sodium chicken or vegetable broth

3 cups diced peeled fresh beets (about 1¹/₄ pounds)

1 cup chopped sweet onion

³/₄ cup chopped carrot

1¹/₂ teaspoons crushed fresh garlic

1–2 tablespoons canola or walnut oil (optional)

¹/₂ cup light sour cream

1¹/₂ teaspoons dried dill, finely crumbled

**Nutritional Facts
(Per 1-Cup Serving)**

Calories: 75
Carbohydrates: 12 g
Fiber: 2.9 g
Fat: 1.9 g
Sat. Fat: 1.4 g
Cholesterol: 7 mg
Protein: 3 g
Sodium: 339 mg
Calcium: 53 mg
Potassium: 370 mg

Diabetic Exchanges

2 vegetable
¹/₂ fat

For All Diets

Garden Gazpacho

For Easy-to-Chew and Soft Diets

1. Place the bell pepper and onion in a food processor, and process until finely chopped. Add the tomato and cucumber, and process again until finely chopped.

2. Combine the vegetable juice, vinegar, olive oil, garlic, and chili powder in a medium-size bowl, and whisk to mix. Add the mixture to the food processor and process for a few seconds to combine. If a smoother texture is desired, process for additional time.

3. Transfer the gazpacho to a covered container and chill for at least 2 hours before serving. Top each serving with a dollop of sour cream, if desired.

For Smooth/Puréed Diets

Working in batches, purée the entire pot of soup in a standing blender until smooth.

For a Change

▪ For a slightly different flavor, try substituting lemon juice for the vinegar. For extra thickness, add a slice of bread to the food processor.

YIELD: 4 servings

1/2 cup diced yellow or red bell pepper

1/4 cup plus 2 tablespoons chopped sweet onion

1 1/2 cups diced fresh tomato

1 cup diced peeled and seeded cucumber

1 3/4 cups V8 vegetable juice

2 1/2 tablespoons red wine vinegar

2 tablespoons extra virgin olive oil

1 1/2 teaspoons crushed garlic

3/4 teaspoon chili powder

1/2 cup light sour cream (optional)

**Nutritional Facts
(Per 1-Cup Serving)**

Calories: 111
Carbohydrates: 12 g
Fiber: 2.6 g
Fat: 7.3 g
Sat. Fat: 1 g
Cholesterol: 0 mg
Protein: 1.9 g
Sodium: 301 mg
Calcium: 27 mg
Potassium: 469 mg

Diabetic Exchanges

2 vegetable
1 1/2 fat

For All Diets

Sweet Cherry Soup

1. Place 1 tablespoon of the water and all of the cornstarch in a small bowl, and stir to dissolve the cornstarch. Set aside.

2. Place the remaining water and the cherries, orange or apple juice, cinnamon, and cloves in a blender, and process until smooth.

3. Transfer the cherry mixture to a 3-quart pot. Stir in the honey and bring to a boil over high heat. Reduce the heat to medium and cook uncovered, stirring frequently, for 5 minutes.

4. Add the cornstarch mixture to the pot while stirring constantly. Cook for a minute or 2, or until the soup comes to a boil and thickens slightly. Transfer to a covered container and refrigerate for several hours or until well chilled. Top each serving with a dollop of sour cream or yogurt, if desired.

Dietary Variations

To reduce calories and carbohydrates:

Replace the honey with sugar substitute equal to six tablespoons of sugar, and you will eliminate 56 calories, 15 grams carbohydrate, and 1 carbohydrate diabetic exchange. (See page 44 for details on using sugar substitutes.)

YIELD: 6 servings

3 cups water, divided

2 teaspoons cornstarch

6 cups fresh or frozen (thawed and undrained) dark sweet pitted cherries

1 cup orange or apple juice

1/2 teaspoon ground cinnamon

1/4 teaspoon ground cloves

1/4 cup plus 2 tablespoons honey

3/4 cup light sour cream or plain low-fat yogurt

**Nutritional Facts
(Per 1-Cup Serving)**

Calories: 216
Carbohydrates: 46 g
Fiber: 3.1 g
Fat: 2.5 g
Sat. Fat: 2 g
Cholesterol: 10 mg
Protein: 3.3 g
Sodium: 21 mg
Calcium: 66 mg
Potassium: 463 mg

Diabetic Exchanges

2 fruit
1 carbohydrate
1/2 fat

For All Diets

Yogurt-Fruit Soup

1. Place the fruit, juice, and sugar or honey in a blender, and process until smooth. Add the yogurt and blend just until mixed.

2. Transfer the soup to a covered container and chill for at least 2 hours. If the cold soup seems too thick, stir in a little more juice. If desired, place some sour cream in a squeeze bottle and drizzle over the top of each serving.

Dietary Variations

To reduce calories and carbohydrates:

Replace the sugar or honey with sugar substitute and you will eliminate 43 calories, 11 grams carbohydrate, and 1 carbohydrate diabetic exchange. (See page 44 for details on using sugar substitutes.)

YIELD: 4 servings

4 cups fresh fruit, such as chopped fresh strawberries, pitted sweet cherries, or blueberries; or 4 cups frozen fruit, thawed and undrained

1/2 cup cranberry juice cocktail, pomegranate juice, or orange juice

1/4 cup sugar or honey

1 1/4 cups low-fat vanilla yogurt

2–3 tablespoons light sour cream (optional)

The Finishing Touch

Any professional chef can tell you that a decorative drizzle of sauce under or over a food is one of the simplest ways to create a stunning presentation as well as a burst of flavor. Simply by squirting a bit of sour cream over your bowl of Yogurt-Fruit Soup (see above), for instance, you will transform this simple dish into a treat for the eyes as well as the palate. Of course, for people on a soft or smooth diet, sauce can be more than decoration. When used on meats, veggies, and other dishes, sauce adds important moisture, making everything easier to swallow. Consider keeping your favorite sauces and condiments in squeeze bottles in your refrigerator. That way, you'll always be ready to add a flavorful finishing touch to your dishes.

**Nutritional Facts
(Per 1-Cup Serving)**

Calories: 182
Carbohydrates: 39 g
Fiber: 3.9 g
Fat: 1.6 g
Sat. Fat: 0.7 g
Cholesterol: 4 mg
Protein: 4.8 g
Sodium: 53 mg
Calcium: 156 mg
Potassium: 449 mg

Diabetic Exchanges

1 fruit
1/2 nonfat/low-fat milk
1 carbohydrate

THE SECRET'S
IN THE SAUCE

The secret of a delicious and easy-to-swallow dish is very often in the sauce. A savory sauce can transform an ordinary bowl of pasta into an extraordinary entrée or side dish, while a sweet sauce can turn a dry piece of cake into a moist, easy-to-eat delight. Sauces can also add color and eye appeal to dishes, enhance aroma, and even boost nutritional value and calories.

Sauces are important for people who have a diminished sense of taste, as well. By using sauces that contain red pepper or other highly flavored seasonings and condiments, you can spice up a variety of dishes. In many cases, a sauce, once prepared, can be stored in the refrigerator for a number of days, allowing you to add a burst of flavor to your meal quickly and with little additional effort.

If you are following a smooth diet, sauce is especially useful since it can be puréed with otherwise dry foods, such as chicken or beef, until they reach the proper consistency. Once puréed, the dish will be far more attractive if you create decorative squiggles of your sauce through use of a squeeze bottle. Just keep in mind that if you must have thickened liquids, you will have to make sure that this condiment is the proper consistency. (See Chapter 6 for more on this subject.)

This chapter presents an array of simple savory and sweet sauces that are designed to perk up your menus. Whether you're trying to add interest to an easy-to-swallow meatloaf, moisten a stack of pancakes, dress a bowl of pasta, or provide a simple topping for a dish of ice cream, you're sure to find a sauce that complements your dish while adding a luxurious gourmet touch.

SAVORY SAUCES

Alfredo Sauce

1. Combine the milk, onion powder, pepper, and nutmeg in a bowl and stir to mix. Set aside.

2. Place the margarine or butter in a 2-quart pot, and melt over medium-low heat. Add the flour and stir to form a paste. Cook for 2 minutes, stirring occasionally, to cook the flour. Do not allow the flour to brown.

3. Remove the pot from the heat and slowly add the reserved milk mixture, whisking until smooth. Return the pot to the heat and cook, stirring frequently, until thickened and bubbly.

4. Remove the pot from the heat and stir in the cheese. Serve hot over pasta, vegetables, chicken, fish, timbales, or soufflés. Store any leftovers in the refrigerator for up to 3 days, reheating the sauce on the stovetop or in a microwave oven.

For a Change

■ Reduce the Parmesan to 2 tablespoons and add ¼ cup shredded Swiss cheese along with the Parmesan.

YIELD: About 1²/₃ cups

1½ cups nonfat or low-fat milk

½ teaspoon onion powder

⅛ teaspoon ground white pepper

Pinch ground nutmeg

2 tablespoons margarine or butter

2 tablespoons unbleached flour

¼ cup grated Parmesan cheese

**Nutritional Facts
(Per ¼-Cup Serving)**

Calories: 72
Carbohydrates: 4 g
Fiber: 0.1 g
Fat: 4.5 g
Sat. Fat: 1.3 g
Cholesterol: 4 mg
Protein: 3.6 g
Sodium: 125 mg
Calcium: 117 mg
Potassium: 99 mg

Diabetic Exchanges

½ nonfat/low-fat milk
1 fat

For All Diets

Cheddar Cheese Sauce

**Nutritional Facts
(Per 1/4-Cup Serving)**

Calories: 94
Carbohydrates: 4 g
Fiber: 0 g
Fat: 5.8 g
Sat. Fat: 3.6 g
Cholesterol: 18 mg
Protein: 6.2 g
Sodium: 130 mg
Calcium: 182 mg
Potassium: 98 mg

Diabetic Exchanges

1 medium-fat meat

1. Place all of the ingredients except for the cheese in a pint-size jar with a tight-fitting lid. Shake until smooth.

2. Pour the milk mixture into a 2-quart microwave-safe bowl. Microwave on high power uncovered for several minutes, stirring after each minute, until the mixture comes to a full boil. Stir again; then heat for an additional 20 seconds.

3. Add the cheese to the milk mixture and stir until melted. Serve hot with soufflés, puréed cauliflower, mashed potatoes, angel hair pasta, macaroni, and other dishes. Store any leftovers in the refrigerator for up to 3 days, reheating the sauce in a microwave oven or on the stovetop.

YIELD: 1 1/4 cups

1 cup nonfat or low-fat milk

1 1/2 tablespoons unbleached flour

1/4 teaspoon dry mustard

Pinch ground cayenne or white pepper

3/4 cup finely shredded sharp Cheddar cheese

Boosting the Calories in Sauces

Besides adding a new layer of flavor and welcome moisture to foods, sauces present a great opportunity to boost calories, should you need to put on pounds or prevent weight loss. Here are some ideas.

If your sauce contains oil or margarine, consider increasing the amount of this ingredient. Each tablespoon will add about 100 calories to the recipe. If the recipe contains mayonnaise, use a full-fat version instead of a light brand to add about 90 extra calories per tablespoon.

If cholesterol and saturated fat are not an issue, you can use extra butter in your butter-based sauce, or substitute full-fat sour cream for your nonfat or light sour cream. You can also substitute evaporated whole milk, half and half, or even cream for the recipe's low-fat milk. With evaporated whole milk and half and half weighing in at about 340 calories per cup, and cream providing 700 to 800 calories per cup, you can easily double or triple the calories in each serving while making your sauce extra smooth, creamy, and flavorful.

For All Diets

Easy Hollandaise Sauce

1. Place the cornstarch in a 1½-quart microwave-safe bowl. Add about 3 tablespoons of the milk and whisk until smooth. Slowly whisk in first the remaining milk, and then the egg yolks and mustard. Add the margarine or butter.

2. Microwave on high power uncovered for about 3 minutes, whisking every 45 seconds, just until the mixture comes to a boil and thickens.

3. Remove the bowl from the microwave oven and whisk in the lemon juice, salt, and pepper. Serve hot over vegetables, fish, soufflés, and timbales. Store any leftovers in the refrigerator for up to 3 days, reheating the sauce in the microwave or on the stovetop.

Dietary Variations

To reduce cholesterol:

Substitute ¼ cup fat-free egg substitute for the egg yolks and eliminate 25 calories, 2.2 grams fat, 107 milligrams cholesterol, and ½ diabetic fat exchange.

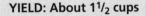

YIELD: About 1½ cups

1½ tablespoons cornstarch

1 cup nonfat or low-fat milk

3 large egg yolks

1 teaspoon Dijon or spicy mustard

¼ cup margarine or butter, cut into small pieces

2 tablespoons fresh lemon juice

⅛ teaspoon salt

Pinch ground white pepper

Nutritional Facts (Per ¼-Cup Serving)

Calories: 122
Carbohydrates: 4 g
Fiber: 0 g
Fat: 10 g
Sat. Fat: 2.1 g
Cholesterol: 107 mg
Protein: 3 g
Sodium: 168 mg
Calcium: 69 mg
Potassium: 92 mg

Diabetic Exchanges

¼ nonfat/low-fat milk
2 fat

For All Diets

Simple Tomato Sauce

For Easy-to-Chew and Soft Diets

1. Pour the olive oil into a 2-quart pot. Add the onion, cover, and cook over medium heat, stirring occasionally, for several minutes, or until the onion softens. Add the garlic and cook for 30 additional seconds.

2. Add the tomatoes, broth, parsley, and basil to the onion mixture, and bring to a boil over high heat. Reduce the heat to low, cover, and simmer for 15 minutes, stirring occasionally. Serve hot over meats, fish, and pasta. Store any leftovers in the refrigerator for up to 3 days, reheating the sauce on the stovetop or in a microwave oven.

For Smooth/Puréed Diets

Use a hand-held blender to blend the sauce until smooth, or, for a smoother consistency, process it in batches in a regular standing blender. (See the inset on page 156 for safety considerations.)

YIELD: About 3½ cups

2 tablespoons extra virgin olive oil

½ cup finely chopped onion

1–2 teaspoons crushed garlic

28-ounce can crushed tomatoes

½ cup vegetable or beef broth

2 teaspoons dried parsley

1 teaspoon dried basil

Making the Most of Canned Tomatoes

Available whole, diced, and crushed, canned tomatoes are a convenient addition to the pantry. To make a quick sauce, simply purée a can of diced Italian- or Mexican-style tomatoes with a few tablespoons of olive oil. Heat and serve over meat, eggs, pasta, rice, and other dishes. Keep in mind, though, that canned tomatoes can be high in sodium. If this is a concern, avoid adding salt to the recipe or choose no-salt-added tomatoes. This will lend your dish rich tomato flavor while keeping it healthful.

Nutritional Facts (Per ½-Cup Serving)

Calories: 76
Carbohydrates: 9 g
Fiber: 2.4 g
Fat: 4.2 g
Sat. Fat: 0.6 g
Cholesterol: 0 mg
Protein: 2.2 g
Sodium: 222 mg
Calcium: 43 mg
Potassium: 357 mg

Diabetic Exchanges

1 vegetable
1 fat

Quick Chicken Gravy

**Nutritional Facts
(Per ¼-Cup Serving)**

Calories: 45
Carbohydrates: 3 g
Fiber: 0.1 g
Fat: 3.4 g
Sat. Fat: 0.3 g
Cholesterol: 0 mg
Protein: 0.5 g
Sodium: 212 mg
Calcium: 0 mg
Potassium: 11 mg

Diabetic Exchanges

½ fat

1. Place the flour and oil in a small bowl and stir until smooth. Slowly stir in 2 tablespoons of the broth. Set aside.

2. Place the remaining broth in a 1-quart pot and bring to a boil over medium heat. Gradually pour the flour mixture into the hot broth, whisking constantly until smooth. Cook and stir for a couple of minutes or until no taste of uncooked starch remains.

3. Serve the sauce hot over puréed chicken, stuffing, or mashed potatoes. Store any leftovers in the refrigerator for up to 3 days, reheating the sauce on the stovetop or in a microwave oven.

For a Change

■ Substitute vegetable or beef broth for the chicken broth.

YIELD: About 1½ cups

3 tablespoons
   unbleached flour
1½ tablespoons
   canola oil
1½ cups plus 2
   tablespoons cold or
   room-temperature
   chicken broth,
   divided

Roasted Red Pepper Sauce

**Nutritional Facts
(Per 2-Tablespoon
Serving)**

Calories: 50
Carbohydrates: 1.2 g
Fiber: 0.3 g
Fat: 5 g
Sat. Fat: 0.7 g
Cholesterol: 0 mg
Protein: 0.2 g
Sodium: 73 mg
Calcium: 2 mg
Potassium: 31 mg

Diabetic Exchanges

1 fat

1. Place all of the ingredients in a blender and process until smooth.

2. Transfer the sauce to a covered container and chill until ready to serve. Serve over chicken, fish, meats, omelets, and soufflés. Store any leftovers in the refrigerator for up to 3 days.

YIELD: About 1 cup

1 cup jarred roasted
   red bell peppers
3–4 tablespoons
   extra virgin olive
   oil
¼ teaspoon salt
¼ teaspoon ground
   black pepper
1 teaspoon balsamic
   vinegar

Sour Cream Dill Sauce

Nutritional Facts (Per 2-Tablespoon Serving)

Calories: 35
Carbohydrates: 1 g
Fiber: 0 g
Fat: 2.9 g
Sat. Fat: 1.8 g
Cholesterol: 9 mg
Protein: 1 g
Sodium: 13 mg
Calcium: 34 mg
Potassium: 44 mg

Diabetic Exchanges

1/2 fat

1. Combine all of the ingredients and stir to mix well. Add a little more milk if you want a thinner sauce.

2. Transfer the sauce to a covered container and chill until ready to use. Serve with seafood and vegetables, storing any leftovers in the refrigerator for up to 3 days.

YIELD: About 2/3 cup

1/2 cup light sour cream

2 tablespoons nonfat or low-fat milk

1/2 teaspoon dried dill, or 1 1/2 teaspoons finely chopped fresh dill

Quick Creole Sauce

Nutritional Facts (Per 1/4-Cup Serving)

Calories: 41
Carbohydrates: 5 g
Fiber: 0.6 g
Fat: 2.3 g
Sat. Fat: 0.3 g
Cholesterol: 0 mg
Protein: 0.6 g
Sodium: 308 mg
Calcium: 11 mg
Potassium: 173 mg

Diabetic Exchanges

1 vegetable
1/2 fat

1. Place all of the ingredients in a blender and process until smooth.

2. Pour the blended tomato mixture into a small saucepan and cook over medium heat for a couple of minutes to heat through. Serve hot over meat, fish, eggs, vegetables, and other savory foods. Store any leftovers in the refrigerator for up to 3 days, reheating the sauce on the stovetop or in a microwave oven.

YIELD: 1 1/2 cups

14 1/2-ounce can stewed tomatoes, undrained

1 tablespoon extra virgin olive oil

2–3 teaspoons Cajun seasoning

For All Diets

Roasted Vegetable Gravy

1. Preheat the oven to 400°F.

2. Place the potato, carrot, and onion in an 8-inch square pan, drizzle with the olive oil, and toss to mix. Bake uncovered, stirring every 10 minutes, for about 35 minutes, or until the vegetables are tender and nicely browned.

3. Transfer the vegetables to a 2-quart pot and add the broth and thyme. Cover and bring to a boil. Reduce the heat to low and simmer for 5 minutes, stirring occasionally.

4. Purée the sauce with a hand-held blender until smooth. Alternatively, process the sauce in batches in a standing blender. Serve hot over meats, vegetables, and other savory dishes. Store any leftovers in the refrigerator for up to 3 days, reheating the sauce on the stovetop or in a microwave oven.

YIELD: 1³/₄ cups

½ cup diced peeled baking potato

½ cup diced carrot

½ medium yellow onion, cut into ½-inch wedges

1–2 tablespoons extra virgin olive oil

1½ cups vegetable, beef, or chicken broth

¼ teaspoon dried thyme

The Goodness of Olive Oil

Throughout this book, olive oil is often used to cook vegetables, moisten sandwich spreads, and even top soups. Why do we use this ingredient in so many dishes?

Olive oil is rich in monounsaturated fat, which has been shown to lower levels of "bad" LDL cholesterol without reducing levels of "good" HDL cholesterol. This golden oil also contains phytonutrients that may help protect against cancer. But olive oil is more than a healthy fat. Unlike most vegetable oils, which are very bland in taste, this product adds its own delicious flavor to foods. Extra virgin olive oil is the least processed and most flavorful form, so if you love the taste of olive oil, this is the type you'll want to buy. If you don't care for olive oil's distinctive flavor, look for a brand that's labeled "light." Just be aware that it's light in flavor, not calories, and that some of the oil's beneficial phytonutrients have been removed to tone down its taste.

Nutritional Facts
(Per ¼-Cup Serving)

Calories: 33
Carbohydrates: 4 g
Fiber: 0.6 g
Fat: 2 g
Sat. Fat: 0.3 g
Cholesterol: 0 mg
Protein: 0.7 g
Sodium: 160 mg
Calcium: 5 mg
Potassium: 92 mg

Diabetic Exchanges

1 vegetable
½ fat

SWEET SAUCES

For All Diets

Fresh Berry Purée

1. Place all of the ingredients in a food processor and process until smooth.

2. Pour the purée into a wire strainer and use a wooden spoon to push the mixture through the strainer into a bowl. Discard the seeds and any coarse bits remaining in the strainer. Add a little orange, pomegranate, or cranberry juice to the sauce if you want a thinner consistency.

3. Transfer the sauce to a covered container and chill until ready to use. Serve over ice cream, pudding, or cake, allowing it to soak into the cake if necessary. Store any leftovers in the refrigerator for up to 3 days.

Dietary Variation

To reduce calories and carbohydrates:

Replace the sugar with a sugar substitute and eliminate 34 calories, 9 grams of carbohydrate, and $1/2$ diabetic carbohydrate exchange. (See page 44 for details on using sugar substitutes.)

YIELD: About 1¼ cups

3 cups fresh or frozen (thawed and undrained) strawberries, raspberries, blackberries, or blueberries

¼–⅓ cup sugar

1½ teaspoons frozen orange juice concentrate

**Nutritional Facts
(Per ¼-Cup Serving)**

Calories: 71
Carbohydrates: 17 g
Fiber: 0.8 g
Fat: 0.1 g
Sat. Fat: 0 g
Cholesterol: 0 mg
Protein: 0.6 g
Sodium: 10 mg
Calcium: 11 mg
Potassium: 92 mg

Diabetic Exchanges

½ carbohydrate
½ fruit

For All Diets

Warm Berry Syrup

1. Place the cornstarch and 1 tablespoon of the juice in a small bowl, and stir to dissolve the cornstarch. Set aside.

2. Place the remaining juice and the berries in a blender, and process until smooth.

3. Pour the fruit purée into a wire strainer and use a wooden spoon to push the mixture through the strainer into a 2-quart pot. Discard the seeds and any coarse bits remaining in the strainer.

4. Stir the sugar into the berry mixture and bring to a boil over high heat. Reduce the heat to a simmer, cover, and cook for 5 minutes, stirring occasionally.

5. Stir the reserved cornstarch mixture into the simmering fruit and cook over medium heat, stirring constantly, for about a minute, or until the sauce is bubbly and has thickened to a syrupy consistency.

6. Serve the sauce warm as a topping for pancakes, or use to moisten pound cake or angel food cake. Store any leftovers in the refrigerator for up to 3 days, reheating the sauce on the stovetop or in a microwave oven.

Dietary Variation

To reduce calories and carbohydrates:

Replace the sugar with a sugar substitute and eliminate 32 calories, 8 grams of carbohydrate, and $\frac{1}{2}$ diabetic carbohydrate exchange. (See page 44 for details on using sugar substitutes.)

YIELD: About 2 cups

1–1$\frac{1}{2}$ teaspoons cornstarch

1 cup white grape or pomegranate juice, divided

2 cups fresh or frozen (thawed and undrained) blueberries, strawberries, raspberries, or blackberries

$\frac{1}{4}$ cup plus 2 tablespoons sugar

Nutritional Facts
(Per $\frac{1}{4}$-Cup Serving)

Calories: 76
Carbohydrates: 19 g
Fiber: 1 g
Fat: 0.2 g
Sat. Fat: 0 g
Cholesterol: 0 mg
Protein: 0.3 g
Sodium: 4 mg
Calcium: 6 mg
Potassium: 44 mg

Diabetic Exchanges

$\frac{1}{2}$ fruit
$\frac{1}{2}$ carbohydrate

For All Diets

Mixed Berry Sauce

For Easy-to-Chew and Soft Diets

1. Place the cornstarch and 1 tablespoon of the juice in a small bowl and stir to dissolve the cornstarch. Set aside.

2. Place the remaining juice, the berries, and the sugar in a 2-quart pot. Cover and bring to a boil over high heat. Reduce the heat to a simmer, cover, and cook, stirring occasionally, for about 5 minutes, or until the berries break down.

3. Stir the reserved cornstarch mixture into the simmering fruit and cook over medium heat, stirring constantly, for about a minute, or until the sauce is bubbly and has thickened to a syrupy consistency.

4. Serve warm as a topping for pancakes, French toast, or ice cream, or use to moisten plain cake. Store any leftovers in the refrigerator for up to 3 days, reheating the sauce on the stovetop or in a microwave oven.

For Smooth/Puréed Diets

After the sauce has simmered in Step 2, use a hand-held blender to process it until smooth. Force the sauce through a wire strainer to remove the seeds, and proceed with the recipe.

Dietary Variation

To reduce carbohydrates and calories:

Replace the sugar with a sugar substitute and eliminate 24 calories, 6 grams of carbohydrate, and $1/2$ diabetic carbohydrate exchange. (See page 44 for details on using sugar substitutes.)

YIELD: About 1³/₄ cups

2 teaspoons cornstarch

$1/2$ cup orange or pomegranate juice, divided

$1 1/2$ cups fresh or frozen (unthawed) chopped strawberries

$3/4$ cup fresh or frozen (unthawed) raspberries

$3/4$ cup fresh or frozen (unthawed) blueberries

$1/4$–$1/3$ cup sugar

**Nutritional Facts
(Per ¹/₄-Cup Serving)**

Calories: 56
Carbohydrates: 14 g
Fiber: 2.1 g
Fat: 0.3 g
Sat. Fat: 0 g
Cholesterol: 0 mg
Protein: 0.4 g
Sodium: 1 mg
Calcium: 9 mg
Potassium: 93 mg

Diabetic Exchanges

$1/2$ fruit
$1/2$ carbohydrate

Cinnamon-Apple Syrup

1. Place the cornstarch and 1 tablespoon of the apple juice in a small bowl and stir to dissolve the cornstarch. Set aside.

2. Pour the remaining apple juice into a 2-quart pot. Add the apples, maple syrup, and cinnamon, and stir to mix. Cover and bring to a boil over high heat. Reduce the heat to a simmer and cook, stirring occasionally, for about 8 minutes, or until the apples are soft.

3. Use a hand-held blender to blend the sauce until smooth, or process it in a regular standing blender. Return the purée to the pot.

4. Stir the reserved cornstarch mixture into the sauce and cook over medium heat, stirring constantly, for a couple of minutes, or until the mixture is bubbly and has thickened to a syrupy consistency. Add the butter or margarine, if desired, and stir until melted.

5. Serve the sauce warm over pancakes or French toast, or use to moisten gingerbread, spice cake, or pound cake. Store any leftovers in the refrigerator for up to 3 days, reheating the sauce on the stovetop or in a microwave oven.

YIELD: About 2 cups

1½ teaspoons cornstarch

1¼ cups apple juice, divided

1 cup chopped peeled apples

½ cup maple syrup

½ teaspoon ground cinnamon

1–2 tablespoons butter or margarine (optional)

**Nutritional Facts
(Per ¼-Cup Serving)**

Calories: 80
Carbohydrates: 20 g
Fiber: 0.3 g
Fat: 0 g
Sat. Fat: 0 g
Cholesterol: 0 mg
Protein: 0 g
Sodium: 3 mg
Calcium: 17 mg
Potassium: 102 mg

Diabetic Exchanges

1 carbohydrate

Cinnamon-Pear Sauce

**Nutritional Facts
(Per 1/4-Cup Serving)**

Calories: 75
Carbohydrates: 21 g
Fiber: 1 g
Fat: 0 g
Sat. Fat: 0 g
Cholesterol: 0 mg
Protein: 0.2 g
Sodium: 3 mg
Calcium: 7 mg
Potassium: 59 mg

Diabetic Exchanges

1/2 fruit
1 carbohydrate

1. Place the undrained pears and cinnamon in a blender, and purée until smooth.

2. Transfer the mixture to a 1-quart pot and stir in the honey or maple syrup. Place over medium heat and cook, stirring occasionally, for several minutes or until heated through.

3. Stir the sauce into hot oatmeal or other cereal or use as a topping for pancakes, French toast, gingerbread, pound cake, or ice cream. Store any leftovers in the refrigerator for up to 3 days, reheating the sauce on the stovetop or in a microwave oven.

YIELD: About 2 cups

15-ounce can pears in juice, undrained
1/2 teaspoon ground cinnamon
1/4 cup plus 2 tablespoons honey or maple syrup

Simple Brandy Sauce

**Nutritional Facts
(Per 2-Tablespoon Serving)**

Calories: 86
Carbohydrates: 13 g
Fiber: 0 g
Fat: 2.1 g
Sat. Fat: 1.3 g
Cholesterol: 8 mg
Protein: 2 g
Sodium: 30 mg
Calcium: 67 mg
Potassium: 88 mg

Diabetic Exchanges

1 carbohydrate

1. Place the condensed milk and brandy in a medium-size bowl and whisk to mix well.

2. Serve at room temperature or chilled, or heat for a couple of minutes in a microwave oven or on the stovetop to warm through, whisking in a little milk if you want a thinner consistency. Serve over bread pudding, apple cake, or other treats. Store any leftovers in the refrigerator for up to 5 days.

For a Change

■ Substitute rum, bourbon, or whiskey for the brandy.

YIELD: 1 1/2 cups

10-ounce can sweetened condensed milk
1/4 cup brandy

For All Diets

Quick Custard Sauce

1. Place the pudding mix and sugar in a medium-size bowl, and whisk to mix.

2. Add half of the milk to the pudding mixture and whisk for 2 minutes. Gradually whisk in first the remaining milk, and then the vanilla extract.

3. Allow the sauce to sit for 5 minutes before serving, or transfer the sauce to a covered container and chill until ready to use, whisking in a little more milk if a thinner consistency is desired. Spoon over pound cake, angel food cake, and other plain cakes. Store any leftovers in the refrigerator for up to 3 days.

For a Change

■ Substitute butterscotch pudding mix for the vanilla pudding mix, and serve the sauce with plain chocolate cake, pound cake, or spice cake.

■ Substitute lemon pudding mix for the vanilla pudding mix, omit the vanilla extract, and replace 1/2 cup of the milk with orange juice, if desired. Serve with pound cake or angel food cake.

■ Substitute white chocolate pudding mix for the vanilla pudding mix, and omit the vanilla extract. Serve with plain chocolate cake or angel food cake.

Dietary Variation

To reduce calories and carbohydrates:

Use sugar-free instant pudding mix and replace the sugar with sugar substitute. (See page 44 for details on using sugar substitutes.) This will eliminate 20 calories, 5 grams carbohydrate, and 1/4 diabetic carbohydrate exchange.

YIELD: 2 1/2 cups

1/2 package (4-serving size) instant vanilla pudding mix

1–2 tablespoons sugar

2 1/2 cups nonfat or low-fat milk

1 teaspoon vanilla extract

**Nutritional Facts
(Per 1/4-Cup Serving)**

Calories: 44
Carbohydrates: 9 g
Fiber: 0 g
Fat: 0.1 g
Sat. Fat: 0 g
Cholesterol: 0 mg
Protein: 2.1 g
Sodium: 103 mg
Calcium: 76 mg
Potassium: 103 mg

Diabetic Exchanges

1/2 carbohydrate

For All Diets

Vanilla Custard Sauce

1. Place the egg yolks, sugar, and salt in a small bowl and whisk for about a minute or until the mixture is pale yellow in color. Set aside.

2. Place the milk powder and cornstarch in a 2-quart microwave-safe bowl. Add about 3 tablespoons of the milk and whisk to mix well. Slowly whisk in the remaining milk.

3. Microwave the milk mixture uncovered on high power, stirring after each minute, for about 4 minutes, or until the mixture comes to a boil.

4. Remove about ¼ cup of the hot milk mixture and slowly whisk it into the reserved egg mixture. Then slowly whisk the egg mixture into the hot milk mixture.

5. Return the sauce to the microwave oven and cook on high power, whisking every 20 seconds, for about 1 minute, or until the mixture comes to a full boil. Stir in the vanilla extract and allow the sauce to cool for 10 minutes, whisking a couple of times.

6. Transfer the sauce to a covered container and chill for several hours or overnight before serving. (The sauce will thicken further as it cools.) Serve over angel food cake, pound cake, and plain chocolate cake. Store any leftovers in the refrigerator for up to 3 days.

Dietary Variations

To reduce calories and carbohydrates:

Replace the sugar with a sugar substitute and eliminate 34 calories, 8 grams carbohydrate, and ½ diabetic carbohydrate exchange. (See page 44 for details on using sugar substitutes.)

To reduce cholesterol and fat:

Replace the egg yolks with 3 tablespoons fat-free egg substitute. This will eliminate 12 calories, 53 milligrams cholesterol, and 1.2 grams fat.

YIELD: About 2 cups
2 large egg yolks
¼ cup plus 2 tablespoons sugar
Pinch salt
¼ cup nonfat dry milk powder
2 teaspoons cornstarch
2 cups nonfat or low-fat milk
2 teaspoons vanilla extract

Nutritional Facts
(Per ¼-Cup Serving)

Calories: 86
Carbohydrates: 14 g
Fiber: 0 g
Fat: 1.4 g
Sat. Fat: 0.5 g
Cholesterol: 55 mg
Protein: 3.9 g
Sodium: 67 mg
Calcium: 86 mg
Potassium: 152 mg

Diabetic Exchanges

1 carbohydrate

Lemon Sauce

1. Place the sugar and cornstarch in a 2-quart microwave-safe bowl and stir to mix. Add about 3 tablespoons of the orange juice and stir to mix. Slowly stir in first the remaining orange juice, and then the lemon juice.

2. Microwave the juice mixture uncovered on high power, stirring after each minute, for about 3 minutes, or until the mixture comes to a full boil.

3. Remove about 3 tablespoons of the hot juice mixture and slowly whisk it into the egg yolks. Then slowly whisk the egg mixture into the juice mixture.

4. Return the sauce to the microwave oven and heat on high power, stirring every 30 seconds, for about 1 minute, or until the mixture comes to a full boil. Stir in the margarine or butter until melted. Pour the sauce through a strainer for the smoothest, silkiest texture.

5. Serve the sauce warm over gingerbread, angel food cake, pound cake, bread pudding, and other treats. Store any leftovers in the refrigerator for up to 3 days, reheating in the microwave oven or on the stovetop.

Dietary Variations

To reduce calories and carbohydrates:

Replace the sugar with sugar substitute and eliminate 30 calories, 8 grams carbohydrate, and $1/2$ diabetic carbohydrate exchange. (See page 44 for details on using sugar substitutes.)

To reduce cholesterol:

Replace the egg yolks with 3 tablespoons of fat-free egg substitute and eliminate all of the cholesterol.

YIELD: 1$1/2$ cups

$1/2$ cup sugar

1 tablespoon cornstarch

1 cup plus 2 tablespoons orange juice

$1/4$ cup lemon juice

2 egg yolks, beaten

1 tablespoon margarine or butter

Nutritional Facts (Per 2-Tablespoon Serving)

Calories: 63
Carbohydrates: 12 g
Fiber: 0.1 g
Fat: 1.6 g
Sat. Fat: 0.5 g
Cholesterol: 35 mg
Protein: 0.6 g
Sodium: 9 mg
Calcium: 7 mg
Potassium: 56 mg

Diabetic Exchanges

1 carbohydrate

For All Diets

Rich Chocolate Sauce

YIELD: 1¼ cups

1. Place 2 teaspoons of the milk and all of the cornstarch in a small bowl, and stir to dissolve the cornstarch. Set aside.

2. Place the remaining milk, brown sugar, and chocolate in a 2-quart microwave-safe bowl. Microwave uncovered on high power for 1½ minutes, or until the milk begins to boil. Whisk until the chocolate is completely melted.

3. Whisk the reserved cornstarch mixture into the chocolate mixture. Microwave on high for about 30 seconds or until the mixture comes to a boil. Whisk in the vanilla extract.

4. Serve the sauce warm or transfer it to a covered container and chill for several hours before using. Serve over cake, ice cream, bread pudding, and other treats. Store any leftovers in the refrigerator for up to 3 days.

¾ cup plus 2 teaspoons evaporated nonfat or low-fat milk, divided

1 teaspoon cornstarch

¼ cup brown sugar

4 ounces chopped dark chocolate or semisweet chocolate chips (about ⅔ cup)

½ teaspoon vanilla extract

For a Change

■ To make Chocolate-Mint Sauce, add 1 or 2 drops of peppermint extract along with the vanilla extract in Step 3.

■ To make Mocha Sauce, add ½ teaspoon of instant coffee granules and ⅛ teaspoon ground cinnamon along with the milk, brown sugar, and chocolate in Step 2.

Dietary Variation

To reduce calories and carbohydrates:

Use a sugar substitute instead of the brown sugar and eliminate 21 calories, 6 grams carbohydrate, and ½ diabetic carbohydrate exchange. (See page 44 for details on using sugar substitutes.)

**Nutritional Facts
(Per 2-Tablespoon
Serving)**

Calories: 90
Carbohydrates: 15 g
Fiber: 0.7 g
Fat: 3.4 g
Sat. Fat: 2 g
Cholesterol: 0 mg
Protein: 2 g
Sodium: 25 mg
Calcium: 64 mg
Potassium: 123 mg

Diabetic Exchanges

1 carbohydrate
½ fat

For All Diets

Quick Caramel Sauce

Nutritional Facts (Per 2-Tablespoon Serving)

Calories: 82
Carbohydrates: 15 g
Fiber: 0 g
Fat: 1.4 g
Sat. Fat: 1 g
Cholesterol: 7 mg
Protein: 2.8 g
Sodium: 39 mg
Calcium: 98 mg
Potassium: 130 mg

Diabetic Exchanges

1 carbohydrate

1. Place the dulce de leche and milk in a 1-quart pot and stir to mix. Cook over medium heat, whisking frequently, for about 4 minutes, or until the sauce is smooth and heated through.

2. Serve warm or chilled over apple or chocolate cake, ice cream, bread pudding, and other treats. This sauce can be stored in the refrigerator for up to 5 days and rewarmed over low heat.

For a Change

■ Substitute rum, brandy, or bourbon for 3 to 4 tablespoons of the evaporated milk.

YIELD: 1½ cups

1 cup dulce de leche*
½ cup evaporated nonfat or low-fat milk

* Dulce de leche is caramelized sweetened condensed milk that has long been popular in South America. It is available near the regular sweetened condensed milk in many supermarkets.

For All Diets

Honey-Date Purée

Nutritional Facts (Per 2-Tablespoon Serving)

Calories: 62
Carbohydrates: 17 g
Fiber: 1 g
Fat: 0 g
Sat. Fat: 0 g
Cholesterol: 0 mg
Protein: 0.3 g
Sodium: 0 mg
Calcium: 5 mg
Potassium: 95 mg

Diabetic Exchanges

1 fruit

1. Place the dates and water in a small bowl, and refrigerate for several hours or overnight to soften.

2. Place the softened dates, along with their soaking water, in a mini-blender. Add the honey and blend until smooth, adding a little more water and/or honey if you want a thinner consistency.

3. Transfer the spread to a covered container and chill until ready to use. Serve with hot cereal, sweet potatoes, pancakes, and other dishes. Store any leftover spread in the refrigerator for up to 5 days.

YIELD: 1 cup

½ cup plus 2 tablespoons chopped pitted dates
½ cup plus 2 tablespoons water
3 tablespoons honey

For All Diets

Cinnamon Honey Butter

1. Place the margarine or butter in a medium-size bowl, and beat with an electric mixer until smooth. Beat in the honey a couple of tablespoons at a time until the mixture is light and creamy. Beat in the cinnamon.

2. Transfer the spread to a covered container and chill until ready to serve. Serve with baked sweet potatoes, winter squash, puréed carrots, hot cereal, and other dishes. Store any leftover spread in the refrigerator for up to 2 weeks.

For a Change

■ To turn this spread into Cinnamon Honey Butter Sauce, continue to beat the margarine or butter and honey together while adding a few tablespoons of milk. Beat until the mixture becomes a thick liquid; then beat in the cinnamon. Use for moistening cakes and breads.

YIELD: ¾ cup

¼ cup margarine or butter, softened

½ cup honey

½ teaspoon ground cinnamon

**Nutritional Facts
(Per 1-Tablespoon Serving)**

Calories: 70
Carbohydrates: 12 g
Fiber: 0 g
Fat: 3 g
Sat. Fat: 0.8 g
Cholesterol: 0 mg
Protein: 0 g
Sodium: 30 mg
Calcium: 2 mg
Potassium: 28 mg

Diabetic Exchanges

1 carbohydrate
½ fat

BREADS, SPREADS, AND SANDWICHES

Breads present a unique challenge to people with swallowing difficulties because they are generally dry and sometimes even crumbly in texture, making them difficult to swallow safely. But if you have already read Chapter 5, you know that this much-loved food can still be enjoyed—even on a puréed diet. The trick is to start with a product that has no nuts or other hard pieces, and to add ingredients that soften and moisten the bread while adding great flavor.

The following recipes were designed to help you make bread part of your daily menus. We begin with recipes that will allow you to prepare your own easy-to-make, easy-to-swallow breads. Through a careful use of ingredients and a variety of cooking methods, including stovetop simmering and steaming, these breads are moister and smoother than many store-bought products. In some cases, you may find these homemade products easy to eat as is. In others, you may want to use margarine, butter, honey, or jelly to further soften or moisten them when sitting down to your meal. If you need a puréed diet, you can use milk, buttermilk, and a variety of sauces and slurries on your bread. If your foods must be even smoother, the saturated breads can be blended in a food processor until the desired consistency is reached.

After the bread recipes, we guide you in preparing some easy-to-swallow bread-based dishes. These dishes combine the staff of life with nutritious and moist ingredients to make treats that will complement a variety of entrées, or can be enjoyed alone. Following this, you will find recipes for smooth and tasty spreads, as well as sandwiches that can be prepared with readily available store-bought breads.

Although you're sure to enjoy the following recipes, feel free to view them as a starting place. By learning the simple techniques described in Chapter 5 and put to use in this chapter, you can create many more satisfying bread dishes, and even convert some of your favorite sandwiches into easy-to-swallow meals. The only limit is your imagination.

BREADS AND BREAD-BASED DISHES

For All Diets

Stovetop Spoon Bread

1. Place the eggs and milk in a medium-size bowl, and whisk to mix well. Set aside.

2. Combine the cornmeal, water, and salt in a 3- or 4-quart non-stick pot, and bring to a boil over high heat. Reduce the heat to medium and cook, stirring constantly, for 3 minutes or until thick. Stir in the margarine or butter.

3. Gradually add the egg mixture to the cornmeal mixture, whisking until smooth. Reduce the heat to low, cover, and simmer, stirring occasionally, for about 10 minutes or until the mixture has the consistency of a thick porridge or hot cereal

4. Remove the pot from the heat and allow to sit for 10 minutes, removing the lid after 5 minutes. Serve hot with margarine or butter and honey, if desired.

YIELD: 6 servings

2 eggs

1 cup nonfat or low-fat milk

1 cup yellow cornmeal

2 cups water

$\frac{1}{2}$ teaspoon salt

2 tablespoons margarine or butter

Margarine Gets a Makeover

In the past, margarine has been a major source of harmful trans fat–a substance that has been linked to heart disease and diabetes. Fortunately, much healthier options are now available. Look for soft trans-free margarines that list liquid canola, soybean, or olive oil as the first ingredient, and avoid products that contain hydrogenated oils.

Where does butter fit in? The latest consensus among health experts is that butter is preferable to hard, trans-fat-laden margarines. However, soft trans-free margarines are an even better choice. Spreads made by blending butter with canola oil are another option for people who want the flavor of butter, with less saturated fat.

**Nutritional Facts
(Per Serving, Without Toppings)**

Calories: 146
Carbohydrates: 18 g
Fiber: 1.5 g
Fat: 6.3 g
Sat. Fat: 1.3 g
Cholesterol: 72 mg
Protein: 5.2 g
Sodium: 280 mg
Calcium: 63 mg
Potassium: 151 mg

Diabetic Exchanges

1 starch
1 fat

For All Diets

Oven-Baked Spoon Bread

For Easy-to-Chew and Soft Diets

1. Preheat the oven to 325°F. Coat four 8-ounce ramekins or a 1-quart casserole dish with nonstick cooking spray, and set aside.

2. Combine the milk and cornmeal in a 2-quart nonstick pot, and bring to a boil over medium heat, stirring frequently. Continue to cook and stir for several additional minutes, or until the mixture is thick and pulls away from the sides of the pot. Remove the pot from the heat and stir in the margarine or butter. Set aside.

3. Place the evaporated milk, egg yolk (reserve the white), honey or sugar (if using), and salt in a small bowl, and whisk to mix well. Slowly add the milk mixture to the hot cornmeal mixture, whisking until smooth. Set aside.

4. Place the egg white in a medium-size bowl, and beat with an electric mixer just until stiff peaks form when the beaters are raised. Fold half of the egg white into the cornmeal mixture. Then fold in the remaining white.

5. Divide the mixture among the prepared ramekins or pour it into the casserole dish. Arrange on a baking sheet and bake for about 25 minutes if using ramekins, and 35 minutes for the casserole dish. The spoon bread is done when the top is puffed and a sharp knife inserted near the center comes out clean. Serve hot, topping each serving with margarine and honey, if desired.

For Smooth/Puréed Diets

Place the baked spoon bread in a food processor and process until smooth, adding a few tablespoons of milk if needed.

YIELD: 4 servings

1 cup nonfat or low-fat milk

½ cup yellow cornmeal

1–2 tablespoons margarine or butter

½ cup evaporated nonfat or low-fat milk

1 large egg, separated

1 tablespoon honey or sugar (optional)

⅛ teaspoon salt

Nutritional Facts (Per Serving, Without Toppings)

Calories: 139
Carbohydrates: 18 g
Fiber: 1.1 g
Fat: 4.1 g
Sat. Fat: 1 g
Cholesterol: 56 mg
Protein: 7.3 g
Sodium: 198 mg
Calcium: 176 mg
Potassium: 268 mg

Diabetic Exchanges

1 starch
½ nonfat/low-fat milk
1 fat

For All Diets

Steamed Buttermilk Cornbread

For Easy-to-Chew and Soft Diets

1. Place the cornmeal, flour, sugar, baking powder, baking soda, and salt (if using) in a medium-size bowl and stir to mix. Add the buttermilk, egg substitute or egg, and oil, and whisk to mix. Set the batter aside for 10 minutes.

2. Coat two 1-pound food cans with nonstick cooking spray and divide the batter evenly between the cans. Cover the cans with aluminum foil.

3. Arrange the cans in a deep pot with 1 to 2 inches of hot water. Cover the pot and bring to a boil over high heat. Reduce the heat to a simmer and steam for about 40 minutes, or until the bread is firm to the touch and a wooden toothpick inserted in the center of the bread comes out clean. (To avoid getting burned, allow the steam to dissipate from the pot before testing.)

4. Remove the cans from the pot and allow to sit for 3 minutes. Run a sharp knife around the edges and invert the loaves onto a cutting board.

5. To serve, slice the cornbread and spread it with margarine or butter before eating. Use regular margarine or butter if you need extra calories, and a light (reduced-fat) product if you're trying to lose weight. Drizzle with honey or maple syrup, if desired.

For Smooth/Puréed Diets

Place a slice of cornbread in a bowl and cover with $\frac{1}{2}$ cup or more of buttermilk or milk. Allow to sit for a minute or more before eating so that the cornbread can soak up the liquid. Pour off any excess milk. For a smoother texture, blend the saturated bread in a food processor until smooth, adding more liquid as needed.

For a Change

■ To bake the cornbread in the oven, increase the buttermilk by 2 tablespoons, and pour the batter into an 8-inch skillet or round cake pan coated with nonstick cooking spray. Bake uncovered in

---

YIELD: 8 servings

$\frac{3}{4}$ cup yellow cornmeal

$\frac{1}{4}$ cup plus 2 tablespoons whole wheat pastry flour or unbleached flour

1 tablespoon sugar

$\frac{3}{4}$ teaspoon baking powder

$\frac{1}{4}$ teaspoon baking soda

$\frac{1}{4}$ teaspoon salt (optional)

1 cup nonfat or low-fat buttermilk

$\frac{1}{4}$ cup fat-free egg substitute, or 1 large egg, beaten

2 tablespoons canola oil

**Nutritional Facts
(Per Serving, Without Toppings)**

Calories: 113
Carbohydrates: 16 g
Fiber: 1.5 g
Fat: 4.2 g
Sat. Fat: 0.5 g
Cholesterol: 1 mg
Protein: 3.5 g
Sodium: 137 mg
Calcium: 66 mg
Potassium: 113 mg

Diabetic Exchanges

1 starch
1 fat

a 350° oven for about 20 minutes, or until a wooden toothpick inserted in the center of the bread comes out clean. Allow to sit for 3 minutes. Then cut into wedges and serve with honey or maple syrup, if desired. This is appropriate for easy-to-chew and soft diets.

For All Diets

Buttermilk Drop Biscuits

For Easy-to-Chew and Soft Diets

1. Preheat the oven to 400°F. Coat a 9-inch cake pan with nonstick cooking spray, and set aside.

2. Place the flours, sugar, baking powder, baking soda, and salt in a bowl, and stir to mix well. Add the buttermilk and oil to the flour mixture, and stir just until the dry ingredients are moistened, adding more buttermilk if needed to make a thick batter.

3. Using a tablespoon, drop 8 mounds of batter into the prepared cake pan, spacing them $1/2$ inch apart. Bake for about 10 minutes, or just until the biscuits are cooked through and the tops are lightly browned.

4. To serve, split open a hot biscuit, arrange the halves on a plate, and, if desired, top with Sausage Gravy (page 134), Cinnamon Honey Butter (page 181), or another moist topping.

For Smooth/Puréed Diets

Remove any hard crust as needed, split the biscuit open, and place it in a bowl. Pour some Cinnamon Honey Butter Sauce over the bread (see "For a Change" on page 181), and allow to sit for a minute or more before eating so that the biscuit can soak up the liquid. For a smoother texture, blend the saturated bread in a food processor until smooth, adding more sauce as needed.

YIELD: 8 biscuits

$2/3$ cup whole wheat pastry flour

$2/3$ cup unbleached flour

2 teaspoons sugar

2 teaspoons baking powder

$1/8$ teaspoon baking soda

$1/8$ teaspoon salt

$1/2$ cup plus 2 tablespoons nonfat or low-fat buttermilk

$2^{1}/2$ tablespoons canola oil

Nutritional Facts (Per Biscuit, Without Toppings)

Calories: 124
Carbohydrates: 18 g
Fiber: 1.6 g
Fat: 4.7 g
Sat. Fat: 0.4 g
Cholesterol: 1 mg
Protein: 3.1 g
Sodium: 167 mg
Calcium: 70 mg
Potassium: 86 mg

Diabetic Exchanges

1 starch
1 fat

Steamed Fig Bread

For Easy-to-Chew and Soft Diets

1. Coat a 1$\frac{1}{2}$-quart casserole dish or three 1-pound food cans with nonstick cooking spray, and set aside.

2. Place 1 cup of hot water in a large saucepan, and arrange a steamer basket over the water. Place the figs in the basket and steam over low heat for about 10 minutes or until soft, adding more water as needed.

3. Place the steamed figs, buttermilk, molasses, margarine or butter, and egg white in a food processor, and process at medium speed until smooth. Set aside.

4. Place the flours, baking soda, and salt (if using) in a medium-size bowl, and stir to mix. Stir in the fig mixture and, if desired, the ground nuts.

5. Pour the batter into the prepared casserole dish or divide among the cans, and cover loosely with foil. Arrange the dish or cans in a 6-quart pot, place about 2 inches of water at the bottom of the pot, and cover tightly.

6. Bring the water to a boil over high heat. Then reduce the heat and simmer for about 1 hour and 15 minutes if using a casserole dish, and 45 minutes if using cans. The bread is done when a wooden toothpick inserted in the center of the bread comes out clean. (To avoid getting burned, allow the steam to dissipate from the pot before testing.)

7. Remove the foil covers and arrange the cans or dish on wire racks for 10 minutes. If using cans, run a sharp knife around the edges and invert the loaves onto a cutting board.

YIELD: 12 servings

I cup dried figs, moderately packed (about 6 ounces)

$\frac{1}{2}$ cup plus 2 tablespoons nonfat or low-fat buttermilk

$\frac{1}{2}$ cup molasses

3 tablespoons margarine or butter

1 egg white

$\frac{3}{4}$ cup whole wheat pastry flour

$\frac{3}{4}$ cup unbleached flour

$\frac{3}{4}$ teaspoon baking soda

$\frac{1}{4}$ teaspoon salt (optional)

$\frac{3}{4}$ cup walnuts or pecans, processed in food processor until finely ground (optional)

1 recipe Lemon Sauce (page 178)

Nutritional Facts
(Per Serving, With 2 Tablespoons Sauce)

Calories: 168
Carbohydrates: 33 g
Fiber: 4.2 g
Fat: 4.2 g
Sat. Fat: 1.2 g
Cholesterol: 35 mg
Protein: 1.8 g
Sodium: 134 mg
Calcium: 74 mg
Potassium: 397 mg

Diabetic Exchanges

1 starch
1 fruit
1 fat

8. Serve the bread warm or at room temperature, topping each serving with 2 tablespoons of Lemon Sauce.

For Smooth/Puréed Diets

Place a serving of bread in a bowl and pierce it several times with a fork before topping with the Lemon Sauce. Allow the sauce to saturate the bread before eating. For a smoother texture, blend the saturated bread in a food processor until smooth, adding more sauce as needed.

For a Change

■ Omit the Lemon Sauce, and spread the warm bread with margarine or butter instead, allowing it to melt and moisten the bread. Alternatively, place the bread in a bowl and spoon a little milk or buttermilk over the top.

Boosting the Calories in Breads and Sandwiches

Although bread may not be the best choice when you're trying to lose weight, it's just what the doctor ordered when you need to put on pounds. And it's easy to boost the calorie count in any bread or bread-based dish.

If you choose to bake your own bread, and cholesterol and saturated fat are not a concern, be sure to use high-calorie ingredients like whole evaporated milk and half and half, rather than their nonfat or low-fat counterparts. Full-fat dairy products can be substituted in any recipe in this book with great results. Whenever you enjoy a slice of bread, boost calories by slathering on plenty of margarine (trans-free, of course), and—as long as high blood sugar is not a problem—sweet toppings like honey and jelly. Again, if cholesterol and saturated fat are not a problem, you can use butter instead of margarine. If you're using bread to prepare a sandwich, include ingredients like regular mayonnaise and cream cheese in your spreads. By simply substituting regular mayonnaise for a nonfat or low-fat brand, you will add up to 90 additional calories per tablespoon of dressing.

Steamed Pumpkin Bread

For Easy-to-Chew Diets

1. Coat two 1-pound food cans with nonstick cooking spray, and set aside.

2. Place the flour, sugar, pumpkin pie spice, baking soda, and salt in a medium-size bowl, and stir to mix well. Set aside.

3. Place the pumpkin, egg substitute or egg, and oil in a small bowl, and stir to mix. Add the pumpkin mixture to the flour mixture, and stir to mix. Stir in the nuts if desired.

4. Divide the batter between the prepared cans. Cover the cans with aluminum foil, spraying the underside of the foil with cooking spray to prevent sticking.

5. Place the cans in a deep pot with 1 to 2 inches of hot water. Cover the pot and bring to a boil over high heat. Reduce the heat to a simmer and steam for about 45 minutes, or until the bread is firm to the touch and a wooden toothpick inserted in the center comes out clean. (To avoid getting burned, allow the steam to dissipate from the pot before testing.)

6. Remove the foil covers and arrange the cans on wire racks to cool for 20 minutes. Invert the loaves onto a cutting board and allow to cool for at least 10 additional minutes before slicing and serving with the topping of your choice.

For Soft and Smooth/Puréed Diets

Place a slice of warm bread in a bowl, and pour some Cinnamon Honey Butter Sauce over it. (See "For a Change" on page 181.) Allow the sauce to soak into the bread before eating. Alternatively, melt together equal parts of margarine or butter and milk, and use the mixture to soften the bread. For a smoother texture, blend the saturated bread in a food processor until smooth, adding more sauce or other liquid as needed.

For a Change

■ To make Steamed Banana Bread, substitute mashed banana for the pumpkin and use ¼ teaspoon ground nutmeg instead of the pumpkin pie spice.

YIELD: 12 slices

1 cup whole wheat pastry flour

½ cup brown sugar

1 teaspoon pumpkin pie spice

¼ teaspoon baking soda

¼ teaspoon salt

¾ cup plain canned pumpkin or cooked mashed pumpkin

¼ cup fat-free egg substitute, or 1 egg

3 tablespoons canola oil

⅓ cup walnuts or pecans, finely ground (optional)

Nutritional Facts (Per Slice, Without Toppings)

Calories: 106
Carbohydrates: 17 g
Fiber: 1.9 g
Fat: 3.6 g
Sat. Fat: 0.2 g
Cholesterol: 0 mg
Protein: 2.1 g
Sodium: 88 mg
Calcium: 16 mg
Potassium: 110 mg

Diabetic Exchanges

1 carbohydrate
½ fat

Cheesy Bread Pudding

1. Preheat the oven to 350°F. Coat a 1½-quart casserole dish or four 12-ounce ramekins with nonstick cooking spray, and set aside.

2. Place the bread cubes and cheese in a large bowl, and toss to mix. Set aside.

3. Place the egg substitute or egg, milk, evaporated milk, and, if desired, the cayenne pepper in a medium-size bowl, and whisk to mix well. Pour the egg mixture over the bread mixture and toss to combine. Set aside for 15 minutes.

4. Pour the bread mixture into the prepared casserole dish or ramekins, and place the dish in a large roasting pan. Fill the pan with hot water so that it comes halfway up the baking dish. Then drizzle the margarine or butter over the top of the pudding, and sprinkle with the paprika.

5. Bake uncovered for about 45 minutes if using a casserole dish, and 30 minutes if using ramekins. The pudding is done when a sharp knife inserted in the center of the dish comes out clean. Allow to sit for 5 minutes before serving.

For a Change

■ Toss in ½ cup finely ground cooked ham along with the cheese in Step 2.

■ At serving time, top the pudding with hot Cheddar Cheese Sauce (page 165) or Roasted Red Pepper Sauce (page 168).

YIELD: 4 servings

3 cups ½-inch cubes day-old oat, sourdough, or other bread, trimmed of crusts (use a smooth-textured bread without nuts, seeds, or pieces of grain)*

1 cup shredded Cheddar cheese

¾ cup fat-free egg substitute, or 3 large eggs, beaten

½ cup nonfat or low-fat milk

12-ounce can evaporated nonfat or low-fat milk

Pinch cayenne pepper (optional)

2 tablespoons melted margarine or butter

Ground paprika

---

* If a finer texture is desired, place the bread cubes in the bowl of a food processor and process into coarse crumbs.

Nutritional Facts (Per Serving)

Calories: 314
Carbohydrates: 22 g
Fiber: 0.9 g
Fat: 15.3 g
Sat. Fat: 7.4 g
Cholesterol: 33 mg
Protein: 21 g
Sodium: 544 mg
Calcium: 517 mg
Potassium: 477 mg

Diabetic Exchanges

½ starch
1 nonfat/low-fat milk
2 medium-fat meat
1 fat

Moist Bread Stuffing

1. Preheat the oven to 325°F. Coat a 1½-quart casserole dish or six 8-ounce ramekins with nonstick cooking spray, and set aside.

2. Place the mushrooms, onion, and celery in a food processor, and process until very finely chopped.

3. Transfer the vegetables to a large skillet and add half the broth and all of the sage, thyme, and pepper. Bring to a boil over high heat. Then reduce the heat to medium, cover, and cook for about 10 minutes or until soft. Add more broth if needed to keep the skillet from drying out.

4. Stir the margarine or butter into the vegetable mixture until melted. Remove the skillet from the heat and toss in the bread crumbs. Slowly pour the remaining broth over the bread mixture while tossing gently. Add more broth as needed until the mixture is moist but not soggy.

5. Spoon the stuffing lightly into the prepared casserole dish or ramekins, cover with aluminum foil, and bake for about 30 minutes if using a casserole dish, and 20 minutes if using ramekins. The stuffing is done when heated through. Allow to sit for 5 minutes before serving hot. If desired, top each serving with 3 to 4 tablespoons of gravy.

For a Change

■ Just after tossing in the bread in Step 4, stir in 8 ounces of cooked, crumbled turkey breakfast sausage.

■ Along with the mushrooms, onion, and celery, include other vegetables that you have on hand, such as grated carrot and chopped bell pepper.

* Start with firm day-old or stale bread, without grain pieces, seeds, or nuts. You will need to tear about eight 1-ounce slices of bread into chunks and process in a food processor. Work in two batches, and stop processing when you have coarse crumbs about ¼ inch or less in size.

YIELD: 6 servings

1 cup sliced fresh mushrooms

¾ cup chopped onion

¾ cup chopped celery

1 cup chicken or vegetable broth, divided

1 teaspoon dried sage

½ teaspoon dried thyme

¼ teaspoon ground black pepper

2 tablespoons margarine or butter

6 cups coarse whole wheat or oat bread crumbs,* or 4 cups crumbled cornbread

1 recipe Quick Chicken Gravy (page 168) (optional)

**Nutritional Facts
(Per Serving, Without Gra**

Calories: 135
Carbohydrates: 20 g
Fiber: 3.2 g
Fat: 4.5 g
Sat. Fat: 1.2 g
Cholesterol: 0 mg
Protein: 4.5 g
Sodium: 368 mg
Calcium: 45 mg
Potassium: 195 mg

Diabetic Exchanges

1 starch
½ fat

SPREADS

For All Diets

Pimento Cheese Spread

For Easy-to-Chew and Soft Diets

1. Place the cottage cheese, mayonnaise, cream cheese, mustard, garlic powder, onion powder, and half of the pimentos in a food processor, and process until smooth.

2. Add the remaining pimentos and the Cheddar to the food processor, and process for a few additional seconds, leaving the spread slightly chunky.

3. Transfer the spread to a covered container and chill for at least 1 hour before serving.

For Smooth/Puréed Diets

In Step 2 of the recipe, continue to process the spread until it is smooth and free of any lumps. Add a little water or milk as needed, spooning the liquid in a tablespoon at a time until the mixture reaches a smooth consistency.

YIELD: 1¾ cups

½ cup nonfat or low-fat cottage cheese

½ cup nonfat or light mayonnaise

¼ cup reduced-fat cream cheese

2 teaspoons Dijon mustard

¼ teaspoon garlic powder

¼ teaspoon onion powder

4-ounce jar diced pimentos, drained, divided

1 cup shredded reduced-fat Cheddar cheese

**Nutritional Facts
(Per ¼-Cup Serving)**

Calories: 92
Carbohydrates: 5 g
Fiber: 0.4 g
Fat: 5.1 g
Sat. Fat: 3 g
Cholesterol: 17 mg
Protein: 8 g
Sodium: 408 mg
Calcium: 144 mg
Potassium: 23 mg

Diabetic Exchanges

1 medium-fat meat

Deviled Ham Spread

For Easy-to-Chew and Soft Diets

1. Place the ham, onion, sweet pickle juice, mustard, and paprika in a food processor. Process, pulsing for several seconds at a time, until the ham is finely ground.

2. Add the mayonnaise and cream cheese to the food processor, and process just until mixed. Add a little more mayonnaise if the mixture seems too dry.

3. Transfer the spread to a covered container and chill until ready to serve.

For Smooth/Puréed Diets

In Step 2 of the recipe, continue to process the spread until it is smooth and free of any lumps. Add a little water or milk as needed, spooning in the liquid a tablespoon at a time until the mixture reaches a smooth consistency.

YIELD: 1½ cups

1½ cups diced lean, reduced-sodium baked ham

1 tablespoon grated onion

1 tablespoon sweet pickle juice

2 teaspoons spicy mustard

½ teaspoon ground paprika

¼ cup plus 2 tablespoons nonfat or light mayonnaise

¼ cup reduced-fat cream cheese

**Nutritional Facts
(Per ¼-Cup Serving)**

Calories: 78
Carbohydrates: 3 g
Fiber: 0.3 g
Fat: 3.9 g
Sat. Fat: 1.8 g
Cholesterol: 17 mg
Protein: 7.4 g
Sodium: 454 mg
Calcium: 11 mg
Potassium: 131 mg

Diabetic Exchanges

1½ lean meat

For All Diets

Chutney Chicken Spread

For Easy-to-Chew and Soft Diets

1. Place the chicken in a food processor. Process, pulsing for several seconds at a time, until the chicken is finely ground.

2. Add the mayonnaise, cream cheese, and chutney to the food processor, and process just until mixed. Add a little more mayonnaise if the mixture seems too dry.

3. Transfer the spread to a covered container and chill until ready to serve.

For Smooth/Puréed Diets

In Step 2 of the recipe, continue to process the spread until it is smooth and free of any lumps.

YIELD: 1½ cups

1½ cups diced cooked skinless chicken breast

¼ cup nonfat or light mayonnaise

¼ cup reduced-fat cream cheese

3–4 tablespoons mango chutney

Food Processing Tips

The food processor can be a powerful friend when you want to chop or grind cooked meats for your easy-to-chew, soft, or smooth diet. For best results, do not add liquid, but simply place diced chicken, turkey, beef, or ham in your processor. Pulse for several seconds at a time until the meat reaches the desired consistency. If you want a truly smooth food, add a small amount of liquid or a high-moisture ingredient such as mayonnaise, cream cheese, or salsa. Approximately two to three tablespoons of liquid will be required for every two ounces (a scant half cup) of meat. Continue to process the mixture as needed, occasionally scraping down the sides of the container so that the food remains in contact with the blades.

**Nutritional Facts
(Per ¼-Cup Serving)**

Calories: 93
Carbohydrates: 4 g
Fiber: 0.1 g
Fat: 3.3 g
Sat. Fat: 1.7 g
Cholesterol: 35 mg
Protein: 11.3 g
Sodium: 166 mg
Calcium: 13 mg
Potassium: 129 mg

Diabetic Exchanges

1½ lean meat

For All Diets

Dilled Chicken Spread

For Easy-to-Chew and Soft Diets

1. Place the chicken in a food processor. Process, pulsing for several seconds at a time, until the chicken is finely ground.

2. Add the mayonnaise, cream cheese, and dill to the food processor, and process just until mixed. Add a little more mayonnaise if the mixture seems too dry.

3. Transfer the spread to a covered container and chill until ready to serve.

For Smooth/Puréed Diets

In Step 2 of the recipe, continue to process the spread until it is smooth and free of any lumps. Add a little water or milk as needed, spooning in the liquid a tablespoon at a time until the mixture reaches a smooth consistency.

YIELD: 1½ cups

1½ cups diced cooked skinless chicken breast

¼ cup plus 2 tablespoons nonfat or light mayonnaise

¼ cup reduced-fat vegetable-flavored cream cheese spread

½–1 tablespoon finely chopped fresh dill, or ½–1 teaspoon dried dill

**Nutritional Facts
(Per ¼-Cup Serving)**

Calories: 84
Carbohydrates: 4 g
Fiber: 0 g
Fat: 2.7 g
Sat. Fat: 1.3 g
Cholesterol: 34 mg
Protein: 11 g
Sodium: 191 mg
Calcium: 19 mg
Potassium: 90 mg

Diabetic Exchanges

1½ lean meat

For All Diets

Classic Hummus

1. Place all of the ingredients except for the parsley in a food processor. Process, pulsing for several seconds at a time, until smooth and creamy. If you want a thinner consistency, mix in a tablespoon or two of liquid from the can of beans, or mix in a few tablespoons of plain yogurt.

2. Add the parsley to the food processor and process for 30 additional seconds or until the herb is very finely chopped.

3. Transfer the spread to a covered container and chill until ready to serve.

Using Your Beans

If you think that beans don't belong on a soft or smooth diet, think again. A good source of protein and cholesterol-lowering fiber, canned beans can be puréed to a creamy consistency in your food processor. For a quick dish, sauté some garlic in olive oil and stir in puréed white beans; combine processed black beans with a little of your favorite salsa; or make a classic hummus with garbanzos (chickpeas), sesame tahini, lemon juice, olive oil, and spices. (See the recipe above.) Keep cans of your favorite beans in the pantry, and you'll always be ready to make a dish that's both flavorful and easy to swallow.

YIELD: 1³/₄ cups

16-ounce can garbanzo beans (chickpeas), drained (reserve the liquid)

¹/₄ cup plus 2 tablespoons sesame tahini

3–4 tablespoons lemon juice

2 tablespoons extra virgin olive oil

1¹/₂ teaspoons crushed fresh garlic

2 teaspoons ground cumin

¹/₈ teaspoon ground cayenne pepper

2 tablespoons finely chopped fresh parsley, or 2 teaspoons dried parsley

Nutritional Facts
(Per ¹/₄-Cup Serving)

Calories: 187
Carbohydrates: 16 g
Fiber: 4 g
Fat: 12 g
Sat. Fat: 1.6 g
Cholesterol: 0 mg
Protein: 6.3 g
Sodium: 110 mg
Calcium: 57 mg
Potassium: 228 mg

Diabetic Exchanges

1 lean meat
1 starch
2 fat

SANDWICHES

For All Diets

Open-Faced Hummus Sandwich

1. Place the slice of bread on a small serving plate. Combine the vegetable juice and olive oil in a small dish, and spread half of the mixture over one side of the bread. Flip the bread over and spoon just enough of the remaining mixture over the bread to make it moist but not soggy.

2. Spread the hummus over the top of the bread and serve immediately. Eat with a fork.

Dietary Variations

To reduce calories:

Use only 1½ teaspoons of olive oil and increase the vegetable juice to 1½ tablespoons. This will eliminate 60 calories, 6.7 grams fat, and 1½ diabetic fat exchanges.

YIELD: 1 serving

1-ounce slice whole wheat bread, trimmed of crusts (use a smooth-textured bread without nuts, seeds, or pieces of grain)

1 tablespoon V8 vegetable juice (more if needed)

1 tablespoon extra virgin olive oil

¼ cup Classic Hummus (page 197) or ready-made hummus

Nutritional Facts (Per Serving)

Calories: 380
Carbohydrates: 30 g
Fiber: 5.9 g
Fat: 26 g
Sat. Fat: 3.6 g
Cholesterol: 0 mg
Protein: 9.2 g
Sodium: 288 mg
Calcium: 64 mg
Potassium: 315 mg

Diabetic Exchanges

2 starch
4 fat
1 lean meat

For All Diets

Peanut Butter and Banana Sandwich

Nutritional Facts (Per Serving)

Calories: 363
Carbohydrates: 48 g
Fiber: 4.5 g
Fat: 16.6 g
Sat. Fat: 2.3 g
Cholesterol: 0 mg
Protein: 10.3 g
Sodium: 176 mg
Calcium: 42 mg
Potassium: 513 mg

Diabetic Exchanges

1 starch
1 fruit
1 carbohydrate
3 fat

1. Combine the honey and water, milk, or juice in a small dish, and stir until smooth. Pour over the bottom of a small serving plate and top with the bread slice.

2. Combine the mashed banana and peanut butter in a small bowl, and stir to mix. Spread the mixture over the bread and allow to sit for a couple of minutes, or until the bread has soaked up the honey mixture and softened. Eat with a fork or spoon.

For a Change

■ Substitute smooth almond butter for the peanut butter.

YIELD: 1 serving

1 tablespoon honey (more if needed)

1 tablespoon water, milk, or orange juice (more if needed)

1-ounce slice whole wheat or oat bread, trimmed of crusts (use a smooth-textured bread without nuts, seeds, or pieces of grain)

¼ cup mashed banana

2 tablespoons smooth peanut butter

For All Diets

Boston Brown Bread and Cream Cheese

Nutritional Facts (Per Serving)

Calories: 123
Carbohydrates: 20 g
Fiber: 2.1 g
Fat: 3.7 g
Sat. Fat: 2.1 g
Cholesterol: 11 mg
Protein: 3.9 g
Sodium: 344 mg
Calcium: 42 mg
Potassium: 158 mg

Diabetic Exchanges

1 starch
½ fat

For Easy-to-Chew and Soft Diets

1. Place the bread on a small serving plate and spread with the cream cheese. If desired, top with the berry sauce.

2. Serve immediately.

For Smooth/Puréed Diets

Blend the bread, cream cheese, and sauce in a blender or food processor until smooth, adding more sauce if needed to get the desired consistency.

YIELD: 1 serving

1½-ounce slice canned Boston Brown Bread, plain

1 tablespoon softened reduced-fat cream cheese

1 tablespoon Fresh Berry Purée, made with raspberries (page 171) (optional)

Pimento Cheese Sandwich

For Easy-to-Chew and Soft Diets

1. Place the slice of bread on a small serving plate. Combine the vegetable juice and oil in a small dish, and spread half of the mixture over one side of the bread. Flip the bread over and spoon just enough of the remaining mixture over the bread to make it moist but not soggy.

2. Spread the Pimento Cheese Spread over the top of the bread and serve immediately. Eat with a fork.

For Smooth/Puréed Diets

Make sure that the cheese spread has been processed until absolutely smooth before spreading it on the bread. Then allow the bread to become well saturated with the juice mixture before eating.

YIELD: 1 serving

1-ounce slice whole wheat or oat bread, trimmed of crusts (use a smooth-textured bread without nuts, seeds, or pieces of grain)

1½ tablespoons V8 vegetable juice or tomato juice (more if needed)

1½ teaspoons extra virgin olive oil or canola oil (more if needed)

¼ cup Pimento Cheese Spread (page 193)

Choosing the Best Breads

When told that they must follow a soft or smooth diet, many people fear that they will have to give up bread. The fact is, though, that by choosing your bread carefully and softening it as described in Chapter 5, you *can* make bread part of your daily menu.

For the greatest health benefits, choose breads made with 100-percent whole grain flours. These products are a good source of the B-vitamins, vitamin E, magnesium, iron, fiber, and other important nutrients. (Note that whole wheat or another whole grain should be the first ingredient listed on the package.) Make sure that the bread is smooth in texture and does not contain pieces of nuts, seeds, fruits, or grains. Trim off the crusts, and soften your bread with the desired spread or slurry before eating. (For detailed information on puréeing breads, see page 76.)

Nutritional Facts (Per Serving)

Calories: 226
Carbohydrates: 19 g
Fiber: 2.5 g
Fat: 13.1 g
Sat. Fat: 4.2 g
Cholesterol: 17 mg
Protein: 11 g
Sodium: 618 mg
Calcium: 167 mg
Potassium: 138 mg

Diabetic Exchanges

1 starch
1 medium-fat meat
2 fat

For All Diets

Deviled Ham Sandwich

For Easy-to-Chew and Soft Diets

1. Place the slice of bread on a small serving plate. Combine the tomato juice and oil in a small dish, and spread half of the mixture over one side of the bread. Flip the bread over and spoon just enough of the remaining juice mixture over the bread to make it moist but not soggy.

2. Spread the Deviled Ham Spread over the top of the bread and serve immediately. Eat with a fork.

For Smooth/Puréed Diets

Make sure that the ham spread has been processed until absolutely smooth before spreading it on the bread. Then allow the bread to become well saturated with the juice mixture before eating.

For a Change

■ Instead of using vegetable juice and olive oil to moisten the bread, combine a tablespoon each of mayonnaise or Dijonaise mustard and water, adding more water if necessary to reach a nectar-like consistency.

YIELD: 1 serving

1-ounce slice whole wheat bread, trimmed of crusts (use a smooth-textured bread without nuts, seeds, or pieces of grain)

1½ tablespoons tomato or V8 vegetable juice (more if needed)

1½ teaspoons extra virgin olive oil or canola oil (more if needed)

¼ cup Deviled Ham Spread (page 194)

**Nutritional Facts
(Per Serving)**

Calories: 212
Carbohydrates: 17 g
Fiber: 2.4 g
Fat: 11.9 g
Sat. Fat: 3 g
Cholesterol: 17 mg
Protein: 10.3 g
Sodium: 646 mg
Calcium: 34 mg
Potassium: 246 mg

Diabetic Exchanges

1 starch
1 lean meat
2 fat

Turkey and Feta Sandwich

For Easy-to-Chew and Soft Diets

1. Place the bread on a small serving plate. Combine the vegetable juice and oil in a small dish, and spread half of the mixture over one side of the bread. Flip the bread over and spoon just enough of the remaining mixture over the bread to make it moist but not soggy.

2. Place the turkey, mayonnaise, and feta cheese in food processor and process to the desired consistency. Spread over the bread and serve immediately. Eat with a fork.

For Smooth/Puréed Diets

When processing the turkey mixture in Step 2, make sure it is absolutely smooth. Then allow the bread to become well saturated with the juice mixture before eating.

For a Change

■ Instead of using vegetable juice and olive oil to moisten the bread, combine a tablespoon each of mayonnaise and water, adding more water if necessary to reach a nectar-like consistency.

YIELD: 1 serving

1-ounce slice whole wheat bread, trimmed of crusts (use a smooth-textured bread without nuts, seeds, or pieces of grain)

1 tablespoon V8 vegetable juice or tomato juice (more if needed)

1 tablespoon extra virgin olive oil (more if needed)

2 ounces roast turkey (scant ½ cup diced)

2 tablespoons nonfat or light mayonnaise

1 tablespoon feta cheese

Nutritional Facts (Per Serving)

Calories: 326
Carbohydrates: 18 g
Fiber: 2.7 g
Fat: 19 g
Sat. Fat: 4 g
Cholesterol: 62 mg
Protein: 21 g
Sodium: 565 mg
Calcium: 79 mg
Potassium: 280 mg

Diabetic Exchanges

1 starch
2 lean meat
3 fat

NEW WAYS
WITH ENTRÉES

The entrée, or main dish, is the centerpiece of a meal, usually providing more protein than any of the accompanying dishes. This is probably why most people associate entrées with meat, poultry, and fish. But can meat and poultry—which can be difficult to chew—be part of soft and smooth diets? The answer is a resounding "Yes." This chapter begins with a selection of delicious poultry dishes, followed by recipes that use beef, pork, or fish to supply the protein that your body needs, as well as the heartiness usually associated with a main dish. Following this, you'll find a variety of satisfying vegetarian dishes, which feature eggs, dairy products, legumes, and tofu. As you'll see, this meatless fare not only offers a healthy dose of protein, but is also easily adapted to a soft or smooth diet. You won't feel like you're being "cheated" when you dig into a cheese soufflé, quiche, or spinach lasagna.

Some of the following dishes were inspired by international fare, while others are classic Americana. Because they include a wide range of ingredients, a few of which are difficult to make absolutely smooth, you'll find that although some of the recipes are suitable for all the diets addressed in this book, others are appropriate only for an easy-to-chew or soft menu. Wherever possible, though, we have included instructions for modifying these dishes to accommodate puréed diets.

The following pages may supply all the entrées you need. But if you find yourself missing the tastes of a favorite family dish, keep in mind that the techniques put to use in this chapter will allow you to adapt nearly any dish to meet your dietary requirements. By mastering a few simple skills, you will be able to enjoy a variety of entrées—some new, some familiar, and all easy to chew and swallow.

CHICKEN ENTRÉES

For Easy-to-Chew Diets

Quick Chicken and Dumplings

1. To make the dumplings, combine the flour and baking powder in a medium-size bowl and stir to mix. Set aside.

2. Place the broth, onion, and carrot in a medium-large nonstick skillet, and bring to a boil over high heat. Reduce the heat to low, cover, and simmer for about 8 minutes, or until the vegetables are tender.

3. Add the condensed soup to the skillet, and stir to mix. Add the chicken and allow the mixture come to a boil. Then reduce the heat to a simmer.

4. Stir the oil and enough of the buttermilk into the dumpling mixture to form a thick batter. Drop heaping teaspoons of the batter onto the simmering chicken mixture, making 12 dumplings.

5. Cover the skillet and cook for about 10 minutes, or until the dumplings are fluffy and cooked through. Adjust the heat if necessary to maintain a gentle simmer. Serve hot.

YIELD: 4 servings

1¼ cups low-sodium chicken broth

⅓ cup chopped onion

⅓ cup diced carrot

10 ¾-ounce can condensed cream of celery soup, undiluted

2 cups diced or chopped cooked skinless chicken breast (about 10 ounces)

DUMPLINGS

¾ cup unbleached flour

1 teaspoon baking powder

1½ tablespoons canola or vegetable oil

½ cup nonfat or low-fat buttermilk

**Nutritional Facts
(Per Serving)**

Calories: 300
Carbohydrates: 26 g
Fiber: 1.7 g
Fat: 8.8 g
Sat. Fat: 1.4 g
Cholesterol: 58 mg
Protein: 27 g
Sodium: 550 mg
Calcium: 216 mg
Potassium: 276 mg

Diabetic Exchanges

1½ starch
2½ lean meat
1 fat

For All Diets

Chicken Timbales

For Easy-to-Chew and Soft Diets

1. Preheat the oven to 350°F. Coat four 6-ounce custard cups or decorative molds with cooking spray, and set aside.

2. Place the margarine or butter in a 1-quart pot, and add the mushrooms, onion, and poultry seasoning. Cover and cook over medium-low heat for about 5 minutes, or until the vegetables are tender.

3. Add the milk to the pot and cook over medium heat, stirring frequently, for a couple of minutes, or just until the milk begins to bubble around the edges.

4. Pour the milk-and-vegetable mixture into a blender, and add the bread, salt, pepper, and garlic powder. Blend until smooth. Then add the chicken and egg substitute or eggs, and blend until the chicken is finely ground.

5. Divide the mixture among the prepared custard cups and arrange the cups in a shallow baking pan. Pour in enough hot water to come halfway up the sides of the cups.

6. Bake uncovered for about 35 minutes, or until a sharp knife inserted in the center of a cup comes out clean. Allow to sit for 5 minutes. Run a knife around the inside of each cup to loosen the edges, and invert onto a serving plate. Serve hot.

For Smooth/Puréed Diets

In Step 4, process the chicken mixture until it is absolutely smooth.

For a Change

■ For added flavor and moisture, top each serving with some Quick Chicken Gravy (page 168), Roasted Red Pepper Sauce (page 168), Quick Creole Sauce (page 169), or Alfredo Sauce (page 164).

YIELD: 4 servings

1 tablespoon reduced-fat margarine or light butter

$\frac{1}{2}$ cup sliced fresh mushrooms

2 tablespoons chopped onion

$\frac{1}{4}$ teaspoon poultry seasoning

1 cup evaporated nonfat or low-fat milk

$1\frac{1}{2}$ ounces (about $1\frac{1}{4}$ medium slices) whole wheat bread, torn into pieces (use a smooth-textured bread without nuts, seeds, or pieces of grain)

$\frac{1}{4}$ teaspoon salt

$\frac{1}{8}$ teaspoon ground black pepper

$\frac{1}{8}$ teaspoon garlic powder

1 cup diced cooked skinless chicken breast

$\frac{1}{2}$ cup fat-free egg substitute, or 2 large eggs, beaten

**Nutritional Facts
(Per Serving)**

Calories: 164
Carbohydrates: 13 g
Fiber: 0.9 g
Fat: 3.1 g
Sat. Fat: 0.9 g
Cholesterol: 32 mg
Protein: 20 g
Sodium: 389 mg
Calcium: 209 mg
Potassium: 409 mg

Diabetic Exchanges

$\frac{1}{2}$ starch
$\frac{1}{2}$ nonfat/low-fat milk
2 lean meat

Home-Style Chicken Pie

1. Preheat the oven to 350°F. Coat a 9-inch deep-dish pie pan with nonstick cooking spray, and set aside.

2. To make the topping, place the potatoes in a small pot, add water to cover, and boil for about 10 minutes, or until the potatoes are soft. Drain the potatoes, reserving $1/3$ cup of the cooking water.

3. Return the potatoes to the pot and add the sour cream, margarine or butter, and salt. Mash or beat until smooth, stirring in just enough of the reserved cooking water to bring the potatoes to a creamy consistency.

4. While the potatoes are cooking, place the soup and milk in a 2-quart pot over medium-high heat. Cook, stirring occasionally, for a couple of minutes, or until the mixture comes to a boil. Stir in the chicken and vegetables, and heat through.

5. Spread the chicken mixture in the prepared pie pan. Using tablespoons, drop the potatoes in 5 mounds over the chicken mixture. Spray the tops of the potatoes with the cooking spray, and sprinkle lightly with the Parmesan cheese.

6. Bake for about 25 minutes or until the pie is bubbly around the edges. Serve hot.

For a Change

■ To make Meat and Potato Pie, substitute 2 cups cooked ground beef for the chicken, and golden mushroom soup for the cream of mushroom soup.

YIELD: 5 servings

10 $3/4$-ounce can reduced-fat condensed cream of mushroom soup, undiluted

$3/4$ cup evaporated low-fat milk

2 cups finely chopped or ground cooked skinless chicken breast

8-ounce can French-cut green beans, drained, or $3/4$ cup soft-cooked fresh or frozen green beans

8-ounce can diced carrots, drained, or $3/4$ cup soft-cooked fresh or frozen carrots

TOPPING

3 cups 1-inch chunks peeled Yukon Gold or russet potatoes (about 1 pound)

$1/2$ cup light sour cream

2 tablespoons margarine or butter

$1/4$ teaspoon salt

Butter-flavored nonstick cooking spray

1 tablespoon grated Parmesan cheese

Nutritional Facts (Per Serving)

Calories: 319
Carbohydrates: 33 g
Fiber: 2.9 g
Fat: 9.3 g
Sat. Fat: 2.6 g
Cholesterol: 58 mg
Protein: 23 g
Sodium: 716 mg
Calcium: 238 mg
Potassium: 687 mg

Diabetic Exchanges

$1^1/2$ starch
$1/2$ nonfat/low-fat milk
1 vegetable
$2^1/2$ lean meat

Pilau (Peppery Chicken and Rice)

**Nutritional Facts
(Per 1½-Cup Serving)**

Calories: 390
Carbohydrates: 46 g
Fiber: 1.2 g
Fat: 10 g
Sat. Fat: 2 g
Cholesterol: 50 mg
Protein: 25 g
Sodium: 401 mg
Calcium: 46 mg
Potassium: 357 mg

Diabetic Exchanges

3 starch
2 lean meat
1 fat

1. Place the chicken, water, onion, pepper, and salt in a 6-quart pot and bring to a boil over high heat. Reduce the heat to a simmer, cover, and cook for 1½ to 2 hours, or until the meat is very tender and falling off the bones. Add more water during cooking if needed.

2. Remove the chicken from the pot, reserving the stock. Set the chicken aside to cool slightly.

3. Pull the meat off the bones in small strips (there should be about 2 cups), discarding the bones.

4. Measure the stock in the pot; there should be about 4 cups. Adjust the amount if necessary by adding or removing water, and return the stock to the pot.

5. Add the rice, chicken, and oil to the pot, and bring to a boil over high heat. Reduce the heat to a simmer, cover, and cook for 25 to 30 minutes, or until the rice is soft and very moist. If a softer texture is needed, add more stock or broth and cook for additional time. Serve hot.

YIELD: 5 servings

½ chicken, cut into pieces (about 2 pounds), skin discarded

5 cups water

1 onion, chopped

1 teaspoon ground black pepper (more or less to taste)

¾ teaspoon salt

1½ cups white rice

2 tablespoons olive or canola oil

Boosting the Calories in Entrées

When you are trying to gain weight or prevent unintentional weight loss, it's important to sneak calories into whatever dish you're preparing. Because most people enjoy relatively large portions of their entrée, it makes particular sense to increase the calorie count of each main dish.

You can begin boosting calories by sautéing your foods in healthful oils, like canola or olive oil. With each tablespoon you use, you'll be adding 120 calories to the dish. You can also increase the amount of margarine or oil in casseroles, and use full-fat mayonnaise instead of nonfat or light. If cholesterol and saturated fat are not an issue, cook with whole eggs, full-fat cheese, and butter rather than their lower-fat counterparts. Also consider substituting evaporated whole milk or half and half (about 340 calories per cup) or even cream (about 700 calories per cup) for the low-fat milk in your recipe. As a crowning touch, and to add extra flavor to your meal, choose a sauce from the selection that begins on page 163 and use it to top your easy-to-swallow dish.

Dilled Chicken Aspic

1. Place the cold water in a medium-size heatproof bowl, and sprinkle the gelatin over the top. Allow to sit for 2 minutes to soften. Add the hot broth and stir until the gelatin is completely dissolved. Stir in the lemon juice, salt, and pepper. Set aside for about 30 minutes to cool to room temperature.

2. Place the gelatin mixture and chicken or turkey in a food processor, and process until finely chopped (for easy-to-chew diets), finely ground (for soft diets), or completely smooth (for smooth/puréed diets). Add the dill and blend just until well mixed.

3. Divide the mixture among five 6-ounce custard cups. Cover and chill for several hours or overnight, until firm.

4. To serve, run a knife around the inside of the cups to loosen the edges, and invert each aspic onto an individual serving plate. If the aspic does not slide out, carefully dip the custard cup just to the rim in warm (not hot) water for about 10 seconds to loosen. Combine the dressing ingredients in a small bowl and spoon the mixture over the aspic.

For a Change

■ Substitute finely flaked cooked crabmeat or salmon for the chicken, and use vegetable broth instead of chicken broth. If the crab or salmon is fine-textured enough, you will not have to put the mixture in a food processor unless you're following a smooth/puréed diet.

■ Substitute V8 vegetable juice or tomato juice for half of the broth.

YIELD: 5 servings

1/4 cup cold water

1 packet (0.25 ounce) unflavored gelatin

1 1/2 cups boiling hot chicken broth

1 tablespoon lemon juice

1/4 teaspoon salt

1/4 teaspoon ground black pepper

1 1/2 cups chopped cooked skinless chicken or turkey breast

1 tablespoon finely chopped fresh dill, or 1 teaspoon dried dill

DRESSING

1/3 cup nonfat or light sour cream

1/3 cup nonfat or light mayonnaise

1 tablespoon finely chopped fresh dill, or 1 teaspoon dried dill

Nutritional Facts (Per Serving)

Calories: 114
Carbohydrates: 4 g
Fiber: 0.3 g
Fat: 3.7 g
Sat. Fat: 1 g
Cholesterol: 39 mg
Protein: 15 g
Sodium: 483 mg
Calcium: 29 mg
Potassium: 180 mg

Diabetic Exchanges

2 lean meat

BEEF ENTRÉES

Meatballs with Mushroom Gravy

For Easy-to-Chew and Soft Diets

1. To make the sauce, place all of the sauce ingredients in a bowl and whisk to mix well. For a smoother sauce, place the ingredients in a blender and blend until smooth.) Set aside.

2. To make the meatballs, place the mushrooms and onion in a food processor, and process until finely ground. Transfer the vegetables to a large bowl, add the ground meat, breadcrumbs, egg substitute, marjoram, garlic powder, and pepper, and mix well. Shape the mixture into 12 meatballs, each about 2 inches in diameter.

3. Coat a large skillet with nonstick cooking spray or 2 tablespoons of canola oil, and preheat over medium-high heat. Add the meatballs to the skillet. Cover and cook for several minutes, turning occasionally, until nicely browned.

4. Pour the sauce over the meatballs and bring to a boil. Reduce the heat to a simmer, cover, and cook, turning occasionally, for about 20 minutes, or until the meatballs are cooked through and their internal temperature reaches at least 160°F. If necessary, simmer uncovered for a few minutes to thicken the sauce a bit. Serve hot with mashed potatoes or tender-cooked noodles, if desired.

Nutritional Facts (Per Serving)

Calories: 250
Carbohydrates: 16 g
Fiber: 1.9 g
Fat: 7.3 g
Sat. Fat: 2.7 g
Cholesterol: 64 mg
Protein: 27 g
Sodium: 734 mg
Calcium: 55 mg
Potassium: 624 mg

Diabetic Exchanges

1 starch
3 lean meat

For Smooth/Puréed Diets

After the meatballs have been fully cooked in Step 4, place the meatballs and sauce in a food processor, and process until completely smooth. Add more sauce or other liquid as needed to obtain a smooth texture. Serve over mashed potatoes or puréed pasta, if desired.

YIELD: 4 servings

1 1/2 cups sliced fresh mushrooms

1/2 cup chopped onion

1 pound 95% lean ground beef

1 cup soft whole wheat breadcrumbs*

2 tablespoons fat-free egg substitute, or 1 egg white, beaten

3/4 teaspoon dried marjoram

1/2 teaspoon garlic powder

1/4 teaspoon ground black pepper

SAUCE

10 3/4-ounce can condensed golden mushroom soup, undiluted

1/2 cup plus 2 tablespoons nonfat or low-fat milk

1/2 cup plus 2 tablespoons water

---

* To make the breadcrumbs, tear about 1 1/2 slices of whole wheat bread into pieces, place in a food processor, and process into crumbs. Choose a firm, smooth-textured bread free of nuts and other hard pieces.

Italian-Style Meatballs

For Easy-to-Chew and Soft Diets

1. Place the mushrooms, onion, and zucchini in a food processor, and process until finely ground. Transfer the vegetables to a large bowl and add the ground meat, breadcrumbs, Italian seasoning, garlic powder, pepper, and egg substitute. Mix well. Shape the mixture into 12 meatballs, each about 2¼ inches in diameter.

2. Coat a large nonstick skillet with nonstick cooking spray or 2 tablespoons of olive oil, and preheat over medium-high heat. Add the meatballs to the skillet. Cover and cook for several minutes, turning occasionally, until nicely browned.

3. Combine the marinara sauce and water or broth in a bowl, and stir to mix. Pour the sauce mixture over the meatballs and bring to a boil. Reduce the heat to a simmer and cover. Cook, turning occasionally, for about 20 minutes, or until the internal temperature of the meatballs reaches at least 160°F (180°F for ground turkey) and the meatballs are cooked through. If necessary, simmer uncovered for a few minutes to thicken the sauce a bit. Serve hot with a sprinkling of Parmesan cheese.

For Smooth/Puréed Diets

After the meatballs have been fully cooked in Step 3, place the meatballs and sauce in a food processor and process to the desired degree of smoothness, adding more sauce as needed. If desired, use a commercial thickener designed for shaping (see page 287) to shape and serve.

For a Change

■ Serve the meatballs over tender-cooked angel hair pasta. To make sure that the pasta is well sauced, increase the pasta sauce from 2 cups to 3 cups.

Nutritional Facts (Per Serving)
Calories: 240
Carbohydrates: 15 g
Fiber: 2.5 g
Fat: 6.5 g
Sat. Fat: 2.7 g
Cholesterol: 63 mg
Protein: 28 g
Sodium: 607 mg
Calcium: 60 mg
Potassium: 892 mg

Diabetic Exchanges
½ starch
2 vegetable
3 lean meat

YIELD: 4 servings

1 cup sliced fresh mushrooms
½ cup chopped onion
½ cup diced zucchini
1 pound 95% lean ground beef or turkey
1 cup soft whole wheat breadcrumbs*
¾ teaspoon dried Italian seasoning
½ teaspoon garlic powder
¼ teaspoon ground black pepper
2 tablespoons fat-free egg substitute, or 1 egg white, beaten
2 cups ready-made marinara sauce or Simple Tomato Sauce (page 167)
½ cup water or vegetable broth
2 tablespoons grated Parmesan cheese

* To make the breadcrumbs, tear about 1½ slices of whole wheat bread into pieces, place in a food processor, and process into crumbs. Choose a firm, smooth-textured bread free of nuts and other hard pieces.

For Easy-to-Chew Diets

Johnny Marzetti

1. Preheat the oven to 350°F. Coat a 7-by-11-inch baking pan with nonstick cooking spray, and set aside.

2. Bring a large pot of water to a boil over high heat and add the whole wheat noodles. Reduce the heat and cook the noodles until tender. Drain thoroughly and set aside.

3. While the water is coming to a boil, coat a large nonstick skillet with nonstick cooking spray. Add the ground beef and cook over medium heat, stirring to crumble, until nicely browned and cooked through.

4. Add the onion, bell pepper, garlic, and black pepper to the skillet. Cover and cook for 5 minutes.

5. Place the canned tomatoes in a blender, and process until smooth. Add to the skillet mixture and heat through. Stir in the noodles and remove from the heat. Cover to keep warm, and set aside.

6. To make the cheese sauce, place the flour in a 2-quart micro-wave-safe bowl, and whisk in about $1/4$ cup of the milk until smooth. Whisk in the remaining milk. Microwave on high power for about 4 minutes, whisking after each minute, until the mixture comes to a full boil. Remove from the microwave and whisk in 1 cup of the cheese until melted.

7. Spread the meat-and-noodle mixture in the prepared pan. Pour the cheese sauce evenly over the top, and bake uncovered for 20 minutes, or until heated through. Sprinkle the remaining $1/2$ cup of cheese over the top and bake for 3 additional minutes, or until the cheese has melted. Allow to sit for 10 minutes before serving.

YIELD: 6 servings

8 ounces whole wheat noodles

1 pound 95% lean ground beef or turkey

$1/4$ cup finely chopped onion

$1/4$ cup finely chopped green bell pepper

1 teaspoon crushed fresh garlic

$1/4$ teaspoon ground black pepper

2 cans ($14 1/2$ ounces each) Italian-style diced tomatoes, undrained

CHEESE SAUCE

2 tablespoons unbleached flour

1 cup nonfat or low-fat milk

$1 1/2$ cups shredded reduced-fat Cheddar cheese, divided

Nutritional Facts (Per Serving)

Calories: 358
Carbohydrates: 40 g
Fiber: 4.1 g
Fat: 8.9 g
Sat. Fat: 4.8 g
Cholesterol: 63 mg
Protein: 32 g
Sodium: 536 mg
Calcium: 318 mg
Potassium: 726 mg

Diabetic Exchanges

2 starch
1 vegetable
3 lean meat

Saucy Meatloaf

For Easy-to-Chew and Soft Diets

1. Preheat the oven to 350°F. Coat a 9-x-5-inch meatloaf pan with nonstick cooking spray, and set aside.

2. Place the mushrooms and onion in a food processor, and process until finely ground. Transfer the mixture to a large bowl.

3. Add the ground meat, breadcrumbs, vegetable juice, egg substitute or egg, Worcestershire sauce, mustard, parsley, and pepper to the vegetable mixture, and mix well. Press the mixture into the meatloaf pan.

4. Bake uncovered for 35 minutes. Top with ½ cup of the sauce or gravy and bake for 30 additional minutes, or until a meat thermometer inserted in the center of the loaf reads at least 160°F for beef, or 180°F for ground turkey.

5. Remove the loaf from the oven and allow to sit for 10 minutes before sliding the loaf out of the pan and slicing. Serve hot with the remaining sauce or gravy.

For Smooth/Puréed Diets

After the meatloaf has been completely cooked in Step 4, place the meat and sauce or gravy in a food processor, and purée to the desired degree of smoothness. If preferred, use a commercial thickener designed for shaping (see page 287) to shape and serve.

Nutritional Facts (Per Serving)

Calories: 243
Carbohydrates: 12 g
Fiber: 1.9 g
Fat: 8.8 g
Sat. Fat: 3 g
Cholesterol: 70 mg
Protein: 28 g
Sodium: 612 mg
Calcium: 59 mg
Potassium: 776 mg

Diabetic Exchanges

½ starch
1 vegetable
3 lean meat

YIELD: 6 servings

2 cups sliced fresh mushrooms
¾ cup chopped onion
1½ pounds 95% lean ground beef or turkey
1½ cups soft whole wheat breadcrumbs*
¼ cup vegetable juice cocktail, like V8 vegetable juice
¼ cup plus 2 tablespoons fat-free egg substitute, or 1 egg plus 1 egg white, beaten
2 tablespoons Worcestershire sauce
1 tablespoon spicy or Dijon mustard
2 teaspoons dried parsley
½ teaspoon ground black pepper
1 recipe Quick Creole Sauce (page 169) or Roasted Vegetable Gravy (page 170), heated

* To make the breadcrumbs, tear about 2 slices of whole wheat bread into pieces, place in a food processor, and process into crumbs. Choose a firm, smooth-textured bread free of nuts and other hard pieces.

For All Diets

Burgers with Barbecue Sauce

For Easy-to-Chew and Soft Diets

1. To make the sauce, place the broth and barbecue sauce in a bowl, and whisk to mix well. Set aside.

2. To make the burgers, place the onion in a food processor and process until finely ground. Transfer the onion to a large bowl.

3. Add the ground meat, breadcrumbs, egg substitute or egg white, parsley, garlic powder, pepper, and salt (if using) to the processed onion, and mix well. Shape the mixture into 4 patties.

4. Coat a large nonstick skillet with nonstick cooking spray and pre-heat over medium heat. Arrange the patties in the skillet, cover, and cook for a couple of minutes, or until the underside is nicely browned. Turn the burgers over and cook until the second side is browned.

5. Pour the sauce over the burgers and bring to a boil. Reduce the heat to a simmer, cover, and cook for 5 minutes. Turn the burgers and cook for 5 additional minutes, or until thoroughly cooked. (The internal temperature of the burgers should reach at least 160°F for beef and 180°F for ground turkey.). Transfer the burgers to a serving plate, and set aside, leaving the sauce in the skillet.

6. Place the cornstarch and water in a small dish, and stir until the cornstarch is dissolved. Whisk the mixture into the sauce and cook and stir over medium heat for about a minute, or until the sauce thickens slightly. Pour the sauce over the burgers and serve hot.

For Smooth/Puréed Diets

Place a cooked burger and some of the sauce in a food processor, and process in brief pulses to the required degree of softness or smoothness. If desired, serve over a slice of crustless bread that has been softened with sauce.

**Nutritional Facts
(Per Serving)**

Calories: 240
Carbohydrates: 19 g
Fiber: 1.2 g
Fat: 5.5 g
Sat. Fat: 2.1 g
Cholesterol: 61 mg
Protein: 26 g
Sodium: 547 mg
Calcium: 26 mg
Potassium: 595 mg

Diabetic Exchanges

1 carbohydrate
3 lean meat

YIELD: 4 servings

$2/3$ cup chopped onion

1 pound 95% lean ground beef or turkey

1 cup soft whole wheat breadcrumbs*

2 tablespoons fat-free egg substitute, or 1 egg white, beaten

2 teaspoons dried parsley

$1/2$ teaspoon garlic powder

$1/4$ teaspoon ground black pepper

$1/4$ teaspoon salt (optional)

SAUCE

1 cup low-sodium beef broth (use chicken broth for ground turkey)

$1/2$ cup barbecue sauce

1 teaspoon cornstarch

1 teaspoon water

* To make the breadcrumbs, tear about $1^{1}/_{2}$ slices of whole wheat bread into pieces, place in a food processor, and process into crumbs. Choose a firm, smooth-textured bread free of nuts and other hard pieces.

For All Diets

Roast Beef Aspic with Horseradish Sauce

1. Place the vegetable juice in a medium-size heatproof bowl, and sprinkle the gelatin over the top. Allow to sit for 2 minutes to soften. Add the hot broth and stir until the gelatin is completely dissolved. Stir in the Worcestershire sauce, salt (if using), and pepper. Set aside for about 30 minutes to cool to room temperature.

2. Place the gelatin mixture and beef in a food processor, and process until finely chopped (for easy-to-chew diets), finely ground (for soft diets), or completely smooth (for smooth/puréed diets).

3. Divide the mixture among five 6-ounce custard cups. Cover and chill for several hours or overnight, until firm.

4. To serve, run a knife around the inside of the cups to loosen the edges, and invert each aspic onto an individual serving plate. If the aspic does not slide out, carefully dip the custard cup just to the rim in warm (not hot) water for about 10 seconds to loosen. Combine the dressing ingredients in a small bowl and spoon the mixture over the aspic.

YIELD: 5 servings

¼ cup vegetable juice cocktail, such as V8 vegetable juice

1 packet (0.25 ounce) unflavored gelatin

1½ cups boiling hot beef broth

1 tablespoon Worcestershire sauce

¼ teaspoon salt (optional)

¼ teaspoon ground black pepper

1½ cups chopped cooked roast beef

DRESSING

⅓ cup nonfat or light sour cream

⅓ cup nonfat or light mayonnaise

1–3 teaspoons prepared horseradish

Nutritional Facts (Per Serving)

Calories: 122
Carbohydrates: 5g
Fiber: 0.4 g
Fat: 4.2 g
Sat. Fat: 1.5 g
Cholesterol: 35 mg
Protein: 15 g
Sodium: 425 mg
Calcium: 29 mg
Potassium: 285 mg

Diabetic Exchanges

2 lean meat

PORK ENTRÉES

For All Diets

Ham Timbales

For Easy-to-Chew and Soft Diets

YIELD: 4 servings

1 tablespoon reduced-fat margarine or light butter

1 tablespoon grated onion

1 cup evaporated nonfat or low-fat milk

1½ ounces (about 1¼ medium slices) whole wheat bread, torn into pieces (use a smooth-textured bread without nuts, seeds, or pieces of grain)

⅛ teaspoon ground cloves or allspice

⅛ teaspoon ground black pepper

1 cup diced lean baked ham

½ cup fat-free egg substitute, or 2 large eggs, beaten

1. Preheat the oven to 350°F. Coat four 6-ounce custard cups or decorative molds with cooking spray, and set aside.

2. Place the margarine or butter and the onion in a 1-quart pot. Cover and cook over medium-low heat for about 5 minutes, or until the onion is tender. Add the milk and, stirring frequently, cook over medium heat for several minutes, or just until the milk begins to bubble around the edges.

3. Pour the milk mixture, bread, cloves or allspice, and pepper into a blender, and process until smooth. Add the ham and egg substitute or egg, and blend until the ham is finely ground.

4. Divide the ham mixture among the prepared cups. Arrange the cups in a shallow baking pan, and pour in enough hot water to reach halfway up the sides of the cups.

5. Bake uncovered for about 35 minutes, or until a sharp knife inserted in the center of the cups comes out clean. Allow to sit for 5 minutes. Run a knife around the inside of each cup to loosen the edges, and invert onto a serving plate. Serve hot.

For Smooth/Puréed Diets

In Step 3, process the ham mixture until it is completely smooth. Then proceed with the remainder of the recipe.

For a Change

■ Top each custard with your favorite smooth sauce, such as Cheddar Cheese Sauce (page 165) or Easy Hollandaise Sauce (page 166).

Nutritional Facts (Per Serving)

Calories: 141
Carbohydrates: 14 g
Fiber: 0.8 g
Fat: 2.5 g
Sat. Fat: 0.7 g
Cholesterol: 18 mg
Protein: 15 g
Sodium: 508 mg
Calcium: 203 mg
Potassium: 285 mg

Diabetic Exchanges

½ starch
½ nonfat/low-fat milk
2 lean meat

Barbecue Pulled Pork

For Easy-to-Chew Diets

1. Sprinkle the roast with the pepper, garlic powder, and dried herbs. Coat a large skillet with nonstick cooking spray, and preheat over medium-high heat. Brown the roast for a couple of minutes on each side.

2. Pour the broth over the roast and cover the skillet tightly with aluminum foil. Bake at 325°F for about 3 hours, or until the roast is very tender and easy to pull apart with a fork. Alternatively, transfer the browned roast to a $3\frac{1}{2}$-quart or larger slow cooker. Use the broth to "rinse out" the skillet, scraping up any browned bits from the bottom, and pour the liquid over the roast. Cover the slow cooker and cook on the low setting for 8 to 10 hours, or until the meat is very tender and easy to pull apart with a fork.

3. Transfer the roast to a large cutting board and allow to sit for 15 minutes. In the meantime, strain the juices from the skillet or slow cooker and discard the solids. Pour the juices into a large skillet and bring to a boil. Cook for several minutes or until reduced to about $3/4$ cup. Stir in the barbeque sauce and set aside.

4. Using two forks, tear the meat into shreds. Then chop the shreds into pieces no longer than $1/2$ inch.

5. Add the meat to the sauce mixture and cook over low heat for several minutes, or until hot and bubbly. Add a little more barbecue sauce or broth if needed, and serve. (Note that any leftovers will freeze well.)

For Soft Diets

After the meat has been shredded in Step 4, chop it very finely before tossing it into the sauce.

YIELD: 9 servings

$2\frac{1}{2}$-pound pork sirloin roast, well trimmed

$1/2$ teaspoon ground black pepper

$1/2$ teaspoon garlic powder

$1/2$ teaspoon dried thyme

$1/2$ teaspoon dried oregano

$3/4$ cup vegetable or chicken broth

$1\frac{1}{4}$ cups barbecue sauce

**Nutritional Facts
(Per $1/2$-Cup Serving)**

Calories: 206
Carbohydrates: 15 g
Cholesterol: 65 mg
Fat: 6.3 g
Sat. Fat: 2.3 g
Fiber: 0.1 g
Protein: 22 g
Sodium: 408 mg
Calcium: 15 mg
Potassium: 375 mg

Diabetic Exchanges

1 carbohydrate
3 lean meat

For Smooth/Puréed Diets

Place the shredded pork and some of the sauce in a food processor, and process in brief pulses until the mixture has the desired degree of softness and smoothness.

For a Change

■ Split open a very soft whole wheat bun, and arrange the halves on a plate. Spoon the pulled pork over the bun and serve. You may need to add more broth to insure that the bread is well moistened.

Supermarket and Deli Shortcuts

Many of the recipes offered in this chapter make use of precooked chicken, ham, or beef. While you can certainly use poultry or meat from last night's dinner to prepare any of these dishes, you don't have to have a refrigerator full of leftovers to turn out a meal quickly and easily. Instead, visit your local deli or supermarket and take advantage of the range of cold cuts and other cooked meats they have for sale.

You probably already know that most delis and supermarket deli counters offer ham, turkey, roast beef, and chicken cold cuts. These are an enormous help to the busy cook. Just ask the salesperson to give you a 1/4-inch slab instead of slicing the meat thinly, and you'll be able to chop or otherwise process the meat to the consistency you desire. If you're trying to reduce sodium, look for a low-sodium brand. Low-fat brands are also available.

If you're going to use ham in your dish, a great option is to buy a packaged lean ham steak. These steaks are fully cooked and all meat (no bone), so they are recipe-ready.

In addition to the chicken cold cuts now produced by several companies, many stores offer grilled boneless, skinless chicken breasts that can be used in any recipe that calls for precooked chicken. Eight ounces of chicken will yield about 1 1/2 cups when chopped. Rotisserie chickens, available in all supermarkets, are another handy item. Pull off and discard the skin and chop as much of the meat as you need for your dish. One rotisserie chicken will yield about 3 cups of chopped meat.

If all else fails, you can quickly poach a boneless, skinless chicken breast for use in your chicken dishes. Place the chicken in a pot or skillet and add enough water or broth to partially cover it. Then bring to a boil over high heat, reduce the heat to low, cover, and simmer for 7 to 10 minutes, or until the interior is no longer pink. If you love chicken, you may want to keep a few poached chicken breasts on hand so that you're always ready to prepare a delicious, easy-to-swallow chicken dish. Sealed in zip-lock plastic bags, the cooked chicken can be stored in your refrigerator for several days.

Ham and Potato Puffs

1. Preheat the oven to 350°F. Coat four 8-ounce ramekins with nonstick cooking spray, and set aside.

2. Place the mashed potatoes in a medium-size bowl. They should be fairly moist, about the consistency of pudding. Add a little milk if necessary. Add the egg yolks, reserving the whites, and stir to mix well. Stir in the ham and cheese. Set aside.

3. Place the egg whites in a medium-size bowl, and beat with an electric mixer until soft peaks form when the beaters are raised. Fold about a quarter of the egg whites into the potato mixture. Then fold in the remaining egg whites.

4. Divide the potato mixture among the prepared ramekins, and spray the tops lightly with the cooking spray. Arrange the ramekins on a large baking sheet and bake for about 30 minutes, or until lightly puffed and beginning to brown. Serve hot.

For a Change

■ Top the baked puffs with Cheddar Cheese Sauce (page 165).

■ Substitute a 6-ounce can of tuna or salmon (drained and flaked) for the ham.

Dietary Variations

To reduce fat and cholesterol:

Use 3 tablespoons of fat-free egg substitute instead of the egg yolks, and substitute reduced-fat Cheddar cheese for the regular Cheddar. This will eliminate 44 calories, 4.4 grams of fat, 2 grams of saturated fat, 102 milligrams of cholesterol, and 1 diabetic fat exchange per serving.

YIELD: 4 servings

1½ cups Home-Style Mashed Potatoes (page 243) or leftover mashed potatoes

2 large eggs, separated

¾ cup finely ground lean baked ham

½ cup finely shredded Cheddar cheese

Butter-flavored nonstick cooking spray

Nutritional Facts (Per Serving)

Calories: 200
Carbohydrates: 15 g
Fiber: 1.1 g
Fat: 9.1 g
Sat. Fat: 4.3 g
Cholesterol: 123 mg
Protein: 13 g
Sodium: 425 mg
Calcium: 146 mg
Potassium: 271 mg

Diabetic Exchanges

1 starch
2 lean meat
1 fat

Crustless Ham and Cheese Quiches

1. Preheat the oven to 325°F. Coat four 12-ounce ramekins with nonstick cooking spray, and set aside.

2. Place the onion and the margarine or butter in a medium-size nonstick skillet. Cover and cook over medium heat for several minutes, or until the onion is soft. Remove from the heat.

3. Stir the ham and milk into the onion. Add the egg substitute or eggs, pepper, and nutmeg. Toss the cheese and flour together, and fold into the onion mixture.

4. Divide the quiche mixture among the prepared cups. Arrange the cups in a 9-by-13-inch baking pan, and pour in enough hot water to reach 1 inch up the sides of the cups.

5. Bake for about 35 minutes, or just until a sharp knife inserted in the center of a quiche comes out clean. Transfer the quiches to a wire rack and allow to sit for 10 minutes before serving.

For a Change

■ Substitute finely flaked cooked crabmeat or finely chopped tender-cooked cauliflower or broccoli for the ham.

■ If you are following an easy-to-chew diet, you can prepare the quiche in a single pie crust. Prick a 9-inch pie crust in several places with a fork and prebake at 400°F for 5 minutes. Pour the filling into the hot crust and bake at 325°F for about 40 minutes, or until a sharp knife inserted near the center of the quiche comes out clean. If necessary, use a pie crust shield to prevent over-browning, or cover the edge of the crust with aluminum foil during the last few minutes of baking.

YIELD: 4 servings

2 tablespoons grated onion

1 tablespoon reduced-fat margarine or light butter

$3/4$ cup finely ground lean baked ham

12-ounce can evaporated nonfat or low-fat milk

1 cup fat-free egg substitute, or 4 large eggs, beaten

$1/8$ teaspoon ground black pepper

Pinch ground nutmeg

$1\frac{1}{4}$ cups shredded reduced-fat Swiss cheese

1 tablespoon unbleached flour

Nutritional Facts (Per Serving)

Calories: 233
Carbohydrates: 13 g
Fiber: 0.1 g
Fat: 6.4 g
Sat. Fat: 2.9 g
Cholesterol: 27 mg
Protein: 29 g
Sodium: 622 mg
Calcium: 583 mg
Potassium: 485 mg

Diabetic Exchanges

1 nonfat/low-fat milk
3 lean meat

SEAFOOD ENTRÉES

For Easy-to-Chew and Soft Diets

Quick Cajun Fish

YIELD: 4 servings

1. To make the sauce, place the tomatoes and Cajun seasoning in a blender and purée until smooth. Set aside.

2. Combine the Cajun seasoning and paprika in a small dish and stir to mix. Rub both sides of each fish fillet with the seasoning mixture.

3. Pour the olive oil into a large nonstick skillet and preheat over medium heat. Add the fish fillets to the skillet; then add the water. Cover and cook for 2 to 3 minutes on each side, or until the fish flakes easily with a fork. Add a little more water if needed to prevent the fillets from becoming crusty. Transfer the fish to a plate, and cover to keep warm.

4. Pour the sauce into the skillet and bring to a boil. Cook and stir for a couple of minutes or until the sauce is heated through and thickened to the desired consistency. Serve the fish hot, topping each serving with some of the sauce and a sprinkling of parsley.

For a Change

■ Substitute Greek or Southwestern seasoning for the Cajun blend.

2 teaspoons Cajun seasoning

2 teaspoons ground paprika

4 cod, flounder, tilapia, or other thin, tender white fish fillets (4–5 ounces each)

2 tablespoons extra virgin olive oil

1 tablespoon water

2–3 tablespoons finely chopped fresh parsley

SAUCE

14½-ounce can no-salt-added stewed tomatoes

2–3 teaspoons Cajun seasoning

Nutritional Facts (Per Serving)

Calories: 192
Carbohydrates: 9 g
Fiber: 2.2 g
Fat: 7.8 g
Sat. Fat: 1.1 g
Cholesterol: 49 mg
Protein: 21 g
Sodium: 576 mg
Calcium: 39 mg
Potassium: 535 mg

Diabetic Exchanges

2 vegetable
3 lean meat
1 fat

For All Diets

Salmon Mousse

For Easy-to-Chew and Soft Diets

1. Place the cold water in a medium-size heatproof bowl, and sprinkle the gelatin over the top. Allow to sit for 2 minutes to soften. Add the boiling water and stir until the gelatin is completely dissolved. Set aside for about 5 minutes to cool slightly.

2. While the gelatin mixture is cooling, combine the sour cream, mayonnaise, dill, lemon juice, onion, paprika, pepper, and salt in a medium-size bowl and whisk until well mixed. Set aside.

3. Beat the gelatin mixture with an electric mixer for about 1 minute, or until light and foamy like soft-whipped egg whites. Fold half of the sour cream mixture into the gelatin; then fold in the remaining sour cream mixture. Fold in the salmon.

4. Divide the salmon mixture among six 6-ounce custard cups or ramekins. Cover and chill for several hours or overnight until firm.

5. To serve, run a knife around the inside of the cups to loosen the edges, and invert onto individual serving plates. If the mousse does not slide out, carefully dip the cups or ramekins just to the rim in warm (not hot) water for about 10 seconds to loosen. Serve with the sauce if desired.

For Smooth/Puréed Diets

In Step 2 of the recipe, combine the sour cream, mayonnaise, lemon juice, onion, and salmon in a food processor, and purée until smooth. Add the dill, paprika, pepper, and salt, and process just to mix in. Prepare and beat the gelatin as directed in Step 3. Then fold half of the salmon mixture into the gelatin. Fold in the remaining salmon mixture and proceed with the recipe as directed above.

YIELD: 6 servings

2 tablespoons cold tap water

1 envelope (0.25 ounce) unflavored gelatin

¼ cup plus 2 tablespoons boiling water

1 cup light sour cream

¼ cup nonfat or light mayonnaise

2–3 tablespoons finely chopped fresh dill, or 2–3 teaspoons dried dill

1 tablespoon plus 1 teaspoon lemon juice

1 tablespoon finely grated onion

½ teaspoon ground paprika

¼ teaspoon ground black pepper

¼ teaspoon salt

2 cups finely flaked cooked salmon, or 14.75-ounce can boneless skinless pink or red salmon, drained and finely flaked

⅔ cup Sour Cream Dill Sauce (page 169) (optional)

Nutritional Facts (Per Serving)

Calories: 144
Carbohydrates: 5 g
Fiber: 0.1 g
Fat: 6.6 g
Sat. Fat: 3.3 g
Cholesterol: 37 mg
Protein: 16 g
Sodium: 220 mg
Calcium: 81 mg
Potassium: 316 mg

Diabetic Exchanges

2 medium-fat meat

Salmon Croquettes

1. Place the celery, bell pepper, onion, and water or broth in a 1-quart pot. Cover and cook over medium heat for several minutes, or until the vegetables are soft, adding more water if needed to prevent scorching. Remove the pot from the heat and drain off any excess liquid.

2. Add the salmon, mayonnaise, seasoning, and 2 tablespoons of the breadcrumbs to the vegetables, and mix well. Stir in the egg white.

3. Divide the salmon mixture into 8 portions and shape each portion into a ball. Place the remaining breadcrumbs in a shallow dish, and roll each ball in the crumbs to coat all sides.

4. Pour the oil in a large skillet and preheat over medium heat. Add the salmon balls and flatten each one with a spatula to create a burger shape. Cook for 2 to 3 minutes, or until the underside is lightly browned. Turn the cakes over and cook until the second side is lightly browned. Serve hot with fresh lemon wedges, Easy Hollandaise Sauce (page 166), or additional mayonnaise mixed with a little seasoning, if desired.

For a Change

■ Substitute finely flaked tuna or crabmeat for the salmon.

YIELD: 4 servings

- 2 tablespoons finely chopped celery (pull strings off before chopping)
- 2 tablespoons finely chopped red bell pepper
- 2 tablespoons finely chopped onion
- 2 tablespoons water or chicken broth
- 2 cups finely flaked cooked salmon, or 14.75-ounce can boneless skinless pink or red salmon, drained and finely flaked
- 1/4 cup nonfat or light mayonnaise
- 1 teaspoon seasoning blend of choice (Cajun, Old Bay, or other spicy favorite)
- 1/2 cup dried seasoned breadcrumbs, divided
- 1 egg white, beaten, or 2 tablespoons fat-free egg substitute
- 2 tablespoons canola oil

Nutritional Facts (Per Serving)

Calories: 249
Carbohydrates: 12 g
Cholesterol: 48 mg
Fat: 14 g
Sat. Fat: 2.2 g
Fiber: 1.2 g
Protein: 20 g
Sodium: 675 mg
Calcium: 51 mg
Potassium: 395 mg

Diabetic Exchanges

1 starch
2 1/2 lean meat
1 1/2 fat

VEGETARIAN ENTRÉES

For All Diets

Angel Hair Alfredo

For Easy-to-Chew and Soft Diets

1. Bring a large pot of water to a boil over high heat, and add the pasta. Cook the noodles until tender, drain thoroughly, and return to the pot. Toss in the margarine or butter, and cover to keep warm.

2. Place the cornstarch and 2 tablespoons of the milk in a 2-quart nonstick pot, and stir to dissolve the cornstarch. Add the remaining milk and place over medium heat. Cook, stirring frequently, until the milk just begins to boil. Cook for another minute, or until the sauce is bubbly and has thickened slightly.

3. Pour the sauce over the pasta. Add the pepper and Parmesan and toss to mix, adding a little more milk if needed. Serve hot, topping each serving with a sprinkling of parsley.

For Smooth/Puréed Diets

After the sauce has been prepared in Step 2, place the cooked pasta and the sauce in a food processor, and process to the desired degree of smoothness.

YIELD: 4 servings

8 ounces angel hair pasta

2 tablespoons margarine or butter

1 tablespoon cornstarch

$1\frac{1}{2}$ cups evaporated low-fat milk, divided

$\frac{1}{8}$ teaspoon ground black pepper

$\frac{3}{4}$ cup grated Parmesan cheese

1 teaspoon dried parsley, finely crumbled

**Nutritional Facts
(Per $1\frac{1}{4}$-Cup Serving)**

Calories: 418
Carbohydrates: 54 g
Fiber: 2 g
Fat: 12.8 g
Sat. Fat: 6.7 g
Cholesterol: 28 mg
Protein: 21 g
Sodium: 489 mg
Calcium: 483 mg
Potassium: 366 mg

Diabetic Exchanges

$2\frac{1}{2}$ starch
1 low-fat milk
1 high-fat meat
1 fat

Cheese Soufflés

For Easy-to-Chew and Soft Diets

1. Preheat the oven to 375°F.

2. Place the onion and the margarine or butter in a 2-quart pot. Cover and cook over medium heat, stirring occasionally, for several minutes, or until the onion is tender.

3. Place the milk, flour, mustard, and pepper in a pint-size jar with a tight-fitting lid, and shake until smooth. Add the milk mixture to the pot and cook over medium heat, stirring frequently, until the mixture comes to a boil and thickens. Remove the pot from the heat and stir in the cheese until melted.

4. Place the egg yolks in a medium-size bowl, reserving the egg whites. Whisk the yolks well. Slowly whisk about $\frac{1}{2}$ cup of the hot milk mixture into the egg yolks. Return the mixture to the pot and whisk to mix well.

5. Place the reserved egg whites in a large bowl, and beat with an electric mixer just until stiff peaks form when the beaters are raised. Fold a quarter of the egg whites into the cheese mixture. Then add the cheese mixture to the remaining beaten egg whites and gently fold to combine.

6. Spoon the soufflé mixture into four ungreased 12-ounce ramekins and arrange them on a large baking sheet for easy handling. Bake for 20 to 25 minutes, or until the soufflés are golden brown, puffy, and set. Serve immediately.

For Smooth/Puréed Diets

Remove any hard crust from the soufflés before serving.

YIELD: 4 servings

3 tablespoons finely grated onion

1 tablespoon reduced-fat margarine or light butter

1 cup nonfat or low-fat milk

3 tablespoons unbleached flour

$\frac{1}{2}$ teaspoon dry mustard

Pinch cayenne or ground white pepper

1$\frac{1}{2}$ cups shredded Cheddar cheese

4 large eggs, separated

Nutritional Facts (Per Serving)

Calories: 303
Carbohydrates: 9 g
Fiber: 0.4 g
Fat: 19.6 g
Sat. Fat: 10 g
Cholesterol: 256 mg
Protein: 20 g
Sodium: 388 mg
Calcium: 410 mg
Potassium: 232 mg

Diabetic Exchanges

$\frac{1}{2}$ starch
1$\frac{1}{2}$ high-fat meat
1 medium-fat meat

For a Change

◼ Top the baked soufflés with Cheddar Cheese Sauce (page 165), Roasted Red Pepper Sauce (page 168), or Quick Creole Sauce (page 169).

◼ To make Ham and Cheese Soufflés, stir $\frac{3}{4}$ cup finely ground cooked ham into the cheese mixture at the end of Step 4.

◼ To make Vegetable and Cheese Soufflés, stir 1 cup finely chopped soft-cooked cauliflower or broccoli into the cheese mixture at the end of Step 4.

Dietary Variation

To reduce calories, fat, and cholesterol:

Use reduced-fat Cheddar cheese, choosing a brand that melts well to keep the texture soft, and substitute $\frac{1}{4}$ cup plus 2 tablespoons fat-free egg substitute for the egg yolks. For each serving, these changes will eliminate 105 calories, 11.5 grams of fat, 5.1 grams of saturated fat, and 232 milligrams of cholesterol. The $2\frac{1}{2}$ high-fat meat diabetic exchanges will become $1\frac{1}{2}$ medium-fat meat and 1 lean meat exchange.

Creamy Risotto

For Easy-to-Chew and Soft Diets

1. Place the margarine or butter in a 3-quart pot, and melt over medium heat. Add the onion, cover, and cook for a couple of minutes, or until the onion softens. Add the garlic and cook for an additional 15 seconds.

2. Add the broth, milk, rice, parsley, and pepper to the pot, and bring to a boil over medium heat. Reduce the heat to low, cover, and simmer for about 25 minutes, or until the rice is soft and most of the liquid has been absorbed. Keep in mind that the rice must be cooked until very soft to insure that it sticks together (is cohesive) when swallowed.

3. Stir half of the Parmesan cheese into the pot. If the mixture is too dry, stir in additional milk until it becomes moist and creamy. Serve hot, topping each serving with some of the remaining cheese.

For Smooth/Puréed Diets

Place the uncooked rice in a blender and process for about 45 seconds, or until it has the texture of grits or coarse cornmeal. Then cook as directed above. If a perfectly smooth texture is needed, transfer the cooked risotto to a food processor and process until the mixture is smooth, adding milk as needed.

For a Change

■ Add 2 cups of finely chopped fresh spinach to the risotto in Step 2, about 5 minutes before the rice is fully cooked. Cook and stir until the spinach is soft and wilted.

■ In Step 3, add 1 cup chopped or ground tender roast chicken to the finished risotto.

■ Drizzle individual servings of the risotto with Roasted Red Pepper Sauce (page 168).

YIELD: 6 servings

2 tablespoons margarine or butter

2 tablespoons grated onion

1 teaspoon crushed fresh garlic

2$1/2$ cups reduced-sodium chicken broth

2$1/2$ cups nonfat or low-fat milk

1$1/2$ cups arborio rice

2 teaspoons dried parsley, finely crumbled

$1/8$ teaspoon ground white pepper

$1/4$ cup grated Parmesan cheese

**Nutritional Facts
(Per 1-Cup Serving)**

Calories: 299
Carbohydrates: 46 g
Fiber: 1 g
Fat: 6 g
Sat. Fat: 2.6 g
Cholesterol: 9 mg
Protein: 13 g
Sodium: 311 mg
Calcium: 265 mg
Potassium: 320 mg

Diabetic Exchanges

2$1/2$ starch
$1/2$ nonfat/low-fat milk
$1/2$ medium-fat meat
$1/2$ fat

For All Diets

Brown Rice Risotto

For Easy-to-Chew and Soft Diets

1. Place the rice in a blender and blend for about 20 seconds or until the grains are coarsely cracked (about the size of bulgur wheat). Set aside.

2. Place the margarine or butter in a 2½-quart pot and melt over medium heat. Add the onion, cover, and cook for about 2 minutes or until the onion has softened. Add the garlic and cook for an additional 15 seconds.

3. Add the reserved rice, broth, milk, and sage to the pot, and bring to a boil over medium heat. Reduce the heat to low, cover, and simmer for 20 to 25 minutes, or until the rice is soft and the mixture is thick.

4. Stir the Parmesan cheese and parsley into the risotto. Add more milk if the mixture seems too dry (it should be moist and creamy), and serve hot.

For Smooth/Puréed Diets

In Step 1, process the uncooked rice in a blender for about 45 seconds, or until it has the texture of grits or coarse cornmeal. Then cook as directed above, adding more liquid as needed. If a perfectly smooth texture is required, transfer the cooked risotto to a food processor and process until the mixture is smooth, adding milk as needed.

For a Change

■ About 5 minutes before the risotto is done, stir in 1 cup of finely chopped fresh spinach. Cook and stir until the spinach is wilted.

■ When the risotto is completely cooked, stir in 1 cup of finely chopped soft-cooked leftover vegetables, such as cauliflower or broccoli.

■ When the risotto is completely cooked, stir in ¾ cup chopped or ground tender roast chicken.

■ Drizzle individual servings of the risotto with Roasted Red Pepper Sauce (page 168).

YIELD: 4 servings

1 cup brown rice

2 tablespoons margarine or butter

2 tablespoons grated onion

1 teaspoon crushed fresh garlic

2½ cups low-sodium chicken or vegetable broth

2 cups nonfat or low-fat milk

½ teaspoon dried sage, finely crumbled

½ cup grated Parmesan cheese

2 teaspoons dried parsley, finely crumbled

**Nutritional Facts
(Per 1-Cup Serving)**

Calories: 311
Carbohydrates: 42 g
Fiber: 1.7 g
Fat: 9.8 g
Sat. Fat: 4 g
Cholesterol: 12 mg
Protein: 13 g
Sodium: 343 mg
Calcium: 336 mg
Potassium: 328 mg

Diabetic Exchanges

2½ starch
½ nonfat/low-fat milk
½ high-fat meat
1 fat

For All Diets

Three-Cheese Manicotti

For Easy-to-Chew and Soft Diets

1. Bring a large pot of water to a boil over high heat, and add the pasta shells. Cook the shells until tender, drain thoroughly, and set aside.

2. Preheat the oven to 350°F.

3. Place the ricotta cheese, mozzarella cheese, half of the Parmesan cheese, and all of the egg substitute and parsley in a medium-size bowl, and stir to mix well. Set aside.

4. To assemble the manicotti, coat an 11-by-7-inch baking pan with nonstick cooking spray, and spread a thin layer of the marinara sauce over the bottom of the pan. Stuff each cooked manicotti shell with about ⅓ cup of the cheese mixture, and arrange the shells in a single layer in the pan. (For ease of filling, place the filling mixture in a 1-quart freezer bag, seal the bag, cut ½ inch from the corner, and squeeze the mixture into the shells.) Pour the remaining sauce evenly over the manicotti, and sprinkle the remaining Parmesan cheese over the top.

5. Bake uncovered for about 25 minutes, or until the edges are bubbly and the dish is heated through. Allow to sit for 10 minutes before serving.

For Smooth/Puréed Diets

Place the cooked pasta shells in the food processor with a small amount of water or olive oil, and process until smooth. Spread the puréed pasta in the prepared dish, and add a layer of the cheese filling, followed by a layer of the sauce. Bake as directed in Step 5 of the recipe.

YIELD: 4 servings

8 manicotti shells

15-ounce container part-skim ricotta cheese

¾ cup shredded part-skim mozzarella cheese

¼ cup grated Parmesan cheese, divided

2 tablespoons fat-free egg substitute

2 teaspoons dried parsley, finely crumbled

2 cups ready-made marinara sauce

Nutritional Facts (Per Serving)

Calories: 409
Carbohydrates: 42 g
Fiber: 3.2 g
Fat: 15.2 g
Sat. Fat: 8.7 g
Cholesterol: 50 mg
Protein: 27 g
Sodium: 767 mg
Calcium: 543 mg
Potassium: 613 mg

Diabetic Exchanges

2 starch
2 vegetable
2½ medium-fat meat

For All Diets

Layered Puréed Black Bean Enchiladas

1. To make the mush, place the cornmeal and milk in a small bowl and stir to mix. Set aside. Place the water in a 2-quart pot and bring to a boil. Slowly add the cornmeal mixture to the boiling water, whisking constantly until the mixture comes to a boil. Reduce the heat to maintain a simmer, cover, and cook, stirring frequently, for about 10 minutes or until thickened.

2. Coat four 12-ounce ramekins with nonstick cooking spray and divide the hot mush among the ramekins, spreading it into an even layer. Set aside. Preheat the oven to 350°F.

3. Drain the beans, reserving the juice. Place the beans and cumin in a food processor, and process until smooth. Add back a tablespoon or 2 of the reserved juice if the mixture seems too thick. Add $\frac{1}{2}$ cup of the cheese and process to mix in. Spread a fourth of the bean mixture over the cornmeal mush in each ramekin.

4. Place the enchilada sauce and the remaining $\frac{1}{2}$ cup of cheese in a blender, and process until smooth. Pour a fourth of the sauce mixture evenly over the bean layer in each ramekin.

5. Arrange the ramekins on a large baking sheet and bake uncovered for about 20 minutes, or until the mixture is heated through and bubbly around the edges. Allow to sit for 10 minutes before serving hot. Top each serving with some sour cream and, if desired, some guacamole.

YIELD: 4 servings

15-ounce can black beans

$\frac{3}{4}$ teaspoon ground cumin

1 cup shredded reduced-fat Cheddar or Mexican blend cheese, divided

$\frac{1}{2}$ cup plus 2 tablespoons canned enchilada sauce

$\frac{1}{2}$ cup nonfat or light sour cream

$\frac{1}{2}$ cup ready-made guacamole (optional)

CORNMEAL MUSH

$\frac{2}{3}$ cup yellow cornmeal

1 cup nonfat or low-fat milk

1-1$\frac{1}{4}$ cups water

Nutritional Facts (Per Serving)

Calories: 272
Carbohydrates: 40 g
Fiber: 6 g
Fat: 7.1 g
Sat. Fat: 3.2 g
Cholesterol: 16 mg
Protein: 16 g
Sodium: 693 mg
Calcium: 347 mg
Potassium: 457 mg

Diabetic Exchanges

2$\frac{1}{2}$ starch
2 lean meat

For All Diets

Layered Puréed Spinach Lasagna

1. Place the orzo in a blender and process for about 1 minute, or until it has the consistency of grits or cornmeal. Set aside.

2. Place the water in a 2-quart pot and bring to a boil. Stir in the olive oil. Whisking constantly, gradually add the ground pasta to the boiling water. Reduce the heat to a simmer, cover, and cook for about 10 minutes, or until the liquid is absorbed and the pasta is tender. If you need a softer texture, increase the water by $\frac{1}{2}$ cup and cook for 5 additional minutes or until the water has been absorbed. Remove the pot from the heat and stir in $\frac{1}{4}$ cup of the Parmesan cheese.

3. Coat four 12-ounce ramekins with nonstick cooking spray, and spread a quarter of the hot pasta mixture evenly in each dish. Set aside. Preheat the oven to 350°F.

4. Cook the spinach according to package directions. Drain the spinach well, pressing out as much of the excess water as possible.

5. Place the drained spinach, ricotta cheese, egg substitute or egg, pepper, nutmeg, and $\frac{1}{4}$ cup of the Parmesan cheese in a food processor, and process until smooth. Spoon a quarter of the spinach mixture over the pasta in each ramekin, followed by a quarter of the sauce. Sprinkle the remaining 2 tablespoons of Parmesan cheese over the top.

6. Arrange the ramekins on a large baking sheet and bake uncovered for about 30 minutes, or until the lasagna is heated thorough and the cheese begins to brown. (The center should reach 160°F.) Allow the ramekins to sit for 5 to 10 minutes before serving hot.

YIELD: 4 servings

$\frac{2}{3}$ cup orzo (4 ounces)

$2\frac{1}{2}$ cups water

1 tablespoon olive oil

$\frac{1}{2}$ cup plus 2 tablespoons grated Parmesan cheese, divided

10-ounce package frozen spinach

1 cup part-skim ricotta cheese

$\frac{1}{4}$ cup fat-free egg substitute, or 1 large egg

$\frac{1}{4}$ teaspoon ground black pepper

$\frac{1}{8}$ teaspoon ground nutmeg

$1\frac{1}{4}$ cups ready-made marinara sauce or Simple Tomato Sauce (page 167)

Nutritional Facts (Per Serving)

Calories: 360
Carbohydrates: 34 g
Fiber: 4.1 g
Fat: 15 g
Sat. Fat: 6.8 g
Cholesterol: 31 mg
Protein: 22 g
Sodium: 759 mg
Calcium: 488 mg
Potassium: 620 mg

Diabetic Exchanges

$1\frac{1}{2}$ starch
2 vegetable
2 medium-fat meat
1 fat

For All Diets

Eggless Egg Salad

For Easy-to-Chew and Soft Diets

1. Place the tofu in a medium-size bowl and mash with a fork to the desired consistency. Set aside.

2. Combine the mayonnaise, mustard, herbs, pepper, and salt in a small bowl and stir to mix well. Add the mayonnaise mixture to the tofu and stir to mix, adding a little more mayonnaise if desired. Cover and chill for 1 hour before serving.

For Smooth/Puréed Diets

For an absolutely smooth texture, omit the dried herbs and process the mixture in a blender.

For a Change

■ Omit the herbs and add 2 to 3 tablespoons of drained sweet pickle relish or finely chopped dill pickles.

■ To make traditional egg salad, substitute 6 mashed hard-boiled eggs for the tofu.

■ Serve the salad on crustless bread that has been softened with thinned mayonnaise or equal parts of olive oil and V8 vegetable juice. Be sure to choose a smooth-textured bread that includes no nuts or other hard pieces. (See page 76 for details on making puréed sandwiches.)

* Sold in shelf-stable aseptic packages in most grocery stores, silken tofu has a softer, smoother texture than regular tofu. Use it in "eggless" egg salad or blend it into soups, sauces, and smoothies.

YIELD: 4 servings

12.3-ounce package silken firm tofu,* well-drained and patted dry

1/4 cup mayonnaise (regular, not low-fat)

2 tablespoons yellow or spicy mustard

1–2 teaspoons dried parsley, crumbled

1–2 teaspoons dried chives, crumbled

1/2 teaspoon dried dill

1/8 teaspoon ground black pepper

1/8 teaspoon salt

**Nutritional Facts
(Per 1/2-Cup Serving)**

Calories: 160
Carbohydrates: 2 g
Fiber: 0.4 g
Fat: 13.6 g
Sat. Fat: 2.4 g
Cholesterol: 10 mg
Protein: 6.4 g
Sodium: 268 mg
Calcium: 38 mg
Potassium: 192 mg

Diabetic Exchanges

1 lean meat
2 fat

SENSATIONAL SIDES

Side dishes are intended to complement the entrée and add interest and substance to the meal. From a nutritional standpoint, though, they can do so much more. While entrées provide the bulk of the protein on the plate, sides that feature healthy veggies, fruits, grains, or beans offer a wealth of vitamins, minerals, and fiber. They also supply beneficial *phytonutrients*—nutritious plant-based compounds. Many of the phytonutrients in plant foods are actually the pigments that give vegetables and fruits their characteristic colors. For example, the orange pigment found in cantaloupe, pumpkin, and sweet potatoes is the healthful antioxidant beta-carotene, while the red pigment in tomatoes is the cancer-fighting substance lycopene. That's why, as a rule, the more colorful the vegetables, the more phytonutrients they contain. By enjoying a rainbow of colors in your meals, you can reap the benefits of nature's full range of phytonutrients.

Whether you're following an easy-to-chew, soft, or smooth/puréed diet, you'll find that side dishes are naturals because so many vegetables can be puréed to a smooth consistency while maintaining both visual appeal and great flavor. In fact, most of the dishes offered in the following pages are appropriate for all three diets without any extra work, and nearly all the sides can be made to fit even the smoothest of menus.

Of course, for most people, the most important part of any dish is the taste. That's why the recipes in this chapter use an assortment of aromatic herbs and spices, tasty broths, creamy cheeses, and other flavorful ingredients to make each dish a true standout. The result is an assortment of sides that are not only easy to swallow, but also easy to love.

Broccoli and Potato Purée

1. Place the potatoes, broth, and garlic in a 3-quart pot. Cover and bring to a boil over high heat. Then reduce the heat to a simmer and cook for 5 minutes.

2. Add the broccoli to the pot and return to a boil. Reduce the heat, cover, and simmer for an additional 7 minutes, or until the potatoes and broccoli are tender. Add a little water during cooking if the pot becomes too dry.

3. Drain any remaining liquid from the vegetables, reserving the cooking liquid, and transfer the vegetables to a food processor. Add the olive oil, margarine or butter, and pepper, and process until smooth. Add enough of the reserved cooking liquid to bring the mixture to the desired consistency, swirling in a few tablespoons of milk, if necessary. Add the Parmesan cheese and process again.

4. Serve the purée hot, drizzling each portion with a little olive oil, if desired.

YIELD: 6 servings

2 cups ³/₄-inch chunks peeled Yukon Gold or russet potatoes (about 12 ounces)

1 cup chicken or vegetable broth

4–5 cloves garlic

4 cups fresh or frozen broccoli florets

1 tablespoon extra virgin olive oil

1 tablespoon margarine or butter

¹/₄ teaspoon ground black pepper

¹/₄ cup grated Parmesan cheese

**Nutritional Facts
(Per ¹/₂-Cup Serving)**

Calories: 100
Carbohydrates: 11 g
Fiber: 2.4 g
Fat: 5.1 g
Sat. Fat: 1.5 g
Cholesterol: 3 mg
Protein: 4.5 g
Sodium: 202 mg
Calcium: 90 mg
Potassium: 329 mg

Diabetic Exchanges

¹/₂ starch
1 vegetable
1 fat

For All Diets

Savory Carrot Purée

1. Place the carrots, potatoes, broth, onion, and savory or marjoram in a 3-quart pot. Cover and bring to a boil over high heat. Then reduce the heat to a simmer and cook for 15 minutes, or until the vegetables are soft. Add a little water during cooking if the pot becomes too dry.

2. Drain any remaining liquid from the vegetables, reserving the cooking liquid, and transfer the vegetables to a food processor. Add the margarine or butter and the pepper, and process until smooth. Add enough of the reserved cooking liquid to bring the mixture to the desired consistency, swirling in a few tablespoons of milk, if necessary.

3. Transfer the purée to a serving dish and, if desired, dot the top with the pesto and swirl with a knife to create a marble effect. Serve hot.

YIELD: 6 servings

4 cups sliced peeled carrots (about 8 medium)

1½ cups ¾-inch chunks peeled Yukon Gold or russet potatoes (about 8 ounces)

1 cup chicken or vegetable broth

¼ cup chopped yellow onion

½ teaspoon dried savory or marjoram

2 tablespoons margarine or butter

Pinch ground white pepper

1½–2 tablespoons prepared pesto (optional)

Veggie Power

You'll notice that many recipes in this book contain lots of vegetables, whether fresh, canned, or frozen. Why? Vegetables are a powerhouse of nutrients, providing vitamin A, vitamin C, vitamin E, potassium, dietary fiber, and more. As you may already know, many of these nutrients, such as vitamins A and C, are *antioxidants*—substances that are known to prevent or slow the oxidative damage that naturally occurs in the body. That is why a vegetable-rich diet may reduce the risk of stroke, type 2 diabetes, kidney stones, bone loss, and several types of cancer.

You may think that vegetables are difficult to include in an easy-to-chew, soft, or smooth diet, but veggies lend themselves well to the creation of silky puréed side dishes, creamy soups, and many other easy-to-chew-and-swallow foods. Flip through the pages of this book to see just how easy it is to include healthful vegetables in your diet.

**Nutritional Facts
(Per ½-Cup Serving)**

Calories: 92
Carbohydrates: 15 g
Fiber: 3.1 g
Fat: 3.2 g
Sat. Fat: 0.9 g
Cholesterol: 0 mg
Protein: 1.5 g
Sodium: 65 mg
Calcium: 26 mg
Potassium: 396 mg

Diabetic Exchanges

½ starch
1½ vegetable
½ fat

For All Diets

Cauliflower Purée

Nutritional Facts
(Per ¹/₂-Cup Serving)

Calories: 89
Carbohydrates: 9 g
Fiber: 3 g
Fat: 4.7 g
Sat. Fat: 1.1 g
Cholesterol: 0 mg
Protein: 3.7 g
Sodium: 193 mg
Calcium: 71 mg
Potassium: 445 mg

Diabetic Exchanges

1¹/₂ vegetable
1 fat

1. Place the cauliflower in a microwave or stove-top steamer, and cook for about 8 minutes or until tender. Drain well.

2. Transfer the cauliflower to a food processor and add the milk, margarine or butter, and salt. Purée the mixture until smooth. Add the sour cream and process until well mixed. Serve hot.

For a Change

■ Stir ¹/₂ teaspoon dried dill or parsley into the puréed cauliflower.

■ Substitute light herb-flavored cream cheese for the sour cream.

■ Add 3 to 4 tablespoons shredded Cheddar cheese along with the milk.

YIELD: 4 servings

5 cups fresh or frozen cauliflower florets (about 1 pound)
¹/₄ cup nonfat or low-fat milk, heated
2 tablespoons margarine or butter
Scant ¹/₄ teaspoon salt
3 tablespoons nonfat or light sour cream

Boosting the Calories in Side Dishes

If you are trying to maintain your weight or even add a few pounds, you'll find it easy to sneak extra calories into your side dishes.

To start, use some extra olive oil when sautéing vegetables, or drizzle the oil over dishes such as puréed carrots or zucchini. A great source of healthful monounsaturated fat, olive oil also packs 120 calories per tablespoon. Another wholesome option is to stir some extra trans-free margarine into mashed potatoes and other hot side dishes. Full-fat versions supply about 100 calories per tablespoon.

If cholesterol and saturated fat are not a concern, use whole eggs, extra full-fat cheese, and extra butter in your sides. You'll be enhancing both the taste and the calorie count of your dish. When preparing mayonnaise-based dressings for aspics and salads, use a full-fat version instead of a light brand to add about 90 extra calories per tablespoon. Finally, when a recipe calls for low-fat milk, feel free to substitute evaporated whole milk or half and half (about 340 calories per cup) or cream (about 700 calories per cup). The results will be creamy and flavorful.

For All Diets

Lima Beans with Sage and Onions

Nutritional Facts
(Per ¹/₂-Cup Serving)

Calories: 156
Carbohydrates: 25 g
Fiber: 7 g
Fat: 2.7 g
Sat. Fat: 0.7 g
Cholesterol: 0 mg
Protein: 8.6 g
Sodium: 185 mg
Calcium: 55 mg
Potassium: 550 mg

Diabetic Exchanges

1¹/₂ starch
¹/₂ fat

1. Place the lima beans, broth, onion, and sage in a 2-quart pot. Cover and bring to a boil over high heat. Then reduce the heat to a simmer and cook, stirring occasionally, for about 15 minutes, or until the lima beans are soft.

2. Add the milk and the margarine or butter to the pot and cook for an additional minute to heat through.

3. Transfer the lima bean mixture to a food processor and purée until smooth, adding a little more milk, if needed. Serve hot.

YIELD: 4 servings

1 pound frozen baby lima beans

³/₄ cup chicken or vegetable broth

¹/₃ cup chopped onion

¹/₂ teaspoon dried sage

¹/₄ cup nonfat or low-fat milk

1 tablespoon margarine or butter

For All Diets

Zucchini-Parmesan Purée

Nutritional Facts
(Per ¹/₂-Cup Serving)

Calories: 85
Carbohydrates: 8 g
Fiber: 2 g
Fat: 5.4 g
Sat. Fat: 1.7 g
Cholesterol: 0 mg
Protein: 2.7 g
Sodium: 93 mg
Calcium: 52 mg
Potassium: 368 mg

Diabetic Exchanges

2 vegetable
1 fat

1. Place the zucchini, water, and garlic in a 2-quart pot. Cover and bring to a boil. Reduce the heat to a simmer and cook for about 10 minutes, or until the zucchini is very tender. Add the margarine or butter and cook until melted.

2. Transfer the zucchini, along with the liquid in the pot, to a food processor. Add the potato flakes, Parmesan cheese, and pepper, and process until smooth. Mix in a little more potato flakes or boiling water if needed to produce a consistency similar to that of mashed potatoes. Allow to sit, covered, in the food processor for 1 minute before serving.

YIELD: 4 servings

4 cups thinly sliced unpeeled zucchini (about 1¹/₄ pounds)

¹/₄ cup water

1 teaspoon crushed fresh garlic

2 tablespoons margarine or butter

¹/₄ cup plus 2 tablespoons instant potato flakes

1¹/₂ tablespoons grated Parmesan cheese

¹/₄ teaspoon ground black pepper

Spinach Soufflés

For Easy-to-Chew and Soft Diets

1. Preheat the oven to 375°F.

2. Cook the spinach according to package directions until tender. Allow to cool, squeeze dry, and chop very fine. Set aside.

3. Place the onion and the margarine or butter in a 2-quart pot. Cover and cook over medium-low heat, stirring occasionally, for 3 to 5 minutes, or until the onion is soft. Set aside.

4. Place the milk, flour, pepper, and nutmeg in a pint-size jar with a tight-fitting lid, and shake until smooth. Add the milk mixture to the onion and cook over medium heat, stirring frequently, until the mixture comes to a boil and thickens. Remove the pot from the heat.

5. Add the Swiss and Parmesan cheeses to the milk mixture, and stir until melted. Stir in the reserved spinach.

6. Place the egg yolks in a small bowl (reserve the whites), and stir in about ½ cup of the spinach mixture. Return the spinach mixture to the pot and stir to mix well. Set aside.

7. Place the egg whites in a large bowl and beat with an electric mixer just until stiff peaks form when the beaters are raised. Fold a fourth of the egg whites into the spinach mixture. Then gently fold the spinach mixture into the remaining whipped egg whites.

8. Spoon the soufflé mixture into six ungreased 6-ounce custard cups or ramekins, and arrange them on a large baking sheet for easier handling. Bake for about 20 minutes or until the soufflés are golden brown, puffy, and set. Serve immediately.

YIELD: 6 servings

10-ounce package frozen chopped spinach

¼ cup grated onion

1 tablespoon reduced-fat margarine or light butter

1 cup nonfat or low-fat milk

3 tablespoons unbleached flour

¼ teaspoon ground black pepper

⅛ teaspoon ground nutmeg

¾ cup shredded Swiss cheese

3 tablespoons grated Parmesan cheese

4 large eggs, separated

Nutritional Facts (Per Serving)

Calories: 165
Carbohydrates: 8 g
Fiber: 1.7 g
Fat: 9.2 g
Sat. Fat: 4.3 g
Cholesterol: 157 mg
Protein: 13 g
Sodium: 212 mg
Calcium: 294 mg
Potassium: 294 mg

Diabetic Exchanges

½ starch
1 vegetable
1 ½ medium-fat meat

For Smooth/Puréed Diets

In Step 5, place the spinach in a food processor before adding it to the milk mixture. Process, adding a few tablespoons of the milk mixture as needed. Then proceed with the recipe. If necessary, remove the crust from the baked soufflés before eating.

For a Change

■ Top the baked soufflés with Alfredo Sauce (see page 164), Easy Hollandaise Sauce (see page 166), or Roasted Red Pepper Sauce (see page 168).

■ Substitute 1 cup of very finely chopped soft-cooked broccoli or cauliflower for the spinach.

■ Substitute Cheddar cheese for the Swiss, and replace the nutmeg with a pinch of ground cayenne pepper.

■ Add ½ cup finely ground lean baked ham along with the spinach in Step 5.

■ To serve the soufflés as an entrée, divide the mixture among four 12-ounce ramekins (instead of the smaller custard cups) and bake for about 25 minutes, or until golden brown, puffy, and set.

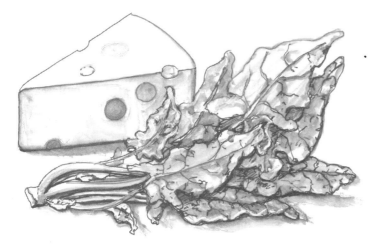

For All Diets

Savory Vegetable Custards

For Easy-to-Chew and Soft Diets

1. Preheat the oven to 350°F. Coat six 6-ounce custard cups with nonstick cooking spray, and set aside.

2. Place the vegetables, onion, and margarine or butter in a $2\frac{1}{2}$-quart pot. Cover and cook over medium-low heat, stirring occasionally, for about 10 minutes, or until the vegetables are tender. Add a little water during cooking if needed, but only enough to prevent the vegetables from browning.

3. Transfer the vegetable mixture to a blender, add the milk, and process until the vegetables are finely chopped.

4. Return the vegetable mixture to the pot and cook over medium heat, stirring frequently, for a couple of minutes, or just until the mixture begins to boil. Remove the pot from the heat and set aside.

5. Place the egg substitute or eggs in a medium-size bowl, and slowly whisk about $\frac{1}{2}$ cup of the vegetable mixture into the eggs. Then whisk the eggs back into the pot. Stir in the Parmesan cheese, salt, pepper, and nutmeg.

6. Divide the vegetable mixture among the prepared custard cups. Fill a large roasting pan with 1 inch of hot water, and arrange the cups in the pan.

7. Bake uncovered for about 25 minutes, or until a sharp knife inserted in the center of a cup comes out clean. Remove the cups from the pan and allow to sit for 10 minutes. Serve hot in the custard cups, or run a knife around the edges and invert onto serving plates.

For Smooth/Puréed Diets

In Step 3, process the vegetable mixture until it is completely smooth. Then proceed with the recipe.

YIELD: 6 servings

- 2 cups chopped fresh or frozen cauliflower, broccoli, or asparagus
- $\frac{1}{4}$ cup chopped onion
- 2 tablespoons reduced-fat margarine or light butter
- 1 cup evaporated nonfat or low-fat milk
- $\frac{3}{4}$ cup fat-free egg substitute, or 3 large eggs, beaten
- 2 tablespoons grated Parmesan cheese
- $\frac{1}{4}$ teaspoon salt
- $\frac{1}{8}$ teaspoon ground black pepper
- Pinch ground nutmeg

Nutritional Facts (Per Serving)

Calories: 83
Carbohydrates: 8 g
Fiber: 1 g
Fat: 2.3 g
Sat. Fat: 0.9 g
Cholesterol: 3 mg
Protein: 8 g
Sodium: 274 mg
Calcium: 171 mg
Potassium: 301 mg

Diabetic Exchanges

$\frac{1}{2}$ nonfat milk
1 vegetable
$\frac{1}{2}$ lean meat

For All Diets

Winter Squash Timbales

1. Preheat the oven to 350°F. Coat six 6-ounce custard cups with nonstick cooking spray, and set aside.

2. Place the onion, margarine or butter, and sage in a 2-quart pot. Cover and cook over medium-low heat, stirring occasionally, for about 5 minutes, or until the onions are tender.

3. Transfer the onion mixture to a blender. Add the mashed squash and milk, and process until smooth.

4. Return the squash mixture to the pot and cook over medium heat, stirring frequently, for a couple of minutes, or just until it begins to boil. Remove the pot from the heat.

5. Place the egg substitute or eggs in a medium-size bowl, and slowly whisk about $\frac{1}{2}$ cup of the squash mixture into the eggs. Then whisk the eggs back into the pot. Stir in the Parmesan cheese and pepper.

6. Divide the squash mixture among the prepared custard cups. Fill a large roasting pan with 1 inch of hot water, and arrange the cups in the pan.

7. Bake uncovered for about 25 minutes, or until a sharp knife inserted in the center of a cup comes out clean. Remove the cups from the pan and allow to sit for 10 minutes. Serve hot in the custard cups, or run a knife around the edges and invert onto serving plates.

YIELD: 6 servings

$\frac{1}{4}$ cup chopped onion

1 tablespoon reduced-fat margarine or light butter

$\frac{1}{2}$ teaspoon dried sage

12-ounce package frozen mashed winter squash, thawed, or 1$\frac{1}{3}$ cups cooked mashed butternut, acorn, or other winter squash*

1 cup evaporated nonfat or low-fat milk

1 cup fat-free egg substitute, or 4 large eggs, beaten

3 tablespoons grated Parmesan cheese

$\frac{1}{8}$ teaspoon ground black pepper

---

* To make this recipe using fresh squash, place 2$\frac{1}{2}$ cups (about 12 ounces) of peeled, cubed squash in a 3-quart pot and cover with water. Bring to a boil; then reduce the heat to a simmer. Cover and cook for about 10 minutes or until soft. Drain well and mash with a potato masher.

Nutritional Facts (Per Serving)

Calories: 98
Carbohydrates: 12 g
Fiber: 1.6 g
Fat: 1.9 g
Sat. Fat: 0.9 g
Cholesterol: 4 mg
Protein: 9 g
Sodium: 209 mg
Calcium: 203 mg
Potassium: 361 mg

Diabetic Exchanges

$\frac{1}{2}$ starch
$\frac{1}{2}$ nonfat/low-fat milk
1 lean meat

Zucchini Custards

For Easy-to-Chew and Soft Diets

1. Preheat the oven to 350°F. Coat six 6-ounce custard cups with nonstick cooking spray, and set aside.

2. Place a large nonstick skillet over medium heat. Add the margarine or butter and cook until melted. Add the zucchini, onion, marjoram, and pepper. Cover and cook, stirring occasionally, for about 10 minutes or until the vegetables are tender. Add a little water if the skillet becomes too dry, but only enough to prevent scorching.

3. Remove the skillet from the heat and stir the milk into the zucchini mixture. Stir in the egg substitute or eggs, and then the breadcrumbs and Parmesan cheese.

4. Divide the zucchini mixture among the prepared custard cups. Fill a large roasting pan with 1 inch of hot water, and arrange the cups in the pan.

5. Bake uncovered for about 30 minutes, or until a sharp knife inserted in the center of a cup comes out clean. Remove the cups from the pan and allow to sit for 5 minutes. Serve hot in the custard cups, or run a knife around the edges and invert onto serving plates.

For Smooth/Puréed Diets

At the end of Step 2, place the zucchini mixture in a blender and process until completely smooth. Then proceed with the recipe.

---

* To make the breadcrumbs, tear about 1½ slices of whole wheat bread into pieces, place in a food processor, and process into crumbs. Choose a firm, smooth-textured bread free of nuts and other hard pieces.

YIELD: 6 servings

1 tablespoon margarine or butter

3 cups shredded unpeeled zucchini (about 3 medium)

2 tablespoons grated onion

½ teaspoon dried marjoram

¼ teaspoon ground black pepper

1½ cups evaporated nonfat or low-fat milk

¾ cup fat-free egg substitute, or 3 large eggs, beaten

1 cup soft whole wheat breadcrumbs*

¼ cup grated Parmesan cheese

Nutritional Facts (Per Serving)

Calories: 122
Carbohydrates: 13 g
Fiber: 1 g
Fat: 3.2 g
Sat. Fat: 1.3 g
Cholesterol: 6 mg
Protein: 11 g
Sodium: 264 mg
Calcium: 266 mg
Potassium: 396 mg

Diabetic Exchanges

1 vegetable
½ nonfat milk
1 lean meat

For All Diets

Home-Style Mashed Potatoes

1. Place the potatoes in a 3-quart pot, add water to cover, and boil for about 10 minutes or until fork-tender. Drain the potatoes, reserving $\frac{1}{3}$ cup of the cooking water.

2. Return the potatoes to the pot and add the milk or sour cream, margarine or butter, salt, and pepper. Mash or beat with an electric mixer until smooth, adding enough of the reserved cooking water to bring the potatoes to the desired consistency. Serve hot.

For a Change

■ Top your hot mashed potatoes with the sauce or gravy of your choice, such as Roasted Vegetable Gravy (page 170), Cheddar Cheese Sauce (page 165), or Quick Chicken Gravy (page 168).

■ Boil 4 to 6 large cloves of garlic along with the potatoes in Step 1, and mash them into the potato mixture.

■ Add 1 teaspoon dried dill or 2 to 3 teaspoons finely crumbled dried chives or parsley to the mashed potato mixture in Step 2.

■ Add $\frac{1}{4}$ to $\frac{1}{3}$ cup grated Parmesan cheese to the mashed potato mixture in Step 2.

■ Substitute extra virgin olive oil for the margarine or butter.

■ Use leftover Home-Style Mashed Potatoes to prepare Ham and Potato Puffs (page 218) or Potato Croquettes (page 244).

YIELD: 8 servings

$1\frac{1}{2}$ pounds peeled baking potatoes such as russet or Yukon Gold, cut into 1-inch chunks (about 5 cups)

$\frac{1}{2}$ cup low-fat evaporated milk or light sour cream

2 tablespoons margarine or butter

$\frac{1}{4}$ teaspoon salt

$\frac{1}{8}$ teaspoon ground white pepper

Nutritional Facts (Per $\frac{1}{2}$-Cup Serving)

Calories: 105
Carbohydrates: 18 g
Fiber: 1.5 g
Fat: 2.6 g
Sat. Fat: 0.9 g
Cholesterol: 2 mg
Protein: 2.4 g
Sodium: 116 mg
Calcium: 46 mg
Potassium: 343 mg

Diabetic Exchanges

1 starch
$\frac{1}{2}$ fat

Potato Croquettes

1. Place the flour in a shallow dish and set aside.

2. Shape ¼ cup of the potatoes into a patty about 2½-inches in diameter. Dip the potato patty in the flour, turning to coat both sides. Repeat with the remaining potatoes to make 6 patty-shaped croquettes.

3. Place the margarine, butter, or oil in a large nonstick skillet, and preheat over medium heat just until a drop of water sizzles when added to the skillet. Arrange the croquettes in the skillet and cook for a couple of minutes, or until the underside is nicely browned. Turn the patties over and cook for another couple of minutes, or until the second side is browned. Serve hot.

YIELD: 6 croquettes

¼ cup whole wheat pastry flour or unbleached flour

1½ cups chilled Home-Style Mashed Potatoes (plain or with any of the suggested variations) or other leftover mashed potatoes*

1–2 tablespoons margarine, butter, canola oil, or extra virgin olive oil

* The potatoes should be well chilled because they must be fairly stiff in order to hold the shape of patties.

Making Perfect Mashed Potatoes

Mashed potatoes are high on nearly everyone's list of comfort foods, and are also a perfect dish for a soft or smooth diet. Here are a few tips for making delicious mashed spuds.

• Choose Yukon Gold potatoes for a golden color and naturally buttery flavor, or use russets for a more traditional look and taste.

• Be sure to cook the cubed potatoes until they can be easily pierced with a fork.

• After draining the potatoes, return them to the pot and add your choice of moist ingredients. Butter, margarine, milk, buttermilk, half and half, cream, sour cream, chicken broth, and even olive oil can help make your spuds moist and creamy.

• Depending on the texture desired, process the cooked potatoes with a hand-held masher, a ricer, or—for the smoothest possible dish—an electric mixer.

Nutritional Facts (Per Serving)

Calories: 82
Carbohydrates: 12 g
Fiber: 1.7 g
Fat: 2.8 g
Sat. Fat: 0.9 g
Cholesterol: 1 mg
Protein: 1.7 g
Sodium: 73 mg
Calcium: 23 mg
Potassium: 199 mg

Diabetic Exchanges

1 starch
½ fat

For All Diets

Cheesy Twice-Baked Potatoes

1. Preheat the oven to 400°F.

2. Scrub the potatoes and pat them dry. Pierce each potato in several places with a fork and arrange on a baking sheet. Bake for about 40 minutes, or until easily pierced with a fork. Remove the potatoes from the oven and allow to cool until they can be easily handled. Reduce the oven temperature to 350°F.

3. Cut the potatoes open and scoop out the flesh, discarding the peel. Place the scooped-out potatoes and the sour cream, milk, margarine or butter, and pepper in a medium-size bowl. Beat with an electric mixer until smooth, adding a little more milk if needed for a smooth consistency. Add the cheese and stir to mix.

4. Coat four 8-ounce ramekins with butter-flavored nonstick cooking spray and divide the potato mixture among the ramekins. Spray the tops with the cooking spray and follow with a sprinkling of paprika.

5. Bake the ramekins for about 15 minutes, or until the potatoes are heated through and the tops are lightly browned. Serve hot.

For a Change

■ Before baking the potatoes in Step 2, lightly spray them with butter-flavored nonstick cooking spray. (This will keep the skins from looking dried out.) When cutting open the baked potatoes in Step 3, neatly slice each in half horizontally to form 2 shells. Once the potato mixture has been prepared in Step 3, spoon it back into the skins instead of the ramekins and bake as directed. Note that you will not be able to eat the skins, but it makes for a nice presentation.

YIELD: 4 servings

4 medium baking potatoes (about 6 ounces each)

1/2 cup nonfat or light sour cream

1/4 cup evaporated nonfat or low-fat milk

1 tablespoon margarine or butter

1/8 teaspoon ground black pepper

1/2 cup shredded reduced-fat Cheddar cheese

Butter-flavored cooking spray

Ground paprika

Nutritional Facts (Per Serving)

Calories: 193
Carbohydrates: 29 g
Fiber: 1.5 g
Fat: 4.9 g
Sat. Fat: 2.3 g
Cholesterol: 8 mg
Protein: 8.9 g
Sodium: 494 mg
Calcium: 187 mg
Potassium: 517 mg

Diabetic Exchanges

2 starch
1/2 medium-fat meat
1/2 fat

For All Diets

Maple Mashed Sweet Potatoes

1. Place the potatoes in a 4-quart pot, add water to cover, and boil for about 15 minutes, or until fork-tender. Drain the potatoes and return them to the pot.

2. Add the maple syrup, margarine or butter, apple juice, and ginger to the potatoes, and mash or beat with an electric mixer until smooth. Add a little more apple juice if needed to create the desired consistency, and serve hot.

For a Change

■ Substitute honey or brown sugar for the maple syrup, and orange juice for the apple juice.

YIELD: 6 servings

2 pounds sweet potatoes (about 4 medium), peeled and cut into 1-inch chunks

3 tablespoons maple syrup

2 tablespoons margarine or butter

2 tablespoons apple juice

1/2 teaspoon ground ginger

The Sweet Benefits of Sweet Potatoes

If you ever thought that sweet potatoes should be confined to the Thanksgiving table, it's time to think again about this brightly colored vegetable. Sweet potatoes, you see, are among the most nutritious foods you can find at your local supermarket.

Sometimes referred to as yams, sweet potatoes supply a wealth of nutrients, including vitamin A, vitamin B$_6$, vitamin D, copper, manganese, potassium, and iron. They are also an excellent source of dietary fiber. Just as important, this root vegetable is a natural for soft and smooth diets. Cook it until fork-tender and mash it with maple syrup, honey, margarine, butter, apple juice, orange juice, applesauce, or crushed pineapple. The resulting dish will be as healthful as it is sweetly satisfying.

**Nutritional Facts
(Per 1/2-Cup Serving)**

Calories: 170
Carbohydrates: 34 g
Fiber: 3 g
Fat: 3.1 g
Sat. Fat: 0.9 g
Cholesterol: 0 mg
Protein: 2.1 g
Sodium: 42 mg
Calcium: 34 mg
Potassium: 414 mg

Diabetic Exchanges

2 starch
1/2 fat

For All Diets

Sweet Potato Pudding

YIELD: 5 servings

2 large or 3 small sweet potatoes (about 1½ pounds), peeled and cut into 1-inch chunks

¼ cup brown sugar

3 tablespoons frozen orange or apple juice concentrate

2 tablespoons margarine or butter

⅛ teaspoon ground cinnamon

⅛ teaspoon ground nutmeg

⅛ teaspoon ground ginger

⅛ teaspoon ground cloves

2 cups mini-marshmallows

1. Place the potatoes in a 4-quart pot, add water to cover, and boil for about 15 minutes, or until fork-tender. Drain the potatoes and transfer them to a medium-size bowl.

2. Add the brown sugar, juice concentrate, margarine or butter, and spices to the bowl. Beat the potatoes with an electric mixer until smooth, adding a little milk if the mixture seems too thick.

3. Preheat the oven to 400°F. Coat a 9-inch pie pan or shallow 1½-quart casserole dish with nonstick cooking spray, and spread the mixture evenly in the pan. Press the marshmallows onto the top of the potatoes, covering the entire surface.

4. Bake for about 15 minutes, or just until the marshmallows begin to lightly brown. (Do not overcook.) Remove from the oven and serve immediately.

For Smooth/Puréed Diets

Omit the marshmallow topping, and serve the potatoes after beating them with the other ingredients in Step 2.

Dietary Variation

To reduce calories and carbohydrates:

Replace the brown sugar with sugar substitute and omit the marshmallow topping. (See page 44 for details on using sugar substitutes.) This will eliminate 95 calories, 24 grams carbohydrates, and 1½ diabetic carbohydrate exchanges.

Nutritional Facts (Per Serving)

Calories: 277
Carbohydrates: 57 g
Fiber: 2.3 g
Fat: 5 g
Sat. Fat: 0.8 g
Cholesterol: 0 mg
Protein: 2.6 g
Sodium: 72 mg
Calcium: 43 mg
Potassium: 325 mg

Diabetic Exchanges

2 starch
1½ carbohydrate
1 fat

Sweet Potato Cakes

1. Preheat the oven to 400°F.

2. Scrub the potatoes, pat dry, and pierce each potato in several places with a fork. Arrange the potatoes on a baking sheet and bake for about 40 minutes, or until easily pierced with a fork. Remove the potatoes from the oven and allow them to cool until they can be easily handled.

3. Peel the potatoes, discarding the peel, and coarsely chop the flesh. Place the chopped potato and milk in a medium-size bowl, and beat with an electric mixer to mix well. Beat in the egg substitute or eggs, and then the baking powder, ginger, salt, and pepper.

4. Preheat a large nonstick skillet or griddle over medium-high heat. Place some of the margarine or butter in the skillet and allow to melt. Drop slightly rounded tablespoons of the sweet potato mixture onto the pan, and spread each into a 2-inch circle, leaving a couple of inches between the cakes. (Do not crowd the skillet.) Cook for about 2 minutes, or until the edges look set and the bottoms are golden brown. Spray the tops with the cooking spray, carefully turn the cakes with a spatula, and cook for 2 additional minutes, or until the second side is golden brown. Repeat with the remaining sweet potato mixture, transferring the cakes to a covered dish to keep warm as they are done. Serve hot.

YIELD: 5 servings (4 cakes each)

2 medium-large sweet potatoes (about 1 pound)

2 tablespoons nonfat or low-fat milk

$\frac{1}{2}$ cup fat-free egg substitute, or 2 large eggs

1 teaspoon baking powder

$\frac{1}{2}$ teaspoon ground ginger

$\frac{1}{4}$ teaspoon salt

$\frac{1}{8}$ teaspoon ground black pepper

2 tablespoons margarine or butter

Nonstick cooking spray

Nutritional Facts (Per 4-Cake Serving)

Calories: 103
Carbohydrates: 14 g
Fiber: 1.7 g
Fat: 3.6 g
Sat. Fat: 1 g
Cholesterol: 0 mg
Protein: 3.6 g
Sodium: 234 mg
Calcium: 31 mg
Potassium: 271 mg

Diabetic Exchanges

1 starch
1 fat

For All Diets

Polenta Parmesan

1. Place the cornmeal, milk, and salt in a 3-quart nonstick pot and whisk to mix well. Add the water and bring to a boil over high heat, stirring constantly. Reduce the heat to low and cover, leaving the lid ajar. Cook, stirring often, for 10 to 15 minutes, or until the mixture is thick and creamy. The cooking time will depend on the texture of the cornmeal.

2. Remove the pot from the heat and stir in the Parmesan cheese and the margarine or butter. Serve hot.

1 cup yellow cornmeal

1 cup nonfat or low-fat milk

$1/4$ teaspoon salt

3 cups water

$1/4$ cup grated Parmesan cheese

1–2 tablespoons margarine or butter

For a Change

■ Drizzle the polenta with Roasted Red Pepper Sauce (page 168).

■ Place the polenta in a bowl and top with Simple Tomato Sauce (page 167) or ready-made marinara sauce. Sprinkle on additional Parmesan cheese and serve as you would pasta.

Say "Cheese"

An excellent source of calcium and protein, cheese can take a dish from ordinary to extraordinary. Be aware, though, that some cheeses are more suitable than others for smooth diets. Firm products like Cheddar, Swiss, and Parmesan must be shredded or grated and incorporated into soft spreads, soups, or sauces. Easier-to-use cheeses include blue cheese, feta, ricotta, cottage cheese, cream cheese, and soft-curd farmer's cheese

If you are following a heart-healthy lifestyle, you'll want to take advantage of the many lower-fat cheeses that are now available. Reduced-fat cheeses offer less fat, cholesterol, and calories than their full-fat counterparts. Try to avoid fat-free cheeses, though, as they can be hard to chew and difficult to melt. Vegan cheeses made from nonanimal foods such as soymilk are another good option, although they may provide less protein and calcium than their dairy-based counterparts. (Check the label.) Again, melting may be an issue, so look for brands that specifically advertise good melting properties.

Nutritional Facts (Per $7/8$-Cup Serving)

Calories: 186

Carbohydrates: 27 g

Fiber: 2.2 g

Fat: 5.9 g

Sat. Fat: 1.9 g

Cholesterol: 6 mg

Protein: 7.2 g

Sodium: 332 mg

Calcium: 166 mg

Potassium: 204 mg

Diabetic Exchanges

$1 1/2$ starch

$1/2$ nonfat/low-fat milk

1 fat

For All Diets

Pasta Purée

1. Place the orzo in a blender and process for about 1 minute, or until it has the consistency of grits or cornmeal. Set aside.

2. Place the water in a 2-quart pot and bring to a boil over high heat. Stir in the margarine, butter, or olive oil and the salt.

3. While whisking constantly, gradually add the ground pasta to the pot. Reduce the heat to maintain a simmer, cover, and cook for 10 minutes, or until the liquid is absorbed and the pasta is tender. If you need a softer texture, increase the water by $1/2$ to 1 cup and cook for 5 additional minutes, or until the water has been absorbed.

4. Serve hot. If desired, top with Simple Tomato Sauce (page 167), ready-made marinara sauce, margarine, olive oil, and/or Parmesan cheese, as you would spaghetti.

For a Change

■ Stir $1/4$ cup of grated Parmesan cheese into the cooked pasta.

■ Stir 2 teaspoons of finely crumbled dried parsley or 2 tablespoons of finely chopped fresh parsley into the cooked pasta.

YIELD: 4 servings

1 cup whole wheat orzo pasta

3 cups water

2 tablespoons margarine, butter, or olive oil

$1/4$ teaspoon salt

**Nutritional Facts
(Per $7/8$-Cup Serving)**

Calories: 188
Carbohydrates: 30 g
Fiber: 6.8 g
Fat: 5.3 g
Sat. Fat: 1.3 g
Cholesterol: 0 mg
Protein: 5.3 g
Sodium: 186 mg
Calcium: 30 mg
Potassium: 110 mg

Diabetic Exchanges

2 starch
1 fat

For All Diets

Savory Brown Rice

1. Place the rice in a blender and process for about 45 seconds, or until it has the texture of grits or cornmeal.

2. Place the ground rice, water (or water and milk), and bouillon granules in a 2½-quart nonstick pot. Cover and bring to a boil over high heat. Reduce the heat to low and simmer, stirring occasionally, for about 20 minutes, or until the rice is creamy and soft. Add a little more water if needed.

3. Stir the margarine, butter, or oil and the parsley into the rice, and remove the pot from the heat. Allow to sit covered for 5 minutes. Serve hot.

For a Change

■ Substitute other whole grains such as barley, spelt, or whole wheat berries for the rice.

YIELD: 5 servings

1 cup brown rice

4 cups water, or 3 cups water plus 1 cup nonfat or low-fat milk

1½ teaspoons chicken, beef, or vegetable bouillon granules

1 tablespoon margarine, butter, or olive oil

2–3 tablespoons finely chopped fresh parsley, or 2–3 teaspoons dried parsley

Whole Grain Goodness

How can you instantly boost the nutrients in your diet? Replace refined grains like white rice with whole grains and whole grain products. While refined grains have been stripped of disease-fighting nutrients, whole grains are loaded with fiber, B-vitamins, minerals, antioxidants, and phytonutrients. For this reason, they can actually reduce your risk of heart disease, diabetes, and many other health problems.

People on soft and smooth diets cannot eat grains in their whole kernel form. However, dry uncooked whole grains such as brown rice, barley, spelt, and wheat can be ground in a blender until they reach a texture similar to that of grits or cornmeal, and then cooked into a creamy dish that is suitable for even the smoothest of diets. Whether used as a savory side dish or a hot breakfast cereal, this can be a palate-pleasing way to get great nutrition.

Nutritional Facts
(Per ¾-Cup Serving)

Calories: 155
Carbohydrates: 29 g
Fiber: 1.3 g
Fat: 2.9 g
Sat. Fat: 0.7 g
Cholesterol: 0 mg
Protein: 3 g
Sodium: 275 mg
Calcium: 11 mg
Potassium: 91 mg

Diabetic Exchanges

2 starch
½ fat

Grits 'n Greens Casserole

1. Preheat the oven to 350°F. Coat a 2-quart casserole dish or six 8-ounce ramekins with nonstick cooking spray, and set aside.

2. Place the water and milk in a 3-quart pot and bring to a boil over high heat. Stir in the grits and reduce the heat to a simmer. Cover and cook for about 7 minutes, stirring every 2 minutes, until tender. Stir in the collard greens, margarine or butter, pepper, bacon, and ¾ cup of the Parmesan cheese.

3. Spoon the grits mixture into the prepared dish or ramekins, and sprinkle the remaining 3 tablespoons of Parmesan cheese over the top. Bake uncovered for about 20 minutes if using a casserole dish, and 12 minutes if using ramekins. The grits are ready to eat when the top is lightly browned. Serve hot.

Dietary Variation

To reduce fat and calories:

Omit the margarine or butter and substitute vegetarian bacon or extra-lean turkey bacon for the pork bacon. This will eliminate 43 calories, 5.6 grams of fat, and 1 diabetic fat exchange from each serving. The high-fat meat exchange will become lean meat.

YIELD: 6 servings

2½ cups water

2 cups nonfat or low-fat milk

1 cup quick-cooking grits

8 ounces frozen chopped collard greens (about 3 cups), cooked according to package directions and well drained, or 2 cups leftover cooked collard greens, drained and chopped

2 tablespoons margarine or butter

¼ teaspoon ground black pepper

6 slices bacon, cooked, drained, and finely crumbled

¾ cup plus 3 tablespoons grated Parmesan cheese, divided

Nutritional Facts (Per ¾-Cup Serving)

Calories: 277
Carbohydrates: 29 g
Fiber: 1.7 g
Fat: 11.4 g
Sat. Fat: 5 g
Cholesterol: 19 mg
Protein: 15 g
Sodium: 480 mg
Calcium: 392 mg
Potassium: 316 mg

Diabetic Exchanges

1½ starch
½ nonfat/low-fat milk
1 high-fat meat
1 fat

For All Diets

Refried Beans

For Easy-to-Chew and Soft Diets

1. Place the beans, vegetable juice, chili powder, and cumin in a food processor, and process until smooth. Set aside.

2. Place the onion and olive oil in a large nonstick skillet, cover, and cook over medium heat, stirring occasionally, for 3 to 4 minutes, or until the onion is soft.

3. Add the puréed beans to the skillet mixture and raise the heat to medium-high. Cook, stirring frequently, for several minutes, or until the mixture is thick. Serve hot, topping each serving with some of the cheese and sour cream.

For Smooth/Puréed Diets

When the beans have finished heating up in Step 3, transfer the mixture to a food processor along with the Cheddar cheese. Process until smooth and serve hot, garnished with the sour cream.

YIELD: 4 servings

2 cans (15 ounces each) pinto or black beans, drained

1/2 cup low-sodium V8 vegetable juice

2–3 teaspoons chili powder

1/2 teaspoon ground cumin

2 tablespoons grated onion

1 1/2 tablespoons extra virgin olive oil

TOPPINGS

1/2 cup finely shredded reduced-fat Cheddar cheese

1/2 cup nonfat or light sour cream

Nutritional Facts (Per 3/4-Cup Serving)

Calories: 279
Carbohydrates: 36 g
Fiber: 9 g
Fat: 8.9 g
Sat. Fat: 2.5 g
Cholesterol: 8 mg
Protein: 15 g
Sodium: 455 mg
Calcium: 223 mg
Potassium: 595 mg

Diabetic Exchanges

2 starch
2 lean meat
1 fat

Easy Vegetable Aspic

1. Place $\frac{1}{2}$ cup of the vegetable juice in a 1-quart heatproof bowl, and sprinkle the gelatin over the top. Allow to sit for 2 minutes to soften.

2. Place the remaining $1\frac{1}{2}$ cups of juice in a small pot and bring to a boil over high heat. Pour the heated juice over the softened gelatin mixture and stir until the gelatin is completely dissolved. Stir in the pepper.

3. Divide the mixture among four 6-ounce custard cups. Cover and chill for several hours or overnight, until firm.

4. To serve, run a knife around the inside of the cups to loosen the edges, and invert each aspic onto an individual serving plate. If the aspic does not slide out, carefully dip the custard cup just to the rim in warm (not hot) water for about 10 seconds to loosen. Combine the dressing ingredients in a small bowl and spoon the mixture over the aspic.

For a Change

■ If you follow an easy-to-chew or soft diet, try stirring $\frac{1}{2}$ cup chopped soft ripe avocado or finely chopped cooked spinach, zucchini, or broccoli into the aspic mixture before pouring the aspic into the custard cups in Step 3.

YIELD: 4 servings

2 cups V8 vegetable juice, divided

1 envelope (0.25 ounce) unflavored gelatin

$\frac{1}{4}$ teaspoon ground black pepper

DRESSING

$\frac{1}{4}$ cup nonfat or light sour cream

$\frac{1}{4}$ cup nonfat or light mayonnaise

2–3 teaspoons finely chopped fresh dill

Nutritional Facts (Per Serving)

Calories: 57
Carbohydrates: 10 g
Fiber: 1.3 g
Fat: 0.5 g
Sat. Fat: 0.1 g
Cholesterol: 2 mg
Protein: 3.3 g
Sodium: 462 mg
Calcium: 35 mg
Potassium: 277 mg

Diabetic Exchanges

1 vegetable

For All Diets

Cherry-Apple Salad

For Easy-to-Chew and Soft Diets

1. Place ½ cup of the apple juice and all of the gelatin mix in a blender. Bring the remaining 1 cup of apple juice to a boil. Pour the boiling juice into the blender and process for about a minute, or until the gelatin is dissolved. Add the walnuts and celery and blend for an additional minute. Add the cherries and blend for another minute.

2. Pour the blended mixture into a bowl and refrigerate for 30 to 40 minutes, or until the gelatin has the consistency of egg whites.

3. Whisk the gelatin mixture well and divide among four 6-ounce custard cups. Cover and chill for several hours or overnight, until firm.

4. When ready to serve, make the dressing by placing the cream cheese in a bowl and slowly beating in the apple juice with an electric mixer. Run a knife around the inside of the cups to loosen the edges, and invert each salad onto an individual serving plate. If the gelatin does not slide out, carefully dip the custard cup just to the rim in warm (not hot) water for about 10 seconds to loosen. Top each salad with some of the dressing and serve.

For Smooth/Puréed Diets

After all of the salad ingredients have been blended in Step 1, pour the mixture through a mesh strainer to remove any coarse bits. Then proceed with the remainder of the recipe.

Dietary Variation

To reduce calories and carbohydrates:

Use a sugar-free gelatin mix and you will eliminate 72 calories, 19 grams carbohydrate, and 1 carbohydrate diabetic exchange per serving.

YIELD: 4 servings

1½ cups apple juice, divided

1 package (4-serving size) cherry gelatin

¼ cup finely ground walnuts

¼ cup chopped celery (remove strings before chopping)

1 cup frozen pitted dark sweet cherries

DRESSING

4 ounces reduced-fat cream cheese

¼ cup apple juice

Nutritional Facts (Per Serving)

Calories: 274
Carbohydrates: 39 g
Fiber: 1.4 g
Fat: 11.2 g
Sat. Fat: 4.5 g
Cholesterol: 21 mg
Protein: 7 g
Sodium: 181 mg
Calcium: 41 mg
Potassium: 228 mg

Diabetic Exchanges

1½ fruit
1 carbohydrate
1 medium-fat meat
1 fat

For All Diets

Mandarin-Banana Salad

For Easy-to-Chew and Soft Diets

1. Drain the oranges, pouring the juice into a 2-cup glass measuring cup. Set the oranges aside.

2. Add enough water to bring the volume of the mandarin orange juice to 1 cup. Microwave for about 2 minutes, or until the mixture comes to a boil.

3. Place the gelatin in a medium-size heatproof bowl and add the boiling juice mixture. Whisk until the gelatin is dissolved. Cover and refrigerate for about 30 minutes, or until the mixture has the consistency of egg whites.

4. Place the cream cheese in a medium-size bowl and beat with an electric mixer until smooth. Beat in the sour cream; then gradually beat in the chilled gelatin. Add the mandarin oranges, and beat until they are broken into small bits. Add the banana and beat to mix in.

5. Divide the mixture between four 6-ounce custard cups. Cover and chill for several hours or overnight, until firm. Serve in the cups or unmold onto serving plates. To unmold, run a knife around the inside of the cups to loosen the edges, and invert each salad onto an individual serving plate. If the gelatin does not slide out, carefully dip the custard cup just to the rim in warm (not hot) water for about 10 seconds to loosen.

For Smooth/Puréed Diets

Purée the banana and mandarin oranges until smooth before adding them to the gelatin mixture in Step 4.

Dietary Variation

To reduce calories and carbohydrates:

Use sugar-free gelatin mix and eliminate 72 calories, 19 grams of carbohydrate, and 1 carbohydrate diabetic exchange per serving.

YIELD: 4 servings

11-ounce can mandarin oranges in juice or light syrup, undrained

1 package (4-serving size) lemon gelatin

$\frac{1}{4}$ cup plus 2 tablespoons reduced-fat cream cheese, softened

$\frac{1}{2}$ cup nonfat or light sour cream

1 banana, mashed

Nutritional Facts (Per Serving)

Calories: 235
Carbohydrates: 43 g
Fiber: 1.3 g
Fat: 5.2 g
Sat. Fat: 3.2 g
Cholesterol: 16 mg
Protein: 6 g
Sodium: 174 mg
Calcium: 79 mg
Potassium: 288 mg

Diabetic Exchanges

1 fruit
$1\frac{1}{2}$ carbohydrate
1 medium-fat meat

DELIGHTFUL DESSERTS

Although desserts are among life's greatest pleasures, they are so often loaded with saturated fats and sugar that many people do their best to avoid them or reserve them for only the most special of occasions. But, as you're about to learn, desserts don't have to be unhealthy. Many of the treats on the following pages feature an abundance of fruit, low-fat milk and cheese, and other wholesome ingredients. Plus, you'll find tips for replacing sugar with sugar substitutes when you need to limit your calorie or carbohydrate intake. Even if you are trying to lose weight, you can have your dessert and eat it, too.

Of course, because your ability to eat has been diminished, we realize that you may be trying to maintain or even gain weight. If so, you'll be happy to know that this chapter was created for you, too. Many of the recipes on the following pages are a good source of calories. You will also find tips for adding extra calories to your desserts—both those desserts found within these pages, and those that you buy ready-made at your local store.

A large number of desserts, such as fruit whips and mousses, are perfect for even very smooth diets because they are designed to have a silky consistency. For that reason, a wide assortment of these little luxuries has been included in the following pages. When a dessert is not absolutely smooth as prepared—Apples and Dumplings, for instance— directions are often offered for adjusting the texture to be compatible with your needs. So whether you're looking for a fluffy fruit mousse, a creamy flan, or a deep chocolate cake, you're sure to find a dessert that is not only delicious but also tailor-made for your easy-to-swallow diet.

For All Diets

Blackberry Doobie
(Steamed Blackberry Pudding)

For Easy-to-Chew and Soft Diets

YIELD: 8 servings

1. Place the flours, sugar, baking powder, and salt in a medium-size bowl and stir to mix well. Set aside.

2. Place the egg or egg substitute in a small bowl and whisk for several seconds. Whisk in first the milk and then the margarine or butter and the vanilla extract.

3. Add the egg mixture to the dry ingredients, stirring just until blended. Set the batter aside for 10 minutes; then stir for several seconds. Fold in the blackberries just until evenly distributed.

4. Coat a 1½-quart casserole dish with nonstick cooking spray and spread the batter evenly in the dish. Cover the dish with aluminum foil, spraying the underside of the foil with cooking spray to prevent sticking.

5. Place the dish in a deep pot with 1 to 2 inches of water. (The pot needs to be large enough to hold the dish with room to spare.) Cover the pot tightly and bring to a boil. Reduce the heat to a simmer, cover, and steam for about 1 hour or until a wooden toothpick inserted in the center of the dish comes out clean. (To avoid getting burned, allow the steam to dissipate from the pot before testing.) Check the water level in the pot after about 45 minutes and add more, if needed, so that it doesn't cook dry.

6. To serve, scoop some of the hot Doobie into a bowl and top with 2 to 3 tablespoons of the sauce.

For Smooth/Puréed Diets

Reduce the milk to ½ cup when making the batter. Place the blackberries in a blender and purée until smooth. Then press through a strainer to remove the seeds. Swirl the blackberry purée into the batter. Do not over-stir or the batter will turn purple. Steam as directed and serve with the Lemon Sauce. If a very smooth consistency is needed, purée the pudding with the sauce.

Ingredients:

- ½ cup plus 2 tablespoons whole wheat pastry flour
- ½ cup plus 2 tablespoons unbleached flour
- ½ cup plus 2 tablespoons sugar
- 2½ teaspoons baking powder
- ¼ teaspoon salt
- 1 large egg, or ¼ cup fat-free egg substitute
- ¾ cup nonfat or low-fat milk
- ¼ cup melted margarine or butter
- 1 teaspoon vanilla extract
- 2 cups fresh blackberries, or 2 cups frozen berries (partially thawed, but not runny)
- 1–1½ cups Lemon Sauce (page 178), warmed

Nutritional Facts (Per ¾-Cup Serving with 2 Tablespoons Sauce)

Calories: 264
Carbohydrates: 47 g
Fiber: 3.5 g
Fat: 7.1 g
Sat. Fat: 2 g
Cholesterol: 62 mg
Protein: 4.6 g
Sodium: 296 mg
Calcium: 135 mg
Potassium: 219 mg

Diabetic Exchanges

3 carbohydrate
1½ fat

For a Change

∎ Substitute blueberries, raspberries, or a combination of berries for the blackberries.

∎ Serve with Vanilla Custard Sauce (page 177), Quick Custard Sauce (page 176), or Mixed Berry Sauce (page 173) instead of the Lemon Sauce.

Dietary Variation

To reduce calories and carbohydrates:

Replace half of the sugar in the batter with a sugar substitute, and use the reduced-calorie version of the Lemon Sauce. (See page 44 for details on using sugar substitutes.) This will eliminate 58 calories, 15 grams carbohydrate, and 1 diabetic carbohydrate exchange per serving.

For All Diets

Frozen Fruit Whip

ional Facts
-Cup Serving)

s: 131
ydrates: 27 g
3.1 g
 g
t: 0 g
terol: 0 mg
: 1.6 g
a: 18 mg
n: 57 mg
um: 262 mg

ic Exchanges

hydrate

1. Place the fruit in a mini-food processor and process for a minute or 2, or until finely ground. Add the remaining ingredients and process for another minute or until smooth. Mix in a little more sour cream, yogurt, or cream cheese, if desired.

2. Transfer the fruit whip to an 8-ounce wine glass or dessert dish and serve immediately.

Dietary Variation

To reduce calories and carbohydrates:

Use a sugar substitute instead of the sugar or honey. (See page 44 for details on using sugar substitutes.) This will eliminate 48 calories, 12 grams carbohydrate, and 1 diabetic carbohydrate exchange.

YIELD: 1 serving

1 cup coarsely chopped frozen (unthawed) fruit, such as strawberries, peaches, blueberries, or pitted sweet cherries

2 tablespoons nonfat or light sour cream, Greek-style yogurt, or reduced-fat cream cheese

1 tablespoon sugar or honey

For All Diets

Apples and Dumplings

For Easy-to-Chew and Soft Diets

1. Place 2 tablespoons of the juice and all of the cornstarch in a small bowl, and stir to dissolve the cornstarch. Set aside.

2. Place the remaining juice and the apples, sugar, cinnamon, and nutmeg in a large nonstick skillet, and stir to mix. Cover and bring to a boil over high heat. Then reduce the heat to medium-low and cook, stirring occasionally, for about 5 minutes or until the apples are tender.

3. Stir the reserved cornstarch mixture and add it to the skillet. Cook and stir for about 30 seconds, or until thickened and bubbly. Remove the skillet from the heat, cover, and set aside to keep warm.

4. To make the dumplings, combine the flour, sugar, and baking powder in a small bowl, and stir to mix well. Add the margarine or butter and stir together, mashing with a fork until the mixture is moist and crumbly. Add the yogurt and stir to mix. Add a little more yogurt, if needed, to form a thick batter.

5. Return the fruit mixture to the heat and bring to a boil. Reduce the heat to a simmer and drop heaping teaspoonfuls of the batter onto the fruit to make 12 dumplings. Cover and simmer without stirring for 10 minutes, or until the dumplings are fluffy and firm to the touch. (Adjust the heat to maintain a gentle simmer if necessary.) Serve warm.

For Smooth/Puréed Diets

If you can tolerate the dumplings whole, make them as moist as possible by cutting them in half and adding more sauce as necessary. If a very smooth texture is desired, you may have to purée the fruit mixture before cooking, or purée the dumplings and fruit mixture together after cooking.

YIELD: 6 servings

1½ cups apple juice, divided

1 tablespoon cornstarch

4 cups diced peeled apples (about 4 medium-large apples)

¼–⅓ cup sugar

½ teaspoon ground cinnamon

¼ teaspoon ground nutmeg

DUMPLINGS

¾ cup unbleached flour

¼ cup sugar

1 teaspoon baking powder

2 tablespoons margarine or butter, softened

⅓ cup vanilla yogurt

Nutritional Facts (Per ¾-Cup Serving with 2 Dumplings)

Calories: 223
Carbohydrates: 48 g
Fiber: 2.3 g
Fat: 3.7 g
Sat. Fat: 1 g
Cholesterol: 0 mg
Protein: 2.3 g
Sodium: 287 mg
Calcium: 161 mg
Potassium: 203 mg

Diabetic Exchanges

3 carbohydrate
½ fat

Dietary Variation

To reduce calories and carbohydrates:

Use a sugar substitute in place of all of the sugar in the filling and up to half of the sugar in the dumplings. (See page 44 for details on using sugar substitutes.) This will eliminate 45 calories, 11 grams carbohydrate, and 1 diabetic carbohydrate exchange.

For All Diets

Cinnamon Applesauce

For Easy-to-Chew and Soft Diets

1. Place all of the ingredients in a 3-quart pot and stir to mix. Bring the mixture to a boil over medium heat. Then reduce the heat to medium-low, cover, and cook, stirring occasionally, for about 20 minutes, or until the apples soften and break down into a sauce. Add a little more juice if necessary.

2. Mash with a potato masher until you have the desired consistency, and serve warm or chilled.

For Smooth/Puréed Diets

For a smoother consistency, use a hand-held blender to purée the mixture. If a very smooth consistency is needed, purée the mixture in a food processor.

Dietary Variation

To reduce calories and carbohydrates:

Either omit the sugar or replace it with a sugar substitute. (See page 44 for details on using sugar substitutes.) This will eliminate 14 calories, 4 grams carbohydrate, and $1/4$ diabetic carbohydrate exchange.

YIELD: 7 servings

6 cups chopped peeled apples (about 6 medium-large apples)

$1/2$ cup apple juice

2–3 tablespoons light brown sugar

$3/4$ teaspoon ground cinnamon

**Nutritional Facts
(Per $1/2$-Cup Serving)**

Calories: 77
Carbohydrates: 20 g
Fiber: 2 g
Fat: 0.3 g
Sat. Fat: 0 g
Cholesterol: 0 mg
Protein: 0.2 g
Sodium: 3 mg
Calcium: 8 mg
Potassium: 141 mg

Diabetic Exchanges

1 carbohydrate

For All Diets

Pear Sauce

For Easy-to-Chew and Soft Diets

1. Place all of the ingredients in a 3-quart pot and stir to mix. Bring the mixture to a boil over medium heat. Then reduce the heat to medium-low, cover, and cook, stirring occasionally, for about 20 minutes, or until the pears soften and break down into a sauce. Add a little more water or juice if necessary.

2. Mash with a potato masher until you have the desired consistency, and serve warm or chilled.

For Smooth/Puréed Diets

For a smoother consistency, use a hand-held blender to purée the mixture. If a very smooth consistency is needed, purée the mixture in a food processor.

Dietary Variation

To reduce calories and carbohydrates:

Replace the sugar with a sugar substitute. (See page 44 for details on using sugar substitutes.) This will eliminate 16 calories, 4 grams carbohydrate, and ¼ diabetic carbohydrate exchange.

YIELD: 6 servings

5 cups chopped peeled pears (about 6 medium pears)

¼ cup water or orange juice

2–3 tablespoons sugar

½ teaspoon ground cinnamon

¼ teaspoon ground nutmeg

Nutritional Facts (Per ½-Cup Serving)

Calories: 98
Carbohydrates: 25 g
Fiber: 3.4 g
Fat: 0.6 g
Sat. Fat: 0 g
Cholesterol: 0 mg
Protein: 0.6 g
Sodium: 0 mg
Calcium: 18 mg
Potassium: 172 mg

Diabetic Exchanges

1½ carbohydrate

For All Diets

Peanut Butter Mousse

1. Place the peanut butter, ricotta cheese or tofu, and powdered sugar in the bowl of a food processor, and process until smooth. Add the vanilla extract, and process to mix well. Add a tablespoon or 2 of milk, if necessary, to create the consistency of a thick pudding.

2. Transfer the peanut butter mixture to a medium-size bowl and fold in half of the whipped topping. Then fold in the remaining whipped topping.

3. Divide the mousse among four small glasses or dessert dishes. Cover and chill for several hours.

4. Top each dessert with a drizzle of chocolate syrup or a sprinkling of grated chocolate, if desired, and serve chilled.

Dietary Variation

To reduce calories and carbohydrates:

Replace the $\frac{1}{2}$ cup of powdered sugar with sugar substitute equal to $\frac{1}{3}$ cup sugar. (See page 44 for details on using sugar substitutes.) This will eliminate 47 calories, 12 grams carbohydrate, and 1 diabetic carbohydrate exchange.

---

* Sold in shelf-stable aseptic packages in most grocery stores, silken tofu has a softer, smoother texture than regular tofu and can be used in desserts, soups, sauces, and smoothies.

YIELD: 4 servings

$\frac{1}{2}$–$\frac{2}{3}$ cup smooth peanut butter

$\frac{1}{2}$ cup nonfat or part-skim ricotta cheese, or 4 ounces silken firm tofu (about $\frac{1}{2}$ cup mashed)*

$\frac{1}{2}$ cup powdered sugar

1 teaspoon vanilla extract

2 cups nonfat or light whipped topping

4 teaspoons chocolate syrup or finely grated chocolate (optional)

Nutritional Facts
(Per $\frac{2}{3}$-Cup Serving)

Calories: 368
Carbohydrates: 31 g
Fiber: 1.9 g
Fat: 18 g
Sat. Fat: 3 g
Cholesterol: 2 mg
Protein: 15 g
Sodium: 205 mg
Calcium: 139 mg
Potassium: 279 mg

Diabetic Exchanges

2 carbohydrate
2$\frac{1}{2}$ high-fat meat

For All Diets

Fabulous Fruit Gelatin

1. Pour half of the juice into a blender and sprinkle the gelatin over the top. Allow to sit for 2 minutes to soften. Place the remaining juice in a small heatproof bowl and microwave for about 1 minute, or until it comes to a boil. Pour the boiling juice into the blender, cover, and process for 30 seconds.

2. Add the undrained fruit and the sugar to the blender and purée until smooth. Pour the purée through a strainer, discarding any seeds or other hard pieces.

3. Divide the sieved mixture among four 6-ounce custard cups or molds. Cover and chill for at least 8 hours, or until firm.

4. Serve the gelatin in the cups or unmold onto serving plates. To unmold, run a knife around the inside of the cups to loosen the edges, and invert the desserts onto individual plates. If the gelatin does not slide out, carefully dip the custard cup just to the rim in warm (not hot) water for about 10 seconds to loosen. Crown each serving with whipped topping, if desired.

Dietary Variation

To reduce calories and carbohydrates:

Use a sugar substitute instead of the sugar and eliminate 48 calories, 12 grams carbohydrate, and 1 diabetic carbohydrate exchange. (See page 44 for details on using sugar substitutes.)

YIELD: 4 servings

3/4 cup cranberry juice cocktail or pomegranate juice, divided

1 envelope (0.25 ounce) unflavored gelatin

2 1/2 cups frozen (thawed and undrained) fruit, such as strawberries, sweet pitted cherries, blueberries, raspberries, or blackberries

1/4 cup sugar

1/2 cup nonfat or light whipped topping (optional)

Nutritional Facts (Per Serving)

Calories: 114
Carbohydrates: 28 g
Fiber: 2 g
Fat: 0.1 g
Sat. Fat: 0 g
Cholesterol: 0 mg
Protein: 1.9 g
Sodium: 6 mg
Calcium: 17 mg
Potassium: 147 mg

Diabetic Exchanges

2 carbohydrate

For All Diets

Creamy Fruit Mousse

| YIELD: 4 servings |

1. Pour half of the juice into a blender and sprinkle the gelatin over the top. Allow to sit for 2 minutes to soften. Place the remaining juice in a small heatproof bowl and microwave for about 45 seconds, or until it comes to a boil. Pour the boiling juice into the blender, cover, and process for 30 seconds.

2. Add the undrained fruit and the sugar to the blender and purée until smooth. Pour the purée through a strainer into a medium-size bowl, discarding any seeds or other hard pieces that get caught in the sieve. Whisk the yogurt or sour cream into the strained fruit mixture.

3. Cover and chill for about $1\frac{1}{2}$ hours, or until firm to the touch. Whisk the gelatin mixture for about 30 seconds, or until it has a pudding-like consistency. Fold in the whipped topping.

4. Divide the mousse among four 8-ounce wine glasses or dessert dishes, and chill for several hours before serving.

$\frac{3}{4}$ cup pomegranate juice or cranberry juice cocktail, divided

1 envelope (0.25 ounce) unflavored gelatin

$1\frac{1}{2}$ cups frozen (thawed and undrained) fruit, such as strawberries, sweet pitted cherries, blueberries, raspberries, or blackberries

$\frac{1}{4}$–$\frac{1}{3}$ cup sugar

$\frac{1}{2}$ cup nonfat or low-fat Greek-style yogurt or sour cream

1 cup nonfat or light whipped topping

Dietary Variation

To reduce calories and carbohydrates:

Replace the sugar in the mousse with a sugar substitute and eliminate 48 calories, 12 grams carbohydrate, and 1 diabetic carbohydrate exchange. (See page 44 for details on using sugar substitutes.)

**Nutritional Facts
(Per $\frac{2}{3}$-Cup Serving)**

Calories: 155
Carbohydrates: 32 g
Fiber: 1.2 g
Fat: 0.1 g
Sat. Fat: 0 g
Cholesterol: 0 mg
Protein: 4 g
Sodium: 26 mg
Calcium: 32 mg
Potassium: 253 mg

Diabetic Exchanges

2 carbohydrate

For All Diets

Mocha Mousse

1. Place the tofu, brown sugar, cocoa powder, vanilla extract, and cinnamon in a food processor, and process until smooth. Set aside.

2. Place the milk and coffee granules in a microwave-safe bowl and stir to dissolve the coffee. Add the chocolate and microwave on high power for about 2 minutes, stirring after 1 minute, until melted and smooth. Add the chocolate mixture to the tofu mixture and process until smooth.

3. Transfer the tofu mixture to a covered container and chill for at least 2 hours. Fold in half of the whipped topping; then fold in the rest.

4. Divide the mousse among six 8-ounce wine glasses or dessert dishes, and chill for at least 1 hour before serving.

Dietary Variation

To reduce calories and carbohydrates:

Replace the brown sugar with sugar substitute and eliminate 35 calories, 9 grams carbohydrate, and $1/2$ diabetic carbohydrate exchange. (See page 44 for details on using sugar substitutes.)

---

* Sold in shelf-stable aseptic packages in most grocery stores, silken tofu has a softer, smoother texture than regular tofu and can be used in desserts, soups, sauces, and smoothies.

YIELD: 6 servings

12-ounce package silken firm tofu,* well drained and patted dry

1/4 cup brown sugar

2 tablespoons cocoa powder

1/2 teaspoon vanilla extract

1/4 teaspoon ground cinnamon

1 tablespoon nonfat or low-fat milk

3/4 teaspoon instant coffee granules

3/4 cup chopped dark chocolate or semisweet chocolate chips (5 ounces)

2 cups nonfat or light whipped topping

**Nutritional Facts
(Per 1/2-Cup Serving)**

Calories: 185
Carbohydrates: 28 g
Fiber: 2 g
Fat: 8 g
Sat. Fat: 4.4 g
Cholesterol: 0 mg
Protein: 5 g
Sodium: 62 mg
Calcium: 41 mg
Potassium: 185 mg

Diabetic Exchanges

2 carbohydrate
1/2 lean meat
1 fat

For All Diets

Rich Chocolate Mousse

1. Place ½ cup of the milk and all of the chocolate in a 2-quart microwave-safe bowl. Microwave on high power for 1½ minutes, or until the milk begins to boil.

2. Remove the bowl from the microwave and whisk until the chocolate is completely melted. Whisk in the remaining milk.

3. Add the pudding mix to the milk mixture, and blend with a wire whisk or electric mixer for 2 minutes. Place the pudding mixture in the refrigerator for about 45 minutes, or until well chilled.

4. Fold half of the whipped topping into the chilled pudding. Then fold in the rest of the topping. Spoon the mousse into six 6-ounce dessert dishes or wine glasses and chill for at least 2 hours. If desired, garnish with additional whipped topping and a sprinkling of ground chocolate just before serving.

Dietary Variation

To reduce calories and carbohydrates:

Replace the regular pudding with sugar-free pudding mix. This will eliminate 55 calories, 14 grams carbohydrate, and 1 diabetic carbohydrate exchange.

YIELD: 6 servings

12-ounce can evaporated nonfat or low-fat milk, divided

⅓ cup chopped dark chocolate (about 2 ounces)

1 package (4-serving size) instant chocolate pudding mix

2–3 cups nonfat or light whipped topping

**Nutritional Facts
(Per ½-Cup Serving)**

Calories: 188
Carbohydrates: 35 g
Fiber: 0.9 g
Fat: 3.3 g
Sat. Fat: 1.9 g
Cholesterol: 2 mg
Protein: 5.1 g
Sodium: 315 mg
Calcium: 170 mg
Potassium: 260 mg

Diabetic Exchanges

2 carbohydrate
½ fat

Raspberry Trifles

For Easy-to-Chew and Soft Diets

1. Place the pudding mix and milk in a small bowl and blend with an electric mixer or wire whisk for 2 minutes. Set aside.

2. Crumble three-fourths of a ladyfinger or half a piece of cake into each of four 8-ounce wine glasses. Top the cake with 1½ tablespoons of the Fresh Berry Purée and ¼ cup of the pudding. Repeat the ladyfinger, berry, and pudding layers.

3. To make the topping, place the whipped topping in a small bowl and fold in the yogurt. Crown each dessert with a fourth of the mixture. Cover and chill for several hours or overnight before serving.

For Smooth/Puréed Diets

Make sure that time is allowed for the cake to become thoroughly moistened before serving. You may need to dilute the Fresh Berry Purée with some juice so that there is sufficient liquid to soak the cake.

Dietary Variation

To reduce calories and carbohydrates:

Use sugar-free pudding mix to prepare the pudding, and make the Fresh Berry Purée with sugar substitute. This will eliminate 96 calories, 24 grams carbohydrate, and 1½ diabetic carbohydrate exchanges.

YIELD: 4 servings

1 package (4-serving size) instant vanilla, cheesecake, or lemon pudding mix

2 cups nonfat or low-fat milk

6 ladyfingers, or 4 slices low-fat pound cake (about ½ ounce each)

¾ cup Fresh Berry Purée (page 171) made with raspberries

TOPPING

¾ cup nonfat or light whipped topping

¼ cup light vanilla yogurt

Nutritional Facts (Per Serving)

Calories: 252
Carbohydrates: 55 g
Fiber: 1 g
Fat: 1.3 g
Sat. Fat: 0.3 g
Cholesterol: 22 mg
Protein: 6.2 g
Sodium: 493 mg
Calcium: 216 mg
Potassium: 316 mg

Diabetic Exchanges

3½ carbohydrate

For All Diets

White Chocolate-Strawberry Parfaits

For Easy-to-Chew and Soft Diets

1. Place the pudding mix and milk in a small bowl and blend with an electric mixer or wire whisk for 2 minutes. Set aside.

2. Crumble a half piece of cake into each of four 8-ounce wine glasses. Top the cake with 1½ tablespoons of the strawberry purée and ¼ cup of the pudding. Repeat the cake, berry, and pudding layers.

3. To make the topping, place the whipped topping in a small bowl and fold in the yogurt. Crown each dessert with a fourth of the mixture. Cover and chill for several hours or overnight before serving. Sprinkle ground chocolate over the top if desired.

For Smooth/Puréed Diets

Make sure that time is allowed for the cake to become thoroughly moistened before serving. You may need to dilute the Fresh Berry Purée with some juice so that there is sufficient liquid to soak the cake. If ground chocolate is not tolerated, top each parfait with chocolate syrup.

Dietary Variation

To reduce calories and carbohydrates:

Use sugar-free pudding mix to prepare the pudding, and make the Fresh Berry Purée with sugar substitute. This will eliminate 85 calories, 22 grams carbohydrate, and 1½ diabetic carbohydrate exchanges.

YIELD: 4 servings

1 package (4-serving size) instant white chocolate pudding mix

2 cups nonfat or low-fat milk

4 wedges (each ¾ inch thick) angel food cake (about ½ ounce each)

¾ cup Fresh Berry Purée (page 171) made with strawberries

TOPPING

¾ cup nonfat or light whipped topping

¼ cup light vanilla yogurt

1 tablespoon finely ground dark chocolate (optional)

Nutritional Facts (Per Serving)

Calories: 260
Carbohydrates: 55 g
Fiber: 1.5 g
Fat: 1.9 g
Sat. Fat: 0.7 g
Cholesterol: 3 mg
Protein: 6.2 g
Sodium: 515 mg
Calcium: 204 mg
Potassium: 320 mg

Diabetic Exchanges

3½ carbohydrate

Saucy Blackberry Crepes

1. To make the crepes, place all of the crepe ingredients in a blender and process until smooth. Set the batter aside for 10 minutes.

2. Coat an 8-inch nonstick skillet or crepe pan with cooking spray and place over medium heat until a drop of water sizzles when added to the pan. Pour a scant $\frac{1}{4}$ cup of batter into the pan. Quickly tilt the pan in all directions so that the batter covers the bottom of the pan with a thin film. Cook for about 1 minute, or until the underside is lightly browned and the top is set. Turn the crepe over and cook for 15 seconds. Repeat with the remaining batter to make 8 crepes. As the crepes are done, stack them on a plate separated by squares of wax paper. (To make the crepes in advance, place the stack in a plastic zip-type bag and refrigerate overnight. Alternatively, freeze the crepes for up to 1 month and thaw overnight in the refrigerator before using.)

3. To assemble the crepes, arrange the crepe pancakes on a flat surface. Spread $1\frac{1}{2}$ tablespoons of cream cheese along the lower end of each crepe. Spoon $\frac{1}{4}$ cup of the pie filling over the cream cheese, and roll the crepe up to enclose the filling.

4. Spoon 2 to 3 tablespoons of the warm syrup over each of 8 dessert plates. Top each plate with one filled crepe (seam side down), 1 tablespoon of syrup, and 2 tablespoons of whipped topping. If desired, add a sprinkling of walnuts. Serve immediately.

For a Change

■ Make the Warm Berry Syrup with raspberries instead of blackberries.

■ Make the crepe pancakes as directed, and fill each with $\frac{1}{4}$ cup sliced banana. To make the sauce, combine $1\frac{1}{2}$ tablespoons honey, $1\frac{1}{2}$ tablespoons orange juice, and 1 teaspoon butter. Heat and pour over the filled crepe.

YIELD: 8 servings

CREPES

$\frac{3}{4}$ cup nonfat or low-fat milk

$\frac{2}{3}$ cup whole wheat pastry flour or unbleached flour

$\frac{1}{4}$ cup fat-free egg substitute, or 1 large egg

1 tablespoon sugar

SAUCE

1 recipe Warm Berry Syrup (page 172) made with blackberries

FILLING

$\frac{3}{4}$ cup reduced-fat cream cheese, softened

2 cups canned apple pie filling, finely chopped

TOPPING

1 cup nonfat or light whipped topping

2 tablespoons finely ground walnuts (optional)

Nutritional Facts (Per Serving)

Calories: 254
Carbohydrates: 48 g
Fiber: 3 g
Fat: 5.2 g
Sat. Fat: 3 g
Cholesterol: 14 mg
Protein: 4.7 g
Sodium: 140 mg
Calcium: 61 mg
Potassium: 184 mg

Diabetic Exchanges

3 carbohydrate
1 fat

■ Make the crepe pancakes as directed, and fill each with $\frac{1}{3}$ cup light vanilla ice cream. Top with $\frac{1}{4}$ cup Mixed Berry Sauce (page 173) or Warm Berry Syrup (page 172).

■ Make the crepe pancakes as directed, and fill each with $\frac{1}{3}$ cup light vanilla ice cream. Top with 3 tablespoons sliced bananas and 2 tablespoons chocolate syrup.

Dietary Variation

To reduce calories and carbohydrates:

Use no-added-sugar pie filling and prepare the Warm Berry Syrup with sugar substitute instead of sugar. This will eliminate 75 calories, 19 grams carbohydrate, and 1 diabetic carbohydrate exchange.

Boosting Calories in Desserts

If you need to gain weight or prevent weight loss, dessert is a luxury you can well afford, so feel free to enjoy the dishes presented in this chapter as well as those available at your local stores. Keep in mind that treats like moist cakes, rich mousses, and premium ice cream will have a lot more calories than puréed fruits or gelatin desserts. But also realize that there are plenty of ways to sneak extra calories into your favorite dessert recipes.

One way to instantly boost the calories in a dessert is to top it with a rich sauce, such as Quick Caramel Sauce (page 180), Rich Chocolate Sauce (page 179), or your favorite smooth store-bought topping. Depending on the sauce and the amount used, this can add 100 calories or more to each serving. Another option is to use cream (45 to 50 calories per tablespoon), melted butter or margarine (about 100 calories per tablespoon), or walnut oil (120 calories per tablespoon) to moisten cakes and sweet breads that are too dry to be easily swallowed. Finally, when preparing your pudding, cake, or other dessert, substitute cream, half and half, or evaporated whole milk for the low-fat dairy products listed in the recipe.

Even if your aim is to put on weight, it's important to consider your overall health goals. If you are trying to reduce blood sugar and cholesterol, for instance, it's vital to emphasize healthful fats and to include only moderate amounts of sugar in your easy-to-swallow desserts.

Tiramisu

For Easy-to-Chew and Soft Diets

1. Place the milk, ricotta cheese, and pudding mix in a medium-size bowl, and blend with an electric mixer or wire whisk for 2 minutes. Set aside.

2. Line the bottom of an 8-by-8-inch dish with half of the ladyfingers, split side up. Combine the liqueur and orange juice in a small bowl. Drizzle half of the liqueur mixture over the ladyfingers, and spread with half of the pudding mixture. Repeat the ladyfinger, liqueur, and pudding layers.

3. Spread the whipped topping over the pudding and sift the cocoa powder over the top. Cover and chill for 8 hours or overnight before serving.

For Smooth/Puréed Diets

Make sure that the ladyfingers and cocoa powder are thoroughly moistened before eating. You may need to increase the amount of juice in the liqueur mixture so that there is sufficient liquid to soak the ladyfingers. Another option is to purée the entire dessert in a food processor.

For a Change

■ Drizzle some Fresh Berry Purée (page 171)—made with strawberries or raspberries—over the bottom of a serving plate before topping with a square of the Tiramisu.

Dietary Variation

To reduce calories and carbohydrates:

Use sugar-free pudding mix and eliminate 29 calories, 7 grams carbohydrates, and ½ diabetic carbohydrate exchange.

YIELD: 9 servings

1½ cups nonfat or low-fat milk

8 ounces part-skim ricotta cheese

1 package (4-serving size) instant cheesecake or vanilla pudding mix

18 ladyfingers (about 4½ ounces), split open

½ cup coffee liqueur

2 tablespoons orange juice

2 cups nonfat or light whipped topping

2 teaspoons Dutch process cocoa powder

Nutritional Facts (Per Serving)

Calories: 215
Carbohydrates: 35 g
Fiber: 0.3 g
Fat: 3.4 g
Sat. Fat: 1.6 g
Cholesterol: 34 mg
Protein: 5.6 g
Sodium: 309 mg
Calcium: 145 mg
Potassium: 117 mg

Diabetic Exchanges

2 carbohydrate
½ medium-fat meat

Cherry Cheesecake

For Easy-to-Chew and Soft Diets

1. Preheat the oven to 325°F.

2. Coat a 9-inch pie pan with nonstick cooking spray and sprinkle the graham cracker crumbs in the pan. Tilt the pan to coat the bottom and sides with the crumbs. Set aside.

3. Place the cream cheese in a medium-size bowl, and add the egg yolk (reserve the white), sugar, flour, lemon juice, and vanilla extract. Beat the mixture with an electric mixer until smooth. Add the evaporated milk several tablespoons at a time, beating well after each addition. Set aside.

4. Place the reserved egg white in a medium-size bowl. Using clean beaters, beat until soft peaks form when the beaters are raised. Fold the egg white into the cream cheese mixture and pour the batter into the pie pan.

5. Bake for about 25 minutes, or until the top is slightly puffed and firm to the touch. Transfer the pie to a wire rack and cool to room temperature. Spread the pie filling over the top, cover, and chill for several hours before serving.

For Smooth/Puréed Diets

Place the pie filling in a food processor and process until smooth before spreading it over the cake.

Dietary Variation

To reduce calories and carbohydrates:

Use no-added-sugar pie filling and eliminate 36 calories, 9 grams carbohydrate, and $1/2$ diabetic carbohydrate exchange.

YIELD: 8 servings

3 tablespoons graham cracker crumbs

8-ounce block reduced-fat cream cheese

1 egg, separated

$1/2$ cup sugar

2 tablespoons unbleached flour

$1^1/2$ teaspoons lemon juice

1 teaspoon vanilla extract

$2/3$ cup evaporated nonfat or low-fat milk

$1^1/2$ cups canned cherry or apple pie filling

Nutritional Facts (Per Serving)

Calories: 232
Carbohydrates: 33 g
Fiber: 0.4 g
Fat: 7.6 g
Sat. Fat: 4.5 g
Cholesterol: 49 mg
Protein: 6 g
Sodium: 171 mg
Calcium: 92 mg
Potassium: 167 mg

Diabetic Exchanges

2 carbohydrate
$1^1/2$ fat

Lemon Custard Cakes

For Easy-to-Chew and Soft Diets

1. Preheat the oven to 350°F. Coat eight 6-ounce custard cups with nonstick cooking spray, and set aside.

2. Place ½ cup plus 2 tablespoons of the sugar and all of the flour and salt in a medium-size bowl and whisk to mix. Set aside.

3. Combine the milk, egg yolks (reserve the whites), and lemon juice in a large bowl and whisk until blended. Add the flour mixture to the milk mixture and whisk until blended. Set aside.

4. Place the reserved egg whites in a large bowl. Using clean beaters, beat until soft peaks form when the beaters are raised. Gradually beat in the remaining ¼ cup sugar and continue beating until stiff peaks form.

5. Gently whisk a third of the egg whites into the batter. Whisk in half of the remaining whites; then whisk in the rest.

6. Divide the custard among the prepared cups and arrange them in a large roasting pan. Fill the pan with enough hot water to come halfway up the sides of the cups. Bake uncovered for 25 to 30 minutes, or until the custards are slightly puffed and browned on top. The tops should not be sticky when lightly touched.

7. Transfer the custard cups to wire racks and allow to cool for 1 hour. Chill uncovered for at least 3 hours or until firm. Then cover and keep chilled until ready to serve. To serve, run a small sharp knife around each custard and invert it onto a serving plate.

For Smooth/Puréed Diets

Remove the browned top layer from the custard before inverting it onto a plate.

For a Change

■ Drizzle a tablespoon or two of Fresh Berry Purée (page 171) over the dessert plate before inverting the custard onto the plate.

YIELD: 8 servings

¾ cup plus 2 tablespoons sugar, divided
¼ cup unbleached flour
Pinch salt
1⅓ cups evaporated nonfat or low-fat milk
2 large eggs, separated
⅓ cup lemon juice

Nutritional Facts (Per Serving)

Calories: 153
Carbohydrates: 30 g
Fiber: 0.1 g
Fat: 1.4 g
Sat. Fat: 0.4 g
Cholesterol: 55 mg
Protein: 5 g
Sodium: 82 mg
Calcium: 131 mg
Potassium: 173 mg

Diabetic Exchanges

2 carbohydrate

Quick Cheesecake Parfaits

For Easy-to-Chew and Soft Diets

1. Place the ricotta cheese, milk, cream cheese, and pudding mix in a food processor and blend for 1 minute, or until smooth.

2. Place a scant ¼ cup of the cheese mixture in each of five 8-ounce wine glasses. Top the cheese mixture with 2½ tablespoons of the pie filling and 1½ teaspoons of the crumbs. Repeat the layers.

3. Serve immediately, or cover and chill until ready to serve.

For Smooth/Puréed Diets

Place the pie filling in a food processor and process until smooth before spreading it over the cheese mixture. Either allow the parfaits to chill for several hours until the graham cracker crumbs are thoroughly moistened, or omit the crumbs entirely.

Dietary Variation

To reduce calories and carbohydrates:

Use sugar-free pudding mix and no-added-sugar pie filling. This will eliminate 114 calories, 29 grams carbohydrate, and 2 diabetic carbohydrate exchanges.

YIELD: 5 servings

1 cup nonfat or part-skim ricotta cheese

1 cup nonfat or low-fat milk

4 ounces nonfat or light cream cheese

1 package (4-serving size) instant vanilla pudding mix

1½ cups canned cherry, blueberry, or apple pie filling, chilled*

¼ cup plus 1 tablespoon graham cracker crumbs

* If using apple pie filling, finely chop the fruit before making the parfaits.

Nutritional Facts (Per Serving)

Calories: 269
Carbohydrates: 53 g
Fiber: 0.7 g
Fat: 1 g
Sat. Fat: 0.2 g
Cholesterol: 7 mg
Protein: 12 g
Sodium: 543 mg
Calcium: 298 mg
Potassium: 279 mg

Diabetic Exchanges

3½ carbohydrate
1 lean meat

Baked Pumpkin Custard

For Easy-to-Chew and Soft Diets

1. Preheat the oven to 350°F. Coat six 6-ounce custard cups with nonstick cooking spray, and set aside.

2. Place all of the ingredients except for the whipped topping in a blender and process for about 30 seconds, or until smooth.

3. Divide the pumpkin mixture among the prepared cups. Arrange the cups in a 9-x-13-inch pan, and add hot tap water until it reaches halfway up the sides of the dishes. Bake for about 45 minutes, or until a sharp knife inserted midway between the center of the custard and the rim of the cup comes out clean.

4. Remove the custards from the pan and set on wire racks to cool. Cover and refrigerate for several hours before serving. If desired, top each serving with some of the whipped topping.

For Smooth/Puréed Diets

If the top of the custard is too hard, remove it before adding the whipped topping.

For a Change

■ Drizzle the chilled custard with honey or maple syrup.

Dietary Variation

To reduce calories and carbohydrates:

Replace half of the brown sugar with sugar substitute and eliminate 31 calories, 8 grams carbohydrate, and $\frac{1}{2}$ diabetic carbohydrate exchange per serving. (See page 44 for details on using sugar substitutes.)

YIELD: 6 servings

1 cup canned or cooked mashed pumpkin

$\frac{3}{4}$ cup fat-free egg substitute, or 3 large eggs, beaten

12-ounce can evaporated nonfat or low-fat milk

$\frac{1}{2}$ cup light brown sugar

$\frac{1}{2}$ cup nonfat or low-fat milk

2 tablespoons maple syrup or honey

2 teaspoons pumpkin pie spice

$1\frac{1}{2}$ teaspoons vanilla extract

$\frac{3}{4}$ cup nonfat or light whipped topping (optional)

Nutritional Facts (Per Serving)

Calories: 169
Carbohydrates: 34 g
Fiber: 1.2 g
Fat: 0.4
Sat. Fat: 0.2 g
Cholesterol: 2 mg
Protein: 8.5 g
Sodium: 148 mg
Calcium: 234 mg
Potassium: 430 mg

Diabetic Exchanges

2 carbohydrate
$\frac{1}{2}$ lean meat

For All Diets

Fabulous Flan

YIELD: 6 servings

1 cup sugar, divided

12-ounce can evaporated nonfat or low-fat milk

3/4 cup nonfat or low-fat milk

3 eggs, beaten, or 3/4 cup egg substitute

2 1/2 teaspoons vanilla extract

1. Place 1/2 cup of the sugar in a 1-quart pot and set over medium-high heat. Cook without stirring for 2 minutes, shaking the pan occasionally, until the sugar begins to liquefy around the edges. Reduce the heat to medium and cook, stirring occasionally, for another couple of minutes, or just until the sugar completely liquefies and turns a golden caramel color.

2. Immediately pour about 1 tablespoon of the caramelized sugar into the bottom of each of six 6-ounce custard cups. (Caution: The liquefied sugar will be very hot.) Swirl to coat the bottom and 1/2 inch up the sides of the cups. Set aside for 10 minutes to allow the sugar to harden.

3. Preheat the oven to 325°F. Place the remaining 1/2 cup of sugar and all of the evaporated milk, milk, eggs or egg substitute, and vanilla extract in a blender and process for about 30 seconds, or until the sugar is dissolved.

4. Divide the milk mixture among the prepared custard cups. Arrange the cups in a 9-x-13-inch pan, and add hot tap water until it reaches halfway up the sides of the dishes. Bake for about 40 minutes, or until a sharp knife inserted near the center of the custard comes out clean.

5. Remove the custard cups from the pan, set on wire racks, and allow to cool to room temperature. Cover and refrigerate for at least 24 hours to allow the hardened caramel sauce to liquefy. To serve, run a sharp knife around the edge of the custards and invert onto individual serving plates, allowing the sauce to flow over and around the custards. Serve immediately.

Dietary Variation

To reduce calories and carbohydrates:

Replace half of the sugar in the custard mixture with sugar substitute, and eliminate 32 calories, 8 grams carbohydrate, and 1/2 diabetic carbohydrate exchange. (See page 44 for details on using sugar substitutes.)

Nutritional Facts (Per Serving)

Calories: 226

Carbohydrates: 42 g

Fiber: 0 g

Fat: 2.7

Sat. Fat: 0.9 g

Cholesterol: 109 mg

Protein: 8.5 g

Sodium: 113 mg

Calcium: 215 mg

Potassium: 277 mg

Diabetic Exchanges

3 carbohydrate

1/2 medium-fat meat

Creamy Bread Pudding

For Easy-to-Chew and Soft Diets

1. Preheat the oven to 350°F. Coat six 8-ounce ramekins with non-stick cooking spray, and set aside.

2. Place the bread cubes in a food processor and process into coarse crumbs. Set aside.

3. Place the egg substitute or eggs, sugar, and vanilla extract in a large bowl and whisk to mix well. Whisk in the milks. Add the processed bread to the milk mixture and stir to mix. Set aside for 15 minutes.

4. Divide the bread mixture among the prepared ramekins. To make the topping, mix the sugar with the cinnamon and sprinkle over the top of the pudding.

5. Arrange the ramekins in a large roasting pan filled with one inch of hot water. Bake uncovered for about 35 minutes, or until a sharp knife inserted in the center of the puddings comes out clean.

6. Remove the puddings from the oven and allow to sit for 30 minutes before serving. Serve warm or chilled.

For Smooth/Puréed Diets

Remove the crust from the top of the puddings. If more moisture is desired, top each serving with Simple Brandy Sauce (page 175), Cinnamon-Apple Syrup (see page 174), Honey-Date Purée (page 180), or Quick Caramel Sauce (page 180). Another option is to place the pudding, including the top crust, in a food processor and purée until smooth, adding sauce or additional milk as needed.

Dietary Variation

To reduce calories and carbohydrates:

Replace half the sugar in the custard mixture with a sugar substitute, and eliminate 32 calories, 8 grams carbohydrate, and $\frac{1}{2}$ diabetic carbohydrate exchange. (See page 44 for details on using sugar substitutes.)

YIELD: 6 servings

6 cups $\frac{1}{2}$-inch cubes day-old oatmeal, oat bran, or French bread, trimmed of crusts (choose a smooth-textured bread without nuts or other hard pieces)

$\frac{3}{4}$ cup fat-free egg substitute, or 3 large eggs, beaten

$\frac{1}{2}$ cup sugar

$1\frac{1}{2}$ teaspoons vanilla extract

12-ounce can evaporated nonfat or low-fat milk

1 cup nonfat or low-fat milk

TOPPING

$1\frac{1}{2}$–2 tablespoons sugar

$\frac{1}{2}$ teaspoon ground cinnamon

Nutritional Facts (Per Serving)

Calories: 221
Carbohydrates: 41 g
Fiber: 1.8 g
Fat: 1.3 g
Sat. Fat: 0.3 g
Cholesterol: 3 mg
Protein: 11 g
Sodium: 287 mg
Calcium: 250 mg
Potassium: 246 mg

Diabetic Exchanges

$2\frac{1}{2}$ carbohydrate
$\frac{1}{2}$ lean meat

For All Diets

Moist Apple Cake

For Easy-to-Chew and Soft Diets

1. Preheat the oven to 350°F. Coat a round 9-inch cake pan with nonstick cooking spray, and set aside.

2. Place the walnuts or pecans in a food processor, and process until finely ground.

3. Place the ground nuts, sugar, flours, cinnamon, baking soda, and salt in a large bowl and stir to mix well. Set aside. Place the oil, egg or egg substitute, apple juice, and vanilla extract in a medium-size bowl and stir to mix. Set aside.

4. Place the apples in the food processor and process until finely chopped. Add the apples and the oil mixture to the flour mixture and stir to mix. Set the batter aside for 10 minutes.

5. Stir the batter for 10 seconds. Then spread evenly in the prepared pan. Bake for about 25 minutes, or just until a wooden toothpick inserted in the center of the cake comes out clean.

6. Allow the cake to cool to room temperature. To serve, top each wedge of cake with 2 to 3 tablespoons of the desired sauce.

For Smooth/Puréed Diets

Place a serving of cake in a bowl and poke holes in it with a fork. Slightly thin several tablespoons of sauce with milk, and pour the mixture over the cake to saturate it. When the cake has softened, eat it with a spoon. Alternatively, purée the cake and sauce in a food processor.

YIELD: 10 servings

¼ cup plus 2 tablespoons walnuts or pecans

¾ cup sugar

½ cup unbleached flour

½ cup whole wheat pastry flour

¾ teaspoon ground cinnamon

½ teaspoon baking soda

¼ teaspoon salt

¼ cup plus 1 tablespoon canola oil

1 egg, beaten, or ¼ cup fat-free egg substitute

¼ cup apple juice

1 teaspoon vanilla extract

2 cups chopped peeled apples (about 2 medium-large apples)

Simple Brandy Sauce (page 175), Honey-Date Purée (page 180), Quick Caramel Sauce (page 180), or Cinnamon-Apple Syrup (page 174)

Nutritional Facts (Per Serving, with 2 Tablespoons Simple Brandy Sauce)

Calories: 299
Carbohydrates: 41 g
Fiber: 1.6 g
Fat: 12.3 g
Sat. Fat: 2.1 g
Cholesterol: 29 mg
Protein: 5.2 g
Sodium: 158 mg
Calcium: 74 mg
Potassium: 178 mg

Diabetic Exchanges

2¹/₂ carbohydrate
2¹/₂ fat

For All Diets

Kahlua Chocolate Cake

For Easy-to-Chew and Soft Diets

1. Preheat the oven to 350°F. Coat a 9-x-13-inch pan with nonstick cooking spray, and set aside.

2. Place the cake mix and cinnamon in a large bowl. Add the water, oil, and eggs or egg substitute, and beat with an electric mixer for 1 minute.

3. Spread the batter evenly in the prepared pan. Bake for about 25 minutes, or until a wooden toothpick inserted in the center of the cake comes out clean.

4. Allow the cake to cool in the pan to room temperature. Using a fork, poke holes in the cake at 1-inch intervals.

5. To make the syrup, combine the sweetened condensed milk and the liqueur in a bowl, and stir to mix well. Slowly spoon the syrup over the top and around the sides of the cake, using the back of the spoon to spread the syrup over the cake so that it can be absorbed. Set aside for 30 minutes.

6. To make the frosting, place the whipped topping in a medium-size bowl and fold in the yogurt. Spread the frosting over the cake. Cover the cake and refrigerate for several hours or overnight before serving. If desired, sprinkle each portion with grated chocolate.

For Smooth/Puréed Diets

Pour several tablespoons of half and half into the bottom of a dessert dish. (Use a fat-free version if you need to cut calories or cholesterol.) Top with a piece of cake and allow it to sit for a minute or 2 to soak up the liquid. Eat with a spoon.

YIELD: 20 servings

1 box (1 pound, 2.25 ounces) chocolate fudge cake mix

3/4 teaspoon ground cinnamon

1 1/4 cups water

1/2 cup canola oil

2 large eggs, or 1/2 cup fat-free egg substitute

SYRUP

14-ounce can sweetened condensed milk

1/2 cup coffee liqueur

FROSTING

3 cups nonfat or light whipped topping

3/4 cup vanilla yogurt

1/4 cup grated dark chocolate (optional)

Nutritional Facts (Per Serving)

Calories: 252
Carbohydrates: 37 g
Fiber: 0.6 g
Fat: 9.1g
Sat. Fat: 2 g
Cholesterol: 26 mg
Protein: 3.4 g
Sodium: 241 mg
Calcium: 82 mg
Potassium: 129 mg

Diabetic Exchanges

2 1/2 carbohydrate
2 fat

Walnut Refrigerator Fudge

For Easy-to-Chew and Soft Diets

1. Place ¼ cup plus 2 tablespoons of the walnuts in a food processor and process until finely ground. Transfer to a shallow dish and set aside.

2. Place the remaining walnuts in the food processor and process until finely ground. Add the powdered sugar and process for 15 additional seconds, or until well mixed and powdery throughout.

3. Place the walnut-sugar mixture in a medium-size bowl. Add the cream cheese and mix well with a wooden spoon. The mixture will be thick.

4. Cover the bowl and place it in the freezer for about 20 minutes, or until the cheese mixture is firm enough to shape into balls. Shape scant tablespoons into 1-inch balls, and roll each ball in the reserved ground walnuts to coat all sides. Alternatively, omit the walnut coating and press the mixture into the bottom of a square 8-x-8-inch nonstick pan.

5. Arrange the fudge balls in a single layer in a shallow container, cover, and chill for several hours or overnight before serving.

For Smooth/Puréed Diets

Omit the walnut coating, and allow the balls to soften at room temperature before eating.

**YIELD: 12 servings
(2 fudge balls each)**

³⁄₄ cup plus 2 tablespoons
  walnuts, divided

1 cup powdered sugar

2 ounces block-style reduced-
  fat cream cheese, softened
  to room temperature

**Nutritional Facts
(Per 2-Ball Serving)**

Calories: 99
Carbohydrates: 11 g
Fiber: 0.4 g
Fat: 5.5g
Sat. Fat: 1 g
Cholesterol: 4 mg
Protein: 2.4 g
Sodium: 19 mg
Calcium: 8 mg
Potassium: 46 mg

Diabetic Exchanges

1 carbohydrate
1 fat

METRIC CONVERSION TABLES

COMMON LIQUID CONVERSIONS

Measurement	=	Milliliters
1/4 teaspoon	=	1.25 milliliters
1/2 teaspoon	=	2.50 milliliters
3/4 teaspoon	=	3.75 milliliters
1 teaspoon	=	5.00 milliliters
1 1/4 teaspoons	=	6.25 milliliters
1 1/2 teaspoons	=	7.50 milliliters
1 3/4 teaspoons	=	8.75 milliliters
2 teaspoons	=	10.0 milliliters
1 tablespoon	=	15.0 milliliters
2 tablespoons	=	30.0 milliliters

Measurement	=	Liters
1/4 cup	=	0.06 liters
1/2 cup	=	0.12 liters
3/4 cup	=	0.18 liters
1 cup	=	0.24 liters
1 1/4 cups	=	0.30 liters
1 1/2 cups	=	0.36 liters
2 cups	=	0.48 liters
2 1/2 cups	=	0.60 liters
3 cups	=	0.72 liters
3 1/2 cups	=	0.84 liters
4 cups	=	0.96 liters
4 1/2 cups	=	1.08 liters
5 cups	=	1.20 liters
5 1/2 cups	=	1.32 liters

CONVERTING FAHRENHEIT TO CELSIUS

Fahrenheit	=	Celsius
200–205	=	95
220–225	=	105
245–250	=	120
275	=	135
300–305	=	150
325–330	=	165
345–350	=	175
370–375	=	190
400–405	=	205
425–430	=	220
445–450	=	230
470–475	=	245
500	=	260

CONVERSION FORMULAS

LIQUID

When You Know	Multiply By	To Determine
teaspoons	5.0	milliliters
tablespoons	15.0	milliliters
fluid ounces	30.0	milliliters
cups	0.24	liters
pints	0.47	liters
quarts	0.95	liters

WEIGHT

When You Know	Multiply By	To Determine
ounces	28.0	grams
pounds	0.45	kilograms

PRODUCTS, MANUFACTURERS, AND DISTRIBUTORS

It can be challenging to meet your nutritional needs when following an easy-to-chew, soft, or smooth/puréed diet. Fortunately, a number of excellent products have been designed to make this task easier.

The Products tables that begin on page 284 list a number of items that can help you follow mechanically altered and thickened liquids diets. The tables include feeding aids such as spill-proof mugs, nutrient-enhanced beverages and foods, liquid and powder vitamin and mineral supplements, ready-made puréed foods, commercial thickeners and pre-thickened foods, and tube feeding formulas. Some of these products have been referred to within this book, while others may be recommended by your health care provider. Once you find a product in which you're interested, check the right-hand column of the table to learn the manufacturer or distributor that offers the item. Then turn to the Manufacturers and Distributors listing, which begins on page 288, to find complete contact information for the company, as well as a description of the firm's other products.

Keep in mind that products are often reformulated or renamed over time, and that companies may merge, change names, or sell their product lines to other firms. If you are unable to find the product you want on the listed website, we urge you to perform a computer search for the item or to ask your health care professional for help. Keep in mind, too, that these are not exhaustive lists and that there may be other suppliers who carry useful items for a soft foods diet. In addition, you may find products in your local pharmacy or medical supply store.

Finally, be aware that some of these products, such as tube feeding formulas, may be covered by your health insurance. Be sure to discuss this with your insurance provider.

PRODUCTS

FEEDING AIDS

If you have a health condition that makes swallowing difficult or that otherwise affects your ability to feed yourself, you may benefit from one of the many products designed to make mealtimes safer and easier. Speak to an occupational therapist or speech therapist to learn which of the following items would be most useful to you.

Feeding Aid Category	Product	Manufacturer or Distributor
Cups and Glasses	Lil' Sip Mug (dispenses a teaspoonful at a time).	Med-Diet Laboratories.
	Nosey cups, spill-proof mugs, two-handled mugs, and weighted cups.	Bruce Medical Supply, CWI Medical, and The Wright Stuff.
Utensils	Curved utensils, easy-grip utensils, flexible utensils, and weighted utensils.	Bruce Medical Supply, CWI Medical, and The Wright Stuff.
Plates and Bowls	Divided dishes, high-sided dishes, plate guards, suction plates, scoop dishes, and weighted bowls.	Bruce Medical Supply, CWI Medical, and The Wright Stuff.

NUTRIENT-ENHANCED BEVERAGES AND FOODS

People who follow easy-to-chew, soft, smooth/puréed, or liquid diets often have difficulty including adequate calories and protein in their meals. If this is true of you, you may benefit from one of the beverages, puddings, or ice creams listed in the table below. Fortified with protein, calories, and/or other nutrients, these products can be consumed either with or between meals to enhance your daily diet. Some of these items also come in modified versions specifically created for people with diabetes, renal disease, or other conditions. Speak to your health care provider and check the information on the company websites to determine which nutrient-enhanced foods will help you meet your dietary needs.

Food/Beverage Category	Product	Manufacturer or Distributor
Fortified Beverages (Clear Liquids)	Resource Breeze fruit-flavored beverage.	Nestlé Nutrition.
	Resource Broth Plus.	
	Enlive fruit-flavored drinks.	Abbott Nutrition.
	Herb Ox High-Protein Broths.	Hormel Health Labs and 4WebMed.
	LiquaCel Liquid Protein.	Global Health Products.
Fortified Beverages (Milk Shake-Type Beverages)	Boost.*	Nestlé Nutrition.
	Carnation Instant Breakfast.*	

	Ensure.*	Abbott Nutrition.
	Mighty Shakes.	Hormel Health Labs and 4WebMed.
	Nutra/Shake.	Nutra/Balance Products and 4WebMed.
Fortified Beverages (Whole Food Beverages)	Resurgex, Resurgex Select, and Resurgex Plus.	Resurgex/Millennium Biotechnologies.
Fortified Puddings	Ensure Pudding.*	Abbott Nutrition.
	Nutra/Balance Pudding.	Nutra/Balance Products and 4WebMed.
	Boost Pudding.*	Nestlé Nutrition.
Fortified, Thickened Ice Cream	Magic Cup Ice Cream.	Hormel Health Labs and 4WebMed.
	Nutra/Balance Ice Cream.	Nutra/Balance Products.
	Resource Ice Cream Plus.	Nestlé Nutrition.

* This product is available in many drugstores and supermarkets.

LIQUID AND POWDER NUTRIENT SUPPLEMENTS

If your diet is lacking in essential nutrients such as vitamins, minerals, or protein, or if you are not getting enough fiber, you may benefit from a liquid or powdered nutritional supplement that can be mixed into beverages or foods. If you need thickened liquids, remember not to take liquid supplements without first mixing them with an appropriately thick pudding, smoothie, or other food. Some supplements can even be added to tube feedings.

Many pharmacies carry at least one liquid vitamin formula, as well as a variety of other nutrient-specific supplements, and may be willing to special order other products for you. You may also be able to find liquid supplements at your local health food store. And, of course, many products of this type can be found online. The following table includes some commonly available brands. Speak to your health care provider about the products that would best meet your nutritional needs.

Supplement Category	Product	Manufacturer or Distributor
Liquid Multivitamin and Mineral Supplements	Centrum Liquid Multivitamin/ Multimineral Supplement.*	Wyeth.†
	Eldertonic Liquid Multivitamin Mineral Supplement.*	Merz Pharmaceuticals.
	Geritol Tonic.*	GlaxoSmithKline.†
Powdered Fiber Supplements	Benefiber.*	Nestlé Nutrition.
	Citrucel.*	GlaxoSmithKline.†

	Fiber Basics.	Hormel Health Labs.
	Metamucil.*	Proctor and Gamble Pharmaceuticals.†
Protein Supplements	ProCel powder.	Global Health Products.
	LiquaCel liquid.	Abbott Nutrition.
	Promod liquid.	
	Propass powder.	Hormel Health Labs.
	Resource Beneprotein powder.	Nestlé Nutrition.

* This product is available in many drugstores or can be ordered by your pharmacist.
† This manufacturer/distributor does not sell its products directly to consumers. If you cannot find the desired item in your local pharmacy, ask your pharmacist to order it for you, or perform an Internet search to locate an online pharmacy or other retailer who offers the item.

PUREED FOODS

This book provides a wealth of recipes for puréed dishes, as well as simple guidelines for puréeing both family favorites and ready-made foods from supermarkets and delis. (See Chapter 5 for step-by-step puréeing instructions.) At times, though, you may appreciate the convenience of ready-to-eat puréed foods and puréed-food mixes. The products in the following table can be big time savers, especially when you need only one serving. Visit the manufacturers' websites to find the items that will best meet your needs.

Pureed Food Category	Product	Manufacturer and/or Distributor
Puréed Ready-to-Heat or Thaw-and-Heat Foods	Canned puréed entrees, vegetables, and fruits.	Thick-It.
	Campbell's TrePuree puréed full-course meals.	Hormel Health Labs and 4WebMed.
	Cliffdale Farms single-serving puréed foods.	
	Thick & Easy puréed shaped fruits, vegetables, and side dishes (in reusable molds).	
	Puréed breakfasts, entrées, and side dishes.	4WebMed.
	Puréed meats and vegetables.	Travis Meats.
Puréed Food Mixes	Resource Purée Solutions Egg & Toast Mix, Bread Mix, and Cereal Plus.	Nestlé Nutrition.
	Thick & Easy Instantized Pasta, Instantized Rice, and Puréed Bread Mixes.	Hormel Health Labs.
Concentrated Fruit Purées	All natural, no-added-sugar fruit purées.	The Perfect Purée of Napa Valley.

THICKENERS AND THICKENED LIQUIDS AND FOODS

The first few sections of the following table list products that will enable you to quickly and easily thicken beverages, soups, and other foods—usually, with little or no effect on taste. The table also lists fortified thickeners and special thickeners that can help you turn puréed foods into attractively shaped dishes. Finally, you will find convenient pre-thickened drinks and ice creams. Be aware that some products are available in two or more levels of thickness. Speak to your health care provider and check the information on the company websites to find the items that are appropriate for your diet. (For information on thickening liquids, see Chapter 6.)

Thickener or Thickened Food Category	Product	Manufacturer or Distributor
Starch-Based Thickeners	Nutra/Balance Regular Instant Thickener.	Nutra/Balance Products.
	Thicken-Up.	Nestle Nutrition.
	Thick & Easy Instant Food Thickener.	Hormel Health Labs.
	Thick-It and Thick-It 2 Instant Food Thickeners.	Thick-It.
Gel-Based Thickeners	Hydra-Aid Liquid Food Thickener.	Med-Diet Laboratories.
	SimplyThick.	SimplyThick.
	Thik & Clear.	Nutra/Balance Products.
Fortified Thickeners	NutraBalance Fortified Instant Thickener (with calcium and vitamin C).	Nutra/Balance Products.
	NutraThik Fortified Instant Food Thickener (with vitamins and minerals).	Hormel Health Labs.
Thickeners for Shaping Puréed Foods	Resource Purée Appeal Puréed Food Enhancer.	Nestlé Nutrition.
	Thick & Easy Shape & Serve Thickener.	Hormel Health Labs.
Thickened Beverages	AquaCareH20 thickened water, coffee, and fruit juices.	AquaCareH20.
	Nutra/Balance thickened shakes, juices, coffee, tea, and water.	Nutra/Balance Products and 4WebMed.
	Resource Dairy Thick, and thickened water, shakes, juices, and decaf coffee.	Nestle Nutrition.
	Thick & Easy fruit juices, iced teas, and coffee.	Hormel Health Labs.
Fortified, Thickened Ice Cream	Magic Cup Ice Cream.	Hormel Health Labs.
	Nutra/Balance Ice Cream.	Nutra/Balance Products.
	Resource Ice Cream Plus.	Nestlé Nutrition.

TUBE FEEDING FORMULAS

If your doctor has put you on tube feedings to supplement or temporarily replace oral foods, a specific product will probably be prescribed for you. Manufacturers create formulas for a wide range of health conditions, including diabetes, renal failure, COPD, wound healing, cancer, HIV/AIDS, and many more, and also gear products for different age groups—infants, children, and adults. Because the array of formulas is so great, the following table offers only a sampling of the most commonly used products from each manufacturer. We recommend that you peruse manufacturer websites, evaluate ingredient lists, and choose products that include whole foods whenever possible. Most important, always secure the approval of your health care provider before using a new formula.

Tube Feeding Formula Category	Product	Manufacturer or Distributor
Standard (Semi-Synthetic) Formulas	Jevity, Glucerna, and other formulas designed for specific conditions.	Abbott Nutrition.
	Isosource, Fibersource, and other formulas designed for specific conditions.	Nestlé Nutrition.
Whole Foods Formulas	Compleat.	Nestlé Nutrition.
	Resurgex Select.	Resurgex/Millennium Biotechnologies.

MANUFACTURERS AND DISTRIBUTORS

Abbott Nutrition (formerly Ross Products)
625 Cleveland Avenue
Columbus, OH 43215-1724
Phone: 800-227-5767
Website: www.abbottnutrition.com
To Order: www.abbottstore.com

Abbott Nutrition produces fortified shakes and puddings, tube feeding formulas, protein and fiber supplements, and other products for a variety of health conditions, including diabetes, HIV/AIDS, renal disease, and more.

AquaCareH2O
6120 Tower Avenue
Superior, WI 54880
Phone: 877-407-2518
Fax: 715-392-9931
Website: http://www.aquacareh2o.com

AquacareH2O offers a variety of xanthan gum-thickened beverages, including water, coffee, and fruit juices. The website features recipes for puréed and thickened liquid diets.

Bruce Medical Supply

411 Waverley Oaks Road, #154

Waltham, MA 02452

Phone: 800-225-8446 or 781-894-6262

Fax: 781-894-9519

Website: www.brucemedical.com

This health and medical supplier offers a wide range of products, including adaptive dinnerware and utensils, food and beverage thickeners, pre-thickened beverages, and puréed foods.

CWI Medical

200 Allen Boulevard

Farmingdale, NY 11735

Phone: 877-929-4633

Fax: 866-588-3337

Website: www.cwimedical.com/nutrition

CWI Medical offers a selection of medical and health care products, including adaptive dining aids, puréed food and beverage thickeners, pre-thickened beverages and foods, protein supplements, and more.

4WebMed

2805 North Commerce Parkway

Miramar, FL 33025

Phone: 877-493-2633

Fax: 954-441-9577

Website: www.4webmed.com

This online store offers a variety of specialized nutritional products made by different manufacturers. Included are thickeners, fortified ice cream, shakes and beverages, and ready-made puréed foods and mixes. In many cases, you will find products that you may not be able to purchase directly from the manufacturer, and you will have the option of purchasing smaller quantities (instead of a whole case), mixing flavors, and combining products from different companies.

Global Health Products, Inc.

1099 Jay Street, Suite 100E

Rochester, NY 14611

Phone: 800-638-2870

Fax: 585-235-8918

Website: www.globalhp.com

Global Health provides a variety of nutritional supplements, including powdered and liquid protein and fiber products, and protein-fortified coffee and broth.

Hormel Health Labs

3000 Tremont Road

Savannah, GA 31405

Phone: 800-617-3482

Website: www.hormelhealthlabs.com

To Order: www.homecarenutrition.com

Hormel Health Labs offers a wide selection of thickeners for foods and beverages, pre-thickened beverages and shakes, fortified ice cream and puddings, instant fiber products and fiber-fortified juices, high-protein broths, instantized rice and pasta, puréed bread mix, and other items for people who need soft and smooth diets. The divisions within Hormel that cater specifically to people on puréed meals include Campbell's TrePuree, Cliffdale Farms, and Thick & Easy Puréed. Hormel products can also be ordered at 4WebMed (see at left).

Med-Diet Laboratories, Inc.

3600 Holly Lane North, Suite 80

Plymouth, MN 55447

Phone: 800-633-3438

Fax: 763-550-2022

Website: www.med-diet.com

Med-Diet Laboratories distributes a variety of products for people with special dietary needs, including dysphagia. The site offers the Lil' Sip Mug as well as food and beverage thickeners, thickened beverages, protein supplements, and more.

Merz Pharmaceuticals

Phone: 888-925-8989

Website: wwwmerzusa.com

To Order: www.merzdirect.com

This company develops pharmaceutical and nutraceutical products, including Eldertonic liquid high-potency vitamin and mineral supplement.

Nestlé Nutrition

13700 Oakland Avenue

Highland Park, MI 48203

Phone: 888-240-2713

Website: www.nestlenutritionstore.com

Nestlé Nutrition offers a variety of items for dysphagia diets, including thickeners for beverages and puréed foods, pre-made thickened beverages, thickened beverage mixes, thickened ice cream, fortified shakes, puréed bread and breakfast mixes, and protein supplements.

Nutra/Balance Products

7155 Wadsworth Way

Indianapolis, IN 46219

Phone: 800-654-3691 or 317-356-5478

Website: www.nutra-balance-products.com

Nutra/Balance produces instant thickeners for hot and cold liquids as well as a range of pre-thickened beverages and foods, including water, coffee and tea, juices, shakes, puddings, and ice cream. Most are available in nectar-like, honey-like, and spoon-thick consistencies. Visit the Nutra/Balance website to find a distributor, or order the products through 4WebMed (page 289).

The Perfect Purée of Napa Valley

2700 Napa Valley Corporate Drive, Suite L

Napa, CA 94558

Phone: 866-787-5233 or 707-261-5100

Fax: 707-261-5111

Website: www.perfectpuree.com

Perfect Purée offers a line of frozen fruit purées and concentrates both to the food industry and consumers. These convenient products can be used to make flavorful sauces, smoothies, and other easy-to-swallow foods.

Resurgex/Millennium Biotechnologies, Inc.

665 Martinsville Road, Suite 219

Basking Ridge, NJ 07920

Phone: 877-737-8749

Fax: 908-604-2545

Website: http://www.resurgex.com

Resurgex produces three nutritional formulas that contain whole foods, including fruits and vegetables, healthy oils, whey protein, and fiber. These products can be used as either beverages or tube feeding formulas.

SimplyThick

200 South Hanley Road, Suite 1102

St. Louis, MO 63105

Phone: 800-205-7115

Fax: 800-508-2990

Website: www.simplythick.com

This company produces SimplyThick, a xanthan gum-based thickener that works in both hot and cold beverages.

Thick-It (Division of Precision Foods)

11457 Olde Cabin Road, Suite 100

St. Louis, MO 63141

Phone: 800-778-5704

Website: www.thickitretail.com

Thick-It offers a line of instant thickeners and ready-made heat-and-serve puréed foods—including entrées, breakfast items, and vegetables—for people with chewing and swallowing difficulties. The company's products can be purchased and special-ordered from many pharmacies, as well as other retail distributors. (See their website for a list.) You can also order Thick-It products through 4WebMed and Bruce Medical Supply (page 289).

Total Care Home Medical Equipment

40 Nassau Terminal Road

New Hyde Park, NY 11040

Phone: 800-698-4990

Fax: 800-856-6931

Website: www.tchomemedical.com

This home medical equipment and supply company offers a wide range of products, including many that are useful for dysphagia. You will find fortified beverages; food and beverage thickeners; thickened beverages; and nutritional supplements that boost protein, fiber, and calories.

Travis Meats, Inc.

P.O. Box 670

Powell, TN 37849

Phone: 800-247-7606

Fax: 865-938-9211

Website: www.travismeats.com

To Order: http://webstore.travismeats.com

Travis offers a variety of heat-and-eat puréed, ground, and chopped meat and vegetable products, including beef pot roast purée, roast turkey purée, carrot purée, and much more. Note that a minimum bulk order is required.

The Wright Stuff, Inc.

111 Harris Street

Crystal Springs, MS 39059

Phone: 877-750-0376

Fax: 662-892-3116

Website: www.thewright-stuff.com

The Wright Stuff provides health care products designed for people with varying physical needs, including feeding difficulties. Product offerings include adaptive plates, cups, and utensils, plus a variety of other helpful kitchen aids.

ORGANIZATIONS AND WEBSITES

As you learn to prepare dishes for easy-to-chew, soft, or smooth eating plans, you are likely to have questions not only about diet, but also about underlying health issues. For that reason, we have created the following listing of organizations and websites. Below, you will find associations, organizations, and Internet sites that can help you learn more about nutrition, swallowing difficulties, and a range of related topics. Be aware that this list represents just a few of the many organizations and sites that can provide you with information, practical advice, and support. A computer search for topics of interest—"ALS support groups," for instance—will lead you to further resources.

ALS Association

27001 Agoura Road, Suite 150

Calabasas Hills, CA 91301-5104

Phone: 818-880-9007

Toll-Free Information and Referral Service:
   800-782-4747

Fax: 818-880-9006

Website: www.alsa.org

Dedicated to helping people better understand and live with the special challenges of amyotrophic lateral sclerosis (ALS), or Lou Gehrig's disease, the ALS Association provides a wealth of information and resources for patients and caregivers. Click on the "Patient, Family, Caregivers" tab to learn what this organization has to offer.

Alzheimer's Foundation of America (AFA)

322 8th Avenue, 7th Floor

New York, NY 10001

Phone: 866-232-8484

Fax: 646-638-1546

Website: www.alzfdn.org

Tips for Feeding: http://www.alzfdn.org/
   EducationandCare/eating.html

The AFA website provides information about Alzheimer's disease, including special support and advice for caregivers. A portion of the website presents tips for dealing with feeding problems. Click on the "Caregiving" tab to find links to a range of topics as well as the Care Connection support service.

American Academy of Otolaryngology— Head and Neck Surgery (AAO-HNS)

1650 Diagonal Road

Alexandria, VA 22314-2857

Phone: 703-836-4444

Website: www.entnet.org

Information on Swallowing Problems:

http://www. entnet.org/HealthInformation/
swallowingTrouble.cfm

AAO-HNS is the world's largest organization representing specialists who treat the ear, nose, throat, and related structures of the head and neck. Included on the academy's website is information about the diagnosis and treatment of swallowing problems as well as other mouth- and throat-related disorders.

American College of Gastroenterology (ACG)

P.O. Box 342260

Bethesda, MD 20827-2260

Phone: 301-263-9000

Website: www.acg.gi.org

The goal of the American College of Gastroenterology is to advance the study and treatment of gastrointestinal disorders. Visit the ACG website to learn more about GI problems such as nausea, heartburn, diarrhea, irritable bowel syndrome, ulcers, and food intolerances. (Click on the "Patients" tab first; then "GI Patient Center" and "Information on GI Health and Diseases.") Or click on "Patients," "Physician Locator" to find a gastroenterologist in your area.

American Dietetic Association (ADA)

120 South Riverside Plaza, Suite 2000

Chicago, IL 60606-6995

Phone: 800-877-1600

Website: www.eatright.org

The world's largest organization of food and nutrition professionals, the American Dietetic Association offers a wealth of information about healthy eating on its website. Click on "Food & Nutrition Information" to find Nutrition Fact Sheets on different topics of interest. If you are looking for a registered dietitian in your area, visit the home page and click on "Find a Nutrition Professional" to perform a search.

American Heart Association

National Center

7272 Greenville Avenue

Dallas, TX 75231

Phone: 800-AHA-USA1

Website: www.americanheart.org

The American Heart Association seeks to reduce the risk and incidence of heart disease, stroke, obesity, and diabetes. The association's website provides links to information about disorders of the heart and cardiovascular system, as well as tips for a heart-healthy diet and lifestyle. Click on the "Healthy Lifestyles" tab to find topics of interest.

American Institute for Cancer Research (AICR)

1759 R Street, NW

Washington, DC 20009

Phone: 800-843-8114

In Washington, DC: 202-328-7744

Fax: 202-328-7226

Website: www.aicr.org

In addition to researching the relationship between diet and cancer, the American Institute for Cancer Research provides nutrition information to cancer patients and their families. Visit the AICR website and find links to dietary recommendations (click on "Cancer Survivors"), submit nutrition questions online, or call the AICR's toll-free number to obtain information from a registered dietitian.

American Parkinson Disease Association (APDA)

135 Parkinson Avenue

Staten Island, NY 10305

Phone: 800-223-2732 or 718-981-8001

Fax: 718-981-4399

Website: www.apdaparkinson.org

The American Parkinson Disease Association focuses its efforts on research, patient support, education, and raising public awareness of the disorder. Visit the website to find APDA chapters in your area, download educational literature, and learn more about Parkinson's disease.

American Speech-Language-Hearing Association (ASHA)

2200 Research Boulevard

Rockville, MD 20850-3289

Phone: 800-638-8255

Fax: 301-296-8590

Website: www.asha.org

ASHA is the professional association for audiologists; speech-language pathologists; and speech, language, and hearing scientists. The ASHA website provides information on a number of issues, including swallowing problems. Click on "The Public" and look for the "Swallowing" link; or click on "Find a Professional" to locate a speech-language pathologist in your area.

Dietary Approaches to Stop Hypertension (DASH) Diet

The DASH Diet is recommended by the National Heart, Lung and Blood Institute (NHBLI) to help reduce blood pressure, and has also been shown to benefit people with other health problems, such as high cholesterol and obesity. To access information on this diet, turn to the entry on the National Heart, Lung and Blood Institute (NHBLI).

Lupus Foundation of America (LFA)

2000 L Street, NW, Suite 710

Washington, DC 20036

Phone: 202-349-1155

Information Requests: 800-558-0121

Fax: 202-349-1156

Website: www.lupus.org

LFA is a national nonprofit organization dedicated to finding the causes of and cure for lupus, and providing support and services for people affected by the disorder. Click on the "Learn About Lupus" tab to access a wealth of information, or click on "Find Resources" to locate local chapters, physicians, and support groups.

Medline Plus

Website: http://medlineplus.gov

Medline Plus is a service of the U.S. National Library of Medicine and the National Institutes of Health. At this site, you will find links to information on a wide variety of health issues, many of which are relevant to people who have difficulties chewing and swallowing. You will also find links to information on prescription and over-the-counter drugs and dietary supplements, a medical encyclopedia, a medical dictionary, and much more. Use the handy "Search Medline Plus" tab to locate discussions of swallowing disorders, nausea and vomiting, dehydration, chronic obstructive pulmonary disease, and other topics of interest.

National Cancer Institute (NCI)

NCI Public Inquiries Office

6116 Executive Boulevard, Room 3036A

Bethesda, MD 20892-8322

Phone: 800-422-6237

Website: www.cancer.gov

A division of the National Institutes of Health, the NCI supports research on cancer and offers information on various types of cancer; cause, diagnosis, prevention, and treatment; and the continuing care of cancer patients and their families. Visit the NCI home page and search for "Diet" or "Nutrition" to find tips for caregivers, recipes, and advice on managing eating problems during cancer treatment.

National Heart, Lung and Blood Institute (NHLBI)

NHLBI Health Information Center

P.O. Box 30105

Bethesda, MD 20824-0105

Phone: 301-592-8573

TTY: 240-629-3255

Fax: 240-629-3246

Website: www.nhlbi.nih.gov

Information on COPD: http://www.nhlbi.nih.gov/ health/public/lung/copd/

DASH Diet Booklet: http://www.nhlbi.nih.gov/ health/public/heart/hbp/dash/new_dash.pdf

A division of the National Institutes of Health, the NHLBI plans and supports research and education projects related to diseases of the heart, blood vessels, lungs, and blood. Visit the institute's website to find information on heart, vascular, and blood diseases, as well as heart-healthy eating—including the DASH diet—and tips for reducing dietary sodium.

National Institute of Allergy and Infectious Disease (NIAID)

NIAID Office of Communications and Government Relations

6610 Rockledge Drive, MSC 6612

Bethesda, MD 20892-6612

Phone: 866-284-4107

TTY: 800-877-8339

Website: www.niaid.nih.gov

A division of the National Institutes of Health, the NIAID conducts research to better understand, treat, and prevent infectious, immunologic, and allergic diseases. The NIAID website provides a wealth of information on allergies and infectious disorders, including AIDS. Click on the "Research" tab and then "Health & Research Topics" to find AIDS/HIV and other topics of interest in the alphabetical listing.

National Institute of Diabetes and Digestive and Kidney Diseases (NIDDK)

Building 31, Room 9A06

31 Center Drive, MSC 2560

Bethesda, MD 20892-2560

Phone: 301-496-3583

Website: www.niddk.nih.gov

NIDDK conducts and supports research on a broad spectrum of metabolic diseases, including diabetes, obesity, digestive problems such as constipation and diarrhea, liver and kidney diseases, and more. Visit the website and click on "Health Education" and then "Easy-to-Read Publications" to find dietary recommendations for people who are dealing with diabetes and kidney disease.

National Institute of Neurological Disorders and Stroke (NINDS)

P.O. Box 5801

Bethesda, MD 20824

Phone: 800-352-9424 or 301-496-5751

TTY: 301-468-5981

Website: www.ninds.nih.gov

NINDS supports research on a broad range of neurological disorders. Click on "Disorders A-Z" to find information on myasthenia gravis, stroke, and other neurological problems, as well as links to other valuable organizations.

National Institutes of Health (NIH)

9000 Rockville Pike

Bethesda, MD 20892

Phone: 301-496-4000

TTY: 301-402-9612

Website: www.nih.gov

Part of the U.S. Department of Health and Human Services, the NIH is the primary federal agency for conducting medical research, and is the umbrella agency for a total of twenty-seven institutes, including the National Cancer Institute; the National Heart, Lung and Blood Institute; and the National Institute of Neurological Disorders and Stroke. The NIH website provides links to information about a wide variety of health topics, including cancer, diabetes, digestive problems, heart disease, kidney disease, weight control, and more.

OncoLink Cancer Resource

Website: www.oncolink.com

OncoLink was developed by the Abramson Cancer Center of the University of Pennsylvania for use by cancer patients and their families, health care professionals, and the general public. To learn more about eating strategies when coping with cancer, search for "diet" or "nutrition" on OncoLink's home page. The site also provides information on specific types of cancer, updates on cancer treatments, and news about research advances. A monthly electronic newsletter—OncoLink eNews—is available free of charge.

U.S. Department of Agriculture—Food Safety and Inspection Service (FSIS)

1400 Independence Avenue, S.W.

Washington, DC 20250-3700

Meat and Poultry Hotline: 888-674-6854

FSIS Website: www.fsis.usda.gov

Food Pyramid Website: MyPyramid.gov

The Food Safety and Inspection Service of the Department of Agriculture is responsible for insuring that the nation's supply of meat, poultry, and eggs is safe. Visit their website and click on "Fact Sheets" for information on safe food handling, or call their hotline for answers to food safety questions. The Department of Agriculture also created the MyPyramid.gov website, which provides nutrition information and helps you create an eating plan tailored to your needs.

U.S. Food and Drug Administration (FDA)— Center for Food Safety and Applied Nutrition

5600 Fishers Lane

Rockville, MD 20857

Phone: 888-463-6332

Food Safety Hotline: 888-SAFEFOOD

Website: www.cfsan.fda.gov

The FDA is responsible for protecting the public health by assuring the safety of foods, drugs, and supplements. As such, it makes available a wealth of information on food safety. Visit the website and click on links such as "Food Safety," "Foodborne Illness," and "Seafood," or call the food safety hotline. To learn about the safety of supplements, click on "Dietary Supplements."

Menu Planning

Eating a balanced diet can be difficult under the best of circumstances, and becomes even more challenging when you're following a soft or smooth diet. If you choose to eat the kinds of foods you have always enjoyed, and simply process them until they are smooth, your health probably won't change measurably. But if you find the processed versions of your regular dishes unappetizing, you may simply avoid eating, and your health will suffer accordingly. One of our intentions in writing this book was to help insure that you continue to take pleasure in your meals whether you are following an easy-to-chew, soft, or smooth/puréed diet. But we also want you to follow a diet that will contribute to your well-being. That's why we have created the following menus. They will guide you in combining easy-to-swallow dishes into meals that include a wise balance of proteins, carbohydrates, fats, and other important nutrients.

When planning meals, keep in mind that people can have very different caloric and nutritional needs. Chapter 7 reviews the basics of a healthy diet and also guides you to MyPyramid.gov, an interactive government website that can help you create a personal eating plan. (See Chapter 7 for more information.) But the best possible option is to work with your physician and/or a licensed or registered nutritionist to fine-tune your diet based on your individual situation. The Nutritional Facts included at the end of each *Soft Foods* recipe will help you choose dishes that meet your needs, and avoid or adjust any dishes that might prove problematic. If you require thickened liquids, of course, you may have to further adjust many of your foods—including the recipes in this book—to create the proper consistency. (See Chapter 6 to learn about thickening liquids of different types.)

The following menus feature recipes from this book as well as some ready-to-eat choices from the supermarket. Feel free to improvise with convenience items when possible. For instance, instead of making lentil soup from scratch, buy a canned variety and purée it to the appropriate consistency. Instead of preparing meatballs in your own kitchen, buy them ready-made from your local deli and process them as necessary. This strategy will allow you to save time and still enjoy variety in your diet. Similarly, although each of our daily menus feature three meals plus one snack, don't hesitate to modify them to suit your goals. If you are trying to gain weight, for instance, you might want to add mid-morning and evening snacks, as well. Use these menus as a starting point, and adjust them to create daily plans that optimize your health and enjoyment.

SAMPLE MENUS

DAY ONE

Easy-to-Chew Diet	Soft Diet	Puréed/Smooth Diet
Breakfast	**Breakfast**	**Breakfast**
Poached Eggs Florentine (page 127)	Poached Eggs Florentine (page 127)	Green Eggs and Ham (page 126)
Chopped ham	Ground ham	Easy Cheese Grits (page 135)
Easy Cheese Grits (page 135)	Easy Cheese Grits (page 135)	Cranberry juice
Sliced strawberries	Sliced strawberries	Coffee, tea, or milk
Coffee, tea, or milk	Coffee, tea, or milk	
Lunch	**Lunch**	**Lunch**
Savory Lentil Soup (page 151)	Savory Lentil Soup (page 151)	Savory Lentil Soup, puréed (page 151)
Pimento Cheese Sandwich (page 200)	Pimento Cheese Sandwich (page 200)	Pimento Cheese Sandwich, puréed (page 200)
Canned pear half topped with sour cream and shredded Cheddar cheese	Diced canned pears	Canned pears, puréed
Snack	**Snack**	**Snack**
Canned apricots with ricotta cheese drizzled with honey	Apricot Frappé (page 110)	Apricot Frappé (page 110)
Dinner	**Dinner**	**Dinner**
Quick Chicken and Dumplings (page 204)	Chicken Timbales (page 205)	Chicken Timbales, puréed (page 205)
Soft-cooked carrots	Lima Beans with Sage and Onions (page 237)	Lima Beans with Sage and Onions, puréed (page 237)
Lima Beans with Sage and Onions (page 237)	Savory Carrot Purée (page 235)	Savory Carrot Purée (page 235)
Raspberry Trifle (page 268)	Raspberry Trifle (page 268)	Parfait of vanilla pudding layered with Fresh Berry Purée (page 171)

DAY TWO

Easy-to-Chew Diet	Soft Diet	Smooth/Puréed Diet
Breakfast	**Breakfast**	**Breakfast**
Cinnamon-Apple Oatmeal (page 140)	Cinnamon-Apple Oatmeal (page 140)	Oat Bran with Peaches and Almonds (page 139)
Sliced fresh peaches	Canned peaches	Canned puréed peaches or applesauce
Coffee, tea, or milk	Coffee, tea, or milk	Coffee, tea, or milk
Lunch	**Lunch**	**Lunch**
Eggless Egg Salad (page 231)	Eggless Egg Salad (page 231)	Eggless Egg Salad, puréed (page 231)
Ready-made hummus drizzled with olive oil	Ready-made hummus drizzled with olive oil	Ready-made hummus drizzled with olive oil
Fruit yogurt	Fruit yogurt	Fruit yogurt (no chunks)
V8 vegetable juice	V8 vegetable juice	V8 vegetable juice
Snack	**Snack**	**Snack**
Peanut butter and banana sandwich	Peanut butter and banana sandwich	Peanut Butter and Banana Sandwich (puréed) (page 199)
Milk	Milk	Milk
Dinner	**Dinner**	**Dinner**
Italian-Style Meatballs (page 210) with tender-cooked angel hair pasta	Italian-Style Meatballs (page 210), with tender-cooked angel hair pasta	Layered Puréed Spinach Lasagna (page 230)
Tender-cooked zucchini with olive oil and garlic	Zucchini Custards (page 242)	Zucchini Custards, puréed (page 242)
Tender-cooked baby carrots tossed with ready-made pesto	Canned carrots mixed with ready-made pesto	Canned carrots, puréed and mixed with ready-made pesto

DAY THREE

Easy-to-Chew Diet	Soft Diet	Smooth/Puréed Diet
Breakfast	**Breakfast**	**Breakfast**
Refried Beans (page 253) topped with poached egg and salsa	Refried Beans (page 253) topped with poached egg and salsa	Refried Beans, puréed (page 253)
Side of ready-made guacamole	Side of ready-made guacamole	Scrambled egg, puréed
Canned mandarin oranges	Orange juice	Side of ready-made guacamole (purée if chunky)
Coffee, tea, or milk	Coffee, tea, or milk	Orange juice
		Coffee, tea, or milk
Lunch	**Lunch**	**Lunch**
Deviled Ham Sandwich (page 201)	Deviled Ham Sandwich (page 201)	Deviled Ham Sandwich, puréed (page 201)
Garden Gazpacho (page 159)	Garden Gazpacho (page 159)	Canned tomato soup
Cherry-Apple Salad (page 255)	Cherry-Apple Salad (page 255)	Cherry-Apple Salad, puréed (page 255)
Snack	**Snack**	**Snack**
Banana-Berry Smoothie (page 115)	Banana-Berry Smoothie (page 115)	Banana-Berry Smoothie (page 115)
Dinner	**Dinner**	**Dinner**
Crustless Ham and Cheese Quiche baked in a crust (page 219)	Crustless Ham and Cheese Quiche (page 219)	Cheese Soufflé (page 224)
Tender-cooked chopped broccoli with olive oil	Tender-cooked chopped broccoli with olive oil	Broccoli and Potato Purée (page 234)
Baked sweet potato with Cinnamon Honey Butter (page 181)	Baked sweet potato with Cinnamon Honey Butter (page 181)	Maple Mashed Sweet Potatoes (page 246)

DAY FOUR

Easy-to-Chew Diet	Soft Diet	Smooth/Puréed Diet
Breakfast	**Breakfast**	**Breakfast**
Fluffy Buttermilk Pancakes (page 130) softened with margarine and Warm Berry Syrup (page 172)	Fluffy Buttermilk Pancakes (page 130) softened with margarine and Warm Berry Syrup (page 172)	Fluffy Buttermilk Pancakes (page 130) softened with margarine and Warm Berry Syrup (page 172)
Orange juice	Orange juice	Orange juice
Coffee, tea, or milk	Coffee, tea, or milk	Coffee, tea, or milk
Lunch	**Lunch**	**Lunch**
Cauliflower-Cheese Soup (page 145)	Cauliflower-Cheese Soup (page 145)	Cauliflower Cheese Soup, puréed (page 145)
Burgers with Barbecue Sauce (page 213) on bun	Sloppy Joe (using packaged mix and ground beef) on bun softened with barbecue sauce	Sloppy Joe (using packaged mix and ground beef on crustless bread softened with barbecue sauce slurry)
Apples and Dumplings (page 260)	Creamy Fruit Mousse (page 265)	Creamy Fruit Mousse (page 265)
Snack	**Snack**	**Snack**
Ice cream	Ice cream	Ice cream
Dinner	**Dinner**	**Dinner**
Flaked steamed salmon with Sour Cream Dill Sauce (page 169)	Salmon Croquettes (page 222) with Sour Cream Dill Sauce (page 169)	Salmon Mousse, puréed (page 221) with Sour Cream Dill Sauce (page 169)
Tender-cooked spinach	Ready-made (frozen) spinach soufflé	Ready-made (frozen) spinach soufflé, puréed
Baked potato with margarine and sour cream	Cheesy Twice-Baked Potatoes (page 245)	Cheesy Twice-Baked Potatoes (page 245)
Steamed Pumpkin Bread (page 190) with Cinnamon Honey Butter (page 181)	Steamed Pumpkin Bread (page 190) with Cinnamon Honey Butter (page 181)	Baked Pumpkin Custard (page 276)

INDEX

THE ACID-ALKALINE FOOD GUIDE
A Quick Reference to Foods & Their Effect on pH Levels
Dr. Susan E. Brown
and Larry Trivieri, Jr.

In the last few years, researchers around the world have reported the importance of acid-alkaline balance to good health. While thousands of people are trying to balance their body's pH level, until now, they have had to rely on guides containing only a small number of foods. *The Acid-Alkaline Food Guide* is a complete resource for people who want to widen their food choices.

The book begins by explaining how the acid-alkaline environment of the body is influenced by foods. It then presents a list of thousands of foods—single foods, combination foods, and even fast foods—and their acid-alkaline effects. *The Acid-Alkaline Food Guide* will quickly become the resource you turn to at home, in restaurants, and whenever you want to select a food that can help you reach your health and dietary goals.

$7.95 • 208 pages • 4 x 7-inch mass paperback • ISBN 978-0-7570-0280-9

TRANSITIONS LIFESTYLE SYSTEM
GLYCEMIC INDEX FOOD GUIDE
For Weight Loss, Cardiovascular Health, Diabetic Management, and Maximum Energy
Dr. Shari Lieberman

The glycemic index (GI) is an important nutritional tool. By indicating how quickly a given food triggers a rise in blood sugar, the GI enables you to choose foods that can help you manage a variety of conditions and improve your overall health.

Written by leading nutritionist Dr. Shari Lieberman, this book was designed as an easy-to-use guide to the glycemic index. The book first answers commonly asked questions, ensuring that you truly understand the GI and know how to use it. It then provides both the glycemic index and the glycemic load of hundreds of foods and beverages, including raw foods, cooked foods, and many combination and prepared foods. Whether you are interested in controlling your glucose levels to manage your diabetes, lose weight, increase your heart health, or simply enhance your well-being, *Transitions Lifestyle System Glycemic Index Food Guide* is the best place to start.

$7.95 • 160 pages • 4 x 7-inch mass paperback • ISBN 978-0-7570-0245-8

JUICE ALIVE
The Ultimate Guide to Juicing Remedies
Steven Bailey, ND and Larry Trivieri, Jr.

The world of fresh juices offers a powerhouse of antioxidants, vitamins, minerals, and enzymes. The trick is knowing which juices can best serve your needs. In this easy-to-use guide, health experts Dr. Steven Bailey and Larry Trivieri, Jr. tell you everything you need to know to maximize the benefits and tastes of juice.

The book begins with a look at the history of juicing. It then examines the many components that make fresh juice truly good for you—good for weight loss and so much more. Next, it offers practical advice about the types of juices available, as well as buying and storing tips for produce. The second half of the book begins with an important chart that matches up common ailments with the most appropriate juices, followed by over 100 delicious juice recipes. Let *Juice Alive* introduce you to a world bursting with the incomparable tastes and benefits of fresh juice.

$14.95 • 272 pages • 6 x 9-inch quality paperback • ISBN 978-0-7570-0266-3

WHAT YOU MUST KNOW ABOUT VITAMINS, MINERALS, HERBS & MORE
Choosing the Nutrients That Are Right for You
Pamela Wartian Smith, MD, MPH

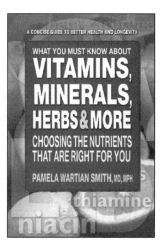

Almost 75 percent of your health and life expectancy is based on lifestyle, environment, and nutrition. Yet even if you follow a healthful diet, you are probably not getting all the nutrients you need to prevent disease. In *What You Must Know About Vitamins, Minerals, Herbs & More,* Dr. Pamela Smith explains how you can restore and maintain health through the wise use of nutrients.

Part One of this easy-to-use guide discusses the individual nutrients necessary for good health. Part Two offers personalized nutritional programs for people with a wide variety of health concerns. People without prior medical problems can look to Part Three for their supplementation plans. Whether you want to maintain good health or you are trying to overcome a medical condition, *What You Must Know About Vitamins, Minerals, Herbs & More,* can help you make the best choices for the health and well-being of you and your family.

$15.95 • 448 pages • 6 x 9-inch quality paperback • ISBN 978-0-7570-0233-5

EAT SMART, EAT RAW
Creative Vegetarian Recipes for a Healthier Life
Kate Wood

As the popularity of raw vegetarian cuisine continues to soar, so does the mounting scientific evidence that uncooked food is amazingly good for you. From healing diseases to detoxifying your body, from lowering cholesterol to eliminating excess weight, the many important health benefits derived from such a diet are too important to ignore. However, now there is another compelling reason to go raw—taste! In *Eat Smart, Eat Raw*, cook and health writer Kate Wood not only explains how to get started, but also provides delicious kitchen-tested recipes guaranteed to surprise and delight even the fussiest of eaters.

$15.95 • 184 Pages • 7.5 x 9-inch quality paperback • ISBN 978-0-7570-0261-8

GOING WILD IN THE KITCHEN
The Fresh & Sassy Tastes of Vegetarian Cooking
Leslie Cerier

Go wild in the kitchen! Be creative! Venture beyond the usual beans, grains, and vegetables to include an exciting variety of organic vegetarian fare in your meals. Step outside the box and prepare dishes with beautiful edible flowers; flavorful wild mushrooms, herbs, and berries; tangy sheep and goat cheeses; tasty sea vegetables; and exotic ancient grains like teff, quinoa, and Chinese "forbidden" black rice. Author and expert chef Leslie Cerier is crazy about the great taste and goodness of organically grown foods. In this exciting cookbook, she shares scores of her favorite recipes that spotlight these fresh, wholesome ingredients.

$16.95 • 240 Pages • 7.5 x 9-inch quality paperback • ISBN 978-0-7570-0091-1

GREENS AND GRAINS
ON THE DEEP BLUE SEA COOKBOOK
Fabulous Vegetarian Cuisine from the Holistic Holiday at Sea Cruises
Sandy Pukel and Mark Hanna

You are invited to come aboard one of America's premier health cruises. Too busy to get away? Well, even if you can't swim in the ship's pool, you can still enjoy its gourmet cuisine, because natural foods expert Sandy Pukel and master chef Mark Hanna have now put together *Greens and Grains on the Deep Blue Sea Cookbook*—a titanic collection of healthful and delicious vegetarian recipes that are among the most popular dishes served aboard the Holistic Holiday at Sea cruises.

$16.95 • 160 Pages • 7.5 x 9-inch quality paperback • ISBN 978-0-7570-0287-8

For more information about our books,
visit our website at www.squareonepublishers.com